Title: Feasting Dragon, Starving Eagle

Author: Peter G. de Krassel

Publisher: CAL Books

Publication Date: May 21, 2010

Price/Page Count: US$25 Canada $25/ 350 pages, 4-color cover

Index

First Printing: 10,000

ISBN: 978-988-97666-9-6

Trim Size Format: 5 ¾" x 9" Publishers Cover

Genre: Non Fiction Current Affairs

Feasting Dragon, Starving Eagle

How China Feeds on Washington and Wall Street Policy Mistakes

and

What We Must Do About It

Peter G. de Krassel

To Stanley,
It indeed was a pleasure
meeting you, Brad & Brian
when Stanley dragged me
along to his luncheon with
you.
Enjoy a literary feast!
All the best!

18 November 2010

CAL Books
Hong Kong, Los Angeles

Published in Hong Kong by CAL Books

Library of Congress Cataloguing-in-Publication Data is available
ISBN 978-988-97666-9-6

THIS BOOK IS DEDICATED TO THE CITIZENS AND
CHILDREN OF AMERICA AND CHINA,
WHO CAN AND MUST LEAD
THE WORLD THROUGH
THE 21st CENTURY.

Engels never flew on an airplane; Stalin never wore Dacron.

– Deng Xiaoping

Contents on the Table

Be not tempted to presume by success: for many that have got largely, have lost all, by coveting to get more.
– William Penn

Bon Appetite – and Enjoyable Read

Our greatest glory is not in never failing,
but in rising every time we fall.
                                        – Confucius

Acknowledgements
Don't You Wish It Was True
– John Fogerty

I have spent many hours over the decades with glass mates debating the merits of U.S. policy toward China because of America's misguided fixation with establishing and maintaining a military presence in Taiwan to fight communist China. I have done so in America, Hong Kong, Macau, Taiwan, China and just about every other country I've been to when people find out I live in Hong Kong. The prolonged disagreements usually ended with me telling them to "kiss my glass" because I had no doubt they were wrong. It cost me – big time over the years – personally and professionally. "Commie," "China lover," and "stooge" are some of the more polite monikers I have been branded with. Time has, regretfully, proven me right.

America was the economic drunkard that went on a binge and must now get into rehab. To all those worldwide glass mates, thank you for the honest political exchanges – especially the many chefs and bartenders with whom I have had the privilege of sharing ideas about the ingredients of their food, drink and politics – most notably the real-live Main Bar at the Foreign Correspondents Club in Hong Kong and the Overseas Press Club in New York City. Living in China and regularly visiting the U.S. is a politically sobering experience.

The revolutionary changes that have taken place the last few years with cocktails at bars around the world, but especially in America – the global political bartender – have been stunning. Not just the martini menu, but a pina colada transformed into a panda colada? That is when I realized that China's global appetite – make that eating and drinking binge – and influence has become a lot more invasive than merely economic.

The ingredients for all good cocktails and meals are selected and determined by the bartenders and chefs who prepare them. Hopefully, they listen to each other and their customers and change their menus according to market prices of seasonal produce and political reality to ensure their customers, citizens and reviewers get the best meal and value for their money. In theory, the same should be true with politics and the politicians who cook up the domestic and foreign policies that govern the lives of their citizens – and the books of the public coffers. But it isn't. The politicians in Washington pay whatever price is necessary to get them re-elected, and their constituents be damned. The result is that America has been devoured by China. America has become China's cheap buffet.

There are four families in particular – petite-foix – whose members have been an integral part of this ongoing dialogue, that of former California Secretary of State March Fong Eu; Kevin and Mary Catherine McBride; Nelson and Angela Wong; and Steve and Taiyun Chicorel. I traveled with the Secretary and her husband Henry Eu to Taiwan, Hong Kong and mainland China in the 1980s. In the course of those travels, I got to know her children, daughter Suyin and son Matt "Kip" Fong, with whom I shared many alcohol-fueled argumentative political debates in California, but especially in Taiwan, where I was the designated drinker for the secretary. After the formal dinners, I would adjourn with Kip, who in 1994 became California state treasurer through 1998, and local Taiwanese politicians and California political activists to debate the pros and cons of America's Taiwan policy. Needless to say, I was the odd man out.

Sitting down to write this book, I spent several memorable visits with Suyin and her husband Jim Stein, son Alaric and daughter Melody in 2008, during the presidential election and right after the vice presidential debates, at their home in Sebastopol, California, reminiscing about those memorable days and how to constructively convey to America why It had better wake up before it is regurgitated by China, or worse, disposed of as waste. Much to my surprise and delight, Alaric and Melody helped restore my faith in America's children with their political awareness and wisdom, which is reflected in the children of many Taiwanese and mainland China children of friends and business associates, who for political reasons have asked that their names not be acknowledged. Hence the dedication of this book to American and Chinese children.

I also spent many a late alcohol-fueled night with Kevin McBride, born and bred in Wilmington, Delaware, and his wife Mary Catherine, who hails from New York – starting in 1984 in my then-wife Gail's restaurant Scratch – through the 2008 U.S. presidential election during my visits to California, when I would stay with them and discuss U.S. and China politics. Their daughter Caitlin was studying global business and Mandarin in Beijing during the 2008-2009 academic year. Mary Catherine was the producer of T.V.'s "Knotts Landing." We worked together on the Jan & Dean In China concert and movie in 1986 and the "Young Indiana Jones in Beijing" episode in the 90s.

While in China, I met Nelson Wong in the early '90s. Nelson was born and raised in Shanghai, China, moved to Hong Kong in the '80s and got into the real estate consultancy and agency business, where he met his future wife Angela. They have two daughters; the older Shu-shu is studying International Relations and Law at the London School of Economics. Nelson maintains residences in Hong Kong and Shanghai, where he and I have also spent many a late night in spas, sweating out our political opinions about America, China, Khazakhstan, North Korea, Japan and Taipei as we soaked in the vodka and whiskeys on offer.

Taipei is where Hollywood producer Steve Chicorel and his wife Taiyun and children Philip and Anabel live. Steve was born and raised in Milwaukee, lived in New York, Hawaii and Los Angeles. He met Taiyun at the airport in Chicago. Steve, Taiyun and I also spent many an alcohol-lit-night on their rooftop or garden in Brentwood, California, Taipei or mine in Hong Kong debating U.S.-China-Taiwan relations.

Today the world accepts China as a re-emerging power that, if it chooses, has the ability to cripple America and the countries it leads and misguides economically. This is nothing new and should not come as a surprise. Like many others, I have been writing, talking to the Eus, McBrides, Steins, Wongs and Chicorels of this world and warnng those who care to listen, for more than three decades now, of the dawning of the age of China at the dawning of the Age of Aquarius at the expense of America.

I want to thank and acknowledge all those citizens who echoed my concern; my editor Jim Houston; political pundit radio talk show hosts Bill Bertenshaw, Scott Hennan, Phil Whelan; and all the other talk radio, broadband, TV, print and other media hosts who invited me as their guest for their courage in allowing me to voice our collective warnings and concerns. That day has arrived.

The first panacea for a mismanaged nation is inflation of the currency; the second is war. Both bring a permanent ruin. But both are the refuge of political and economic opportunists.
                                                    – Ernest Hemingway

Preface
Civilizations, countries or corporations
collapse because they are led by morons.
– Andy Xie

Starving Stupidity

Muted revelry across the world rang in the New Year of 2009, and for good reason. People in America and the world it leads finally realized that the reason we are in the economic and financial mess we are confronted with today is because We the People have allowed idiots to become our political and corporate leaders. Watching the world leaders who created the global meltdown get together at the G-20 summits in December 2008, April 2009 and September 2009 to cure the disease they created gave me a severe case of indigestion.

America's corporate titans – the chefs who cooked the global financial meltdown, a dog's breakfast of thousands of failed companies, millions unemployed and retirees penniless without health care in their wake – rewarded themselves with multi-million dollar caviar and champagne-laden golden parachutes and bonuses while taxpayers and their children and grandchildren pick up the tab. They obviously forgot what happened to Marie Antoinette, who had her head guillotined like a sausage because she said of the starving masses who didn't have bread, "Let them eat cake."

America's corporate and political leaders are incompetent, greedy, self-serving and corrupt. How can so many ruthless and incompetent people be running the world at the same time? asked Andy Xie, an independent economist in an editorial he wrote in November 2008. I concur. That is why China is the feasting dragon at the expense of the starving eagle – America and the global financial soup it over cooked, fell into and boiled itself.

One thing that suprises me is that President Barack Obama, the man who promised "change we can believe in," has put into positions of power the same bureaucratic chefs who spoiled the soup in the first place. Obama reappointed Federal Reserve Chairman Ben Bernanke to a second term, named former New York Fed chief Timothy Geithner as Treasury secretary, and chose the well-travelled Lawrence Summers, as director of the National Economic Council.

Nassim Taleb, author of *The Black Swan,* asks a question that I have repeatedly echoed: "Bernanke, Geithner and Summers didn't see the crisis coming so why are they still there?"

Starving Eagle

Flying across America and driving the length of California, as I did several times in 2008, especially in November and December – after Barack Obama won the presidential election during the global financial meltdown – I was flabbergasted at the range of human rage and emotions expressed by family members, friends, business associates and fellow travelers at America's career politicians and China. It didn't matter if it was a clear moonlit night, bright sunny day, chilly downpour or bitter snowfall. The anger and rage at corrupt, self-serving career politicians was weather-neutral but vehement. Fear, self-doubt and insecurity about their future and that of their children or grandchildren, coupled with their fear and distrust of China, was frankly a shocker for me as an American living in China.

Tainted food for people and their pets, lead in children's toys, finger-chopping strollers, drywall that smells like rotten eggs and corrodes pipes, undervalued currency, human rights violations and Tibet policy were magnified because of the perception in America that China is hoarding U.S. dollars and expanding its global presence at America's expense – especially in America's own backyard. Cuba, Venezuela, Peru, Brazil, Mexico and Canada were the countries mentioned most. There is no doubt America has dropped the economic, financial and geopolitical ball and China has picked it up and is scoring too many touchdowns for Americans' comfort.

But let's put the blame where it belongs, on Washington's career politicians and their corporate Wall Street financial backers. The reality is that China, like America, has become a top global geopolitical brand. China will survive the 21st century. Can the same be said for America? Unless it changes course, the answer is a resounding "YES, Peter!" Mary Catherine said as she loudly interrupted me as I was sharing my concerns about America with her and her husband Kevin at their home, after a book talk I gave at Barnes

& Noble in Westlake Village, California, in the fall of 2008.

"You ask in your book and talk tonight 'will America survive?' Kevin and I give you a resounding YES." Before I could question Mary Catherine on the reasons for her emphatic answer, Kevin, a teamster who works the Hollywood studio cars driving the stars and trucks that carry what makes the stars look good, added: "The world might be in the middle of a huge shakeup after a colossal shakedown from big business crooks, but in the end we'll come out fresher, wiser, more focused, alert, and with a deeper understanding and commitment that will allow America to soar again, only now with a friend and ally, the Eagle and the Dragon – united!" Kevin yelled as he hoisted his glass to ours as they clanked in mid-air.

"How the hell did we allow this to happen?" Kevin asked, his voice full of angst as he continued with his question, "How did America get into this mess as China moved ahead so fast?"

"Greed versus obedience," Mary Catherine responded before I could open my mouth. I just kept sipping my wine knowing Kevin would interject his thoughts as he paced the room.

"Goddamn it, is there any doubt in anyone's mind that America is not burned out and will survive?" Kevin asked.

"Yeah," I responded. "Its infrastructure – physical, political, cultural, military – is outdated and irrelevant to the 21st century and cannot keep up with its Chinese banker."

The point was brought home to me on more than one occasion in American airports at the charging terminals for phones and computers. The Chinese and Chinese-Americans have the latest and best toys, while their multi-ethnic American counterparts have models that are several months or years old, kind of like mine.

America is behind the eight-ball technologically and busted – broke. U.S. financial losses from the credit crisis might reach more than $3.6 trillion, suggesting the banking system is effectively insolvent. Bank of America Corp., the largest U.S. bank by assets, posted a fourth-quarter loss in 2008 of $1.79 billion and received $45 billion in cash and $118 billion in asset guarantees from the government's TARP program because it reluctantly bought Merrill Lynch, knowing if it didn't it would not get the taxpayers multi-billion dollar lifeline. The ongoing financial and economic meltdown that brought America's eagle crashing to earth in 2008 was all the more dramatic because of the Chinese dragon's awesome and expensive multi-billion-dollar Olympic Games extravaganza that opened on 8/8/8 – and its record-breaking gold medal performance.

Hungry Dragon Reaching for Mars Bar
The spectacular opening and closing ceremonies of the Beijing 2008 Olympics – and China's record haul of gold medals – was a millennium wake-up call and a reminder that the dragon has risen from its sleep and has a ravenous appetite for all commodities, not just gold.

The national pride radiated after the Olympics was given an added dose of technological pride a month later when China's third manned space mission in five years culminated in a spacewalk, making China only the third country to accomplish the feat, after the United States and Russia. Hong Kongers all around me, like all Chinese, were glued to television screens watching the walk and applauding and cheering when it was completed. Thousands of Hong Kong students of all ages enthusiastically greeted the astronauts and their Shenzhou VII re-entry module when they visited Hong Kong in December 2008.

China's first Mars probe, Yinghuo-1, is expected to be launched in the second half of 2009. It will ride aboard a Russian carrier rocket. Why not a U.S. launch vehicle? Yinghuo-1 will go into Martian orbit in 2010 after a 10-month, 380-million-kilometer journey. The mission hopes to discover why water disappeared from Mars and explain the planet's other environmental changes. China has come a long way fast since Russia launched Sputnik in 1957 and started the space race.

Joan Johnson-Freese, an expert on the Chinese space program at the Naval War College in Newport, Rhode Island, said it best: "The Chinese have read the Apollo playbook. They understand everything the U.S. got from the lunar program." That was evident when China's first lunar probe crashed into the moon in March 2009 in a controlled collision after completing a successful 16-month mission. Mao Zedong is reported to have complained in 1957 that China couldn't launch a potato into space, much less a rocket.

Gearing Up & Winding Down
China is also gearing up to stage the largest world expo ever in the fair's 158-year history: the 2010 World Expo in Shanghai. The expo used to be

known as the World's Fair. The city plans to spend $45 billion, more than Beijing spent on the 2008 Olympics. The Expo is also advancing a larger government goal of turning Shanghai into a world-class city and premier global financial center. By the time the six-month-long Expo opens, Shanghai will have two new airport terminals, a subway system nearly as large as New York's, a new cruise ship terminal and a $700 million promenade in its historic Bund riverfront district. New parks, roads and bridges have already opened.

I visited Shanghai in September 2009 and was stunned by the changes that have taken place in China's largest city in preparation for the World Expo. The transformation is nothing short of mind-boggling, especially for someone like me who has been visiting the city for more than 20 years. Shanghai was dubbed "the Paris of the East" back in the 1930s. But now, with the Bund transformed into a pulsating mix of old and new, the traditional and the trendy, the moniker has become outdated. Shanghai has become The 21st Century City.

Shanghai officials believe they can make a profit from the World Expo even though it may wind up costing more than the Beijing Olympics. The total cost of the Expo is estimated to be $45 billion compared to the $40 billion Beijing spent on the Summer Games. The profits will come from the redevelopment of the site after the exposition closes. The infrastructure is being put in place. More than 200 billion yuan is being invested in the transportation system, with the subway network being doubled. The local power company has invested 26 billion yuan to upgrade the city's electricity network, including high-efficiency substations and underground cables to ensure a stable power supply to the residential developments that will be built on the site.

China's biggest worry is that the United States may not be able to participate in the exposition which takes place every five years. Because of a U.S. federal law that restricts the use of government funds, American participation in an exposition depends on donations and corporate sponsors. Washington is supporting a nonprofit group trying to raise $61 million to build and operate an American pavilion. Secretary of State Hillary Clinton has joined the effort to raise the money from corporate sponsors. As of the writing of this book in December 2009, the U.S. managed to raise only $30 million. Nevertheless, the U.S confirmed in July, two months after the May deadline, that it will attend the expo.

According to the original plan, the U.S. national pavilion, under the theme "Celebration 2030," is expected to provide a glimpse of an American city of the future with a focus on clean energy, healthy living, sustainable farming and green technologies. The project is a source of embarrassment as the weeks and months go by without ground being broken. It's the latest indication of how truly hungry capitalist America is compared to China. The capitalist eagle desperately trying to make another loaf out of corporate crumbs while the dragon feasts.

While trying to raise funds for the U.S. pavilion, Clinton fell and broke her elbow on the way to a meeting at the White House – on the heels of Britain's former Prime Minister Margaret Thatcher breaking her arm a week earlier. This was interpreted by the Chinese as a bad omen for America and the June 30 deadline for countries to start work on their pavilions was postponed five months to allow America more time to raise the necessary funds. To many China watchers, it was a reminder of Thatcher's fall on the steps of the Great Hall of the People in 1984, when she was negotiating with the Chinese government to renew Hong Kong's lease, which expired in 1997. Her fall then was interpreted as an omen that Britain was doomed in its negotiations and the lease would not be renewed – and it wasn't. Hopefully, Clinton will have better luck.

While Shanghai is gearing up for the World Expo, the city of Guangzhou is also spending feverishly preparing to be a lavish host of the 2010 Asian Games. It plans to improve upon Beijing's blueprint for clear skies at the 2008 Olympics. The city plans to close or relocate 123 heavy polluting manufacturers by the end of 2009. The government is keen to use the Asian Games as an opportunity to invest in environmental protection.

The Eclipse

I support any endeavor that invests in true environmental protection. I made that commitment on July 23, 2009, during the longest solar eclipse in our lifetime. I watched the eclipse with my normal reading glasses because I had not prepared myself for a proper eclipse watch, since in Hong Kong it was only a partial eclipse. The advisory reports recommended wearing protective eyewear. Possible damage includes blurred vision, central visual field loss, seeing an after-image, and reddening of the image. Sounds like the way I feel the morning after a heavy drinking session at the Main Bar at the Foreign Correspondents Club in Hong Kong. Having said that, I did wish I had gotten the right eye gear which is why I am now a firm believer in any investment in environmental protection.

The cosmic alignment of July 2009 was the most-watched eclipse in history because of its path over Earth's most densely inhabited areas, including India and China. The cone-shaped shadow, or umbra, created by the total eclipse first made landfall on the western Indian state of Gujarat just before 6.30 am. It then raced across India, blacking out the holy city of Varanasi on the banks of the Ganges, squeezing between the northern and southern tips of Bangladesh and Nepal before engulfing most of Bhutan, traversing the Chinese mainland and slipping back out to sea off Shanghai.

A total solar eclipse usually occurs every 18 months or so, but the spectacular July 2009 eclipse was special because of its maximum period of "totality" – when the sun is totally covered – of six minutes and 39 seconds. Such an extended totality will not be matched again until the year 2132. An eclipse is a perfect natural alignment of the sun, moon and earth.

My home in Hong Kong was perfectly situated to watch the solar eclipse as it has a clear view to the east. Knowing the eclipse in Hong Kong would be partial and start at 8.15 am, end at 10:46 am and peak sometime between 9:36-10:00 am, I decided to take a break from writing and take my dog Spud for a run on the beach at 8:14 am, making a point of getting back to my rooftop garden that faces east before 9.

I poured myself a generous ration of American bourbon and prayed. Many superstitious and religious believers view the eclipse as a sign of potential doom, especially after September 9, 2009, when fiery Saturn moves from Leo into Virgo. There is a high probability for unrest or war to break out in years of a solar eclipse. Over the last 200 years, whenever Saturn has gone into Virgo, there has been either a world war or mini-war.

In ancient China, eclipses were often associated with disasters, the death of an emperor or other ominous events, and similar superstitions persist today. According to legend, during a lunar eclipse the moon is eaten by a celestial dog.

I decided to call Nelson Wong in Shanghai right after the eclipse, which was a gamble as Nelson is usually a late riser. Calling him a little after 10 am, I was pleasantly surprised that he had actually witnessed the eclipse. He couldn't believe all the tourists, especially Americans, who had come to China to witness the eclipse. "Why?" I asked. "Just because China is eclipsing America around the world, is that reason enough for Americans interested in astrology and science to stay away from China?" I prodded Nelson knowing he would find my comment both annoying and amusing.

After he finally stopped laughing, he said, "No, it is their commitment to their scientific passion to come all the way to China to experience a once in a lifetime opportunity, even though they might miss it because of rain like happened here in Shanghai today."

To many it was anticlimactic and a disappointment because of the clouds and rain. "I'm not sure how many Chinese would go to America to watch the eclipse if it were to take place there," Nelson said as we shared our experiences of the morning. "With you promoting the tours and tying it into a real estate buying junket, I'm sure there will be record-breaking crowds lining up," I responded.

Many well-heeled Chinese and tourists weren't taking any chances. They boarded special charter flights that chased the lunar shadow from above the clouds. Others boarded regularly scheduled flights along the path of the eclipse.

Staying on top of an eclipse, any eclipse, but especially a geopolitical eclipse, is essential for America's survival as a superpower. The time is long overdue for all citizens of Earth, but especially American and Chinese, to carefully study the Sino-American eclipse taking place today the way scientists study a solar eclipse. Failure to do so will result in higher taxes being imposed by failing and faltering blind-sided career politicians to cover the costs of their shortsighted policies.

Starved for Cash
Enjoying the great fireworks displays put on by the government of Hong Kong each year and by Beijing during the 2008 Olympics, I was saddened to hear that most cities in the U.S. were forced to cancel their 4th of July fireworks shows because of their budget deficits.

As if canceling firework shows in America wasn't bad enough, what horrified me was reading a couple weeks later that state governments across the country were shutting down rest stops in their bids to save money. As someone who enjoys driving across America, I use the rest stops to answer nature's call and to stretch out. Ouch, I thought to myself. Well, like many other drivers across America, I will just have to do my fair share to irrigate and fertilize the plants on America's highways to help state governments save even more money.

While Shanghai and Guangzhou spend billions on their upcoming events, my home state of California, America's most populous and trendsetting Golden State, with an economy that would be the eighth-largest in the world if it were a country, was forced to pay its debts, including tax refunds, with IOUs because it is bankrupt. The Census Bureau report released in September 2009 showed that America lost ground on every indicator. Median income slumped. The poverty rate increased. The percentage of Americans without health insurance rose – as did unemployment, which topped 10% in October 2009.

Nearly 40 million people in America lived below the poverty line in 2008 as the recession smoked out jobs, dragged down incomes and boosted the poverty rate. The poverty rate of 13.2 percent was the highest since 1997, according to the Census Bureau. The poverty threshold for one person in 2008 was just under $11,000 and for a family of four was $22,025.

Forty-nine million people in American households – one in six – went hungry or had insufficient food at some point in 2008, the highest number since the government began tracking the problem in 1995.

Food stamp applications are surging and food bank shelves are emptying at an unprecedented rate.

A home is foreclosed every 13 seconds in America. There are more than 6,600 home foreclosure filings per day, according to the Center for Responsible Lending, a non-partisan watchdog group based in Durham, North Carolina. More than six million families could face foreclosure over the next three years. So, although the U.S. economy seems to be recovering from its worst recession since the Great Depression, mortgage delinquencies continue to rise on the back of mounting unemployment. The U.S. has lost 7.2 million jobs since the recession began in December 2007.

America is a welfare state, and its future is precarious. The Congressional Budget Office projects the federal debt to double as a share of the economy (gross domestic product) to about 80 percent of GDP by 2019. The system has promised more than it can deliver. America is borrowing not to finance investment in the future but to pay for today's welfare – present consumption. The U.S. welfare state is weakening; insecurity is rising.

Los Angeles, host of the profitable 1984 Olympics, which I supported as a member of the Olympics Finance Committee, is awash from broken water mains, part of its aging infrastructure. One burst pipe dated from 1917. The deluges have buckled streets, flooded businesses and homes, exasperated residents, blocked traffic and has Angelinos worried that they will soon be floating out to sea.

In the thick of all that, the city announced it could not afford to pay for a victory parade for the 2009 NBA champion Lakers. Said City Council-woman Jan Perry: "How could we make a decision (to cut) people's jobs and then sponsor the parade?" Finally, private donors stepped in to pick up the tab.

The city, faced with a deep budget deficit, was contemplating worker lay-offs and cuts in services and did not think it appropriate to sponsor the cel-ebratory parade. Barbara Maynard, a spokeswoman for the city's employee unions, agreed, telling the paper: "We do not believe it's appropriate in this economic climate for taxpayers to be funding a parade." The parade finally went ahead, funded by the Lakers and the private sector as fans got drunk and junked out on drugs and unhealthy food.

Buried Alive in Junk Food

Paying for a parade? How about paying for a decent burial or cremation? Bodies are left unclaimed, stacked high in morgues across America, un-claimed by families who cannot afford a burial or cremation. One family that can still afford an extravagant funeral is the family of Michael Jack-son. The pop star's untimely death brought attention and again focused the global lens on America's impoverished state of affairs a few weeks later with Jackson's memorial service.

The service took place at the Staples Center in downtown L.A. and was beamed worldwide and watched by more than a billion fans. The world learned that the City of Angels was in financial trouble and unable to pay for the security required to control his grieving fans. The tab was picked up by Hollywood. Meanwhile, Shanghai announced it was going to build a version of Michael Jackson's Neverland Ranch on an island near the city that will include a man-made lake, movie theater and zoo.

While Jackson's fans mourned his untimely, drug-induced death, they con-tinued to stuff themselves with more political junk – and junk food. Food and how it is produced and its negative impact on the planet – not to men-tion waistlines – has triggered a social movement of people disgusted at government's failure to properly nourish and take care of its citizens.

America's hunger and appetite is metaphorically exemplified by the public's obsession of where foodie President Obama and his wife Michelle eat out. How's this for a healthy political appetite: pizza in St. Louis, pancakes in Pittsburgh, soul food in Chicago, and chili dogs and cheese fries in Washington? But, hey, that's America and that's what it takes to get elected and hold onto high popularity ratings while America is starving. Any wonder Gourmet magazine, long considered the grande dame of culinary publishing, went out of business? What is more amazing is that P.F. Chang's simple Chinese recipe for profits actually features ingredients that would never be found in Chinese restaurants, like chocolate, cheese, melon balls ,and that the "P.F." stands for company founder Paul Fleming. A smart Yankee that others should take note of, especially the career politicians in Washington.

China certainly offers America – and the world it leads – the most diversified, phenomenal and constantly changing cutting-edge nourishing and delicious cuisine. The same holds true on the political front. China is again moving to center stage as it returns to the historical norm in which it is the world's largest economy, as it was for 1,800 years. The New World Disorder created by America needs to be reorganized with a fused Chinese recipe.

Skip Lunch

Chinese recipes are very healthy – yes, I know about MSG, but having been raised on the Mediterranean diet, I also know and appreciate the pure organic taste of exotic Chinese dishes. I am constantly disappointed and angered when I dine in Chinese restaurants in America and experience the Americanizing of Chinese food in an unhealthy way. As more Americans go Chinese with their dietary appetites, my hope is their hunger to better understand China is also satisfied and that China's rich history, culture, capitalist and political development is correctly digested.

The time for a new culinary and political order in America is long overdue.

Let's start with food for now. Dr. David Kessler, the former commissioner of the U.S. Food and Drug Administration, has no kudos for mass-produced American cuisine. He is highly critical of its nutritional imperialism. Americans steal Asian cuisines, import them with fanfare, and then absolutely destroy them with harmful additions and additives. He trashes Americans' penchant for large quantities of mayonnaise-topped tempura shrimp wrapped evilly in rice as a faux sushi roll. He says Americans imperialize so many world cuisines that they should be ashamed of themselves.

"American Chinese food is not Chinese," he complains. I agree wholeheartedly. The classic dish General Tso's chicken, after mass-Americanization, is poisoned with sugar: "Hunan cuisine is not sweet," Kessler rails. The same applies to Chinese politics, which is misrepresented in America.

Fast food chains like Panda Express corrupt otherwise healthy Chinese dishes with piles of sugar and fat. Across America, trendy fused pan-Chinese restaurants, well marketed and much ballyhooed by the media systematically spoil every cuisine they touch.

Fusion cuisine, like fusion geopolitics, can be good for everyone's health, but only depending on how skillfully and carefully it is all put together. The trick is to take the best of China and combine it with the best of America. Continue going the other way around – with the worst of America – and you have a major mishmash and nutritional meltdown. Much like the economic and financial meltdown-tsunami the world has been force-fed by Washington politicians and their bankers.

Michelle Obama is the ideal political animal First Lady by making food a prime area of interest – especially with her new White House kitchen garden. There the president can down a beer to drown out the ugly specter of racism in America, which festers despite his historic election.

Stockpiling Food and Guns

What also struck me during my late 2008 visits to the U.S., but especially my February 2009 visit after the Obamas moved into the White House, was the talk of people stockpiling food, planting home gardens and buying guns and ammunition. Being a graduate of an agricultural high school, I received several offers to join friends who were seriously thinking and planning on buying farms and starting family communes.

People are afraid of the future. Afraid of not being able to buy food and afraid they could lose all personal possessions to burglars and thieves. The fear was fueled by various talk show hosts I would listen to on satellite-radio as I channel surfed while driving up and down the Golden State. People were convinced that the economy was going to get worse – much worse. A financial apocalypse that would render the dollar worthless and normal commerce impossible, leading many people to make contingency plans that included stockpiling food, planting gardens, buying guns and investing in gold and silver.

Prophets of doom have always existed, of course, but today their voices are easier to hear because of the Internet and talk radio. The consensus of the various doomsayers was that the first things to be affected by the continued economic meltdown would be America's food supply. "If you don't have the ability to grow your own food next year, your life may be in danger," was a common theme by talk show hosts and seed sellers who are driving the growing number of home vegetable gardens and gun sales.

The other apocalyptic warnings that caught my attention were not from right-wing nut cases, but Nobel Laureate scientists. The scientists are finally speaking out and raising the alarm of our impending doom because of global warming – unless we reverse course, soon and fast.

The biblical Apocalypse of God destroying the world to rebuild it is being brushed aside by scientists who are criticizing heretofore uncriticized theological assumptions. James Carroll, Jesuit priest and author-columnist, summed it up best for the religious front. "The overwhelming message of the Bible, read critically, is that this world is the world that counts. Any notion of afterlife that suggests otherwise, undercutting care for the home planet, must be discarded, along with the habits that have put us at this precipice."

Buffet Power Lunch

Zhao Danyang, a Hong Kong-based hedge fund manager, made the winning bid of $2.11 million in 2008 on eBay to have lunch with Warren Buffet, chairman of Berkshire Hathaway, in June 2009. Zhao's winning bid was three times the amount paid at the previous auction, which raises money for the Glide Foundation, a San Francisco charity that provides food and shelter for the needy an d for which Mr. Buffet's late wife volunteered.

The three-hour multi-million-dollar lunch at Manhattan's Smith & Wollensky, one of my favorite New York watering holes, was good value and an experience that could not be "measured by money," said Zhao, who was accompanied by his wife, son and friends. He said a Chinese-language book called *Warren Buffet: From $100 to $1.6 billion* that he read during the Asian financial crisis in the 1990s gave him new perspectives on his investment philosophy. He said he owed his firm's 600 percent return over the past six years to lessons he learned from Buffet. "Buffet is my teacher," Zhao said. "In my heart, I am really thankful to him."

The Chinese leadership has developed domestic and foreign policies that have propelled China and its citizens to the head of the geopolitical dining table while career politicians in Washington pursue shattered foreign policies and broken domestic policies that have left America standing at the same table with its hand out, begging for the leftovers – much like the panhandlers outside Smith & Wollensky and countless other street corners across New York City and America. America continues to finance a bankrupt, starving Treasury indebted to foreign bondholders, including China, its largest creditor, with more debt as more Americans go hungry.

Now that billionaire Buffet, who wears Chinese made suits, has agreed to share his insight with children by tutoring tots about finance in an Internet cartoon series to be aired by 2010, future generations of American, Chinese and all young adults around the world, the future political and business leaders, will learn the mistakes of earlier generations and not repeat them. Buffet's character will host the *Secret Millionaire's Club,* where kids "have adventures in business and learn financial lessons."

Feasting Dragon
The number of U.S. companies featured in the annual Fortune 500 list of top global companies released in July 2009 fell to its lowest level ever, the business magazine said, while a record number of Chinese firms appeared. China saw its fortunes rise across the board with oil giant China Petroleum & Chemical Corp. appearing in the top 10 for the first time. Seven of the top 10 were oil firms. Overall, China had 37 companies featured on the list, with nine new entries and others climbing in the rankings. The number of U.S. firms in the top 500 fell to 140, the lowest since *Fortune* began the list in 1995.

The Industrial & Commercial Bank of China is the world's largest lender by market value and also the biggest by deposits. ICBC overtook JPMorgan Chase, the biggest U.S. bank by deposits, and Mitsubishi UFJ Financial Group of Japan. ICBC overtook Citigroup as the world's largest bank by market value in July 2007 after less than a year as a public company. Citigroup, once the world's No. 1 bank, is worth about the same as a second-tier commercial bank in China.

ICBC was also the world's most profitable bank in 2008 and 2009 as of the publication of this book, followed by China Construction Bank, the second most profitable global financial institution.

Chinese banks increased their combined profit by 31 percent in 2008 to

583.4 billion yuan, after the government lifted lending curbs to stem a slow-down in economic growth. A far cry from what leading U.S. banks were doing with their hands out for taxpayer bailout funds.

Chinese financial institutions are now being encouraged to also help bail out failed American banks by buying small and midsize institutions. More than 100 U.S. banks have already been seized by regulators during the financial crisis and more seizures are under way.

In October 2007, Minsheng Banking agreed to buy 9.9 percent of UCBH, which is based in San Francisco, for more than $200 million. It was the first investment in a U.S. bank by a mainland Chinese bank. China is finally being allowed to enjoy U.S. banks for lunch.

According to a 2008 study by the U.S. research organization Carnegie Endowment for International Peace, China's economy will overtake that of the U.S. by 2035 and be twice its size by mid-century.

Watching America get clobbered by a re-emerging China on the economic and geopolitical front – and get further indebted to it – as career politicians in Washington are paralyzed by their Wall Street financial backers and the lobbyists they are beholden to, oblivious to the global political morass they have created as America nose-dives toward the precipice to Armageddon, is a millennium wake-up call for change. And this is just the appetizer.

New Economic and Political Global Order
China is the new super-sized political and economic kid on the world stage. It is the world's largest producer of coal, steel and cement, the second largest consumer of energy and the third largest importer of oil. China's exports to the U.S. have grown more than 2,000 percent since 1990. There have been two great shifts in global power over the past 400 years before China's current rise. The first was the rise of Europe, which around the 17th century became the richest, most enterprising and ambitious part of the world. The second was the rise of the U.S., in the late 19th and early 20th centuries when it became the single most powerful country in the world – the decisive player in economics and politics.

Historically, when the world's leading power is challenged by a rising one, there is friction.

The perfect economic and political spicy tempest in a teapot is brewing in

America that has allowed China to rise: disparity between growth in productivity and gross domestic product on the one hand and growth in wages for the average American worker on the other, with Sino-U.S. relations on the verge of either rupturing or becoming Siamese twins with the geopolitical realignments that crystallized with the swearing in of Barack Obama as president in January 2009.

Globalization died in the last decade of the 20th century. It was a 19th-century model of economics based on scarcity, but the whole world was in surplus. Yet America insists on clinging to an economic theory it created and globalizes – even though it has brought about its economic and financial demise. China has rejected the globalization economic model, just as it did with rural communism, and is forming a harmonious Confucian-capitalist- social economic order for its citizens and Chinese expatriates around the world.

Since the global financial meltdown, Chinese women have lost interest in Western men as potential husbands, according to two independent surveys. Cynical Western men, like me, who are divorced from Chinese wives, didn't find the news that newsworthy.

This while America's Latino backyard hemisphere, which Monroe and his 1823 doctrine so vigorously defended as America's "sphere of influence," made a radical left turn to China's warm embrace. America is simply not living up to its proud ideals and is in fact becoming politically anorexic – while its citizens starve as China's darling one-child princes and princesses become obese.

Smash-Mouth Rhetoric

While career politicians and bureaucrats continue to mouth off in Washington and further inflame the world with their smash-mouth political rhetoric and political spin, the price of oil hit a record high of $150 a barrel, and then dropped to $50 before the 2008 presidential and congressional elections as the world economy collapsed while America and China compete to corner the world's dwindling supplies of energy, with China winning.

Everybody is pummeling America these days, especially China, in politics, economics, sports, political esteem, image and perception. This was best witnessed at the Beijing 2008 Olympics where China won 51 gold medals to America's 36. America couldn't even win a gold medal in its national pastime, baseball. It had to settle for bronze as it watched South Korea take the gold and Cuba the silver. The smash-mouth media in America emphasized the fact that Team USA won more medals overall – 110 to China's 100. But the rest of the world media counted the gold medal haul and proclaimed China the winner.

Brazen tough cowboy talk does not change the fact that America, notwithstanding its unsurpassed military machine, has become a second-rate economic power. This was highlighted the day after the Beijing 2008 Olympic closing ceremonies, when China's Premier Hu Jin-tau visited South Korea, winner of the gold medal in baseball and host to thousands of American troops stationed there. China, not America, is South Korea's largest trading partner.

To make matters worse and really hammer the point home, in August 2008, Iraq, where over 120,000 U.S. troops are stationed and where more than 4,250 have given their lives, gave its first major oil contract to a foreign firm since the fall of Saddam Hussein – not to America – but China.

The China condom conundrum was an ever bigger blow to America. The U.S. Agency for International Development, which distributes millions of AIDs preventing condoms, decided to stop buying them in America and gave the order instead to China.

Wrong Ingredients – Assumptions

Many of America's home-grown political nightmares and geopolitical daydream assumptions at the sunset of the 20th century and dawn of the 21st were wrong – because the ingredients used were wrong. For example, *The New York Times* disbelief in 1972 that the Watergate burglary was known and orchestrated by then President Richard Nixon and Attorney General John Mitchell. Reading that the 250-room Watergate Hotel, part of the complex made famous by Nixon's Watergate scandal that brought the president down, was sold in a foreclosure auction in 2009 for a mere $25 million, was just another indicator of how the world's best spin doctors couldn't spin America out of a disastrous Bush-Cheney recession; or how before 1989, virtually all Sovietologists agreed that the USSR was very stable and a growing threat to America. Before 2001, few Middle East scholars worried that America was vulnerable to a major terrorist attack. Before 2003, neocon hawks were convinced that Saddam Hussein had weapons of mass destruction and before 2008, few economists doubted the fundamental soundness of the U.S. financial system. So it should come as no surprise if America's assumptions about China are also wrong.

Twenty years after Tiananmen Square, the Chinese Communist Party is strong, stable and a threat to America and the world. Nothing could be further from the truth. It is therefore no surprise that China-bashing is on the rise and China more conciliatory on both the economic, nuclear and military fronts.

While we explore more closely the wrong assumptions about China, let's also delve into the wrong perceptions in America about the respective roles Washington and Wall Street played in the Great U.S. Recession and global financial meltdown – a topic debated in New York since the founding of the Republic when Alexander Hamilton's vision of U.S. financial power was not shared by the other Founding Fathers.

Who is to blame more, the Wall Street bankers or the Washington politicians? It has to be the politicians who rewrote the rules governing regulation and allowed them to melt away and allow bankers' insatiable greed to run amok. AIG contributed directly to elected officials and parties $9.3 million from 1989 to 2009, and the top recipients of money include the chairs of the Senate Finance and Banking Committees. Talk about rotten conflict of interests. America's political GPS financial contribution laws definitely have to be recalibrated. As a former member of the Finance Council of the Democratic National Committee in the 1970s, and a member of the Steering Committee of Democrats for Reagan, I personally experienced what the high-paying customers at the political fund raisers, not only national, but state, county and city, expected in return for their overpriced "rubber chicken" meals, which today have become politically correct and include vegetarian options.

It's easy to see how America's financial meltdown came to pass. The Federal Reserve comes in for a big share of the blame. It allowed the housing bubble to inflate and then burst. Between January 2001 and June 2003, the Fed slashed the federal funds rate from 6.5 percent to 1 percent. It then began nudging the rate back up over the ensuing three years, until it hit 5.25 percent. During that time, housing price inflation ran wild, ranging from 7 percent to 17 percent a year, right up until January 2006.

As if that wasn't bad enough, the Federal Reserve Bank of New York, then headed up by Treasury Secretary Timothy Geithner, gave more financial breaks and financial support to banks and bankers, paid for with U.S. tax dollars and Chinese loans, to save A.I.G. from bankruptcy.

The New York Fed gave up and buckled in under pressure from A.I.G. and its trading partners – which are banks. That's according to the most inflammatory episode in the rescue of A.I.G., released in November 2009 in a U.S. government report prepared by the Troubled Asset Relief Program.

This A.I. G. episode is a good example of how quickly and easily career politicians, their financial supporters and designated incompetent bureaucrats, give up taxpayer dollars to the financial institutions that brought the world to its economic and financial knees, without *We the People's* input or approval. The government paid out 100 cents on the dollar to the Wall Street banks, including Goldman Sachs and others and top foreign banks like UBS. Incidentally, besides banking and sheltering a lot of illicit U.S. taxpayer dollars, UBS was the only bank that volunteered to take a modest loss, a haircut in bankers jargon — two cents on the dollar – and it wasn't allowed to.

It gets better. The UBS gesture was quashed by Goldman Sachs and the top French bank regulator. They argued, on behalf of all A.I.G. bank-trading partners, that it would be improper and perhaps even criminal to force A.I.G.'s banks to bear losses outside of bankruptcy court. The banks and French regulator were confident that the New York Fed was not going to push A.I.G. into bankruptcy because it had already put up $85 billion to keep the insurer afloat. They were right.

It was a shameful disgrace to make A.I.G.'s bank-trading partners whole when the taxpayer public had to take painful losses in the financial markets, because of the bankers they then had to bail out and make whole. I have a problem with this logic. I believe the government got things bassackwards. It is the bankers who should be making the taxpayers they duped whole.

The Fed acted like a creditor instead of the regulator it is. It should not have gone to the banks asking them for voluntary concessions. It should have mandated the terms of their haircut and looked out for the best interest of taxpayers.

Why weren't the banks treated like GM and Chrysler? Why didn't the government negotiate as aggressively with the banks as it did with the car manufacturers?

Meanwhile, the Securities and Exchange Commission under Christopher Cox – a world-class China-basher when he was a congressman – allowed leverage in the banking industry to spiral out of control.

Then there's Freddie Mac and Fannie Mae, which imploded after amassing risky, highly leveraged loans while Congress looked the other way.

Why does America insist on continuously appointing well connected career politicians to regulatory enforcement positions they are clueless about? Why not appoint competent officials who will do the job to vigorously enforce the law and protect citizens and the politicians and their financial supporters be damned?

Then, of course, there's the Bush-Cheney White House with its brilliant media-managing spin that carried the tagline: "We want everybody in America to own a home," as George W. Bush put it in October 2002. What he neglected to add was " ... In order to finance the wars against terrorism in Iraq and Afghanistan ... and, of course, my buddies in the oil and pharmaceutical business who have brought me so much happiness."

In the words of economic historian Niall Ferguson, author of *The Ascent of Money: A Financial History of the World,* "Washington sold itself to Wall Street."

Oh, and let's not forget the regulatory quagmire when you have the Comptroller of the Currency, the SEC, the Office of Thrift Supervision, the FDIC, the banking regulatory authorities of all 50 states – all more interested in protecting and expanding their own turf than regulation.

The cocktail of politicians seeking re-election at any price and bankers making money at the same price is a financial kamikaze – green in color. Add to that publicly listed companies getting away with falsifying their financials because of the lax and confusingly contradictory regulatory language and the kamikaze becomes a volcano. All in all, a bunch of stupid, arrogant, incompetent and greedy hogs that got slaughtered because not only did they pig out at the trough, they got drunker on the liquor constantly being added to the financial derivatives punchbowl by the Fed to wash down the pork.

What really surprised and upset me was the fact that as the economy was getting worse and heading to the precipice of meltdown, the bad news was repeatedly spun by the media as good. It reminded me of the financial analyst who had a heart attack, which was then described by politicians and colleagues as a "cardiac correction." That is how career politicians in Washington are describing the current "economic correction" caused by the un-regulated toxic assets, now described as "legacy" assets, that triggered the global financial crisis.

Alex Berenson, an investigative business reporter for *The New York Times,* blames Wall Street and contrasts its miserable performance to the stellar U.S. airline industry that has regulated itself as one of the safest in the world, putting safety first. By comparison, Wall Street was run by a bunch of greedy children for 10 years who, because they were making millions for a year's work, don't have much incentive for *The Long Run* – one of the great Eagles songs. Another Eagles hit, *Take It to the Limit,* summarizes Wild West unregulated capitalism. The minute capitalism allows the quantity of transactions to justify compensation more than quality due diligence, it is inevitable that the system will collapse.

And as if the collapse wasn't bad enough, Washington decided to wean the greedy bankers and U.S. consumers off their addictions with a huge federal bailout package that works like a giant methadone clinic dispensing to a population of heroin addicts. "By artificial stimulus of the economy, the U.S. administration has dulled the withdrawal symptoms – but the challenge of weaning the population off its heroin addiction still lies ahead. And even the U.S. does not have the resources to continue dispensing methadone indefinitely," said David Dodwell, chief executive officer of Strategic Access, Hong Kong.

What Flu and Whose?

One of the most frequently asked questions I was confronted with during my visits to the U.S. in the fall of 2008 and early 2009 was: "Aren't you worried about bird flu and those other killer Chinese diseases? You are living in the epicenter of every pandemic that originates in China. Why don't you move back to the U.S. where it is so much safer?"

"Because of swine flu" is what I would have answered had it broken out a few weeks earlier. Instead, I had to settle for "C'mon, that's an exaggeration. The biggest pandemic we have experienced in our lifetime is the financial pandemic killing industry and employment for millions, which originated on Wall Street – not China."

With the exception of the first swine flu case to reach Hong Kong with a man who arrived from Mexico via Shanghai, every confirmed swine flu case in Hong Kong and mainland China came aboard flights from the United States, with a few exceptions from Canada. The swine flu pandemic is the first global outbreak declared by WHO since 1968 – and America is the hardest hit country.

Digesting the news stories about the thousands of children across America spending their time in summer camp in quarantine because they had come down with the H1N1 flu symptoms and the resulting havoc for parents and camp counselors alike, all I could think of is how America's children are being prepared for the country's next biological war created by Tamiflu come the fall. For someone like me who is supposed to be in the U.S in November on a business trip and to help launch this book, the news was disconcerting.

What worries doctors about swine flu is that it mixes pig flu viruses from three continents with human and bird flu and people have no natural immunity to it. Hong Kong is the only place to have quarantined an entire hotel because of the first case that arrived and checked in before going to the hospital and being confirmed. Hong Kong took such a tough approach because of its experience in dealing with SARS in 2003.

Having lived through the SARS experience and the earlier bird flu outbreak in 2000, when the government culled all poultry in the territory, I felt very comfortable heading back to Hong Kong while the world was awaiting the arrival of a bird flu pandemic from China.

"I can't think of a safer place to be if bird flu does break out," I would tell my Chinese detractors and concerned friends. "It is the one place that has tackled it effectively in the past and I have no doubt they will do so again should the need arise. I'm not sure I can say the same about America."

My concern was confirmed when the U.S. government failed yet again to deliver on its political-spun promise to its citizens of 100 million swine flu vaccine doses by the winter flu season. Hearing that only 11 million doses were available at the end of October 2009, forcing Americans to line up at 3 a.m. to get the under-promised flu shots – while Wall Street banks received the vaccine for their in-house clinics – all I could do was hang my head in shame when asked to explain the U.S. governments' hypocritical shortfall to my Chinese inquisitors.

China-Bashing and Fear Mongering
Presidential candidates Senators John McCain and Barack Obama both

took political swipes at China in answering questions submitted to them by the American Chamber of Commerce in Beijing during their 2008 campaign and published in the chamber magazine. Both conveniently overlooked the yuan's more than one-fifth appreciation against the dollar over the past three years. Surprisingly, the candidates were not asked during their presidential debates to comment on how they proposed to deal with China. That's surprising, since China is the scapegoat blamed for everything wrong with America. It is a convenient political football. Both presidential candidates did, however, take a swipe at China during their second debate. In the vice presidential debate that followed, China was blamed for causing global warming and pollution. While China is the worst of the carbon dioxide emitters, the U.S. is a close second, a fact that was conveniently overlooked.

China is portrayed as the villain for keeping the value of the yuan artificially low to maintain a trade advantage over U.S.-based manufacturers and for causing higher prices for raw materials, including oil, and for increasing exports of cheap manufactured goods that have condemned America's work force to redundancy because of outsourcing, and for global warming.

After all, no U.S. congressman worth his vote is going to admit global warming is the result of decades of hyper-consumption in a small number of Western economies led by the U.S. when he can instead blame it on 1.3 billion Chinese who also have had the temerity to strive for affluence. Nor is a U.S. politician going to accept blame for the global economic recession when 1.3 billion Chinese can be blamed for saving too much and consuming too little.

The fact is that most of the factories that once polluted American skies to supply U.S. consumers with their needs have now relocated – "outsourced" – to China. Congress also wants to impose sanctions on China for its inclusion since 1999 on a U.S. blacklist of "severe" religious freedom violators.

U.S. politicians habitually make sure that whatever blame is directed their way for their "voodoo economics" is deflected and redirected at China – especially during the current financial meltdown and recession. The fact that much of the bashing and fear mongering is untrue is overlooked or deliberately ignored by America's media.

For example, former U.S. Vice President Dick Cheney, claimed that China, at Cuba's behest, was drilling for oil in waters less than 60 miles from the Florida coast. In a speech to the U.S. Chamber of Commerce in June 2008, Cheney said that waters in the eastern Gulf of Mexico, long off limits to oil companies, ought to be opened to drilling because China was already there pumping oil.

"Oil is being drilled right now 60 miles off the coast of Florida,"Cheney said. "We're not doing it; the Chinese are in cooperation with the Cuban government. Even the communists have figured out that a good answer to high prices is more supply."

Independent energy experts say that Cheney's claim is an exaggeration at best and a lie at worst. Jorge Pinon, a senior energy fellow at the University of Miami specializing in Latin America, said China was being painted as an unnecessary "bogeyman by drilling proponents."

Talk of China drilling in waters within 60 miles of Florida has been a common Republican theme. "China, thanks to a lease issued by Cuba, is drilling for oil just 50 miles from Florida's coast," Republican Congressman George Radanovich wrote in 2008 in *The Modesto Bee*. House Republican leaders echoed this false claim throughout the 2008 campaign and George Will wrote about it in his newspaper column. Thankfully, neither presidential candidate nor the public took the bait.

The end of the election season did not bring an end to China-bashing. China was blamed as the source of the 2009 Mexican swine flu outbreak. Since China doesn't export pork to either Mexico or America, it would be an easy thing for news outlets to check before reporting it as fact. Some press reports quoted the governor of the Mexican state of Veracruz, Fidel Herrera, as telling reporters the virus began in China. The fact is that China gave Mexico $5 million in aid to help fight the outbreak.

China-bashing is not limited to politicians. Respected professors living in self imposed isolated ivory towers far removed from reality contribute their fair share of fear mongering. One such agent provocateur is historian Niall Ferguson of Harvard, whom I respect and quote periodically on subjects we agree upon. He spoke at the Aspen Ideas Festival in June 2009, where he argued that the economic friction building up between America and China will lead to conflict and potential catastrophe.

Ferguson claims the Internet has made young Chinese more nationalistic.

China is acquiring resources around the world and with them, willy-nilly, an overseas empire that threatens U.S. interests. And China is building up its navy, a historic precursor to expanded ambitions and global conflict. Think of China, Ferguson concluded, as Kaiser Wilhelm's Germany in the years before the first world war: a growing, aggressive, nationalistic power whose ambitions will tear through pre-existing commercial ties and historic friendships.

The Falun Gong spiritual movement helped further inflame anti-China sentiments in its weekly *The Epoch Times,* with stories of prisoners making everything from umbrellas to children's clothes. They are not alone. Political pundits, whose predictions on just about everything, especially China, are almost always wrong, are right there on every talk show and news program dispensing their erroneous conclusions. Philip Tetlock, a research psychologist at Stanford University who studies cognitive styles and pundits, concluded that the most popular predictors, the ones feted the most by the media, have the worst accuracy. No surprise there. However, they do unjustly inflame the protectionism debate when it comes to China.

The rise of protectionist sentiment in America over the trade deficit with China could have devastating consequences for the global economy. Quotas on textiles and televisions from China will not save U.S. jobs. The quotas will only increase imports from other low-cost manufacturing centers that have lost market share to China. This will raise the prices paid by U.S. consumers. The fact is that affordable Chinese textiles and goods are an integral part of the American lifestyle. If the U.S. insists on messing with Chinese currency and quotas, Americans will end up wandering around like the Timorese – the poorest people on earth.

America seems to have forgotten a certain 1980s Japan trade history lesson. Low-cost, fuel-efficient Japanese cars terrified Detroit so much back then that the U.S. automakers persuaded Congress to impose quotas on them. The Japanese then started to make luxury cars, which are far more profitable. The result is that Japan's Infinitis, Lexuses and other luxury makes along with their reliable, fuel-efficient smaller cars – have bankrupted the Detroit automakers and their part suppliers.

China-bashing, sanctions and quotas will not help America's economy recover. On the contrary, it will only expedite the current economic and financial meltdown should China decide to retaliate by dumping its vast holdings ofdollars and treasuries. Not only that, China-bashing doesn't help improve

America's global image.

America's global image is more negative than China's, according to a BBC World Service 2008 survey. At the dawn of the 21st century, China's image has enjoyed steady improvement at America's expense. The election of Barack Obama to the White House has helped temper the erosion of America's image, according to the Pew Global Attitudes Project released in mid-2009 – though not enough though to keep Chicago from finishing last in the first vote in its bid for the 2016 Olympics – a humiliating Olympic-sized embarrassment for Barack and Michelle Obama, who made personal appearances in support of America's bid, along with Oprah Winfrey and many other American dignitaries and celebrities.

The shock award of the 2009 Nobel Peace Prize to Obama in the wake of the Olympic trashing helped burnish America's tarnished image, and rightly so.

"Very rarely has a person to the same extent as Obama captured the world's attention and given its people hope for a better future," the committee said. The prize was more for America's idealism and promise to the world than its performance – realpolitik.

Historical Reality

While America's Founding Fathers were waging their struggle for independence in 1776, China was already not only the most populous, but the wealthiest nation on earth. China was the leading high-tech civilization in the 10th and 13th century in silk, the compass, navigation, book-printing and porcelain and the furnaces used to make it. China has a big balance of payments surplus today, as it had in the 18th century, when it accumulated gold, silver and credits from the West in payment for its silk, porcelain and other luxury goods. The West, and Britain in particular, was able to offset this only by exporting opium to China.

The lesson for companies and countries is that old established firms, like political parties and dated ideologies – despite ample capital and technical know how – often don't dominate new industries or geopolitics if they forget the lessons of history. Google, Microsoft, eBay and Yahoo rule the Internet, not General Motors, Ford, Chrysler, Sears or Disney. The same holds true when it comes to America and China.

This is best exemplified by how America squandered billions of dollars under the Bush-Cheney administration on bullets and guns and all kinds of military hardware to be wasted in the deserts of Afghanistan and Iraq. Meanwhile, China spent its money on education and infrastructure, a lesson it learned from America's Franklin Delano Roosevelt and his New Deal – hence the phenomenal sports venues and related infrastructure the world witnessed during the Beijing Olympics. Who made the better investment is plainly evident.

The political neglect and lack of regulatory oversight that lit the fire under America's economic meltdown led to the loss of trillions of dollars, as risky, heretofore unknown financial instruments cooked up by Wall Street went south. Among those burned were thousands of Chinese investors who put more than $3 billion into Lehman Brothers investment products that became worthless.

The U.S. Treasury was forced to step in with a trillion-dollar-plus bailout for Wall Street and the banking industry, as well as riding to the financial rescue of Detroit's Big Three automakers. All this has not only made the market meltdowns of Mexico in 1994 and Asia in 1997 look like chump change, but has allowed China to take giant steps in the industries that America once dominated. That includes not only automobiles, but aerospace as well. China's homemade jumbo passenger jet is to take to the skies in five to 10 years.

China is challenging and marginalizing America's role as the dominant industrial and geopolitical player.

Today America and China must develop a new successor model to free-market capitalism and interlocalism. Globalization is benefiting only a handful of the richest people and impoverishing the rest of the world. A new economic and political system that is in tune with the new global economic reality thrust upon us by the worldwide Internet is necessary to get the global economy back on track.

China is re-emerging as a global economic and military power. It is a power America should embrace in a strategic alliance. The alternative is a futile and costly exercise of containment and encirclement that is doomed to fail. America is trying to do to China today what Britain and France tried to do to contain the rapid growth of Germany before World War I. Britain and France formed an alliance with Russia to encircle Germany. The U.S. is trying to form a similar alliance with Japan and India to contain China.

But China, unlike Germany, has no desire to conquer the world. This is a historical fact that I address in detail in my book *Custom Maid Knowledge*. America's thinking is outdated. It didn't work for Britain and France and it won't work for America. The only outcome, just like in 1914, is an avoidable war.

"You snooze, you lose" America, just as China did in the 19*th* century. Is it any wonder Americans have awakened to find themselves threatened on the home front as impoverished debtors at the mercy of creditors in China?
High Hopes

In my previous books, I questioned and challenged the futility and self-destructiveness of China fear-mongering and bashing – especially during presidential and congressional elections. Thankfully, in the 2008 presidential election, Obama and McCain avoided a China-bashing strategy. Compared to previous campaigns, it was milder than mild – virtually nonexistent. China's conspicuous absence from the campaign speaks volumes about the maturity of the Sino-America relationship. The fact that senior Chinese envoys met with both candidates during the campaign to discuss issues of mutual interest and concern – and attended the Democratic National Convention for the first time as observers – are significant developments. America seems to have grudgingly accepted its dependence on China and doesn't want to inflict any more economic or geopolitical pain on itself. By the same token, China's Communist Party has expressed its desire to learn from America's experienced political parties how to modify its rigid structure.

During my travels across California in late 2008, I took the scenic highways across the Santa Cruz mountains and through the California redwoods, fir trees and occasional eucalyptus, interspersed with leaves in bright shades of purple, orange, pink, yellows and reds brought on by the unseasonably cold winter, actually the coldest to hit the Western United States and Canada in several decades. The leaves changed colors, depending on whether the sun was out or it was overcast and raining. The weather, like the political mood, was unpredictable, but hope was in the air awaiting the inauguration of President-elect Obama. I also drove the scenic routes across the Sacramento Delta where, like the Monterey Peninsula, the smell of freshly plowed fields filled the air.

During the election campaign, and still today, I am disturbed by the periodic discussions by reputable media talking heads and elected politicians about the possibility of Obama being assassinated. The fact that Facebook launched an online poll asking whether Obama should be assassinated reaffirmed my concern about how depraved and racist many Americans are.

Driving from Los Angeles to the Sacramento Delta via the Monterey Peninsula, where I was to meet a business associate for lunch, I decided to stop off in Paso Robles for the night and catch up with long-time friend Ralph Herman.

Ralph and I don't agree on much of anything or anyone political, which always results in stimulating discussions over a few good bottles of local wine. I shared with Ralph what I was concluding in this book about starving Americans being hoodwinked by their governing elite. He suddenly interrupted, saying: "I've got a good one for you. Have you heard about the Indian who walked into a café with a shotgun and a buffalo?" I hadn't. "Well," Ralph continued, "an Indian walks into a café with a shotgun in one hand pulling a male buffalo with the other. He says to the waiter. 'Want coffee.' The waiter says, 'Sure Chief. Coming right up.' He gets the Indian a tall mug of coffee. The Indian drinks the coffee down in one gulp, turns and blasts the buffalo with the shotgun, causing parts of the animal to splatter everywhere, and then just walks out. The next morning the Indian returns. He has the shotgun in one hand pulling another male buffalo with the other. He walks up to the counter and says to the waiter 'Want coffee.' The waiter says 'Whoa, Tonto! We're still cleaning up the mess from yesterday. What was all that about anyway?' The Indian smiles and proudly says: 'Training for position in United States Congress: Come in, drink coffee, shoot the bull, leave mess for others to clean up, disappear for rest of day.' "

"Good one, Ralph" I said, laughing and raising my glass of pinot in a toast to his timely sense of humor. Then we got back to the subject of the deepening U.S. recession and its consequences. I told him how stunned I was at the number of panhandlers and homeless people seeking handouts at the intersections and freeway ramps of urban America, even here in relatively affluent Paso Robles. I also shared with him my depressing observations on this visit of people living in makeshift roadside encampments and at the highway rest stops.

Interlocalism

I also stopped off for a couple of days in Isleton, a small town in the Sacramento Delta region, to visit my daughter Alexandra's father-in-law, Ron Swepston, who lives there. The drive took me through Sacramento, the

California state capitol and home to America's most notorious homeless tent city. This is what the capital of the Golden State has become – like the rest of America – bankrupt and home of the hungry, homeless and free.

Driving across the Delta toward Isleton, I was again reminded of the long collaborative and constructive history between Chinese and Americans. Iselton is a small town of 900 people that attracts hundreds of thousands of tourists every Father's Day weekend to the Crawdad Festival. The town is equidistance between San Francisco, Stockton, San Jose and Sacramento. It sits below water level on the Sacramento River and best represents the term interlocalism, which I coined and devoted a chapter to in my book *Custom Maid Knowledge*.

Interlocalism is the proposed interaction between different local communities promoting their collective well-being with minimum government participation. The concentric circles start with the local village, town or city and expand over the county, country and compatible global communities. It is the fusion of local strengths spread widely over similar- minded and compatible people. From the San Fernando Valley, Los Angeles, California, Mexico, the Americas, Quebec, Hawaii, Scotland, Wales, Ireland, Italy, Indonesia, Cyprus, Germany, Korea and China. The Chinese have perfected this with their Chinatowns worldwide, exemplified in Isleton.

Globalism died in the last decade of the 20th century. It was a 19th-century model of economics based on scarcity, but the whole world was in surplus. The debates over globalization, secession or separatism must therefore be replaced with an all-encompassing discussion on interlocalism. Interlocalism will accelerate as the economic benefits and natural growth of the model become evident in the 21st century.

Interlocalism adapts and expands the industrial concept of "clusters." Compatible communities competing and collaborating in a network of mutually supportive, global-wired urban hubs that recognize and accept that economics – fueled by the natural resources that empires, countries, communities, tribes and villages have gone to war over – are, and always have been, the underlying driving engine of the locomotive of politics and senseless wars that get innocent, uneducated children killed because of their parents' ignorance.

China has rejected the globalization economic model, just as it did with rural communism, and is forming Confucian humanist city clusters as the essential national cornerstone of its future interlocal cluster economic model. Most Chinese mega-cities such as Beijing, Shanghai and Wuhan – already home to millions of people – have room to grow. Smaller cities around the mega-cities – especially those with populations of around one million – will become an integral part of the city cluster as sustainable ruralism expands simultaneously.

City clusters have already formed on the Yangtze River Delta and the Pearl River Delta, with Hong Kong, Shanghai and Guangzhou as their respective cores with rapidly expanding sustainable rural communities on their fringes. The key to successful growth is good management. Hong Kong is the best-managed city in China, probably the world. It has the population density of most cities in China, yet it is the most efficient and functional. A great place to raise and enjoy children and pets – not by eating them – but loving, bonding, teaching and learning.

Interlocalism Isleton-Style

Native Americans occupied the Isleton area until the American Civil War in the 1860s, when the Delta was settled by farmers and workers from China who helped tame the rivers and transform the marshy land into working farms. The Chinese, many of whom had worked to build the railroad network across the West, built the levees and created the channels across the Delta with the techniques they learned in China taming the Yangtze River. As farmers moved into the Delta, the Chinese also took on the back-breaking labor on the farms and built their own community in Isleton. The Chinese laborers' contribution to California and America's economies, like the countless Chinese treasures in antique stores across California that they and many other Americans brought from China, is priceless.

A recent story in Hong Kong that caught my attention as a millennium reminder of how industrious the Chinese are was that of 72-year-old Fung Kan-chuen. Fung worked as a cleaner-handyman in a tenement building that didn't have an elevator. He is a slim man, 1.52 meters tall. He carried a tenant's 1.82-metre-high refrigerator on his back down five flights of stairs, each comprising 24 steps.

Isleton's Chinatown became a vibrant hub replete with Chinese customs, traditions and family values. The two-block Main Street hub of the Chinese community still stands and is registered today as a national historic district. The Tong building, a large two-story structure in the middle of Main Street, was the "government" of the Chinese community and today houses the Isleton Historical Society after being deeded to the city by the Bing Kong Tong Association of San Francisco.

This small-town continuous historical collaborative history between Chinese, Chinese-Americans and other ethnic Americans – and the phenominally prosperous California economy they helped build, like many communities across California where Chinese settled to build the railroads, levees and farms – is a microcosm of the global economy that China and America can continue to build together.

The long and distinguished list of Chinese-Americans who have contributed to America's global rise and stature include architect I.M. Pei, cellist Yo-Yo Ma, Anna Chennault, the diplomatic lobbyist who promoted Sino-U.S. relations to U.S. Presidents Richard Nixon and Ronald Reagan, former Labor Secretary Elaine Lan Chao and current U.S. Commerce Secretary Gary Locke, the grandson of such laborers and the first Chinese-American governor in U.S. history, and Energy Secretary Steven Chu. Chu is a Nobel Prize-winning physicist and former director of the Lawrence Berkeley National Laboratory, the oldest government research institute in California with over 4,000 employees and a budget of $650 million. During his tenure, the lab focused research on alternative energy, energy efficiency and reduction of greenhouse gases, the backbone of America's new environmental and economic agenda.

Many Chinese-Americans are going into politics and public service these days, not only in Chinatowns, but across lily-white America. This is exemplified by Hank Eng, who ran as a Democrat in Colorado's 6th Congressional District, an overwhelmingly white and Republican district – one of three Chinese-Americans to run for U.S. Congress in 2008. To make matters more interesting, he is also Jewish, having converted to his wife's religion on a visit to Beijing. Eng lost, but made a strong run in a district dominated by Republicans.

Sino-U.S. relations are now on a new constructive plateau, notwithstanding their vastly different values and political systems. Hopefully, with the new Obama administration, the cooperative relationship will continue to grow and rise to higher plateaus. The fact is, with all the outsourcing America does today, why can't its economic and geopolitical policies also be outsourced in partnership with China?

The disturbances in Tibet did not stop President Bush and other world leaders from 80 countries from attending the Beijing 2008 Olympics. America and China have come a long way to embrace each other since World War II and 1979, when the U.S. established diplomatic relations with Beijing. Both countries still have a long way to go to become equal global leaders that jointly lead their respective global constituencies to cooperate and work with each other as one.

My hope is that this book contributes to the tighter embrace.

Hold My Hand
– Hootie and the Blowfish

Chapter 1

The Palate Cleansers
– Bittersweet Aftertastes

*When the tyrant has disposed of foreign enemies by
conquest or treaty, and there is nothing to fear from
them, then he is always stirring up some war or
other, in order that the people may require a leader.*
– Plato

Bad Dim Sum Call

The cancellation of President Hu Jin-tao's visit to
the White House in September 2005 – Hurricane Katrina being the convenient excuse – was a worrisome reminder of the continued discord between America and China. After all, the two presidents were only going to
spend half a day together, hardly enough time to warrant canceling the visit.
Katrina was a convenient excuse, albeit a major crisis of George Bush's
presidency. The cancellation only complicated the already delicate Sino-
American relations at the dawn of the 21ˢᵗ century.

The usual state visit includes an arrival ceremony on the White House
South Lawn accompanied by a customary 21-gun salute for a head of state,
a summit meeting in the Oval Office and a state dinner. The U.S. agreed to
welcome Hu with the salute, but drew the line in the salad at a state banquet
– no state dinner, just a lunch.

Hu was the first Chinese leader not to get the full state visit treatment on
his maiden trip to the U.S. as head of state. Because the visit was cancelled,
they had to settle for a photo-op meeting in New York during the U.N. 60ᵗʰ
anniversary's wasteful wake. It was no surprise therefore that China locked
the doors on all of the issues America pressed for during Bush's later visit to
China in November 2005 – not just the door to his news conference in that
hilarious moment when he was trying unsuccessfully to escape – but the
doors to discussions on currency revaluation, human rights and piracy.

When Hu finally did make his landmark visit to the White House's South Lawn in April 2006, his "symbolic" visit was greeted with pomp and pageantry but was riddled with gaffes. It was interrupted by a Falun Gong protester and the White House announcer referred to the mainland as the "Republic of China" – the official title of Taiwan. To make matters worse, Bush's speech was translated into Chinese in a halting, stuttering fashion that had Chinese officials shaking their heads in disbelief. Apparently, while the Chinese had provided the Americans with an advance copy of Hu's remarks, the Americans had not reciprocated with Bush's speech. Maybe that was one of the reasons Bush did not make it onto Time Magazine's 100 most influential people list in 2006. Hu made the list along with six others of Chinese descent.

Wrong Sushi Call
When Japan's Prime Minister Junichiro Koizumi visited the White House in June 2006, not only was the red carpet rolled out with a gala official state dinner, but President Bush accompanied Koizumi and gave him a ride on Air Force One to Memphis, Tennessee, for a tour of Graceland because Elvis Presley is a musical hero of the former prime minister. It was the ultimate state reception and a slap to the Chinese face – a tremendous loss of face. The presidents of Mexico, Poland, the Philippines and Kenya were also honored with White House state dinners while Hu was treated to a mere "social lunch."

Is this any way for America to treat China, America's third-largest export market, ahead of fourth-place Japan – and the leading buyer of U.S. treasuries, the bedrock of American deficit spending?

It should therefore not have come as a surprise when President Barack Obama, even though he is the first U.S. president to visit China during his first year in office, was denied his signature town hall meeting in Shanghai which he wanted to broadcast live on the Web, and also a news conference at the end of his official visit to China in November 2009. Obama's joint appearance before the media with President Hu Jintao was billed as a news conference, but since when do such conferences not allow even one question from any member of the press? It was a position statement announcement, not a press conference.

Watching President Obama tour the Forbidden City and Great Wall alone, without any important Chinese officials, speaks volumes about how isolated and far apart the two countries are. China is eating America's economic and sole superpower status for lunch.

Japan's denial of its wartime history is a dark, ugly regional shadow that will be replaced by a bright rising sun only when Japan comes clean. I visited the Nanjing Memorial Museum in 2005 with Nelson Wong and Pauline Taylor. The museum is dedicated to the Chinese slaughtered in the city by the Japanese in World War II. I asked Wong, who studied in Nanjing, how he felt about the fact that the Japanese had not apologized for their atrocities.

"Idiotic, incomprehensible stupidity and denial that is just making matters more difficult for both China and Japan [which] do want to work together but have to deal with an America that wants them to fight," Nelson responded.

"Over Taiwan?" I asked. "Or do you mean over all containment?"

"Both" he answered without any hesitation.

Shortly after that Nanjing visit, I shared my experience with Bruce Grill, an American who lives in Hong Kong and is in the shoe business in China. We had got together at the Main Bar of the Foreign Correspondent's Club on a Friday night. Grill, a native New Yorker, wasted no time in expressing his opinion. Japan's failure to apologize for those wartime atrocities, he said, "is unforgivable, and I can understand completely why the Chinese are so angry. … Can you imagine how Jews would feel if the Germans didn't apologize [for the Holocaust], not to mention pay reparations?"

Sitting next to us at the bar was Hugh van Es, the Dutch photojournalist who took the iconic picture of the rooftop helicopter evacuation in Saigon in 1975 as the victorious North Vietnamese rolled into the south in 1975. He had picked up on our conversation.

"The fucking Japs deserve the fucking shit they are getting!" he declared. "Everyone knows what they did but they pretend it didn't happen. What bullshit!"

Van Es died in May of this year. He was one of my sponsors when I joined the the Foreign Correspondent's Club in the early 1990s. He also took the photo that appears on the back cover of my 2005 book *Custom Maid War*. In that book, I describe a chance meeting with Hugh in Ho Chi Min City in

1993, and the impromptu tour he gave me of his old wartime haunts in the former Saigon. He pointed out a souvenire shop that was selling copies of some of his wartime photos.

Vanes, as he was known, was passionate about life and harbored strong beliefs about injustice, racism and human suffering, reflected in his photographs. He understood that people have to change if the world is to survive. He was born and raised in Holland, where he was first exposed to Americans, the U.S. troops who had helped to liberate Europe from the Nazi scourge. Vanes, despite his habit of sprinkling his conversation liberally with profanities, was keenly articulate in his condemnation of racism and religious prejudice. His family, at the risk of death, had sheltered Jews during the Nazi occupation of Holland. Later he would be inspired to take up the camera himself in the cause of truth and justice, having seen a 1950s exhibition of the wartime work of filmmaker Frank Capra.

I was thinking about Vanes' remarks about Japan when his wake was held at the Foreign Correspondent's Club last May. His wife Annie, a petite Hong Kong businesswoman, summed the man up perfectly when she said of her husband, "He said it and pictured it as he saw it in his heart and mind.

American Chop Suey

With America getting its sheriff's badge ripped from its shirt and handed back in Vietnam, Afghanistan and Iraq, China is clearly a major beneficiary of U.S. geopolitical and economic quagmire, which America is finally reluctantly acknowledging.

Sadly, Hu's U.S. visit was a lost opportunity because America continues to believe "that the Chinese dragon will prove to be a fire-breather. There is a cauldron of anxiety about China," according to former Deputy Secretary of State Robert Zoellick.

The most challenging conundrum facing America is how to balance the growing conflict between free trade and national security concerns. This has already impacted everything from Chinese direct investment in America, the European Union's subsidies of a new search engine to challenge Google and Yahoo, and for Airbus to challenge Boeing, as well as barriers to trade in the high-tech sector and agricultural policy in developing countries.

Washington's use of "essential security" interests has become an excuse for protectionism. How far should America go in allowing considerations of national security to interfere with trade and commerce?

Washington's decision in September 2009 to impose a 35 percent tariff on Chinese tires for a year, then down to 30 percent the second year, and 25 percent the third before returning to the normal 4 percent in 2012, resulted in China filing a complaint with the World Trade Organization challenging America's tariff. The tire case is the first American use of the special clause of the 1999 "accession" agreement that brought China into the WTO, which makes import limits unusually easy. This clause, known as 421 for its place in the big green book of the Federal Register that governs trade laws, allows U.S. companies and unions to appeal for tariffs on fast-growing Chinese imports – not on grounds of unfair trading practices, but simply to provide a crutch in a period of rising imports and competition – in other words, to challenge free trade. Section 421, like most U.S. foreign policy agendas, is temporary, lasting only until 2013. China's concern is that, since "421" cases are relatively easy to file, more trade unions will file complaints the next few years.

Beijing's decision to challenge Washington is a meaningful development in the relationship, as China is acknowledging the value of the rule of law. China lodged its complaint against the U.S. in the wake of a WTO ruling in August 2009, that it must open up its entertainment sector to more foreign competition, which China is appealing. China has learned how to wield the sword of Western justice in international judicial bodies.

My personal favorite is China's challenge to a blatant inconsistency in U.S. trade law – the Commerce Department treats China as a "nonmarket economy" when considering anti-dumping cases, but is willing to view it as a "market economy" when investigating whether China should be subject to countervailing duties as a result of subsidies for exporters. The result of this legal contradiction is higher U.S. duties on Chinese exports that run afoul of anti-dumping rules. Several Chinese cases against this regulation are currently winding their way through Geneva.

When China first joined the WTO, it adopted a watch-and-learn strategy. It did not file any cases. When it did decide to get involved in the judicial process, first with the steel case only after several other countries, including the EU did so first – it did so as a "third party observer." This gave China a chance to observe from the sidelines how the wheels of Western justice work in practice.

Beijing is now making a concerted effort to train a crop of lawyers with relevant expertise for WTO litigation and other venues that govern trade policy. A Chinese judge now sits on a WTO appellate panel.

China's challenge of the U.S. tire tariff at WTO in Geneva signals a lot more litigation, which will rapidly become much less litigious and lead to a more constructive trade cycle, since most trade laws being passed in America and the West are focused on rising protectionism – against China their banker. All China has to do is withdraw its financing and America's litigious nature, like it's wars, are no longer sustainable.

The Obama administration decision to impose a three-year tariff on Chinese tires can become a marker for one of the first steps towards a 1930s-style closure of world markets. What is worrisome about the China tire tariff is that only one-third of tires imported by the U.S. come from China.

Three paper companies and the United Steelworkers filed an anti-dumping case against China in September 2009 alleging it has been dumping tons of shiny, coated paper, making good the union's threat to protect other U.S. industries. As a former union worker myself, I respectfully disagree. The union is actually filing a case against the largest union in the world that can become its biggest ally in unionizing workers worldwide, another short-sighted example of U.S. global misjudged Sino-realpolitik.

In October 2009, the U.S. launched a probe to consider slapping almost 100 percent tariffs on imported seamless steel pipes from China. A spokesman at the Chinese Ministry of Commerce said: "The rising trade protection-ism is worrying. The U.S. should be aware that trade protectionism is a double-edged sword and will do no good to either side." China followed up its warning by making U.S. toothbrushes and nylon socks the latest vic-tims of the U.S.-China trade skirmish. China imposed a 36 percent tariff on American-made Nylon 6, a synthetic filament that winds up in a wide array of products including auto parts, toothbrushes, socks and Glock handguns. Nylon-6 followed the tariffs China imposed on chicken meat and car parts after the U.S. imposed the tire tariff.

Considering the fact that the United Steelworkers represent only 6,000 hourly workers at plants in nine U.S. states operated by three companies, one has to question the wisdom of the filings. With the upcoming G-20 taking place in Pittsburgh Steelers home town, the steel capital of America –and once the world – C'mon why is anyone surprised? That is not the point. The point is let's analyse it and question its prudence for the future of interlocal economic and financial superbowls. These free-trade sanctions are a bad replay of what happened in 2007, under the dictatorial executive orders of Obama's predecessor George Bush. Where did it get America then and what is different today? America is digging itself a deeper hole for the Chinese barbeque and hot pot. America, the host of the G-20 in Pittsburgh in September 2009, overlooked its promises at not only this G-20 summit, but the two earlier ones in London and Washington by yielding to local political vested interests and imposing protectionist measures that merely add fuel to the fire cooking up extra costs and delays to internationalized production and supply chains in America.

The tariffs imposed by the Obama administration are understandable when viewed in the context of the Herculean domestic agenda that Obama has to get passed by Congress to adress unemployment, economic recovery and healthcare reform. Union votes and lobbying efforts can make a significant difference – so let the Chinese and American consumers take the hit again. Hopefully, China understands and appreciates this domestic political imperative and does not allow the U.S. and its other powerful political constituencies to accelerate the protectionism spiral into a ful-blown trade war. Just like America is trying to restore the cumulative 7.2 million job losses, China is trying to protect the interests of its producers and workers. The difficult economic environment in both countries makes more trade disputes possible, but hopefully, unlikely. Both countries" political leaders do have to pander to their base constituencies to advance their domestic agendas, but do recognize that they cannot afford to jeopardize their bilateral relationship. Nevertheless, tit-for-tat retaliation is a dangerous flirtatious affair that can lead to protectionism. Announcing the tire tariffs shortly before the September G-20 economic summit in Pittsburgh only made it harder to combat protectionism.

China-U.S. bilateral trade stands at more than $400 billion in 2009. Trade with China accounts for about 12 percent of total U.S. trade, while China's trade with the U.S., accounts for 13 percent of its total. Thus, if the trade dispute spreads to other sectors, it will have a substantial negative impact on global trade, which is already predicted to contract by about 10 percent in 2009.

America's decision to change its trade policy toward China began in early 2007 with the filing of the widest-ranging WTO trade case ever put forward by Washington against Beijing. It followed up by imposing countervailing duties on Chinese coated paper – paper that has been treated to give it certain qualities, including weight and surface gloss, smoothness or ink absorbency. They were the first imposed in 23 years by the U.S. of so-called countervailing duties in response to subsidies in a "non-market economy," as China is classified by America. The U.S. Commerce Department's long-standing position had been that it is difficult to determine subsidy levels in a non-market economy. Though China's coated paper exports to the U.S. account for less than 1 percent of the total bilateral trade, the duty could be followed by similar action against Chinese steel, textiles and other products because those U.S. industries claim cheap imports from China have hurt them. America then follows up with another WTO lawsuit against China for piracy and counterfeiting of U.S. goods and blocking access to American movies, music, books and other publications.

Washington is blasting Beijing with both barrels – granted a lot quieter in these days of desperate cash needs. Hearings have looked into everything from Beijing's test of an anti-satellite weapon, military build-up, policy on forced abortions, support of ruthless regimes, "cheating" on its trade commitments, undervaluing its currency, repatriation of North Korean refugees in violation of international law, and even one to end normal trading relations with China.

Anti-China trade legislation reached a fever pitch less than six months after the U.S. 2006 midterm election, with at least 15 bills in Congress seeking to punish Beijing. The presidential election campaigning in 2007 re-ignited unprecedented China-bashing, especially when the yuan reached a post-revaluation high on May Day 2007. It was the highest intraday level since it was revalued and freed from the dollar peg in July 2005. The yuan has risen more than 20 percent in value since being de-linked from the dollar.

A bipartisan bill introduced by Senators Max Baucus, Chuck Grassley, Charles Schumer and Lindsey Graham is designed to tackle the huge trade deficit with China by requiring the Treasury Department to identify fundamental misaligned currencies – driven by explicit government policies. However, the senators acknowledge that reducing the U.S. trade deficit will require a lot more than punishing China – at the expense of U.S. consumers.

The bill, if passed into law, would permit companies to seek anti-dumping duties on rival Chinese imports based on the undervaluation of the currency and calls for a new trade case to be brought by the U.S. at the World

Trade Organization, alleging that the depressed yuan amounts to an illegal subsidy. China again became the scapegoat of U.S. economic and political anxiety. The reevaluation of the Chinese currency will not help reduce America's trade deficit. It will merely shift the source of imports to other low-cost countries. American consumers will be the victims of the trans-Pacific trade crossfire.

Americans have to boost national savings, promote U.S. exports and invest in responsible education and healthcare policies if we are to curb the trade deficit with China. It hit a record $300 billion in 2008, and continues to rise. It is important to keep in mind that after China joined the World Trade Organization in 2001, many companies from other low-cost manufacturing countries in Asia moved their operations to China, bringing with them their long-standing trade surpluses with the U.S.

About 60 percent of China's exports by value are produced or assembled by foreign firms, American, European and Latino. But most are from Hong Kong, Taiwan, South Korea, Japan and Southeast Asia. The actual added value of mainland inputs is no more than 30 percent of the total value of mainland exports. That is why passage of the legislation will penalize mainly foreign firms, including American. Protectionism will have global and interlocal repercussions that will paralyze the international trading system. Protectionism is just so not American. It is totalitarian.

Protectionism flies in the face of international agreements to reduce or eliminate trade tariffs and capital controls, legalize subsidies and lower transport costs.

Chinese Butcher?
As if that wasn't bad enough, the U.S. media, led by Fox News, were quick to blame a Chinese student for the Virginia Tech shooting rampage in April 2007. Other news outlets picked up the story and ran with it without verifying its authenticity. They were all wrong. The murderer at Virginia Tech was of Korean ancestry, not Chinese. Rupert Murdock's Fox News must have had a lot of explaining to do to the boss after his Chinese-born wife got through with him that night. Dragon lady Wendy must have been a sheer delight to come home to.

The same thing happened again in April 2009, when 13 people from eight countries were killed while taking an English-language class run by the American Civic Association in Binghamton, New York, by a fellow Vietnamese student who was angry at being ridiculed for his poor English. Many media outlets blamed the killings on a Chinese student. The fact that four Chinese students from the mainland were among the dead, including a well respected professor from Shenzhen who was in the States as a visiting schola,r was conveniently overlooked.

"Yeah, it is amazing how we Americans think all Asians are Chinese. Can you tell the difference?" Kevin McBride asked me one evening as he got off the phone with his daughter Caitlin, who was studying in Beijing and rejoined Mary Catherine and I, who were in the midst of one of our ongoing debates about racism in America. Before I could answer, Kevin hit me with another question. "Did you hear the one about the two Afghans who immigrated to America and agreed to meet in a year and see who had become more Americanized?" I hadn't. "Well, when they met up again a year later, one tells the other how he takes his son to Mickey D's for breakfast every Sunday before taking him to his Little League baseball game, grills burgers and hotdogs on the 4th of July for his family and neighbors and drinks beer with his buddies when watching Monday night football. 'So what do you think, I'm very American hey bro? What about you, 'Fuck off, towel head, responds the second Afghan."

When we all stopped laughing, Mary Catherine got back to the subject at hand.

"Your books invoke frustration with our American system, but for us it helped fuel a feeling of patriotism for our red, white and blue. The Chinese made me realize just how many things we have in common, not how very different we are," she said.

Consumable Subsidies

What about the billions of subsidized tax breaks, soft loans and offsets that U.S. industries like agriculture, steel and many others have been living on for decades? For Washington to claim that American farmers suffer because of China's subsidies on manufactured goods, as former U.S. Commerce Secretary Carlos Gutierrez said, especially in light of the billions of dollars in annual U.S. farm subsidies that flood the global markets with below-cost American foodstuffs to the detriment of struggling farmers in every poor corner of the world, is not only hypocritical but counter-productive.

America's first "MBA president" and the Democratic-led Congress botched things up again. America is picking the wrong fight. A careful analysis by

Lawrence Lau and his team at the Stanford Center for International Development is objective and persuasive. They argue that the U.S. actually benefits more from the trade imbalance because there is more value added to the U.S. economy from America's exports to China, than to the Chinese economy from its exports to the U.S.

China's decision to end its bid for the U.S. oil firm Unocal, because of opposition in Congress on the grounds of national security, highlighted Washington's intolerance of China's economic resurgence. Had the acquisition been concluded, China would not have posed any threat to U.S. energy supplies. What has been created is a precedent for China, and other countries, to keep U.S. firms out of their own energy sectors on similar grounds. China's quest for oil should not lead to a military clash with the U.S., as many pro-Japan and anti-communist disinformation propagators predict.

Is it any wonder then that Beijing is becoming protectionist and, like America, concerned about economic nationalism? This became patently obvious in March 2008 when Coca-Cola's $2.4 billion bid for China Huiyuan Juice Group was blocked because of "a negative effect on competition" and the sale may "force consumers to pay higher prices." A sneak preview to Coke's bid getting bottled up was given to America in 2006 when U.S. private equity fund Carlyle agreed to buy half, rather than 85 percent of a state-owned construction firm, after Beijing intervened.

Beijing also booted Starbucks from the Forbidden City. Kicking Starbucks out is not of earth-shaking importance. After all, the Forbidden City is of historical significance. Would America allow a Starbucks in Independence Hall in Philadelphia, or any other important historical monument for that matter? Why should China?

China and America must weave their geopolitical strategic alliance to match the Chinese goods woven into the fabric of American life and the U.S. treasury bonds woven into the Chinese economy. Hopefully, what the Chinese delegation that signed $4.3 billion in deals in the U.S. in May 2007, primarily in the high-tech field, buying knowhow, software, semiconductor and telecommunications equipment for its rapidly expanding economy, was the first of many more such delegations to help shrink the U.S. deficit. The delegation was made up of executives from more than 200 mainland companies who met their U.S. counterparts in 24 cities across 23 states. Not a bad start.

Morgan Stanley estimates that U.S. consumers have saved $600 billion in the past decade by buying goods made in China. A reality U.S. Senators Lindsay Graham, Tom Coburn and Charles Schumer reluctantly acknowledged after their fact-finding trips to Beijing in early 2006. They went to Beijing to pressure China to liberalize its yuan policy and to threaten punitive sanctions if Beijing didn't comply, but came back believers and withdrew their bill after they realized the 27.5 percent tariffs they proposed would ultimately be paid by the U.S. consumer.

China's growth is an inevitable historical process that America grudgingly acknowledged during Hu Jintao's April 2006 state visit. China is more than a "stakeholder" in the new economy and global community. It is the dominant player with which America must form a long term strategic partnership.

The U.S. political landscape has to stop looking like a political Disneyland.

Chinese Wrap
Indeed, the world is changing. When Greece and Turkey announced a joint gas pipeline, with the Greek prime minister visiting Turkey to announce the deal – the first visit by a Greek leader in 40 years – it signaled the irrevocable arrival of change. A pipeline planned through Pakistan to India, from Bangladesh to India, and from Egypt to Israel, bringing Myanmar and eventually Iran into the global loop, was another seal of approval for change.

With America's enemies, North Korea and Iran – China's friends – going nuclear, a major geopolitical realignment is taking place that America must come to terms with. A nuclear Shiite Iran next door to Shiite Iraq, next to nuclear neighbor Israel, will trigger a nuclear arms race among the neighboring Sunni Arab states. The same will happen in Asia with a nuclear North Korea. Japan and South Korea will also be compelled to go nuclear.

The only solution to avoid Armageddon is for America and China to partner, cooperate and for America to accept the fact that the center of gravity has moved to Asia in the 21st century with China at the controls. This was made clear during the North Korea denuclearization talks. North Korea was the catalyst in getting the U.S. and China to work together for a common goal and get closer to each other.

"Not bad for a couple years' work," Secretary of State Condoleezza Rice said, referring to the period of time Washington and Beijing worked together on the North Korean nuclear issue.

I wonder what she would say today now that the shortsighted U.S. approach to North Korea has ended in failure again?

China acknowledges and accepts its importance and role in working with America to secure a peaceful and harmonious world. China voted twice in three months with the U.S. and its allies on the U.N. Security Council for a resolution denouncing North Korea. Gone forever are the days when Beijing would describe its relationship with North Korea as being as close as that between lips and teeth.

America and China are better off forging a strategic partnership to prevent a bipolar nuclear world instead of backing any regional nuclear grouping on opposite sides. America and China are both better off working together to ensure a nuclear-free Asia and Middle East. The alternative is Armageddon.

America is ready for another "Nixon on China." When President Richard Nixon and Chairman Mao Zedong signed the historic Shanghai Communique in 1972, the rapprochement was not only long overdue but far-sighted. Both countries benefited from the peace and prosperity that followed.

The right-wing Republican rule that uncomfortably settled over America after the 2004 and 2006 elections was reminiscent of China's Cultural Revolution and the "Red Peril" that Nixon embraced. If China is prepared to embrace America even closer, why is America rejecting the gesture? America must again overcome the red scare that career politicians and the "military industrial complex" have instilled in the country.

China is more universally popular today than the U.S., according to a 2005, 2006 and 2008 survey of global attitudes conducted by the Washington-based Pew Research Center and BBC World Service, because it is perceived as not posing a military threat. Paradoxically, the U.S. is more unpopular around the world than it has ever been. Over the last seven years, since 2002 – post 9/11 sympathy factor – favorable ratings of the U.S. have decreased "in 26 of the 33 countries for which trends are available," Pew said. By embracing China, America can begin the journey to redeem its popularity and standing in the world, a concept and perception the Obama administration understands, grasps and is changing.

"What's funny is how many Chinese restaurants I have eaten at in places faraway from China," Suyin Stein said one evening as we compared U.S. diplomacy to China's. She had worked at the Canadian High Commission in Nairobi in the 1980s. "In Nairobi, I would often get a party of 10 together from our High Commission and phone in a banquet lunch. The owner was from Hong Kong and would regularly get Chinese cooks in. The Chinese embassy was also famous for its dinner parties. Everyone, everywhere wants to eat Chinese and seeks out a Chinese table at which to share friendship." Why not American?

Chinese Debit Card

U.S. foreign policy can no longer afford to ignore or alienate China, either politically or economically. Sino-U.S. cooperation – a strategic alliance –is essential for America to survive the 21st century. America and China can and must be friendly, cooperative competitors pursuing a mutual goal of peace and prosperity. Shanghai Communiqué IV is long overdue.

The U.S. dollar hit a 15-year low against a basket of currencies in August 2007. It is only a matter of time before the yuan will overtake the U.S. dollar as the most accepted currency among the world's central banks. The People's Bank of China has accumulated over $2 trillion of reserves. Because in the past it had no domestic use for them, it turned around and lent them back to the U.S. which recycled them back into the housing loan market. This meant that both Treasury borrowing costs and mortgage interest rates were lower than they otherwise would have been. American homeowners and taxpayers became the beneficiaries. If China did comply with U.S. pressure to revalue its currency, American consumers would face an even worse fiscal apocalypse.

China let its currency rise very quickly and quietly – it even broke through 7.9 to the dollar for the first time in September 2006. It appreciated at a daily rate of 0.8 percent, which works out to an annualized rate of 10 percent. That was quite a contrast to the annual pace of 2 percent to 2.5 percent during most months after China's 2.1 percent revaluation on July 21, 2005. The acceleration came at a time when the Chinese economy settled down to sustained but controlled growth, which made Chinese officials more willing to experiment with the value of the yuan. Some China watchers gave the credit to the quieter U.S. policy advocated by Treasury Secretary Henry Paulson Jr., who with decades of China experience, pursued a much more low-key approach to the currency issue.

The fact is that at the dawn of the 21st century, the Chinese yuan is already an internationally recognized currency that is giving the dollar a run for its money. The dollar slid to a 12-year low against a basket of currencies, and a 26-year low against the British pound in July 2007. The yuan is quietly becoming a universal currency at the expense of the dollar. It delivers everyday economic values without devaluation. There is enough of the currency to finance capital anywhere and anytime – and it does.

There is even talk that the yuan may be the next reserve currency. The U.S. dollar has had a relatively short run so far as the global reserve currency. It assumed the position after World War II and the establishment of the Bretton Woods system of global monetary stability. Back then, the dollar was pegged to gold – at $435 an ounce – and was established as the fallback monetary unit that underpinned the postwar era of economic growth around the world until the Iraq war fiasco.

China, the world's third-largest gold producer, is poised to surpass the U.S. to become the second-largest producer of the precious metal. It produced more than 260 tons in 2007.

All China would have to do today is pass laws that all its exports be purchased in yuan instead of dollars. The currency would then begin a serious push for reserve status. China could bring down the U.S. greenback. With $2 trillion in currency reserves, it holds the ultimate bargaining chip.

With inflation on the rise in America, oil prices rising, with a depression looming on the horizon because of concerns of a major Persian Gulf supply disruption, and America's trade deficit growing, China may just be tempted to make the yuan the global reserve currency.

The U.S. trade deficit and gap in other international transactions keeps growing, with about a third of that deficit with China. There always seems to be a discrepancy of approximately $100 billion annually between the U.S. and Chinese figures, largely because the U.S. counts the cost of shipping and insurance in its figures, which China objects to because most of that business goes to non-Chinese firms. America manages to survive each year economically because of the higher interest rates it pays foreign buyers of the treasury notes that have financed its rapidly widening deficits.

America needs more than $2 billion of foreign cash every day to plug the deficit gap. This is unsustainable as the European Central Bank and Japan raise their interest rates and attract many of the investors now financing America's deficit. For Congress to consider more unpaid-for tax cuts in the 2008 election year – instead of pursuing ways of developing an economic and political partnership with China – is economic suicide. To continue this tax policy as part of the Obama economic recovery plan is a Dr. Kevorkian-style economic assisted-suicide program.

Over the past 20 years up to 2008, China's economy has grown by nearly 10 per cent a year, lifting some 377 million people out of poverty. In 2009, it is expected to grow by 8 percent. Even the rampant fraud that exists in the Chinese banking system can't slow economic growth. U.S. manufacturers, farmers and service providers have seen exports to China grow an average of 22 per cent a year since China joined the WTO in December 2001. The rise of protectionism in America has triggered a rise in economic nationalism in China that could undercut the mainland's promises to the WTO. China can and will backtrack on free market reforms if America continues to change its economic tune.

China's economy hit an 11-year high in July 2007. It grew by 11.9 percent in the second quarter. It produced an output of $2.9 trillion in 2006. China's economy surpassed Germany's in 2007, leapfrogging ahead of the 2010 date most economists predicted, and will exceed Japan's by 2020, becoming the world's leading economy by 2040. China's overall economy is larger and healthier than that of five G-8 members – and its people richer – than current government figures show.

By another measure, known as purchasing-power parity, China is already the world's second-biggest economy. If exchange rates are adjusted to equalize the cost of goods in different countries, then the value of China's total output was $10 trillion in 2006, according to estimates by the IMF. That eclipses Japan's $4.2 trillion and Germany's $2.6 trillion, and is hot on the heels of America's $13 trillion.

It is not just the Chinese government that has trillions of dollars in reserves. So does the consuming public – who are savers. In fact, China depositors are stuffing more money into banks than they can possibly lend or invest, endangering bank profitability and operations in general. The People's Bank of China, the country's central bank, has more than $3.5 trillion in individual savings accounts.

It is a banker's nightmare because the bank must pay interest to depositors while unable to put the cash to work to generate income for the bank. Gross national saving in China amounts to more than 40 percent of gross domestic product, suggesting that Chinese households are much more frugal than their U.S. counterparts, who are swamped by debt after chasing the American dream and designer lifestyle. Eight out of 10 mainlanders are satisfied with the way things are going in China, the 2006 Pew Global Attitudes Project concluded. The 81 percent satisfaction rate is an increase from the 72 percent recorded in 2005 – and the polar opposite of dissatisfied Americans.

America is characterized by the opposite imbalance: an excess of gross domestic investment over domestic savings. If and when these basically symbiotic imbalances becomes unsustainable, tinkering with the yuan/dollar exchange rate will have little impact. Quite different policy changes must be made by the career politicians in Washington to boost the U.S. savings rate, while lowering China's. To do so without triggering a depression in America and inflation in China is the challenge.

In the 1970s, a middle-class existence in America didn't include central air conditioning, computers, mobile phones or cable television. Today, new drugs and surgeries raise the cost of health insurance, reducing coverage and take-home pay. From 1991 to 2005, the cost of fringe benefits, mainly health insurance, rose nearly twice as fast as wages. American household budgets have been stretched beyond the breaking-point by huge repayments and the impact of rising interest rates, mortgage payments and inflation that led to a housing bust and recession in 2007-2008. America has seen its heyday in the sun and its citizens are desperately trying to spend their way there again.

The subprime mortgage meltdown in America led to recession, financial meltdown and Wall Street implosion in the run-up to the 2008 U.S. presidential election. The U.S. housing boom that turned to bust is inflicting great pain. Higher interest rates and falling home prices do not bode well for America. About 80 percent of the increase in employment and almost two-thirds of the growth in the gross domestic product in recent years stemmed directly or indirectly from property. Homes became ATMs in the "net equity extraction" game, financed and backed by banks and hedge funds to the tune of more than $100 billion that will be wiped out. Bear Stearns, the Wall Street investment bank, was the first major casualty, followed by Fannie Mae, Freddie Mac, Lehman Brothers, AIG, Washington Mutual, Wachovia and dozens of regional and local banks.

In late July 2007, the New York Stock Exchange's worst meltdown in five years triggered a record one-day plunge in world markets. It was a sneak preview of more to come: Wall Street's October 2008 surprise – a worst-ever one-week performance.

With the U.S. Federal Reserve, the U.S. central bank, injecting $38 billion into the financial market in August 2007 to sustain liquidity, followed by the $700-billion-plus government bailout of October 2008, not to mention FDIC multi-billion-dollar bank takeovers, it only brought bigger smiles to the Chinese creditors.

By contrast, in China, the precautionary motive for saving is very strong among households because of the lack of an adequate pension system and the sharply rising costs of healthcare. Sound familiar? The need to finance education has also bolstered saving. Corporate savings in China have also risen and now account for almost half of national saving. Corporations in China, unlike America, have an incentive to retain their earnings in order to finance their investment.

American Credit Card

"Come on, gents, get real. The U.S. is bankrupt, out of Benjamins," U2 frontman Bono tells a visibly shocked President Hu Jintao at a Beijing concert. "It's cool to be charitable to the downtrodden and you have trillions in currency reserves. Just ask that Confucius cat." After years of fighting African relief debt, Bono has found an unlikely new cause: America.

President Hu, although visibly angry, is thinking: You know, he's right. The once high and mighty U.S. is a mess. Enron, Lehman Brothers, AIG, General Motors. Some cradle of capitalism. More like the cradle of cronyism. Some superpower. America built this massive house on the foundation of Milton Friedman and his fellow market fundamentalists. Now China holds the mortgage – almost $800 billion worth of U.S. Treasuries that are losing value by the day. Talk about a subprime investment.

Forget Bernard Madoff and his $65 billion fraud, Hu thinks. I'm on the hook for 12 times that, and party members are getting worried. I like that Timothy Geithner. Nice to have a Treasury secretary who speaks a bit of Putonghua and flies to China to stroke me. It's not good enough. America is running a Ponzi scheme the likes of which Madoff couldn't fathom.

"I'm sure you know, President Hu, that American poverty is rising and the ranks of the homeless are increasing," Bono continues. "Soon it won't be able to pay for education and health care. Surely you agree, America's hands are full. China has the power. You can relieve U.S. debts."

Hu's steely gaze gives way to a smile as he ponders how to say no. "Thanks for stopping by, Bono. I suspect that when you leave Beijing, you will remember this as one of those times when you still haven't found what you are looking for."

That"s from a great satirical piece written by William Pesek in June 2009, about a dream U2 concert taking place in Beijing in June 2010 attended by Chinese officials.

Stuffed to the Gills

It is impossible for a developing country as large as China with its vast underground economy to report accurate gross domestic product figures. It is estimated that as much as 4.4 trillion yuan of personal income in China is not reflected in the official figure, suggesting that potential growth in consumer spending and the property and stock markets may be stronger than perceived. One thing is certain: China is the world's fastest-growing economy. It's GDP is second only to the U.S. – the world's largest economy. But the gap is shrinking and it won't be long before China's economy surpasses that of the U.S.

China's gross domestic product grew by 10.8 percent in 2007. That was the fastest pace of expansion in 12 years and almost 3 percentage points higher than the 8 percent target. Monetary policy in China has fallen so far behind that it may be too late to achieve a soft landing. The collapse, if it comes in 2009 or 2010, will resemble the 19th-century U.S. boom-busts when there was no U.S. Federal Reserve managing the business cycle.

The last time the Chinese economy seriously overheated – from 1993 to 1995 – the annual inflation rates were 15 percent, 24 percent and 17 percent, respectively.

China is the world's third-largest consumer of luxury goods after Japan and the U.S. Yet China's widening of the urban-rural gap since 1987 has been one of the most worrisome accomplishments to China's economic miracle. If the bubble grows for another couple of years, the unsustainable demand and gap may become too large for a soft landing. Chinese stock market investors found out the hard way in 2008 that what goes up does come down and not everyone gets rich.

China's growth strategy has been different from Japan's. When Japan rose to economic power after World War II, it did so in a predatory fashion, pushing its products and investments in other markets but keeping its own market closed. China has done the opposite, opening itself up to foreign trade and investment.

Chapter 2

Soup – Taiwanese Beef Noodles

*Red China is not the powerful nation seeking to
dominate the world*
– General Omar Bradley

Reunited

The future reunification of Taiwan with the mainland
was metaphorically symbolized by Lee Fu-tang, the 92-year-old groom who
tied the knot again with Kuan Wen-ying, his 85-year-old bride, after being
separated for more than six decades by the Chinese civil war. The wedding
took place in Lee's home in Taiwan.

Lee and Kuan had their first wedding in their hometown in the northern
province of Shandong on the mainland. Three years later, Lee left his wife
and newborn son to join the Nationalist army to fight the Japanese and then
moved to Taiwan with the Nationalists. The couple had no contact again until 1993, when Lee was able to contact Kuan and their son. Both had remar-
ried and both their spouses had passed on. Lee went to Shandong in 2007,
to bring Kuan to Taiwan to renew their wedding vows and start a new life.

In 2008, after 60 years of separation, China and Taiwan set up direct air, sea
and postal links. Both Presidents Hu Jintao of China and Ma Ying-jeou of
Taiwan reiterated in their 2009 New Year's addresses their desire to forge
even closer ties. Hu said Beijing was even willing to develop military ties
with Taiwan to ease tensions across the Taiwan Straits. Both leaders' remarks reflect a dramatic change, given that relations were once so bitter the
two sides came to the brink of war.

In July 2009, Taiwan's military removed anti-tank and anti-landing-craft
barricades deployed along about 350 meters of the coast at Shuangkou on
Lesser Quemoy, the former defense outpost, to allow 100 swimmers from
Taiwan and the mainland to hold their first official cross-strait swimming

competition on August 15 between Quemoy and Xiamen, Fujian province. "The great meaning of the competition is that it is an event for peace," said Lee Juh-feng, a Quemoy county magistrate and organizer of the swim.

The mainland fired more than 470,000 shells at Quemoy over 44 days in 1958, killing 618 people, in an attempt to take over the small group of islets, the closest of which is just 2 kilometers from Xiamen.

Today mainland property developers are exploring investment opportunities in Taiwan. Mainland business executives, doctors and mine owners are spending millions of dollars buying rare Taiwanese orchids. Mainland tourists are welcome, as are the spouses of Taiwanese returning home after spending time doing business on the mainland. Taiwan's unofficial investment in China increases annually and now exceeds $200 billion.

During my stay in Shanghai in the early '90s, I had the privilege of sharing several quiet dinners with Wang Daohan, the former mayor of Shanghai and the former head of the Association for Relations Across the Taiwan Strait, who negotiated the 1992 Hong Kong Consensus. "The promotion of peaceful economic development and stability between us and our brothers and sisters in Taiwan is how we will become reunited," Wang said in response to my question about the possibility of China invading Taiwan. "There is no need for a military conflict, unless, of course, Taiwan declares independence," he continued as we toasted the peaceful reunification of Taiwan.

Unification is only a matter of time. In the meantime, as the mainland and Taiwan get closer, U.S. concerns that China will attack Taiwan are pure political spin to justify U.S. arms sales to Taiwan while stopping the Europeans from selling arms to China. All America is doing is marginalizing itself in the region. The U.S. should reverse course and promote and expedite unity by halting military sales and support for Taiwan. By promoting unification, America can maintain its presence in the region and be a major participant in maintaining peace, stability and prosperity.

Only a handful of countries in the world recognize Taiwan, and that number is eroding. They are a handful of small and poor countries in Africa, the Pacific and Latin America. Taiwan buys this recognition. The Vatican is Taiwan's only European ally. To make matters even more dysfunctional, Taiwan dropped Mongolia from its map even though its constitution still claims Mongolia as part of the Republic of China. Unlike Beijing, which recognizes Mongolia's independence, Taiwan claims to be the government of all China and continues to claim Mongolia. Beijing is recognized by more than 160 countries.

Throughout most of its history, Taiwan, which means "terraced bay" in Chinese, was inhabited by different ethnic aborigines and was not considered Chinese. Some Chinese settled there about the year 500. In 1517, the Portuguese christened the island "Ilha Formosa" – beautiful island. It was only in the 1600s that Taiwan attracted interest as a settlement by the Chinese and Europeans. The Portuguese were followed by the Dutch, Spanish and then again the Dutch. In 1623, Dutch traders asked China for a trading post on the coast, similar to the Portuguese post in Macau.

The Chinese gave them Taiwan. Forty years later, during the civil war in China, a half-Japanese general named Koxinga, like Chiang Kai-shek later, fled there and he ridded the island of the Dutch. His family ruled until 1683, when mainland armies invaded and took over. It was treated as a distant Chinese colony for the next 200 years. Only in 1887 did China upgrade Taiwan to a full province. Eight years later, in 1895, it was taken over by the Japanese. After World War II, the Allies agreed that Taiwan belonged to China.

Few people expect reunification in the near future. Many in fact fear reunification because of the potential negative impact on the island's labor market. During Taiwan's boom years from the 1960s to the 1990s, unemployment was seldom on the agenda, but has now emerged as a major political issue. So far in 2009, the unemployment rate in the crisis-battered economy has been 5.82 percent, nearly double the 2.99 percent recorded in 2000.

But as Foreign Correspondent's Club regular Frank Ching, a columnist for the *South China Morning Post,* points out: "By talking to each other, they are leaving the door open. The only alternative to a dialogue is the virtual certainty of war some time in the future."

Taiwan's idea that its ties with the mainland should be "state to state" is a bad joke. It is a province of the mainland. They are not Siamese twins. China ceded Taiwan to Japan in the 1895 Treaty of Shimonoseki and the island was returned to Chinese sovereignty under terms of the 1945 Cairo Declaration. The fact that America helped create democracy in Taiwan does not entitle Taiwan to become an independent country – or America going to its defense if it does and China were to attack. America has been put on notice by Chinese Army Maj. Gen. Zhu Chenghou that China "would not hesitate to use nuclear weapons against the United States" if it came to the defense of Taiwan.

The reality that Americans must come to terms with is that Taiwan is a convenient U.S. military base in China's backyard. The U.S. military-industrial complex's insistence on continued arms sales to Taiwan is nothing short of installing American military hardware on the base – and having someone else pay for it.

America appears to be ignoring the change and insisting on the same reheated and rehashed geopolitical soup, pretending nothing has changed. America's insistence and determination to sell more military hardware to Taiwan and maintain a military presence there is an outdated policy of the 20th century that is no longer relevant – or constructive for Sino-U.S. relations.

Panda Diplomacy

A pair of goodwill diplomacy pandas first offered to Taiwan in 2005, but rejected by then President Chen Shui-bian, finally arrived in Taiwan on Dec. 23, 2008. The pair, named Tuan Tuan and Yuan Yuan, which when linked together means "reunion," is another sign of the warming of relations. In return, Taiwan will send a pair of Formosan sika deer and a pair of Formosan goats to the mainland. Panda diplomacy is doing for China-Taiwan relations what table tennis diplomacy did for U.S.-China relations in 1971. Coincidentally, as the pandas arrived in Taipei, the U.S. and China celebrated 30 years of diplomatic ties with a table tennis match between the U.S. and China teams, with former players from the American and Chinese teams of 1971 present. The pandas represent a further step in cross-strait rapprochement and reconciliation.

Burned Out

The Cold War between communism and democracy has burned out both the East and West. Democracy won, but paid a tremendous price financially, emotionally, socially and politically. The West's victory in the Cold War has produced not triumph but exhaustion. As the West's primacy erodes, much of its power will simply evaporate and the rest will be diffused on a regional basis among the several major civilizations and their core states. The most significant increases in power are accruing to Asian civilizations, with China gradually emerging as the society most likely to challenge America for global supremacy. This is a reality America has to deal with sensibly and in a timely manner, especially when it comes to China-Taiwan and

U.S.-Taiwan relations.

The U.S. doesn't want to repeat the mistakes it made in Vietnam, Korea and Iraq with China over the geopolitics of the Pacific, especially Taiwan. The U.S. must not interfere in an internal civil war. If it does, it should expect the same result as its other post-World War II military excursions in Asia.

Taiwan Folly

The U.S sent the 7th Fleet carrier task force to the Taiwan Straits when China was about to begin large-scale military exercises in 2000. President Bush said America would do "whatever it takes to help Taiwan defend herself." Why send U.S. warships while China is testing missiles prior to the Taiwan elections or conducting military exercises? That Taiwan is considering a referendum on independence is reason enough for China to threaten military action to preserve its national unity. It's a domestic issue. For Therese Shaheen, former chairwoman of the American Institute in Taiwan, America's de facto embassy in Taipei, to declare that the Bush administration had never said it "opposes Taiwan independence" is diplomatically and politically counterproductive.

It reminds me of another U.S. diplomat's famous message to Saddam Hussein that declared as official U.S. policy: "We have no opinion on Arab-Arab conflicts like your border disagreement with Kuwait." A few weeks later Saddam's tanks rolled into Kuwait.

How would America react if China started selling arms to Native Americans? After all, their reservations are sovereign territories. How would the U.S. like it if the Chinese sent a naval fleet to North America to resolve regional disputes, let alone a domestic dispute? Imagine a Chinese naval fleet cruising into San Francisco Bay to contribute to the resolution of a Native American dispute over Alcatraz. How would the U.S. react if China said that it never said it "opposed Native-American independence?" It's ludicrous.

Why isn't America abiding by President Reagan's 1982 agreement to reduce and eventually end arms sales to Taiwan? When America agreed to sell submarines to Taiwan, no U.S. shipbuilder was building them in America. When asked by America, the Germans refused to build the eight diesel submarines America promised to sell Taiwan, so Washington must now either reactivate long dormant shipyards or find another builder to honor its military commitment to Taiwan. What is the point? Is Taiwan really worth becoming America's 21st century Vietnam?

The fact that former Senator Jesse Helms and the Republicans seriously considered passing the Taiwan Security Enhancement Act in 2001, which would have expanded military cooperation between the U.S. and Taiwan and create a de facto military alliance between Washington and Taipei – in violation of the Taiwan Relations Act – is worrisome.

Sen. James Jefford's defection from the Republican Party gave the Democrats a majority in the Senate and allowed them to replace Jesse Helms as chairman of the Foreign Relations Committee with former Senator Joe Biden and reversed America's perilous military pursuit. Is this delicate personal partisan political balance something America can afford to perpetuate in the New World Order? Does it make sense for one person committed to financial supporters in Taiwan to have the power to send America to war and *We the People* be damned, especially when we risk a nuclear war? News leaked of a Pentagon review that envisaged the use of nuclear weapons against China in the event of a war in the Taiwan Straits. Isn't this perilous risk something we must sweep out in the 21st century?

What is even more absurd and dangerous is the law signed by Bush that identified Taiwan as one of America's "allies," an illogical position since officially Washington does not even recognize the government of Taiwan. The legislation bars U.S. troops from being sent to countries that cooperate with the International Criminal Court, exempts members of NATO, Japan, South Korea, and other U.S. allies, including Taiwan.

After the nationalist Kuomintang fled the mainland in 1949 for Taiwan, many officers crossed the border from Yunnan province to Burma. There they got into the heroin trade to fund their early military purchases from America. Their heroin factories in the Golden Triangle were conveniently overlooked by the U.S. government, even though their output was killing Americans in every city and suburb.

Burma provided sanctuary for many KMT officers and their troops after China's civil war. Until his death in the 1980s, Gen. Tuan Shi-wen, the late KMT 5th Army commander, claimed that opium trading was needed to finance the war against the Communists – at the expense and lives of capitalist America.

Regional U.S. Hardware

U.S. warships are finally making port calls again at Vietnam's Cam Ranh Bay after the Russians pulled out in 2002. America couldn't keep its ships in the port it built in Vietnam, or U.S. troops in the country. Yet U.S. military planners think they would be able to sustain a Navy in the Taiwan Strait in the event of a war with China over Taiwan.

The U.S. currently has bases and aircraft in Tajikistan and Kyrgyzstan, used as hubs for operations in Afghanistan, and also has received unprecedented over-flight rights from Vietnam, Pakistan and Laos in its war on terrorism in Afghanistan. Coupled with the increased number of aircraft carrier groups and submarines equipped with guided missiles cruising the Pacific, one can understand why China is suspicious of U.S. intentions.

Let's not forget the annual "Cobra Gold" combined war games by the U.S., Thais and Singaporeans; "Team Challenge," which also includes the "Balikatan-Shoulder to Shoulder" U.S.-Philippine exercise, and the "Tandem Thrust" U.S.-Australian exercise. Other military exercises include South Korea and India with Mongolia and a dozen other nations invited to observe. With all this military activity in Southeast and East Asia, can China be blamed for wondering what the true U.S. intentions are in the area? Is it going to be another war over the oil in the South China Sea under the guise of defending Taiwan and bringing about regime change in China?

What could America do if China gave Taiwanese civilians 48 to 72 hours to go to defined "safe zones" or leave Taiwan before a Chinese attack? Redeploy troops from Iraq or Afghanistan?

America clearly does not have adequate forces to come to the defense of Taiwan. Of the 10 divisions in the active U.S. Army, eight are deployed or are deploying to Iraq, Bosnia and Afghanistan. Of 12 aircraft carrier battle groups, five are deployed in the Persian Gulf region, three are usually undergoing maintenance, leaving only four for action for the defense of Taiwan. That assumes none is deployed in a war on the Korean Peninsula. The fact is that U.S. military forces are spread "beyond the danger point into crisis," military historian Frederick Kagan wrote in an editorial.

It is estimated that at least two divisions – and possibly many more – will be required to maintain peace in postwar Iraq and help maintain a new government there. By the three-to-one logic of deployments (in which one unit is deployed, one is recovering from its deployment and one is preparing for deployment), it would take six to 10 divisions just to maintain two in Iraq. With Afghanistan, Bosnia and North Korea on America's plate, does it really need to add Taiwan?

It makes no sense for America to form a military alliance, sell arms to or share codes with Taiwan. What is truly amazing is that the U.S. announced the military sales to Taiwan in 2003 before the parliament there even approved funding for the purchases – and then repeatedly refused to do so. Furthermore, public opinion polls show the Taiwanese themselves are opposed to such sales. Taiwan's cabinet finally approved the purchase in 2005 after China passed the Anti-Secession Law. Why push military sales that create political hostility to a reluctant buyer?

Meanwhile, U.S.-China relations suffer. The annual announcements of new military sales agreements between America and Taiwan, the latest being in 2008, fueled by the annual reports that China is becoming a military threat to the U.S., Taiwan, the Philippines and Japan, serve no purpose other than a justification for a further U.S. military buildup in the region.

The U.S. couldn't defeat North Korea, North Vietnam, find Osama bin Laden in Afghanistan or defeat the insurgents in Iraq. So how does it think it can defeat China? Building an anti-missile defense network and a so-called "missile-proof" Taiwan is a step that could trigger a war between China and the U.S. To Beijing's delight, Taiwanese voters voiced a similar concern in the 2008 parliamentary and presidential elections when President Chen Shui-bian's pro-independence parties lost as the voters chose stability over the prospect of war with China. The defeat of Taiwan's Democratic Progressive Party reaffirmed that peaceful reunification with mainland China makes more sense than wasting billions of dollars on military equipment and a futile war.

Beijing issued a paper entitled China's National Defense in 2004 highlighting Japan's "increased military activities abroad" as a main security factor in the region and pledging to "resolutely crush... at any cost" Taiwanese attempts to move toward independence. The paper also said the U.S. was "sending the wrong signal" to Taiwan by increasing arms sales to the island as well as its new military alliance with Japan to defend Taiwan.

The U.S.-Japan Security Alliance that governs cooperation in defense and the concept of establishing a separate U.S. Northeast Asian command, which would include the Korean Peninsula as well as Taiwan, is absurd. For

America and Japan to even think of joining Taiwan's computer-simulated war games, linking Taiwan's military with the U.S. Pacific Command and Japanese and South Korean forces, is both politically and militarily a self-defeating exercise.

To argue that security in the Taiwan Strait is a "common strategic objective" is merely window dressing for the real issue – containing China's military modernization and buildup. To demand that China be more "transparent" about its military buildup is ridiculous. Are Japan and America transparent about their military programs?

China's New Toys

China's response to the U.S.-Japan defense of Taiwan is to spend billions buying sophisticated bombers, destroyers and submarines from Russia and the development of its own shashoujian, or secret "killer" weapons.

China launched a new class of ballistic missile submarine in July 2004, "China's first truly intercontinental strategic nuclear delivery system," a U.S. defense official said. It became fully operational in 2006, well ahead of the Pentagon's estimate of 2010. The Type 094 submarine is based on Russian designs and is equipped with new JL-2 nuclear missiles.

China is also developing the means to blockade Taiwan electronically through attacks on the island's vital utilities, the Internet and other communications networks, said Richard Lawless, former deputy U.S. under-secretary of defense. "Taiwan could be electronically blockaded, isolated from the world, creating a kind of perfect storm in which the U.S. could not communicate with Taiwan, or Taiwan with the world." Lawless said such a strategy could be called an "acupuncture" attack, aimed at the "destruction of a national will" with the "insertion of a hundred needles."

The fact is that prosperous China can and will outspend Taiwan on weapons systems – just like America did with the Soviet Union. By the middle of the 21st century, China will probably be able to even outspend an impoverished America if Washington doesn't clean up its political, economic and military act.

Taiwan won't be able to keep up. It is just a matter of time. Who can blame China for going on a weapons-buying spree and developing long-range missiles that can reach American cities if the U.S. repeatedly threatens to come to the defense of Taiwan?

In a strange geopolitical circumstance, it's like the Japanese trying to provoke Hawaii and thinking the U.S. would tolerate it. "Amid mounting umbrage at American 'arrogance' abroad, even some close U.S. friends complain that Yankee Doodle is not minding his step, or the music," columnist James Walsh said of America's brazen foreign policy.

The late Sen. Alan Cranston of California justly criticized America in 1992 for wanting to be "the only main honcho on the world block, the global Big Enchilada," when America drafted a planning document outlining how it could maintain military hegemony. As a result, the planning document was withdrawn. The same document has now resurfaced as the National Security Strategy to fight terrorism. However, it doesn't call for a temporary wartime buildup to fight terrorism. It calls for a permanent policy of maintaining U.S. military hegemony.

Harvard University professor Michael Ignatieff summed it up best in an article in *The New York Times* magazine in 2003. ("The U.S.) is the only nation that polices the world through five global military commands; maintains more than one million men and women at arms on four continents; deploys carrier battle groups on watch in every ocean; guarantees the survival of countries from Israel to South Korea; drives the wheels of global trade and commerce, and fills the hearts and minds of an entire planet with its dreams and desires."

Why then are U.S. politicians surprised and alarmed when China's leaders respond by acquiring submarines and jets from Russia to thwart America?

Is it any wonder Chinese leaders visit Libya and Iran to strengthen diplomatic and military ties? Is it worth pushing China closer to Iran and other rogue states over the Taiwan question? Is it really worth supporting Taiwan or trying to suppress China? Is it in America's national interest to alienate China and push it closer to Iran and the Arab dictatorships? How does this benefit America and keep it secure from terrorism?

While America is obsessed with its anti-China policy, its neighbors in Latin America are forging military links with Beijing. Latin American officers who used to travel to the U.S. for training are now going to China instead. The mainland has stepped into a void created by the U.S. policy to cut military aid to countries that refused to exempt U.S. citizens from the jurisdiction of the International Criminal Court. The result is the U.S. faces the prospect of losing contact with a whole generation of Latin American military officers now being trained by China.

America should keep in mind poet Rudyard Kipling's admonition to Britain against imperial hubris when Britain was the greatest power in the world in 1900 and failed in trying to spend its way to maintaining hegemony.

> *Far-called, our navies melt away; / On Dune and headland sinks the fire:*
> *Lo, all our pomp of yesterday / Is one with Ninveh and Tyre!*
> *Judge of the Nations, spare us yet, / Lest we forget – lest we forget.*

One China

The political-saber rattling over China's adoption of the Anti-Secession Law in 2005 was much ado about nothing. The law changed nothing. It merely reaffirmed China's long-standing policy and the Taiwan constitution. The legislation says that its purpose is to oppose and check "Taiwan's secession from China." It also says that "both the mainland and Taiwan belong to one China," a phrase first used by Taiwan's own Kuomintang government and repeated by both governments over the years. This was a phrase I heard uttered many times by Taiwan government officials on my visits to the island with American trade delegations led by U.S. elected officials – and in China.

China's President Hu Jintao, in speeches supporting adoption of the law, pointed out that "the existing regulations and documents in Taiwan" also support a "one-China" principle. For example, even the additional articles in the Taiwan constitution adopted in 1991 assume that Taiwan will eventually be reunited with China. They also say that the territory of the Republic of China includes both the mainland and Taiwan. Ironically, Taiwan's own laws do not allow secession. The National Security Law promulgated in 1987 says the public "must not violate the constitution, advocate communism or the division of the national territory."

With more than $200 billion invested in China today by the more than one million Taiwanese doing business there, and with more than $100 billion in annual China-Taiwan trade, it should not have been a surprise when Taiwanese tycoons and senior advisors to Taiwan's former President Chen Shui-bian, Shi Wen-long and Stan Shih, announced their public support of China's Anti-Secession Law as Chen joined thousands to march and denounce the law. Yet the nation and its leaders were shocked.

Shi said: "We should all feel more relieved." He said Taiwan could not do without the mainland and that any independence movement would only lead to war. Shi went further. He said: "Taiwan cannot develop its economy without the mainland." Both resigned as advisers to President Chen. If Abraham Lincoln could go to war in 1861 to prevent secession, why can't China?

Shi is not the only influential community member to speak up for unity. He is joined by Everett Chu, whose father fled the mainland for Taiwan, where he founded Want Want, now the world's largest maker of rice crackers, with 34 factories and more than $1.5 billion in annual sales. The mainland accounts for 90 percent of those sales. The younger Chu says that, if relations stay friendly, "we have a unique opportunity to become the No 1 food and beverage company in the world."

Master Hsing Yun, Taiwan's best-known monk and a strong advocate of reunification with the mainland, believes Buddhism, not rice crackers will lead the way.

"Those Chinese with a good conscience all approve of a unified China, Hsing Yun says. "But this is not a unification in which I take over you or you take over me. It is based on peace and equality."

The Anti-Secession Law is a catalyst for diplomacy and peace. This was confirmed two days after President Chen led protesters in denouncing the law, when the opposition Kuomintang (KMT) party sent a delegation to visit the memorial for martyrs of the failed 1911 uprising in the Huanghua Gang Commemoration Park in Guangzhou, China. The uprising was led by KMT founder Sun Yat-sen, the father of modern China. The 34-strong member delegation – the first to visit the mainland since the nationalists fled Taiwan in 1949 – was a giant first step toward peaceful reunification. The invitation extended by China to "all parties in Taiwan" to come to China for talks on reunification was the second step. The acceptance of the invitation by KMT Chairman Lien Chan was a home run. "Political development promoted by economic ties" has always been the long-term, de facto strategy for Beijing to assimilate Taiwan.

What is constantly overlooked is that China's Communist Party and Taiwan's KMT were once allies in the struggle to build a united China. In 1923, Sun Yat-sen, the KMT's founding president, embraced the then much smaller Communist Party. Mikhail Borodin, Moscow's emissary to China, advised both parties on organizational and propaganda matters, which accounts for the striking similarity in their structure. And in the same year, Chiang Kai-shek, America's darling who was to assume the mantle of KMT leadership, was shipped off to Moscow for training.

Chiang lost the civil war with the communists back home despite massive U.S. assistance and support and was forced to flee to Taiwan in 1949, where he ruled with an iron fist until his death in 1975. America has backed the wrong Chinese political horse from the very outset of the post-World War II Sino-U.S. relationship.

Arm Thy Enemy

What is truly amazing is the way the media distort how China is getting its military capabilities. The U.S. congressional commission's report identifies the American, European, Japanese and, most ironically, Taiwanese, chip-making firms that are providing China with advanced semiconductor fabrication technologies. The U.S. Commerce and State departments are approving the export of new chip-making technologies equal to the industry standard in the U.S. without any coherent export control policy. As U.S. businesses increase their investments in China, the commission sees a danger of America's defense industrial base becoming ever more dependent on Chinese-controlled companies.

Meanwhile, retired Taiwanese officers are defecting to China because they receive offers of higher rank, better pay and housing for their families. The "using Taiwan to conquer Taiwan" strategy is designed to obtain valuable Taiwanese military operators as well as inflict psychological damage on morale. These defectors are teaching tactics on how to invade the island in China's military academies. China has been practicing an attack on Taiwan that is aimed at killing or capturing the island's leaders in a "decapitation" action modeled on the U.S. action in Iraq to capture Saddam Hussein. Computer simulation games in military academies in China, Taiwan and the U.S. all indicate that Taiwan could be captured in a few days.

Dozens of retired generals from the mainland and Taiwan – including Deng Xianqun, the younger sister of late leader Deng Xiaoping and a retired high-ranking officer in the General Political Department – gathered in Xiamen on the mainland in May 2009 for a golf tournament aimed at initiating talks on forming a cross-strait military trust mechanism. Up to 37 former generals led by Qian Shugen, former deputy chief of the People's Liberation Army General Staff, and Huang Hsing-chang, Taiwan's former army commander-in-chief, attended the five-day tournament.

President Hu Jintao urged Taipei to start work on establishing a mechanism of mutual trust in the military field when he met the visiting chairman of Taiwan's Kuomintang party, Wu Po-hsiung, on May 26. The mechanism is the first step in Hu's three-step approach to peaceful reunification. The second step is to formally announce the end of confrontation and the final step is to sign a peace accord.

Taipei is asking Beijing to remove the hundreds of missiles currently targeting Taiwan to further extend the deepest thaw in cross-strait relations to date – and Beijing probably will.

Taiwan's concern about China's missiles is understandable in light of the spate of its own military corruption, sex, intelligence and damaged missiles scandals. Taiwan's air force had to discard the rocket engines of several of its medium-range, air-to-air missiles made in the United States because they were damaged during delivery by the Taiwan Railway Administration in 2007. On the intelligence front, the bureau has shifted its focus from gathering intelligence on the mainland to gathering headline news because it believes it no longer needs to spy on the mainland.

Taiwan acknowledges it is helpless to defend itself against a mainland missile attack. "If necessary, they can be used to strike Taiwan in waves of precision missile attacks," Taiwan military spokesman Yu Sy-tue said in October 2009 after the release of the Defense Ministry annual report.

If Taiwanese military personnel are acknowledging the futility of their military buildup, joining the island's capitalists and business people in building China's military and economic capability, shouldn't the U.S. political establishment be doing the same rather than provoking and again siding with the loser? U.S. business icons like Motorola, Intel, Kodak, General Motors, Nike and countless others are invested in China to the tune of more than $50 billion. China has also amassed more than $2 trillion in foreign reserves, much of which it has invested in U.S. treasuries. Classifying Taiwan as "a major non-NATO ally," which allows it to enjoy the same treatment as Japan, New Zealand and Australia, is suicidal. As George Strait says, you can't put it all on the line unless you've got an ace in the hole. Under current U.S. policy, what is America's ace when it is in the hole?

Even though the U.S. doesn't appear to get it, Taiwan does. That's why

Taiwan decided to end its decades-old military draft by 2015 in an attempt to trim its force to 200,000, despite the mainland's double-digit-percentage rise in defense spending. To uphold the quality of Taiwan's volunteer army, all recruits must be at least high school graduates.

Watching Taiwan and the mainland get battered by Typhoon Morakot in August 2009, I had no doubt the tragedy would bring the two sides closer together on both the aid and military fronts, and it did. Taiwan was ill-prepared for the typhoon, which was the worst natural disaster to hit the island in 50 years. The typhoon brought record rainfall that triggered deadly mudslides and killed at least 670 islanders.

"Now our enemy is not necessarily people across the Taiwan Strait, but nature," the island's president said. "In the future, the armed forces of the country will have disaster prevention and rescue as their main job."
President Ma made clear that the armed forces would undergo intense disaster-response training. Their budget, manpower, equipment and strategy would be retooled to focus on disaster relief and prevention.

The fallout from the Morakot disaster, not just for the military, but for Ma, has far-reaching implications for his political future and cross-strait relations. The mishandling of the preparation and rescue efforts, not to mention the destruction caused by the Morakot fiasco, caused Prime Minister Liu Chao-shiuan to resign, followed a few days later by the rest of his cabinet. By then, Ma's approval rating, which stood at nearly 60, percent plummeted to 20 percent – a dangerous level for any incumbent.

The parallel between Ma's misfortunes in the aftermath of Morakot and President George W. Bush's after Hurricane Katrina is unavoidable. Bush's mishandling of the rescue efforts in New Orleans greatly escalated public doubt about his judgment in appointing high-level officials and his overall competence as president. He was never able to erase that perception and it is possible that Ma will experience a similar problem. Beijing's approval of the Dalai Lama's visit to the island to pray for the victims is an indication of just how concerned Beijing is about Ma's political future.

The change of emphasis for Taiwan's military mirrors that facing the People's Liberation Army in the wake of the devastating 2008 Sichuan earthquake. Following the quake, which prompted the military's biggest peacetime mobilization, President Hu said disaster relief and reconstruction was the key mission and responsibility of the army. Shouldn't the U.S. be making the same change in view of what happened in the wake of Hurricane Katrina?

Lin Chong-pin, Taiwan's deputy defense minister, has said that "2010 to 2015 [will be] when the PLA will have such a supremacy in both qualitative and quantitative comparison of forces that it may feel confident to move". So what is the point of America continuing to waste political capital on arming Taiwan and vowing to go to its defense?

Mainland Chinese and Taiwanese military officers met in August 2009 for the first time at the U.S. Pacific Command think-tank in Honolulu. The meeting in Hawaii marked the first formal exchange between the rival forces in six decades. China resisted at sending officials to the centre because officials from Taiwan had been in attendance since 2002.

America is poorly served by its fragmented, inconsistent and superficial China policy, wielded in compulsive secrecy and plagued by dismal crisis management, a bipartisan congressional commission warned. The U.S.-China Economic and Security Review Commission said in its first annual report that U.S.-China relations, often testy and tainted by mutual suspicion, suffered from an uncoordinated approach among the branches of the U.S. government.

Richard D'Amato, chairman of the commission set up by Congress, said: "U.S. policy toward China has been and is fragmented, lacking consistency and depth. It has often been driven solely by commercial interests, or by specific human rights issues, or by a particular military crisis – rather than by a comprehensive examination of all the issues which impact this relationship." Is this any way for the U.S. government to be doing business with China?

Retired U.S. Army Colonel Al Wilhelm was among the first uniformed officers sent to the mainland at the height of the Cold War in the 1980s to provide advice and weaponry to the People's Liberation Army. Wilhelm is still on a mission of peace. "China is going to become a superpower. What the hawks say about China having the potential to threaten America is true. The key is how we find a way to coexist, he says.

"Unless we develop mutual trust and friendship, it's likely my eight grandchildren will be fighting in a war against China," Wilhelm said in an interview in Hong Kong. I agree. In my case, my grandchildren will be fighting each other.

The two-China policy the U.S. is trying to straddle is doomed to fail. China is determined to become a major power again, and will. The U.S. cannot stop this geopolitical reality. America's Taiwan policy is only fueling, expediting and facilitating China's military machine. America must embrace the one-China policy and work with Beijing as its Pacific partner, as it has done on the Atlantic front with Europe.

Why can't America withdraw its support of Taiwan in exchange for China withdrawing support to North Korea to help bring nuclear disarmament and stability to the region? Why should China encourage North Korea to disarm without a U.S. trade-off?

America has shown that when it acts decisively and brings its full military capabilities to bear, others will listen and follow. However, let's not get overconfident and too cocky for our own good when it comes to China in the 21st century. "The supreme art of war is to subdue the enemy without fighting," Sun Tzu, the Chinese military strategist, wrote in 400 B.C.

Taiwan's polemic dialogue advocating independence or a confederation between China and Taiwan is a nonstarter. The 1992 Hong Kong Consensus – the tacit agreement reached by the mainland and Taiwan in Hong Kong – got both parties to agree that there is only one China. Taiwan's Kuomintang party now has an office in Beijing to serve the needs of Taiwanese investors on the mainland.

Taiwanese military ships and aircraft were allowed into Chinese waters and airspace in 2002 to search for victims of the Taiwanese China Airlines plane that crashed as it headed for Hong Kong. Two mainland vessels helped in the search for bodies carried into Chinese territorial waters by strong currents.

As the two former rivals draw closer, there is a story about Mao Zedong, who is said to have admitted that he made a mistake in proclaiming the establishment of the People's Republic of China in 1949. "If I had only kept the name Republic of China," he is said to have lamented, "the Taiwan problem would not have existed." It certainly would make it easier to invade under the theory of "renegade province."

Arrogant Head Chef

The mass resignation in January 2006 of 34 Taiwan cabinet members led by Premier Frank Hsieh, over former President Chen's hardline New Year's speech about his future policy toward China, was a clear signal that Taiwan does not want to provoke Beijing. Chen's decision to scrap the island's National Unification Council on February 27, 2006, resulted in a mass rally opposing his decision and a motion in the legislature to unseat him.

Chen's decision was a brazen breach and betrayal of his own so-called "five nos." He delivered his famous five nos after his presidential election wins in 2000 and 2004, committing himself not to declare independence, not change Taiwan's national title, not hold a referendum or institute a new constitution specifying Taiwan's statehood, and not to scrap the Unification Council. Although Chen may want to go down in history as the leader of Taiwan's independence movement, he will go down in history as the first former Taiwan president sent to jail for embezzlement, money laundering, fraud, influence peddling, blackmail and corruption.

Fasting Prisoner

Chen had defiantly refused to step down amid the scandal even as his wife, Wu Shu-chen, was being prosecuted for alleged financial corruption. Chen himself was suspected of involvement in the scheme, but enjoyed immunity from prosecution as the sitting president. The minute he left office, he was charged with collaborating with his wife to embezzle, forge documents, bribery, influence peddling, blackmail and laundering at least $21 million. He and many of his immediate family members were indicted and tried for the crimes.

During the course of his trial in 2009, prosecutors added new charges of taking bribes and illegal donations. If convicted he and his relatives could face life imprisonment. His political allies in the Democratic Progressive Party urged him to plead guilty to the corruption charges to mitigate the political fallout. His wife, son and daughter-in-law have pleaded guilty to money laundering and other charges. Chen's wife also urged him to plead guilty and get the charges against their children dropped to end their suffering.

Chen is the first former Taiwanese president to be arrested, jailed and criminally prosecuted. He tried but failed to force three other former presidents, including Ma Ying-jeou, to testify in an attempt to prove that corruption was commonplace in previous governments, thus mitigating his own misdeeds.

Adding to the scandal swirling around Chen, his son-in-law, Chao Chien-ming, was charged with insider trading in a high-profile case involving the Taiwan Development Corp. Chen's daughter and son-in-law, meanwhile, were accused of perjury and using government funds to pay their household maids.

Besides Chen and his wife, at least a dozen Chen family members were eventually charged in the case. Several pleaded guilty to money-laundering or corruption charges as the investigation unfolded.

As if that wasn't enough, in an embarrassing turn of events while Chen was president, his son Chen Chih-chung and his pregnant wife Huang Jui-ching were forced to scrap plans to have their baby born in the United States because it conflicted with a vow made by Chen that he would never be the grandfather of an American. The political fallout forced the couple to return home and have their child born in Taiwan. They were forced to return again after Chen left office to explain how $21 million wound up in their bank account. They pleaded guilty to money-laundering.

Prosecutors performed a satirical skit mocking the former president at a Taiwan Law Day dinner attended by the justice minister and other leaders of the island's legal community in January 2009, a dangerous slippery slope if the true rule of law is to prevail without prejudicing the judges and public opinion.

The political fallout stands as an astounding testimonial to the vagaries of democracy. A truly independent prosecutor's office, backed by legislators like the KMT's Chiu Yi, is determined to expose and prosecute corrupt elected officials and civil servants if enough evidence can be gathered to stand up in court. Chen faces 30 years to life in prison if convicted. That is what the true rule of law is all about.

Hundreds of thousands of people took to the streets around the presidential palace in Taipei demanding that Chen resign when the charges were first made public. But Chen refused, knowing that the split makeup of Taiwan's 221-seat legislature made it impossible for the opposition to muster the votes necessary to remove him through a recall or impeachment. He just had to serve out his term before his arrest, imprisonment and prosecution.

While the political circus raged over the pros and cons of removing Chen from office, the president took off in September 2006 on a tour of South Pacific island allies to shore up diplomatic support for Taiwan and keep them from switching their loyalties to mainland China as he laundered more money. He used three different airplanes for his visits to Palau, Nauru and Guam. He attended a summit in Palau with the leaders of six South Pacific allies, including Palau, Nauru, the Solomon Islands, Marshall Islands, Tuvalu and Kiribati – all great diving and fishing areas where Taiwanese and Indonesian fishermen are repeatedly arrested for poaching – and where I have spent time with U.S. and Chinese business people trying to poach the islands natural resources.

Chen was stashing his cash – more than $40 million of ill-gotten gains – in Palaun banks and then wiring the funds to the U.S. He allegedly used the presidential jet to smuggle the cash into the country. Not an unusual practice in Asia. Thailand's exiled former president Taksin Shinawatra, the Philippines, Ferdinand Marcos, Myanmar's ruling generals, Indonesia's former dictators and many other regional leaders smuggle their corrupt gains aboard government planes, courtesy of the taxpayers who pick up the tab.

Having lived and worked in Palau, on and off for a couple of years in the early '90s, I couldn't help but chuckle when I read that six former Guantanamo Bay detainees, who were held without trial as "enemy combatants," were resettled in Palau in 2009. Not a bad halfway house for the Uygurs who were among 22 Chinese Muslims picked up by U.S. forces in Afghanistan and Pakistan in 2001 on suspicion of terrorism.

Palau is creating the world's first shark sanctuary, a biological hot spot to protect great hammerheads, leopard sharks, oceanic white-tip sharks and more than 130 other species fighting extinction in the Pacific Ocean because of Greater China's ravenous appetite for shark fin soup. I dove many times in Palau and swam with these beautiful, gentle creatures which are much tamer than the political and business sharks in Washington and on Wall Street.

When Chen returned to Taiwan, he arrived in fighting mode. On the eve of the 60th anniversary of the so-called 228 Incident, he assailed Chiang Kai-shek and his Kuomintang Party for violating the human rights of native Taiwanese. That massacre took place on Feb. 28, 1947, when Taiwanese police pistol-whipped an elderly woman for selling contraband cigarettes outside the Taipei train station. The episode set off rioting throughout Taiwan, which Kuomintang security forces brutally suppressed, killing thousands of civilians in the process. Chen went on national television to accuse the Kuomintang Party of failing to accept responsibility for the incident. His vicious attacks on Chiang resulted in people removing statues of the late Nationalist leader from public parks and buildings. Those that remained were defaced. Tourists from the mainland now appear to be the only ones interested in visiting the discarded busts and statues of Chiang in a quiet hillside park in northern Taiwan.

Chinag Kai-shek's failed attempts to recapture the mainland in the 1960s, were declassified and made public in May 2009 with the opening of Back Tzuhu, the seven-hectare crescent-shaped restricted section of the Chiang Kai-shek Mausoleum in Tzuhu in the northern county of Taoyuan. The site served as a wartime command center for Chiang during Project Kuokuang, or the Project of National Glory, in 1964 and 1965.

Chiang believed the right moment had arrived because the Communist government had botched the economy with the disastrous "Great Leap Forward." Also, the Vietnam War had broken out, and there was the prospect that the mainland would soon have a nuclear weapon. On August 6, 1965, two naval vessels carrying special operation troops for a reconnaissance mission along the mainland's coast were intercepted and sunk off Dongshan Island near Fujian province. The troops were virtually annihilated, with about 200 killed.

In November of the same year, Chiang ordered two other naval vessels to pick up wounded soldiers from Makung and Wuchiu, offshore islands of Taiwan. The vessels were attacked by mainland ships and sunk. Some 90 soldiers were killed. The encounter also sank Chiang's ambitions to retake the mainland.

Chen's brazen and arrogant decisions, and his stone-walling in the face of corruption charges against himself and members of his family, are in the tradition of Chiang Kai-shek, whom Chen vilified as he fought for his political survival. It's a lesson in political brinkmanship. And, as if he didn't have enough on his plate at home at the time, Chen decided to goad China again by calling for Taiwan independence and holding military exercises to practice against a large-scale invasion. Chen's ruling Democratic Progressive Party, in the midst of all this scandal, fared better in the local elections than expected. It proved that Chen was better at scamming the vote and the public than he was at scamming his fellows in the legislature.

Chen and his wife Wu Shu-chen were sentenced to life in prison on Sept. 11, 2009, and collectively fined NT$500 million. His daughter and son-in-law were sentenced to jail for one year and eight months and two years respectfully and each were fined NT$150 million. Their appeals are expected to last five years. Chen's request to post bail and be released from jail pending his appeal was rejected.

Chen filed a lawsuit against President Barack Obama in September 2009, accusing him of failing to uphold U.S. jurisdiction over Taiwan and permitting a "government in exile" in Taiwan to illegally issue court rulings on the island. Chen contends in his lawsuit that Taiwan's courts are illegal, that its legitimate ruler is the U.S. military and that U.S. President Barack Obama and Defense Secretary Robert Gates should be hauled before an American judge to explain why the Pentagon has failed to uphold its jurisdiction. Chen vows to take the pair to court as a means of securing his release from life imprisonment. Chen insisted that the U.S. was Taiwan's "principal occupying power." He even claimed he had to "accept the instructions of the U.S. on many occasions even when their instructions interfered with my presidential decision making."

Chen withdrew the lawsuit after it was rejected by a U.S. military court. Chen now also faces the prospect of treason charges after denying the legality of the government he once led. Lu Hsueh-chang, secretary general of the ruling Kuomintang caucus, filed a lawsuit in the Taiwan High Court against Chen for alleged treason.

Creative New Chef

Taiwan's current president, Ma Ying-jeou, former mayor of Taipei and head of the Kuomintang party, overcame his own legal problems before his election in 2008 to succeed the disgraced Chen Shui-bian. Ma was acquitted of misusing mayoral funds. He had visited the U.S. in March 2006, securing his status as Washington's favored candidate as the island's next leader.

Ma has touched on three themes that will define his China policy: accommodating the mainland; ending self-imposed isolation from China, and waiting for conditions that would make unification palatable to the Taiwanese. Ma had vowed in 2008 that if his party came to power he would seek a peace deal with the mainland. He has repeatedly come out against military arms purchases from the U.S. He believes the purchases are unnecessary because he recognizes that China does not pose a military threat unless provoked by Taiwan declaring independence.

Ma started cross-strait talks to improve relations even before his inauguration on May 20, 2008. The "ice melting" trip by Vincent Siew Wanchang to the Boao Forum in Hainan in mid-April, a couple of weeks before his swearing in as vice president, let the world know the ice was gone. Siew's meeting with President Hu Jintao on the sidelines of the Boao Forum –dubbed the highest-level contact between the mainland and Taiwan in six decades – opened a new chapter in Beijing-Taipei relations.

The relationship got off to a rocky start when Zhang Mingqing, vice president of Beijing's Association for Relations Across the Taiwan Strait, was shoved to the ground during his Taiwan visit at the Confucius temple in Tainan by a Democratic Progressive Party city councilor who favors Taiwanese independence and opposes warmer ties with Beijing.

Notwithstanding that confrontation and continued demonstrations against closer ties which promise to go on during the remainder of President Ma's term in office, high-level cross-strait meetings between both sides continued in Beijing and Taipei, where President Ma Ying-jeou met with Chinese Senior envoy Chen Yunlin. Ma also did a radio interview in December 2008 that was broadcast direct to the mainland netizens. He called on Beijing not to ban *Cape No. 7,* the award-winning Taiwanese feature film. The film addresses the inter-relations between the Japan that ruled Taiwan for 50 years from 1895 to 1945 and the Taiwan that China censors feel might offend nationalists on the mainland. The film does point out the cultural differences across the strait – especially the conflicting views and feelings towards Japan.

Beijing and Taipei signed agreements in 2008 that resulted in direct trade, direct flights, shipping, air cargo, food safety and postal services and cross-strait representative bureau offices in Beijing and Taipei. Cross-strait links were further expanded in April 2009 in Nanjing on the mainland during the third summit between Taipei and Beijing. Agreements expanding aviation routes, the number of flights, financial services and joint efforts to fight organized crime were signed.

Talks between the two semi-official organizations representing the mainland and Taiwan will now be held every six months. Taiwanese banks now offer yuan exchanges, the first since 1949. Taiwan has a lot more to gain economically from the relationship than does China. It is therefore no surprise that Taiwanese President Ma Ying-jeou called for a wide-ranging economic pact with the mainland as part of his government's measures to fight the island's recession.

The "Economic Co-operation Framework Agreement" which came into effect May 1, 2009, permits the free flow of goods, services and capital across the 160 kilometer-wide Taiwan Strait. The pact cleared the way for mainland businesses to invest in Taiwan, ending a ban that had existed since 1949. China Mobile, the world's largest mobile carrier by users, has agreed to buy a HK\$4.07 billion stake in one of Taiwan's leading telecom service providers, the first direct investment on the island by a mainland state-owned company in six decades. A flood of cross-strait mergers and acquisitions is expected to take place on the recession-hit island.

Beijing also dropped its objection to Taiwan joining the World Health Organization as an observer in May 2009 under the name Chinese Taipei. This was the first time that Taiwan has been able to take part in the activities of any U.N. agency since 1971, when it was expelled from both the General Assembly and Security Council. The invitation does not offer Taiwan permanent observer status. Beijing can withdraw the benefit at any time in the future if the pro-independence DPP party returns to power. Taiwan now has its eyes fixed on joining other U.N. agencies and the International Committee of the Red Cross. Good reasons for Taiwan in 2009 to drop its annual bid to join the U.N. as a separate entity that is not part of China – for the first time in 17 years.

Taiwan and the mainland are even in discussions to build a cross-straits bridge. The bridge would span 8.6 kilometers and link Kinmen with Xiamen, Fujian province.

Party Animals

Hu Jintao is not only the president of China, but the general secretary of the Communist Party of China Central Committee. It is in that capacity that he met with Wu Poh-hsiung, Taiwan Kuomintang chairman, in May 2009 in Beijing. Both parties agreed to set up a cross-straits economic cooperative mechanism to help check the slump in Taiwan's economy.

While in China, Wu received an honorary degree from Nanjing University, where he told students Taiwan and the mainland were tied by cultural links that could not be erased. "We must advance the spirit of human culture, treasure this golden opportunity of developing cross-strait relations and create together a new age of cultural values," Wu said.

In Nanjing, Wu attended a ceremony at the Sun Yat-sen Memorial to mark the 80th anniversary of Sun's death. Sun, founder of the KMT and father of modern China, is one of the few historical Chinese politicians to be revered both in Taiwan and the mainland. At the memorial, Wu indicated he would step aside as KMT chair and make way for President Ma Ying-jeou to take control of the party – which he did. Now that Ma, like Hu, is both president and head of his party, it is only a matter of time before these two political animals meet as party heads and bring Taiwan and the mainland even closer towards reunification. The congratulatory telegram Hu sent Ma after Ma's election as party chairman in July 2009 was the first of many future direct communications between the two leaders.

The communication between the two men was the first direct public exchange in 60 years, paving the way for a new era of cross-strait engagement. "I sincerely hope that our two parties will continue to push for cross-strait peaceful development, further increase mutual political trust and jointly work for the well-being of the people across the strait so as to lead to the great renaissance of the Chinese people," Hu said. Ma thanked Hu and echoed his call for continued efforts to promote cross-strait peace.

By addressing each other in their capacity as ruling party leaders, rather than as heads of state, they circumvented the disputed issue of Taiwan's sovereignty. Both party leaders are now in a position and on the road to start cross-strait political talks and address the issue of reunification, notwithstanding their public protestations to the contrary. The growing economic and cultural exchanges are paving the way over the thorny issue of reunification. It is only a matter of time before both leaders meet face to face.

"Right on," Steve Chicorel said as I shared my views about reunification with him when he stopped off in Hong Kong to visit me after attending the Shanghai TV Festival in June 2009. "Except you are missing that on the ground, the realities of the pride of the people is the biggest obstacle toward reunification," Steve continued. "As I've told you on numerous occasions – and recently experienced in Shanghai – when referring to my wife. A guy asked me if my wife is Chinese. I paused and hesitated and said yes. He asked why the pause? I told him that when people in the States ask her if she is Chinese, she quickly says, 'No. I am Taiwanese'." He had a point. I have heard her say that on several occasions.

"So what are you saying. Reunification won't happen?" I asked.

"No," he said. "Theoretically your argument is valid and powerful. The social obstacle is strong and eventually as cross-straits relations build, reunification will occur, but in 10-20 years, I predict," Steve concluded as we raised our glasses of tequila and toasted reunification.

"I disagree," I said as we put our glasses down and continued to puff on our cigars. "It's going to be a lot quicker than 10 years."

No Taiwan administration can hold political talks with the mainland without the support of the vast majority of the population. Today, most of the 23 million people on Taiwan do not want reunification, but a continuation of the status quo. The reality, however is, that China does not accept the status quo. It wants reunification and the year 2012 looks like a watershed year because of two critical political events. The end of Hu Jintao's term, with Hu eager to leave a historic legacy; and if Taiwanese President Ma Ying-jeou fails to get re-elected in 2012 and the pro-independence party wins.

Trading Cooking Ingredients

The Economic Co-operation Framework Agreement between Taiwan and the mainland will help Taiwan's sagging economy, which like America's turned out to be worse than thought. Taiwan's economy shrank a record 10.24 percent in the first quarter of 2009 from a year earlier. It was the worst decline since records began in 1962. The expectation is that Taiwan will recover rapidly and ride out the export slump faster than South Korea or Japan because of its fast-paced economic, trade and investment support from Beijing. The mainland's multi-billion dollar spending spree in Taiwan by its procurement missions is intended to stimulate Taiwan's sagging economy and make a strong political statement about the benefits of reunification.

This was highlighted by the 2,000 lighting projects at about 200 locations in Beijing during China's National Day celebrations on Oct. 1, 2009. The bulbs used to light up the capital for 11 days were 12 watt, 50,000-hour bulbs that were designed in Taiwan and manufactured in Zhuhai, China.

The Taiwan Trade Fair held in September 2009 in Nanjing, the historic capital city of Jiangsu province, was the major attraction at the 20th Nanjing Golden Autumn Economic and Trade Fair. The fair has a different theme each year to encourage foreign investment in the province. The 2009 trade fair was dedicated to creating closer ties with Taiwan. More than 4,000 Taiwanese businessmen from 750 enterprises attended the fair.

Taiwan also opened a pavilion for the first time at the 13th China International Fair for Investment and Trade in Xiamen in 2009. Xiamen, the closest city to Taiwan in terms of distance, is preparing to become the first currency settlement center for yuan and New Taiwan dollars.

Beijing's National Palace Museum shipped 37 prized cultural artifacts to its rival institution in Taiwan. The items formed part of a joint exhibition with Taipei's National Palace Museum focusing on the Qing dynasty emperor Yong Zheng, who ruled China for 13 years until 1735.

The exchange was the first since the civil war ended in 1949 with Nationalist armies carting off to Taiwan crates of some of the finest imperial treasures once housed in Beijing's Forbidden City. The loss of the items has long been a sore point with Beijing. The Taipei museum has said it will not lend any of its collection of more than 655,000 Chinese items spanning 7,000 years to Beijing before the two sides reach an agreement exempting the items from confiscation.

That it was no surprise when Taiwan's National Palace Museum refused to accept two donated imperial Chinese bronze heads, a rat and a rabbit head that were looted when Beijing's Summer Palace was razed by invading French, British and American forces in 1860 during the opium wars. That it was pilloried as "gutless" by the opposition Democratic Progressive Party. President Ma Ying-jeou was criticized for rejecting the pieces in order to "please China."

Pierre Berge, partner of the original owner, the late French fashion designer Yves Saint Laurent, offered the two pieces to the museum after the buyer of the pieces at a Paris auction refused to go ahead with the purchase. No other buyers have stepped up to the plate.

With cross-strait maritime links improving, there are now 68 harbors on the mainland authorized to conduct direct trade with Taiwan. The economy of Taiwan is being integrated into that of the mainland at a breathtaking pace. So much so that the island of Quemoy is considering building Taiwan's first casinos, which could draw millions of gamblers from the mainland and transform the island county that has long been the frontline in cross-strait tensions into a tourist destination for millions of mainlanders just 20 nautical miles away.

Quemoy has close ties with Xiamen, which provides much of its food and consumer goods. An estimated 20 percent of Quemoy's population have bought flats in Xiamen, while some of its students attend university there. Conversely, major Taiwan universities are now recruiting mainland students to enroll starting in September 2010.

The Connecting Bridge

The haixi region of the mainland which includes Fujian and parts of Zhejiang, Guangdong and Jiangxi provinces is the bridge that will integrate Taiwan into the mainland, with Fujian being the cornerstone. Haixi, which translates as "west bank of the Taiwan Straits," is a top economic development priority of the Chinese government.

"Do you think Taiwan and the mainland will reunite anytime soon?" I asked Nelson Wong in 1995 as he and I were walking along the waterfront in Fuzhou with the head of the Fujian redevelopment agency. We were preparing a feasibility study on the best use of a prime 25-hectare site for the government. Tensions were high across the strait at the time with China test firing missiles and the U.S. repeatedly reminding China it would come to Taiwan's defense if China invaded.

"They will," Nelson responded. "The only question is when and how. Peacefully or by force. I believe it will be peacefully," Nelson added.

"When do you guestimate" I asked.

"Hard to tell. Ten, 20, 30 years but definitely in our lifetime. There's too much common business interests. What is your American expression you always say 'Money talks and bullshit walks?' That is the case with Taiwan. It is only a matter of time."

Today, Nelson has Taiwanese business partners and an office in Taipei.

In May 2009, the State Council approved plans to support the setting up of a haixi economic zone, a project championed by the provincial authorities in Fujian since 2004. The nation's cabinet said in its pronouncement setting up the HEZ that: "The major positive changes that have taken place in the cross-straits relationship have provided significant opportunities for boosting the development of the HEZ." The move will transform Fujian from a military frontline into advancing cross-straits exchanges and cooperation into eventual reunification.

It is believed that 80 percent of Taiwan natives can trace their families back to Fujian. A 30-minute boat ride is all that separates the two. By April 2009, Taiwan companies had invested more than $20 billion in Fujian industries, including electronics, manufacturing and electronics. In the early 1980s, Fujian's economy was just 2.5 percent the size of Taiwan's. Today it stands at 40 percent. "If it continues improving as it has been doing, Fujian's economy will surpass Taiwan's in the future," said Lu Zhangong, Fujian's Party secretary.

To expedite the process, Beijing and Taipei are working on a standardized dictionary that will help further build cross-strait ties. The plan calls for academics to standardize technical terms and create computer software to translate traditional Chinese characters into simplified ones and vice versa. Taiwan primarily uses traditional characters and the mainland simplified ones.

Mixed and Matched

Ma, like his counterparts in China, knows that Hong Kong is proof that the one-country, two-systems model works. He was born in Hong Kong. With the passing of the 10-year anniversary of the July 1, 1997, handover, Hong Kong is economically stronger and politically more open and vocal with free, uncensored press that covers all political views, whether or not they support Beijing. Capitalism and socialism have fused harmoniously and the principle of "high autonomy of Hong Kong people governing Hong Kong" has been successfully implemented. Hongkongers enjoy wider democracy today than during the colonial period. Hong Kong's economy on the 10-year anniversary of the handover was its best in 20 years, enjoying high growth and low inflation for three consecutive years leading up to that anniversary.

Hong Kong has witnessed average annual growth of 4 percent for the 10 years since the handover, and also 7.6 percent for the past few years, following the recession after the Asian financial crisis. It also remained the freest economy for the 13 years leading up to the handover anniversary celebrations, and the unemployment rate has remained at a low 3 percent. Like the rest of the world, unemployment has since risen because of the global meltdown of 2008.

Relations between Taiwan and Hong Kong have warmed considerably since Ma's election in 2008. They really heated up when Hong Kong's Secretary for Constitutional and mainland Affairs Stephen Lam Sui-lung visited Taiwan in June 2009. It was the biggest breakthrough in relations in 12 years. He was the first minister from Hong Kong to visit Taiwan since the handover. Meanwhile, Sean Chen, chairman of Taiwan's Financial Supervisory Commission, visited Hong Kong in June 2009, the first Taiwanese ministerial-level official to visit Hong Kong. Now more than 90 percent of applications by Taiwanese officials for Hong Kong visas are successful. By contrast, more than 95 percent of applications were rejected before the warming of ties.

In his October 2009 policy address, Hong Kong's Chief Executive Donald Tsang announced plans to establish a Hong Kong-Taiwan Economic and Cultural Cooperation and Promotion Council to promote multi-faceted and multi-level exchanges with Taiwan.

Both governments are setting up business cooperation committees to boost trade, investment and tourism. Taiwan's financial regulator approved in May 2009 the issuance of Hong Kong exchange-traded funds in the island's stock market, a move expected to accelerate cross-strait investments. An ETF is an investment product backed by a portfolio of stocks trading on the domestic exchange. It is now clear that the stock exchanges of Taiwan, Hong Kong and the mainland are compiling a greater China index as a benchmark for ETFs.

During the past 20 years, Hong Kong has been the largest source of overseas investment in the Chinese mainland. Capital from Hong Kong or from foreign countries via Hong Kong accounted for 41 percent of the mainland's total. It is the safest business center in the world with world-class universities that share their research worldwide. Hong Kong is the global standard of a harmonious, functional city. Hong Kong native Jackie Chan infuriated many Taiwanese with his remarks in April 2009 that Chinese needed "control" because too much freedom could lead to chaos, "like in Taiwan."

Hong Kong, with over 200 professors with Taiwanese backgrounds teaching in Hong Kong's eight universities, is the ideal hub for scholarly exchanges between academics from across the strait because it has freedom of speech, a good geographic location and a common language.

That is why the "referendum" periodically promoted by former Taiwan leader Chen Shui-bian over whether the island should join the U.N. under the name "Taiwan" was a nonstarter. The Taiwanese won't vote for de jure independence and the U.N. won't accept Taiwan as a sovereign nation. Is it any wonder China treats Taiwan as recyclable and reuseable-hazardous waste?

What does the U.S. do in this situation? It turns up the heat on Taipei by allowing high government contacts that push Taiwan to buy the $10-billion arms package the U.S wants to sell it. Naturally, activists protest, China objects and says the U.S. lawmakers trying to lift the ban on high-level U.S. contacts with Taiwan are committing a "serious violation" of the basis of Sino-American relations, and America looks dumb yet again in a place it shouldn't be in the first place. The meeting between Ma's predecessor as head of the Kuomintang party, Lien Chan, and Chinese President Hu Jintao in Beijing in 2005 when Hu headed the Chinese Communist Party, ended the Chinese civil war, a fact America has not come to terms with, yet alone accepted.

If Mao and Chiang Kai-shek could shake hands and toast Japan's defeat in the Chung King Foreign Correspondents Club in 1946 – and after the treachery they exchanged during the battle against the Japanese, to many it was a sham of a handshake – so can today's Chinese and Taiwanese leaders. They can toast their reunification and unified political, economic and military dominance over Japan in the New World Order as they share a Nobel Peace Prize.

Chapter 3

Salad – Chopped, Tossed and Mixed
Bushleaguer
– Pearl Jam

Sliced and Diced

The Council on Foreign Relations in New York is-
sued an excellent report in June 2007 on the state of relations between
Washington and Beijing. It says that the growth of U.S.-China economic
ties "is occurring against the backdrop of a shift in the structure of U.S.
employment from manufacturing to services." The 2009 bankruptcy of
General Motors, America's corporate icon and the outsourcing of its manufacturing to China confirmed the Council's findings.

China is by no means the only cause of this transition, nor is it a major
source of U.S. job losses the report said. Unfortunately, America's perception is different and wrong. An enlightening paragraph in the 106-page report says: "A growing number of Americans believe that trade with China
harms the U.S. economy, and that the U.S. trade deficit with China is mainly
the result of unfair Chinese trade practices. Both notions are false."

America's foreign policy consensus, released in October 2005, encouraged
closer U.S.-China ties – a policy that Congress is finally starting to pursue.
The U.S.-China Working Group in the House of Representatives was set
up in the middle of 2005 to make the U.S.-China relationship the primary
bilateral relationship in the 21st century. What started out as a 35-member
bipartisan group received bipartisan support and encouragement from their
colleagues in the U.S. Senate, where a similar working group was formed in
January 2006. In 2009 the group members grew to 55 and are actually being
constructive for a change.

On the other hand, the Quadrennial Defense Review, published by the
Pentagon in February 2006, concluded: "Of the major and emerging pow-

ers, China has the greatest potential to compete militarily with the United States…. Shaping the choices of major and emerging powers requires a balanced approach, one that seeks cooperation but also creates prudent hedges against the possibility that cooperative approaches by themselves may fail to preclude future conflict."

Reality Check

One of the hardest adjustments that may have to be made over this new century is the U.S. accepting at some point that it is no longer the world's sole superpower and that such a status is no longer pertinent to unfolding conditions in various regions. America finds itself in a position that the British used to occupy with its Royal Navy. Any other state that came close to rivaling Britain in power and scope was perceived as a threat to peace. The same holds true today in the eyes of the U.S. because of China's expanding naval capabilities.

The world is going through a geopolitical economic and political transformation. The global awakening has caught America off guard. "Just how we got to this point is an experience we must study and learn from. The almighty truth is that both America and China have to change and work together in order to grow from here," Mary Catherine McBride said in our continuing rambling discussion that has been going on since we took Jan & Dean to China in 1986. "Right on, sister," her husband Kevin piped in. He had been in China in 1994 to film a video of XCL, the hottest foreign band Mary Catherine and I brought from California to China at the time. They played at the Shanghai Hilton 24/7 express restaurant from 9pm to whenever hotel guests or neighbors complained – usually between 3 and 4am.

Just like U.S. rock 'n roll connected with China, so can U.S. geopolitics with the right political beat. The U.S. does have a chance to join up with China and lead the transformational charge. It is time America accepts China as a partner and a part of a larger world the two can lead together.

China's strong and stable economic performance drives regional development and has lifted millions out of poverty. This economic performance has shifted world attention to China. The one thing Asia does not want to experience again is the financial crisis of 2008. Driven by the Beijing 2008 Olympics and the World Expo 2010 Shanghai, the Chinese economy can be expected to continue to grow and attract more international capital. China is like a giant elephant riding a bicycle – it must maintain speed at its own pace – otherwise it will crash.

The reality is that the People's Bank of China is bankrupt, bust. It has a bare 22 billion yuan in capital to support total assets of more than 14 trillion on its balance sheet. If the U.S. dollar falls by 5 percent against the yuan and 80 percent of China's reserves are in U.S. dollar instruments, then the value of those reserves falls by more than $50 billion.

"This represents many multiples of the bank's capital. How can the central bank absorb this hit without going bust?" former columnist Jake van der Kamp asks. In other words, China's Central Bank, the holder of the world's largest dollar reserves, is bankrupt. Thus it should come as no surprise that China is in no rush to revalue its currency and literally break its own bank.

"I wish you could meet my friend Kevin McBride, who lives in L.A.," I responded as we continued our lunch at the Foreign Correspondents Club in Hong Kong. "I get into late night discussions with Kevin and his wife Mary Catherine when I visit them in L.A. It usually revolves around why the U.S is bust and China is so prosperous. Your take puts a whole new spin on financial reality that no one seems to address," I added.

Diversified Reserves

China announced in January 2006 that it could begin to diversify its massive and rapidly growing foreign currency reserves away from the U.S. dollar and government bonds – a potential shift with significant implications for U.S. and global financial and commodity markets. It is estimated that more than 70 percent of China's reserves are in U.S. dollar assets, which has helped sustain America's deficits. If China were to stop acquiring such a large proportion of dollars with its reserves – currently accumulating at about $15 billion a month – it would put heavy downward pressure on the greenback.

When China sold off a record $6 billion of U.S. treasuries in June 2007, the first drop in holdings since October 2005, world markets took notice – as did the 2008 U.S. presidential contenders, who wisely concluded that China bashing was counter-productive.

Chinese held over $2 trillion worth of U.S. assets, mostly in Treasury debt, at the end of 2008. If China decided to use its reserves to finance infrastructure projects in China and clean up state-owned enterprises, or to invest in higher-yielding assets rather than financing U.S. borrowing, America's economic downspin would go into freefall.

"God damn bankers, make that wankers, who got us into this mess," Kevin McBride said in a very Scottish Billy Connolly accent as he got up to answer his phone. Kevin had been Connolly's driver on a couple of movies and became a real fan.

Rich nations need to try to capitalize on the inevitable emergence of what already is the engine of the world's economic activity before it is too late. Somewhere between 2030 and 2040, China will become the largest economy in the world, leaving the United States behind. "The U.S. bankers are now screwing the U.S. banks the way they did the world," Kevin continued as he rejoined us. By 2050, China's current $2 trillion GDP is set to balloon to $48.6 trillion. In comparison, the $13 trillion U.S. economy would expand to $37 trillion, more than $10 trillion behind China's.

In light of these forecasts, it is clear that Washington is not investing enough in educating the next generation to be able to take advantage of the coming realignment.

The realignment became blatantly obvious on Feb. 27, 2007, when a one-day drop in the Chinese stock market – an 8.8 percent plunge in the Shanghai stock market and 8.5 on Shenzen's – had an enduring negative impact on major stock markets around the world. The world realized overnight just how important China's economic might has become. U.S. stocks lost about $900 billion in value that week, almost 5 percent – another good reason for U.S. 2008 presidential candidates to stop bashing America's lead banker.

Overseas markets used China as an excuse for corrections in their overheated economies. America's economic vitality and financial stability depends on China's continued purchases of U.S. Treasury and dollar investments. The U.S. cannot afford to have China start selling its Treasury holdings or significantly diversifying its greenback purchases. That would spark a run on the U.S. dollar that would destabilize America's financial stability. It is a real possibility, and something China can afford to do. Can America? Do we want to find out? If America continues to alienate China by refusing to distance itself from Japan and Taiwan, we well may.

Cooking Oil
Cash-rich China is using the economic crisis – and the period of low oil prices it heralds – to improve its energy security and ensure that its economy has the oil-based fuels it needs to sustain growth when the recovery takes hold. Oil prices reached a record level of $147 a barrel in July 2008

before falling to under $33 a barrel in February 2009. China, the world's third-biggest oil importer, is taking advantage of the buyer's market.

Since February 2008, China has committed more than $50 billion to loans-for-oil agreements with Russia, Kazakhstan, Venezuela and Brazil. If the deals go through, China will gain access to more than 1.5 million barrels a day of extra oil. In 2009, China imported 4.1 million barrels a day.

Beijing is using government-owned banks with deep pockets and access to mountains of cheap credit to fund the loans-for-oil deals. The form of partnership, which offers foreign oil producers money for development without ceding direct control of their energy resources, is attractive at a time when Western banks are constrained by the credit crunch from lending.

China National Petroleum Corp, the mainland's largest oil and gas producer, offered between $13.2 billion and $14.5 billion for a 75 percent stake in the Argentine unit of Spanish oil company Repsol-YPF in June 2009. The initial reaction from Repsol's board was receptive. If it is successful, the deal could be a win-win for both the Chinese and Argentine companies. CNPC will acquire a sizable oil-producing asset while YPF's aging oilfields will be helped by mainland experience in rehabilitating its more than 40-year old Daqing oilfield in northeast China.

What differentiates China's aggressive state-owned acquisition approach from Western oil firms is that China is eager to reduce its U.S. dollar holdings through overseas acquisitions to hedge its currency risks.

China has also been invited by Iran to get involved in several huge oil projects worth more than $42.8 billion. The projects comprise upgrades and expansions of refineries, construction of seven new ones and building a 1,640-kilometer oil pipeline from Neka on the Caspian Sea in the north to Jask on the Gulf of Oman in the south. Iran hopes to boost its petrol production capacity to 190 million litres per day by 2012 from 44 million.

The Iranian government is offering sweeteners to attract investment for its projects from China, such as a 5 percent discount on the price of crude fed to the refineries, an eight-year tax exemption, and free and unlimited transfer by foreign investors of their profits from the projects. The most attractive component is that foreign investors will be entitled to raise their equity holding by up to 80 percent in all the new refinery projects and even higher for existing refineries that will be privatized.

The invitation extended to China by Iran came on the heels of Sinopec's successful $7.2 billion bid in June 2009 for Addax Petroleum Corp, which has oil reserves in Africa and Iraq.

In 1979, when I first rode a horse in Los Angeles to protest the high price of oil, Big Oil lorded over 75 percent of global reserves and 80 percent of output. Today they control 6 percent of oil reserves and 25 percent of production, while national oil companies in Asia, the Middle East, Africa and Russia have the rest and are now dealing with China. A classic example of how pigs get fat and hogs get slaughtered.

China's oil diplomacy may be bad for Big Oil, but it is good for the global oil market. It is increasing the oil supply, helping to ensure that when economic recovery comes, there will be enough oil to meet demand and keep prices from going sky-high again.

Venturing into countries in the Middle East and Africa in its quest to quench its thirst for cooking oil is not without risk. In Iraq, where China made the first major investment in the Ahdeb oil field in southeastern Iraq, it was confronted by angry farmers complaining that the drilling has damaged their property and asking for security jobs to protect the drilling equipment from being damaged "accidentally." Without a petroleum law in place that spells out the legal rights and responsibilities of foreign investors, it is up to the parties to negotiate a mutually acceptable price for harmony.

In Africa, the price China has to pay for harmony is much higher, as there it has had to periodically pay ransom for the release of its kidnapped workers.

Chinese "Marshall Plan"
China is using its foreign-exchange reserves to finance infrastructure projects in the developing world. As foreign banks and Western governments retreat to their home markets to deal with domestic issues, China has stepped in to fill the void out of necessity. Necessity stems from the challenges China faces in investing nearly $2.3 trillion worth of foreign reserves. Over 65 percent is invested in U.S. assets, and thus exposed to the risks of a weak dollar or rising yields. Diversification is necessary. Investment in foreign infrastructure offers a viable alternative.

China is seen as the natural leader of the emerging world as it challenges America's economic hegemony.

Yeast – China Rising

China was the world's leader in the 10 centuries between 500 and 1500, although without global reach. Only in the last half of the last millennium was it overtaken by Europe and America. The Asian Development Bank has calculated that in 1820, at the beginning of the Industrial Age, Asia generated an estimated three-fifths of world product. By 1940, this had fallen to one-fifth. China is reemerging as a global power, leading an Asia that America cannot afford to alienate or continue a future relationship based on fear. America must always keep in mind Thucydides' warning more than two millennia ago that belief in the inevitability of conflict can become one of its main causes. Each side, believing it will end up at war with the other, makes reasonable military preparations that are then read by the other side as confirmation of its worst fears.

China has encroached openly, capitalistically and transparently onto the U.S.'s political, military and geopolitical patches in Asia and Latin America as the U.S. flounders trying to manage two wars and the meltdown of its corporate icons of capitalist might and financial firepower, as it watches them slide into bankruptcy to restructure to become financially viable contenders again.

"I can't friggin believe General Motors, the symbol of America's corporate and global power, is going into bankruptcy and its jobs outsourced to China," McBride said as we read the news that its bankrupcy filing was imminent one morning over coffee.

"Who would have ever have believed it when we were growing up?" Mary Catherine added."

"Yeah, and in the meantime, China is not only benefiting from America's financial meltdown financially and economically, but politically as well, and is moving very aggressively into the U.S.'s traditional spheres of influence," I responded. "Not only Taiwan, one of America's main military allies on China's doorstep, but Australia, its regional ally and in America's backyard, its "hemisphere of strategic influence in Canada, South and Central America.

Kangaroo Bar-B-Q

The rapidly growing economic cooperation between China and Australia is breathtaking. The state visits of Australian Prime Minister John Howard to China and Premier Wen Jiabao's visit to Australia in 2006 cemented the relationship. They are partners in a $25-billion natural liquefied gas project in Guangdong, China. Beijing is also set to become a key buyer of Australian uranium. Australia has the world's largest uranium deposits.

China's state-owned Aluminum Corp. of China tried to invest more than $20 billion in Rio Tinto, Australia's second-largest resource company, to acquire an 18 percent stake in the company. Although Australians, according to the Sydney-based Lowy Institute's 2009 annual foreign policy survey, feel the government has "a responsibility to ensure major Australian companies are kept in majority Australian control" and "a majority of Australians oppose major foreign ownership," the government looked like it was going to approve the deal when Rio Tinto decided to pull out at the last minute because of the unexpected rapid rise of commodity prices that suddenly presented Rio Tinto with alternatives to China. The deal ultimately collapsed for business reasons, not political ones.

Rio Tinto approached Chinalco in February 2009, at the height of the financial crisis, to help repair a balance sheet weighted down by $38.7 billion in debt. A payment of $8.9 billion was due in October 2009. At the time, Chinalco was Rio Tinto's only source of salvation. The rise of commodity prices in the summer of 2009 presented Rio with new investment alternatives that it did not have in February.

The sticking point was the failure to reach agreement on a $7.2 billion convertible bond issue that was a key part of the deal that favored Chinalco. Unfortunately for Chinalco, it seized a timely investment opportunity but did not execute and close the deal fast enough.

China is naturally disappointed that it was unable to close the deal, but it is not a real concern about ensuring a steady, reliable, competitively priced iron ore. Analysts estimate that steel production capacity would shrink 50 percent in 2009 and it will take another 10 years for the world steel industry to return to 2008 levels. China has many good options because of the unprecedented iron ore glut in the global market in 2009. Unlike Japan, South Korea and Taiwan, it did not rush to sign any benchmark price deals to ensure its supply of 2009-2010 iron ore.

China's fat and rich dragon approach to the iron ore dispute backfired and the country's steel mills had to pay as much as 80 percent higher prices on the spot market than those on offer and signed by other steel producing countries who agreed to a benchmark price. China's failure to agree on a benchmark price that its steel mills pay the world's top three iron ore producers – Vale, Rio Tinto and BHP Billiton – resulted in Chinese mills having to pay millions more on the spot market. China sought a 45 percent reduction on 2008-09 prices, even after a 33 percent cut in benchmark iron ore prices had already been set with steel mills in Japan, South Korea and Taiwan. Beijing felt that as the world's biggest importer, it deserved a bigger price reduction.

China's iron ore and oil imports reached record highs in July 2009. Oil imports climbed by 18 percent to 19.6 million tons from June, and iron ore rose by 5 percent to 58.1 million tons, up 35 percent from the same period a year earlier. China spent a combined $13.8 billion on the two commodities, 15 percent of the country's total imports for the month. China's exports in July exceeded $100 billion for the first time in 2009, up 10.4 percent compared with June.

While in the middle of talks with Rio Tinto, China arrested four employees of the Anglo-Australian mining group in the company's Shanghai office – the firm's main center in China and its chief base in the country for iron ore sales and marketing – including one Australian passport holder, on charges of bribing government officials to obtain "state secrets" about China's iron ore needs. The state secret charges were later dropped when they were "formally" arrested. They were charged with obtaining trade secrets about the steel and iron industry through "improper means," in other words, bribery.

Killer Party Spirit

Drinking at banquets is an unspoken rule for doing business in China – even if it kills you. Communist Party officials regularly binge on alcohol and kill themselves on the job. In 2009, there were three such publicly announced deaths that highlight the problems of a drinking culture connected with government and business activities. Chinese officials spend an estimated 500 billion yuan of public funds every year on boozy banquets.

I have experienced first-hand the ganbei business culture and can testify how hard it is to survive. Guo Shizhong, a family planning official from Xinyang, Central China's Henan Province, is one of the Communist Party members who died in 2009. He was honored posthumously as an "excellent Party member and given a merit award for dying with "honor."

A lot of business is conducted at official banquets. The Chinese prefer to make decisions at the dinner table rather than the boardroom table. I wonder who President Obama's designated drinker, if any, was during his official state visit in November 2009?

The Rio Tinto criminal case is a dangerous precedent for what other companies in China and "developing" countries will be doing to foreign firms that signed exploitive contracts.

This is especially true with derivative contracts. Many state-owned enterprises racked up huge losses on the trades, prompting the state-owned Assets Supervision and Administration of the State Council to announce in September 2009, its support for legal efforts by some state-backed Chinese companies to break loss-making contracts with foreign banks. Abrogating contracts with foreigners in pursuit of domestic policy goals is a time- honored tradition in China. Regretfully, I know this first hand.

"Contracts are legally binding and where the line will be drawn between the rule of law and the rule of pigs get fat and hogs get slaughtered remains to be seen," I told Nelson Wong when he asked me what impact the arrests would have on the validity of contracts in the future.

"Everybody who does business in China knows that there is collusion between foreign firms and unscrupulous state-owned company executives who are more than happy to share information for the right price," Nelson told me in response to my question about what he thought about the arrests, which had rattled many businessmen and companies doing business in China. "You know what it's like," he continued. "How many officials have you invited to dinner, karaoke and to the U.S. on business trips before closing deals?" he asked. "It's the way business is done."

"I know *guanxi*," I responded. No different than what pharmaceutical companies do in America with doctors and politicians to push their drugs while fighting a national health program.

Taking government officials and Chinese business executives on foreign "business trips," paying their children's tuition fees in foreign universities, or just taking them to dinner, karaoke bars and drinking is an integral part of doing business in China. Drinking has always been a key way of bonding and building guanxi – one of the reasons I did so well in China. There are definitely times when the lines between entertainment and bribery do blur, or maybe it's just the alcohol.

Which Menu?

In most cities in China, there are two menus and two sets of prices – one for locals and one for foreigners. The same holds true for business. There does seem to be a double standard for Western multinational firms when it comes to doing business in China. This was highlighted in August 2009 when U.S. label maker Avery Dennison admitted it bribed Chinese officials to get contracts. Bribes in China are the quickest shortcut to winning a contract or getting business information. Foreign companies were involved in 64 percent of the 500,000 corruption cases tried from 1999 to 2009 in China.

"My take on the whole incident is that since the Rio Tinto executives were arrested by the Shanghai branch of the secretive Ministry of State Security, it means mainland officials must have had hard evidence implicating the four," I said to Nelson, knowing he probably knew more about the case than he was willing to discuss on the phone.

China's Ministry of State Security – the mainland equivalent of the U.S. CIA and National Security Agency combined – has sweeping powers and uses the most advanced eavesdropping technology to target and detain anyone on the mainland suspected of buying or selling state secrets. Charges of leaking state secrets were usually confined to political dissidents, journalists and foreign correspondents. The arrest of the Rio employees changes the paradigm and extends the definition to what is referred to in the West as industrial espionage – with a twist over drinks.

"So do you think there was a political agenda and motivation behind the arrests because of Rio's refusal to close the deal with Chinalco?" I asked. "I hear on the news that Hu Jintao himself approved the arrest. That's pretty unusual for a simple bribery case isn't it?" I pressed as Nelson remained silent and evasive.

"Who knows," he finally said. "It's possible."

What is interesting is that Chinese steel mills preferred to import more iron ore from Brazil rather than Australia after the detention of the four Rio Tinto employees. Spot iron ore vessel bookings from Brazil to China surged to a record 39 in July 2009, from 24 in the previous month. Vessel bookings from Australia's main iron ore ports to China dropped to 31, down from 40 in June, the lowest reading after the Rio Tinto scandal. Chinese steelmakers have begun to cut their imports from Australian mines and are switching to Brazilian ore instead.

But the Rio Tinto dispute has not deterred China's determination to acquire mining companies in resource-rich Australia. Yanzhou Coal Mining was reportedly close in August 2009 to sealing a multi-billion dollar-deal to buy Australian coal miner Felix Resources, but its bid was rejected. China Non-ferrous Metal Mining was also blocked from buying more than 50 percent of Lynas Corp., a prospector for rare earths, amid concerns about Chinese control of that market. Mainland Chinese investors announced more than $12 billion in investments in Australia in the first five months of 2009, almost four times the amount they invested in all of 2008. Nevertheless, several Chinese investments have been rejected.

Wugang Australia Resources, a wholly owned subsidiary of Wuhan Iron and Steel Corp., tried to buy 21.1 million shares in Western Plains, and half of Western's Hawk Nest magnetite mine, for A$45 million. The Australian government blocked the sale in September 2009 on grounds that the mine, near an outback missile-testing range, posed a security risk because the mine was in the missile firing line, and not because the buyer was Chinese.

"On the one hand, Australia welcomes Chinese investment as it knows its economic development cannot ignore China, but on the other, it hopes it can get the most benefits in the cooperation and is reluctant to see Chinese companies taking the major stake in the resources sector," said Yu Liangui, director of research center at Mysteel.

It was the second time in 2009 that the Australian Defense Department had vetoed an application from a Chinese company for investment near the Woomera prohibited area. In March 2009, the government blocked China Minmetals Non-ferrous Metals Co. from buying Australian miner Oz Minerals Ltd. for A$2.6 billion because one of the assets, the Prominent Hill gold and copper mine, was within the range area. China Minerals eventually bought Oz Minerals minus the mine for A$1.7 billion.

Yanzhou Coal Mining resubmitted its application in October 2009 to buy Felix Resources for $3.2 billion to the Australian Foreign Investment Review Board. The board, an advisory body to the Australian treasurer, has been flooded with applications by Chinese state companies, including a bid by Sinochem for the farm chemicals group Nufarm and Baosteel's plan to buy 15 percent of iron ore explorer Aquila Resources.

Australia recognizes that China is in the process of making a transition from communism to capitalism, that its state-run companies are becoming more independent and that foreign investment helps build a Chinese middle class that will demand more freedom. More importantly, China's economic growth is good for Aussies because it has helped underpin the nation's continued growth cycle and may enable Australia to weather the worst effects of the global financial storm.

Prime Minister Kevin Rudd, a Mandarin speaker, is aggressively pushing Australia's relationship with China and the region beyond the economic and strategic – many Australians think too aggressively. The first ministerial resignation for Rudd in June 2009 was that of Defense Minister Joel Fitzgibbon, triggered by his close friendship with a Chinese-born business-woman who had given him flight tickets to China and a suit, which he failed to report. An official investigation found there was no security breach in the relationship.

China-Australia relations deteriorated further when Chinese students in Australia started mysteriously disappearing and getting murdered in 2008. Chinese students in Australia today are afraid for their safety. There are about 120,000 Chinese students studying in Australia. The country's A$15.5-billion international education market is its third-largest "export" industry.

Rudd strongly believes Australia's future lies predominantly in developing deep relationships with China.

"Will China democratize? How will China respond to climate change? How will China deal with crisis in the economic and financial systems? How will China respond domestically to the global information revolution? And how will Chinese culture adjust to the array of global influences now washing across its shores?... How China responds to these forces will radically shape the future course of our country," said Rudd. He added, "I am committed to making Australia the most Asia-literate country in the collective West."

He is hitching his horse to the rising dragon. Why isn't America?

Granted, the task of getting average Aussie Joe Six-Pack to speak fluent Putonghua and watch Chinese movies is no easy challenge. Australia is a country of 21 million people, most of whom are racist and xenophobic toward China. Sino-Australian relations hold promising prospects for mutual prosperity. China's soft approach is not limited to Asia or Australasia. It is reaching out of the region to Europe, Africa and Latin America as well.

Canadian Club

Canadians know their whiskey and know how to drink it with the best whiskey ganbaiers in America, China, actually anywhere. I've hoisted a few with Canadians across China and the U.S. They do get touchy when told they are America's 51st state – because of their oil and water. It should therefore come as no surprise that Canada is America's No. 1 trading partner and China's new primary reserve currency.

China, with the world's largest currency reerves of $2.3 trillion, is buying Canadian dollars with U.S. dollars to protect itself against the declining dollar – a great hedge for China. Being in America's backyard is an extra super bonus point. The Canadian dollar gained 15 percent in 2009 against the U.S. dollar. One Canadian dollar purchases 94.58 U.S. cents. Canada's currency is predicted to appreciate to parity with the U.S. in 2010.

Canadian banks, like Chinese banks, remained on a solid financial footing during and after the global financial meltdown, because they never bought into the U.S. banks subrime Ponzi scheme. Canada also had the lowest debt levels among the Group of Seven nations, making its currency a relatively safer investment.

PetroChina, the country's largest oil company, bought in 2009 its first stake in the Canadian oil sands, paying C$1.9 billion for 60 percent of a project run by Athabasca Oil Sands Corp. Teck Resources, Canada's biggest base metal producers, sold a 17 percent stake to China's sovereign wealth fund for C$1.74 billion in July, 2009.

Canada sits on the largest pool of oil reserves outside the Middle East and is also a major exporter of other commodities such as gold.

Prime Minister Stephen Harper, seeking to cut dependence on the U.S., traveled to China a few weeks after President Obama's visit to secure more contracts for oil, natural gas, uranium and other commodities. Canada is also a primary immigration destination for Chinese nationals.

Sichuan-Salsa

Trade between China and Latin America reached a record of more than $140 billion in 2008, 40 percent higher than the $101 billion of 2007. China's overall investment in Latin America is relatively small when compared to that of the U.S. – but it is growing. China's investment in Latin America and the Caribbean at the end of 2008 was more than $40 billion, compared to America's more than $300 billion.

A decade ago China was almost invisible in Latin America. Today it is building cars in Uruguay, donating a soccer stadium to Costa Rica and lending billions to Brazil. Beijing's main interest in Latin America has been guaranteeing access to the regions raw materials – principally oil, iron ore, soy beans and copper – to fuel its continued rapid growth. Beijing's increased presence in Latin America has alarmed policymakers in Washington. However, China has been careful not to establish a military presence in the region, knowing it will antagonize Washington, which considers Latin America to be in its sphere of influence since the Monroe Doctrine of 1823.

Beyond trade, China is suddenly rivaling the World Bank and Inter-American Development Bank as a major lender to Latin America at a time when Beijing is flush with cash and many companies cannot get access to bank loans.

China's growing ties to Latin America, especially Brazil, are helping tackle the global economic crisis and chart the road to a new international order. The declining influence of the United States in Latin America has made China's task easier. Latin countries no longer want to be dependent only on the U.S.

China replaced the United States as Brazil's largest trading partner in the first four months of 2009. China has become Brazil's No. 3 export destination after the U.S. and Argentina. Those exports include iron ore, airplanes, soy beans and pulp. China also plans to invest more than $3 billion in Brazilian infrastructure – ports, roads and railways – while Brazil's Foreign Ministry has hinted at some $5 billion in direct investment in China. These investments will be in reals and yuan, a worrisome concern for the U.S. dollar.

The link between Brazil and China connects the biggest emerging markets of the Western and Eastern hemispheres. In the words of Celso Amorim, Brazil's foreign minister, it could be part of a "certain reconfiguration of the world's commercial and diplomatic geography."

This was confirmed in February 2009, when Brazil and China signed a landmark agreement that will ensure long-term supplies of oil to China in exchange for China financing the development of the enormous reserves of oil and gas discovered in Brazil's coastal waters. Brazil will supply China with between 100,000 and 160,000 barrels of oil a day in exchange for Beijing's $10 billion loan.

China signed a similar deal with Venezuela in February 2009. A $6 billion China-Venezuela development fund created in 2007 was renewed with an additional $6 billion. Venezuela's President Hugo Chavez told the Chinese delegation: "All the oil China needs for the next 200 years, it's here. It's in Venezuela."

Venezuela is the third-largest foreign supplier of oil to the U.S., and owns Citgo, one of the largest refinery complexes and gas distribution networks in America. Chavez has threatened to replace the U.S. oil market with China on more than one occasion – and emphatically so after Christian commentator Pat Robertson called for Chavez's assassination and the Bush White House's deafeningly silent rebuke. Condemning the incendiary remarks would have been the decent thing to do and in the U.S. national interest.

The Bush alternative option was again another example of America's misguided foreign policy. What happened? Chavez, in mid-May 2007, continued to aggressively nationalize Western energy companies, including BP, Chevron, Conoco, Exxon, Total and Statoil, forcing ExxonMobil, the largest U.S. oil company, and Conoco Phillips, the third largest, to end their participation in exploration ventures. In the past the global oil companies paid only 1 percent in royalties for the crude they extracted in the country's oil-rich Orinoco Belt. After Chavez was elected in 1998, royalties increased to 33.2 percent, while taxes went up from 34 percent to 50 percent. Chavez also re-nationalized American-owned telecoms and electricity companies.

With the extra revenue, it was only a matter of time before Chavez would propose his plan for a Banco del Sur – Bank of the South – a development bank funded and run by Latin American countries. He periodically threatens to leave the Organization of American States and pull out of the IMF. It would be nice if Chavez spent the people's money developing their education and health systems, infrastructure and lives in general, instead of just glorifying and enriching himself.

China has increased its investments in Venezuela along with the amount of oil it is buying from the country. Chavez threatened to give China and Cuba 22 U.S.-made F-16 jets after the U.S. refused to sell Venezuela spare parts for the planes. Venezuela bought the F-16s in the early 1980s and for a long time was the only Latin American country to possess the sophisticated warplanes, a reflection of how bad the relationship between Venezuela and the U.S. has become. A deal Venezuela made with Israel to buy the needed parts was cancelled after America intervened. Chavez brought up the possibility of giving the planes to China and Cuba in 2005 to mark the signing of a satellite production agreement with China.

China launched the communications satellite on October 29, 2008 as the two countries continued to strengthen their political and economic ties. Venezuela reportedly paid China $400 million to join the satellite club – another breakthrough for China in the international satellite market. China has already jointly built satellites with Brazil, launched a commercial satellite for Nigeria, and signed a satellite-building and launching pact with Pakistan. China is direct to the point as to why. "We launched satellites for Nigeria and Venezuela because they both have oil and we need it," said Wang Xudong, satellite designer and adviser to the China Aerospace Science and Technology Corp.

Chavez has been desperately trying to find an alternative buyer to the U.S. for his oil. China is happy to accommodate him. Exports to China will more than treble to 1 million barrels a day by 2012. China also sees Venezuela's substantial undeveloped oil reserves as an attractive long-term source for ensuring energy security.

The Sino-Venezuelan bond got tighter when Chavez described himself as a "Maoist" and predicted the "collapse of global capitalism" on his fifth trip to Beijing in September 2008, when he announced he was expanding his energy ties to China by building a refinery with them in Venezuela. China imported 380,000 barrels of oil a day from Venezuela at the end of 2008. Chavez said he wanted to expand this to 1 million barrels per day by 2013. He also announced that the joint Sino-Venezuela investment fund would be doubled in size to $12 billion. Bilateral trade between the two countries in 2008 exceeded $8 billion.

During Chavez's April 2009 visit to Beijing, he declared that the world now revolved around China as he praised the nation for driving the global economy amid the "capitalist" crisis.

While Venezuela and the U.S. rattle their war sabers, because of the military bases the U.S. is building in Colombia that Venezuela perceives as a military threat, China is getting ready to tap even deeper into Colombia's oil and gas fields.

Colombia, best known for its coffee, cocaine and narco-terrorists, is also South America's fourth-largest oil producer. The energy rich nation is expected to produce 700,000 barrels of oil a day in 2009. Its oil consumption has been relatively steady, ranging between 222,000 and 240,000 barrels a day, with the bulk of its exports going to the U.S. That may all change now that China has been invited to join the Colombian oil exploration dinning and poker tables.

China Petrochemical Corp formed a joint venture with India's ONGC in 2006 to acquire Colombian oil firm Omimex, which has proven reserves of 60 million barrels. In August 2009, Sinochem bought British-based Emerald Energy, which has oil exploration rights in Colombia.

Colombia is estimated to have 100 to 115 million hectares of onshore and offshore areas with sedimentary formations that may have trapped oil and gas. The country plans to open 170 exploration areas for development in 2010.

Colombia aims to raise its daily production to more than 1,000,000 barrels a day by 2015. Foreign firms can own 100 percent of oil projects and are only required to pay a royalty fee of 20 percent.

The "eternal friendship" expressed by China's Defense Minister General Cao Gangchuan at the start of his 2007 visit to Cuba was aimed at bolstering strategic ties. The long-standing friendship between China and Cuba heated up when China's Hu Jintau and Cuba's Fidel Castro announced after the 2004 APEC meeting in Chile that China would mine Cuba's nickel as Castro cut off the use of U.S. dollars. Today Cuba sells China nickel, sugar, medicines and crude oil.

President Hu visited the ailing 82-year-old Cuban icon in November 2008, during a visit to Havana to boost economic ties between the two nations. It was Hu's second visit to Cuba. Earlier he had met Fidel's brother Raul Castro, who led 200 Chinese students learning Spanish at a Cuban school in an impromptu sing-a-long of a Chinese song about the late Chairman Mao Zedong. The two leaders oversaw the signing of dozens of trade and investment deals. China agreed to further defer for 10 years payment of a trade debt Cuba ran up in 1995 and a credit facility granted in 1998.

Hu brought a large business delegation with him to pursue deals despite the global financial crisis – continuing a trend that has seen Beijing's trade with Latin America rise from $10 billion in 2000 to $103 billion in 2007. China is now Cuba's second-largest trading partner, after Venezuela, with a figure of $2.3 billion in 2007.

Bolivia's President Evo Morales, inaugurated on Jan. 22, 2006, embarked on a 10-day victory tour of Spain, France and China before his swearing-in ceremony. China pledged to strengthen bilateral ties with Bolivia by developing partnerships in investment and trade. Morales said the Bolivian people regard China as a trustworthy friend and partner.

"Expanding relations with China will be a priority among the policy goals of my presidency," Morales promised. "I made a priority of answering the invitation of China because I consider it to be a political, ideological and programmatic ally of the Bolivian people," Morales told Hu as the two leaders shook hands.

Morales invited China to help Bolivia develop its vast gas reserves. Bolivia has the second-largest natural gas reserves in Latin America and is also rich in silver, tin and other minerals.

In 2005 China joined the Inter-American Development Bank, giving its construction companies access to the bank's infrastructure projects.

China is developing strong relationships in Latin America because of U.S. neglect and alienation of goodwill in the region. Washington's relations with Argentina, Brazil, Cuba and Venezuela are anything but cordial – which some Latin American countries have decided to exploit.

The U.S. failure to get a free-trade agreement at the 2005 34-nation Summit of the Americas in Argentina was the latest indication of how little goodwill America has even in the Americas. Washington tried to revive negotiations on a free-trade area stretching from Canada to Chile and failed. Venezuela's Chavez led the attack against America and the agreement. Chavez also managed to block a U.S. push to set a date to resume negotiations.

Things didn't go much better for America in its efforts to push through the Central American Free Trade Agreement, which would eliminate most trade barriers and open up trade valued at $32 billion between the U.S. and Costa Rica, El Salvador, Honduras, Guatemala, Nicaragua and the Dominican Republic. The twin defeats, coming on the heels of America's earlier defeat in its choice of secretary general of the Organization of American States, is unprecedented. It was the first time in the organization's history that a candidate initially opposed by the U.S. will lead that regional grouping.

The OAS was founded in 1948, part of the same post-World War II American effort to construct a multilateral foreign policy that also led to the creation of entities like NATO. The U.S. contributes about 60 percent of the OAS's $76-million annual budget and has traditionally played the dominant role in the group, whose missions include monitoring elections and mediating political disputes in member countries. With left-leaning parties winning elections in Nicaragua and Ecuador and their leaders joining the Castro-Chavez bandwagon, America is spending millions of dollars to finance its political foes instead of mending its political fences there.

The Russians Are Here

Today the Russians are back. Russian President Dmitry Medvedev visited Cuba in December 2008 to show the U.S. that Russia is prepared to meddle in Washington's backyard in response to U.S. support for governments such as the Ukraine and Georgia that Russia considers to be in its sphere of influence. Russia is back with a vengeance and emulating China's strategy of broadening ties in Latin America – and China.

Russia is in an aggressive mode to expand its collaboration with China in the trade, energy and military sectors – while supporting one another's measures to safeguard national sovereignty and territorial integrity. China, sees Russia, the world's ninth-biggest economy, which like America, is struggling to recover from the global financial meltdown, as a valuable strategic counterweight to U.S. influence, and believes Russian energy, resources and markets will remain important in the future. Is it any wonder the U.S. is repeatedly checkmated at the U.N. Security Council by one or both countries?

Talk about the *The Times They Are a-Changing*. Today there is a New Word Disorder that has to be recognized by America. Russia, not Saudi Arabia, is the world's biggest energy producer, and neighboring China, not Japan, is the world's second-largest energy consumer after the U.S.

The North Korean nuclear crisis, which has obsessed the U.S. political and military establishments, could be easily resolved by the U.S., China and

Russia if their respective negotiators sat down in a room over exquisitely cooked meals from chefs from all three countries, generously washed down with bourbon, vodka and mao tai, with beer chasers.

Russia sealed Chinese oil contracts in 2009 valued at more than $100 billion, and is negotiating an agreement that would make China its biggest customer for natural gas. China currently buys no Russian gas. The two countries' ties are based on mutual economic gain – economic and political. Bilateral trade totaled a record $56 billion in 2008, a six-fold increase in six years.

One of the oil deals signed in 2009 calls for $25 billion in Chinese funding to support construction of a pipeline from Russia's vast untapped reserves to China. In exchange, China was guaranteed a 20-year supply of crude oil. A similar credit-deal was done with Russia's state-run natural gas monopoly, Gazprom, to get started on gas pipelines for its Kovykta project, one of the largest undeveloped gas fields in eastern Siberia with estimated reserves of 2 trillion cubic meters of gas and more than 83 million tons of gas condensate.

Russia and China are basically telling the Western powers, especially Europe, to get used to the new Cold War. Get used to being left out in the cold.

The bad news for America is that China and Russia stressed optimization of their trade structures and financial cooperation by using the two countries' currencies for settlement – no more U.S. dollars.

When will America sweep in the foreign policy changes needed for the country to again be embraced by its Cuban and Latino neighbors, not to mention Russia and China?

African Chicken

China is also challenging the U.S. in Africa, according to an independent study released by the Council on Foreign Relations at the end of 2005. It has become a key U.S. competitor for oil there as other world supplies have dwindled. China issued its first-ever African Policy Paper in January 2006 to promote long-term growth of China-Africa relations. The New Partnership for Africa Development has drawn up an aggressive and encouraging plan of rejuvenation and development. Among the total of 53 countries in Africa, 48 have established diplomatic relations with China. The stragglers are being wooed away from Taiwan.

Premier Wen Jiaobao offered Africa $10 billion in concessional loans over a three-year period at the Forum on China-Africa Cooperation in the Egyptian resort of Sharm el-Sheikh in November 2009. He also announced Beijing would cancel the government debts of some of the poorer countries. Having enjoyed snorkeling in the local Red Sea with American and Israeli politicians and businessmen, usually to clear the head from the banquet festivities of the night before, I know how commitments can increase. The aid is double that offered by President Hu Jintao in Beijing in 2006.

The weekend Forum on China-Africa Cooperation in November 2006 for the heads of state of the 48 African nations was the biggest red-carpet event China ever hosted. The routes along which the heads of state traveled were blocked off for the likes of Zimbabwe's Robert Mugabe to drive unimpeded. The summit was held on the occasion of the 50th anniversary of the inauguration of diplomatic relations between China and Africa, and celebrated more than 1,000 years of ties dating back to Ming Dynasty explorer Zheng He, who took his fleet to the east coast of Africa.

After China established diplomatic relations with Egypt in 1956, it spread its influence across the continent, following Mao's famous advice to "teach how to fish instead of giving developing countries the fish," with aid, public health, education and infrastructure projects. One of its most ambitious projects was the 1,848km TanZam railway linking Zambia's copper belt to the Indian Ocean port of Dar es Salaam in Tanzania, which took about 16,000 Chinese workers five years to construct and opened in 1976.

Another major infrastructure project that Chinese firms are involved in is the rebuilding of the 1,344-kilometer Benguela railway, linking Angola's coast and the copper belt that straddles Zambia and Congo. The railway has been inoperable for most of three decades because of the numerous civil wars along its route and the stringent conditions of multilateral institutions for infrastructure financing.

Beijing dispatched the first medical teams to Algeria in 1964 and has since sent more than 15,000 doctors to about 47 countries and treated more than 180 million people. Isolated jungle villagers, like Gabon's pygmies, are benefiting from China's insatiable appetite for raw materials and are thrilled that someone cares. They are getting medical attention, roads, public buildings, schools and libraries. At the other extreme, in countries like Zambia,

China's policy of importing Chinese workers is breeding resentment, hostility and accusations of a "new colonialism."

China now ranks as Africa's second-largest trading partner behind the United States. Trade between China and Africa surged from $10.6 billion in 2000 to $107 billion in 2008. China's financing investments in Africa rose from less than $1 billion per year before 2004 to about $7 billion in 2006 and $45 billion in 2007. Africa registered 5.8 percent economic growth in 2007, its highest ever, in part because of Chinese investment, according to the World Bank. China's $4.5 billion infrastructure investment in 2007 was more than the Group of Eight countries combined, according to the Public Private Infrastructure Advisory Facility, a multi-donor organization managed by the World Bank.

In the Democratic Republic of Congo, China agreed to build railways and dams in exchange for mineral rights. Not all deals worked out in China's favor. More than 40 Chinese-run copper smelters are standing idle after their owners fled the country without paying taxes or wages when commodity prices collapsed at the end of 2008.

"Some serious companies remain with metallurgical plants. I don't have any problem with them. But they are 10 percent of the Chinese who were here. Ninety percent have gone," said Moise Katumbi, governor of Katanga province, which is bisected by Congo's copperbelt, dismissing them as "speculators."

The Congo is trying to meet the criteria to join the IMF's highly indebted poor countries scheme, where it could be relieved of the majority of its multilateral and bilateral debt burden. The use of the Congo's mineral reserves as a guarantee for the infrastructure projects constitutes external debt that prevents the Congo from qualifying, according to the IMF. The Congo face-off between China and the IMF is a reminder that despite international criticism, Beijing's rising global economic might is being welcomed in countries bypassed these days by U.S. investors.

China's increasingly deep pockets mean international agencies such as the IMF risk being edged out of Africa. The IMF may be able to provide short-term finance for the Congo, but some say the Chinese deal is more suited for the long-term development of the country.

"Those who oppose Chinese investment...All they need to do is to equal the help we are getting from China," the late Zambian President Levy Mwana-wasa told a business forum in 2007. "We only turned to the East when you people in the West let us down. I know of no strings attached to Chinese investment."

China is encroaching on international financial institutions' domain of traditional influence and their potential control of domestic policy and affairs of debtor nations.

The latest and best example is China's October 2009, $7 billion lifeline to Guinea's military junta, the West African country led by Captain Moussa Dadis Camara, who seized power in December 2008, through a Hong Kong mainland controlled company. The deal gives Guinea's junta a major source of revenue, even though it faces isolation from the international community after soldiers opened fire in September 2009 at demonstrators opposed to Camara running in the January 2009 election. It is estimated that more than 100 people died in the streets as women were being raped on the same streets.

The African Union suspended Guinea's membership.

Guinea is the world's largest producer of bauxite, the raw material used to make aluminum, and also produces diamonds and gold. New power plants, railway links and aircraft were part of the deal.

China is focused on the development of transportation, communication, water conservation, electricity and education. It is also committed to go all out with its African Human Resources Development Foundation to train Africans. The aggressive student exchange programs between China and Africa will continue in the 21st century. China will increase the number of government scholarships for African students, continue to send teachers to Africa to teach Africans the Chinese language – and carry out educational assistance programs in every technical and vocational field – through the teachers it sends and by distance learning while encouraging more student and teacher exchanges and cooperation between Chinese and African educational institutions.

When most countries in Africa became independent in the 1950s and '60s, their economies were based on the export of natural resources, oil and agricultural products and the import of manufactured goods and services. Africa's primary trading partners were their former colonial masters. The system worked relatively well until the late 1970s, when prices for export commodities from Africa tumbled on world markets while the cost of imported goods and services increased. As a result, despite the increase in export volume, revenues decreased, making it difficult for African countries to buy the equipment needed to build up their own modern infrastructure and manufacturing sectors.

Today, China's emergence as a major trading power has given Africa an unprecedented opportunity to sell its natural resources at higher prices than it received from its former European colonial occupiers. This powers China's economy and allows Africa to buy cheaper manufactured goods from China – a win-win for all. In 2004, Sino-African trade volume reached $29.5 billion compared with $19 billion in 2003; nearly 60 percent growth in just one year. In 2005, trade volume reached $40 billion, then $50 billion in 2006 –and is growing fast. It is estimated it will reach $100 billion by 2010.

China imports a third of its foreign oil from Africa. Angola passed Saudi Arabia in 2006 to become China's top oil supplier.

African countries need investment to exploit their resources for economic development and China is willing to cooperate. It has more than 800 infrastructure projects in Africa. How many does America have? Zippo. America needs a good lighter to spark an enlightened contemporary and relevant Africa policy. Hopefully, Barack Obama, with real African roots, can light the necessary fire.

China describes its relationship with Africa as "all-weather friends and partners." In Zimbabwe, Chinese farmers are settling on tobacco farms abandoned by white owners who were driven off by Mugabe's government to make room for landless Africans. In Nigeria, China has struck a deal to export 30,000 barrels of crude oil a day to China. China is willing to pick up where the colonial forerunners left off.

"The Chinese are willing to work the dregs," said Lyal White, Asia specialist at the South African Institute for International Affairs. Mineral concessions worked to exhaustion and abandoned as unprofitable are all game for the Chinese. "They are prepared to go in and start operations in places that the French, British and Americans have long given up on," said White.

But many are also paying with their lives. Today, China is paying the discounted human price that colonial powers did in the 19th and 20th centuries. One of the worst incidents took place in Ethiopia, where a Chinese-run oilfield was attacked in 2007 and 77 people were killed, including nine Chinese nationals. Seven Chinese nationals in the remote and barren southeast Ogaden region were kidnapped by the Ogaden National Liberation Front, ethnic Somalis fighting for independence for the Somali-majority province since 1984. The killings and kidnappings occurred nine months after nine Chinese workers were abducted and released in Nigeria.

China is Ethiopia's largest trading partner, with bilateral trade exceeding $600 million.

With the mainland's hunger for mineral and oil unlikely to abate any time soon, resource-rich Africa will continue to be a major international priority for Beijing as it works at overtaking the U.S. as Africa's top trading partner.

The good news about what China is doing is that, because of China's strong growth and investments in Africa and Latin America, African and Latino countries, for the first time in modern history, haven't been worst hit by the gringos' global meltdown. America and Europe were the one's worst hit by their bankers' greed and lack of government supervision.

China doesn't lecture other countries on human rights, degradation of the environment or corruption. It doesn't make improvement a condition for building roads or factories. It only wants to do business – and African countries like that.

During my December 2005 visit to Brisbane, I asked Abel Stoltz, a South African doctor who immigrated to Australia, what will happen to Africa and how it can lift itself out of poverty.

"China will take over and make it part of China. They are everywhere. That's the only way," Abel replied.

My South African and Rhodesian neighbors, friends and business associates in Hong Kong agree.

Chapter 4

The Main Course – Political Cook-Off
John Brown
– Bob Dylan

Regional Overview

The Pentagon's 2006 Quadrennial Defense Review contains this saber-rattling passage: Of "the major and emerging powers, China has the greatest potential to compete militarily with the United States and field disruptive military technologies that could, over time, offset traditional U.S. military advantages [without] U.S. counter-strategies." Then in 2009, a U.S. Defense Department report accused China of developing "disruptive military technologies, including those for anti-access/area-denial, as well as for nuclear, space and cyber warfare." The report also said that China's military buildup was shifting the balance of power in Asia. Beijing dismissed the report as fear-mongering.

The fact is that America, with its only permanent overseas-based carrier group in Japan, with additional ships, planes and thousands of military personnel based in Guam, Japan and South Korea, remains Asia's biggest military power – one that is concerned that China is emerging as a credible long-term challenge. America's Asia-based military could be mothballed in the near future, much like Russia's once intimidating global naval power was, if America goes bust because of Washington's misguided foreign, economic and military policies.

The last thing America and the world needs in the 21st century is a Sino-U.S. war. In the first half of the 20th century – from the outbreak of World War I to the famine that followed Mao Zedong's Great Leap Forward – about one in every 10 people alive on the planet was shot, gassed, stabbed, burned or starved to death by fellow human beings. The religious and political differences that inflicted so much pain and suffering in the Old World Disorder, many of which have been passed on to our wired 21st century, must be replaced with religious and political tolerance, understanding and respect for human life and basic human rights.

The good news is that cadets at West Point are now being taught to seek a better understanding of the post-9/11 enemy. The Combating Terrorism Center, set up in the wake of 9/11, aims to prepare cadets at the nation's premier military academy to confront the shifting geopolitical realities of the 21st century. It was inspired by the precept of the ancient Chinese warlord Sun-Tzu, "to know your enemy."

America and China can no longer afford miscommunication and cross-cultural misunderstandings. America must recalibrate its geopolitical compass to develop a strategy that will forge a partnership with China if it is serious about regaining international legitimacy and being a significant player in the New World Order. America must accept that it is no longer "a city upon a hill" that the rest of the world will emulate as it did since isolationist, idealistic Puritan John Winthrop first spoke those words in 1630. It must accept the geopolitical reality that it is no longer the strategic center of global gravity. Pax Americana has been replaced by interlocalism, with Sino-U.S. pillars at the center of gravity. China, working together with America, can forge peace deals with North Korea, Iran and the Middle East. America and China have to become the "double engines" driving world peace and prosperity.

The U.S.-Japan military alliance embracing the security of Taiwan does not benefit either America or China. The primary beneficiary is North Korea. America must do militarily what it did economically with China. It must open its door wider to U.S.-China military ties and cooperation. The fond farewell America bid Japan's Junichiro Koizumi during his last visit to the U.S. as prime minister in 2006 is the same type of farewell America should bid the U.S.-Japan relationship as it embarks on the fusion of American capitalism with Confucian capitalism as both countries' executive chefs in the White House and Great Hall of the People come up with the creative new recipes needed in the New World Order.

Discussing the matter with Jim and Suyin Stein in Sebastopol, California, Suyin said: "I actually think that China and the U.S. are not part of the problem but could be the Iron Chefs that are part of the solutions worldwide. China has 'manpower' and the U.S. has an obsession of being the world's 911. Together they should jump in and fix entire communities. They should be cooking together."

America and China should begin to build military establishments that are complimentary and compatible with each other. Why continue to compete to develop mutually incompatible, destructive and wasteful military hardware and strategies? The fact that the first defense talks between Beijing and Washington after Barack Obama took office were the most productive in more than a decade bodes well for full cooperation. Hopefully, America won't mess up this new constructive beginning by selling F-16 fighter aircraft to Taiwan – or any other military hardware that will jeopardize the new relationship.

America and China can and must cooperate, share intelligence on Islamic terrorists, track and interdict financial transactions that may support terrorism, and join together in many other ways to contain common enemies – starting in the Middle East, where both countries sell their military hardware and software.

The more than $60 billion worth of arms, ammunition, bombs, missiles and warships America committed to sell to countries in the Middle East, while China tries to compete and keep up, can only lead to disaster.

The U.S. military industrial complex is ecstatic about the arms sales and the extra income and jobs, which, they claim, would otherwise have gone to China. Isn't it time that the governments of arms-producing countries sit down with each other and draw up policies that control which regimes their arms merchants can do business with? Policies that apply to all members and are uniformly enforced.

For the U.S. to continue a policy of selling arms to unreliable allies, weapons that are then often turned against American troops, is insane, and must be challenged to avoid the abyss of Armageddon.

What the career U.S. politicians don't seem to grasp is that, by continuing to spin China as a threat, it risks losing China as an ally in the global war on terrorism. Beijing could easily and gladly withdraw its support for the cause. America must turn away from Taiwan and stop its hypocritical, incessant beating of the human rights drum.

Doing so can help propel peace and prosperity and open the way for a new dawn on a vibrant, energetic and constructive Sino-American century and beyond.

America doesn't want to repeat with China the mistakes that got it into Iraq. In the words of former CIA Director George Tenet, Dick Cheney and other administration officials pushed to invade Iraq without a "serious debate" about whether Saddam Hussein was an imminent threat. There was never "a significant discussion" about containing Iraq without an invasion. America definitely does not want to repeat that mistake with Japan against China over Taiwan and North Korea.

The Japanese are concerned about a new "Nixon shock" – the surprise 1972 rapprochement between China and the U.S. – this time concerning North Korea. It is long overdue. The long-term military relationship America is pursuing with Japan is unsustainable because it is unlikely that Japan's aging society will be prepared to spend the money needed to maintain a robust military alliance down the road. An "Obama shock," realigning U.S. relationships in Asia, is hopefully on the horizon with the election of Yukio Hatoyama and his Democratic Party of Japan.

Checking Out the Kitchen
The same can be said about unnecessary, repeated reconnaissance missions by unarmed planes or ships. The U.S. flies more than 400 such missions a year directed at China. Surely there are less intrusive ways to collect information. America's satellite, land-based and submarine surveillance capabilities give it the necessary access to the Chinese communications information it is trying to collect.

The U.S. National Security Agency also operates a signals intelligence facility on Yangmingshan Mountain in suburban Taipei, Taiwan. It was established in the mid-1980s and is able to intercept radio communications within 500 kilometers. One really can't blame the Chinese for not accepting America's claim of a "right of espionage" and for taking offense to U.S. spy planes regularly flying 19 kilometers off their coast listening in on their military, mobile phone, fax and Internet communications. The U.S. listed China in September 2009 as one of the key targets for espionage for the next four years, a significant shift by the Obama administration and one that offers a rare insight into the motives of America's spies.

The National Intelligence Strategy produced by new intelligence director Dennis Blair groups China with Iran, North Korea and a resurgent Russia as nations with the ability to "challenge U.S. interests in traditional and emerging ways." The previous National Intelligence Strategy produced under George W. Bush in 2005, made no mention of any nation and instead focused on the threat of terrorism and the need to integrate U.S. spying efforts.

"China shares many interests with the United States, but its increasing natural-resource-focused diplomacy and military modernization are among the factors making it a complex global challenge," Blair's report states. Really, what was your first clue, Hawkeye?

Beijing responded quickly, with a Foreign Ministry official repeating a warning that Washington is stuck in a cold war mentality. "We urged the U.S. side to abandon its … bias and stop issuing remarks that mislead the American people and harm mutual trust between China and the United States," Foreign Ministry spokeswoman Jiang Yu said.

If the situation were reversed and China flew spy planes off the coast of California, the U.S. would bring them down.

"We seem to be conducting something we cannot control very well. If planes were flying 20 to 50 miles from our shores, we would be very likely to shoot them down if they came in closer, whether through error or not," said President Dwight Eisenhower in 1956. He was speaking after the Chinese shot down a U.S. spy plane over the East China Sea, killing all 16 crewmen.

The Chinese don't provoke the U.S. by sending spy planes from Cuba over U.S. shores. In fact, the U.S. enforces a 200-mile territorial rule. Why should the U.S. be the only military power that does? What if China did the same? Why create and then provoke an unnecessary enemy that happens to be America's major creditor in the 21st century?

In 2003, when China shipped weapons and explosives to Cuba as the two countries increased their cooperation, the U.S. was outraged and threatened to impose sanctions. Why is it OK for the U.S. to sell weapons to Taiwan and not for China to do the same with Cuba? How would America react if China imposed sanctions on the U.S. for selling weapons to Taiwan and dumped billions of dollars worth of U.S. debt instruments it holds on the world financial markets? Why run the risk of another accident – military or financial? After all, it was a U.S. government surveillance plane that ordered a Peruvian jet to shoot down a single-engine Cessna 185 over Peru in 2001, killing Veronica "Roni" Bowers, an American missionary, and her 7-month-old daughter, Charity.

It was also faulty U.S. radar information that resulted in the downing of an Iranian passenger jet, killing all 298 people on board in 1988 over the Persian Gulf. Repeated civilian casualties from misguided bombs in Afghanistan, Pakistan and Iraq have become the norm. Does America need to further risk such mistakes in the Pacific or the Taiwan Strait with China?

Although China supported the U.S.-led war to rid Afghanistan of the Taliban and capture or kill Osama bin Laden, respected conservative columnists and politicians in America, including George F. Will and Rep. Henry Hyde, were still arguing that China was a future military threat to America.

Beijing and Tokyo have reached an agreement concerning permitted naval activity in exclusive economic zones, which reach 220 nautical miles from shore. Shouldn't Washington and Beijing be doing the same?

President Eisenhower apologized for the flight of captured American spy pilot Francis Gary Powers over Russia and ended the U-2 flights over that country. Why couldn't President Bush have done the same when the U.S. reconnaissance plane crash-landed on Hainan Island in March 2001? Why couldn't he just have picked up the phone and discussed matters amicably with Jiang Zemin? Why was the first American spokesman Admiral Dennis Blair, commander of U.S. forces in the Pacific? Why did the U.S ambassador in Beijing, Adm. Joseph W. Prueher, handle the negotiations? Why was the U.S. defense attaché to Beijing, Brig. Gen. Neal Sealock, wearing his military uniform at his first news conference? Was this diplomacy or a not-so-subtle military reminder and threat?

Fly Fishing
When a Russian pilot defected with his MiG-25 in 1976 to Japan, American experts spent nine weeks stripping the plane and examining every part. The Russians eventually got the plane back in boxes. Why was the U.S. surprised then that the Chinese examined that downed U.S. spy plane in 2001? Isn't that part of the risk in the espionage game? Besides, if all the hardware and software was destroyed per the "checklist," as claimed by the American crew before the Chinese got access to the plane, what is the big deal? It is face. Symbolic value – it is just as important to the U.S. as it is to China.

What is the point of America pairing and starting to operate radar-evading B-2 bombers and F-22 fighters in the Pacific for the first time in February 2009? More to the point, what is the point in sending the surveillance-spy ship Impeccable with 2-km-long underwater receiver and source cables, off Hainan Island to gather acoustic data on China's submarine movements from its main submarine base on Hainan in March 2009? Whether the ship was in China's exclusive economic zone or in international waters is irrelevant.

The end result is the same – an unnecessary confrontation with five Chinese vessels that, luckily, ended without any casualties, but triggered the U.S. to send the destroyer Chung-Hoon to protect its "surveillance" vessels. China responded by sending its largest "fishery patrol ship" China Yuzheng 311 "on a routine mission" in the South China Sea and deciding to convert mothballed naval vessels to fishery patrol ships – all this at the dawn of a new U.S. presidential administration. It was a similar provocation to what happened with the spy plane that crash-landed at the dawn of Bush's first term in office. Why does the U.S. military insist on provoking China while the White House and State Department are trying to get the two countries to work closer to resolve the global financial and various geopolitical crisis?

There is no point anymore in the 21st century for the U.S. to continue resorting to outdated 20th century surveillance and provocative harassment tactics that ruffle the seas and diplomatic relations.

An accident that could have led to a military confrontation happened in June 2009 when a Chinese submarine collided with an underwater sonar array towed by the U.S. destroyer John S. McCain in the South China Sea in international waters near the Philippines due to a "misjudgment" of distance. An "inadvertent encounter." The sonar array, used to listen for and locate underwater sounds, was damaged in the incident, but fortunately the ship and sub did not collide. The U.S. Navy did not consider the incident an intentional provocation by Beijing, as it would have been extremely dangerous had the array got caught in the sub's propellers. The Chinese knew what they were doing.

A reasonable conclusion is that the U.S. destroyer failed to detect the submarine, while the sub set its distance based on the assumption that the ship wasn't carrying or deploying sonar arrays.

The Pentagon says U.S. ships and aircraft operate regularly within China's exclusive economic zone without incident. Really? As if to prove its point, the U.S. sent the sub hunter Victorious into China's exclusive economic zone in May 2009, within just a few weeks of its last confrontation with China. A military confrontation was avoided when the two Chinese vessels that came to within 27 meters of the U.S. vessel only used high-intensity spotlights several times to warn it off. The American crew responded by aiming their fire hoses at the Chinese during the hour-long incident.

The U.S. claimed the Victorious was operating in international waters, about 193 kilometers off the mainland. The area is within China's exclusive economic zone under the U.N. Convention on the Law of the Sea, which the U.S. refuses to ratify. There have been repeated incidents and there may be more. Disputes over military activities in China's zone could trigger a more serious crisis as China's military capabilities grow and, with them, its desire to keep the U.S. Navy out of its backyard. After all, wouldn't America do the same?

China has asked the U.S. to reduce and eventually halt air force and naval surveillance close to its shores. The request was made during a special session on maritime safety between the two countries' militaries in August 2009. After six confrontations between Chinese vessels and U.S. surveillance ships, it is a reasonable request to ensure there are no more similar incidents in the future.

Why is it that the U.S. insists on pursuing its bullying "sonar signature" trip for every Chinese submarine off Hainan Island and in the Taiwan Strait? Is it in denial about its reluctant withdrawal from the wars in Korea and Vietnam or is it deluding itself about its "victories" in Afghanistan, Iraq and the former Yugoslavia? After all, who really won? Based on what happened in Korea, Vietnam, Iraq, the Balkans and Afghanistan, does America really think it can pursue gunboat diplomacy with China over Taiwan or other regional or geopolitical goals and win?

Japan's Constitutional Folly

It makes no sense for America to keep upgrading its relationship with Japan in the hope that together they can contain China. This is especially true after the uncertainty created by the electoral win of the Democratic Party of Japan in August 2009, and the swearing in of its new anti-U.S. Prime Minister Yukio Hatoyama. He has publicly stated that he believes Japan should maintain its economic and political independence now that the American influence is declining and China is rising.

Jitsuro Terashima, a Hatoyama adviser who heads a Tokyo think tank, has said: "Since Japan is under the protection of the U.S. nuclear umbrella, the Japanese government is not able to form its own foreign policy." He suggested that Japan should require the U.S. to reduce or withdraw its military forces from Japan. "It is unusual that Japan still allows the U.S. to keep forces in Japan more than 60 years after the end of the war," he wrote. "Japan should go back to common sense and not let a foreign force stay in this sovereign nation." He proposed that the U.S. shift its forces to Guam and Hawaii.

Japan's new Foreign Minister Katsuya Okada said: "It will be the age of Asia and in that context it is important for Japan to have its own stance, to play its role in the region."

The Japanese, like America, voted for "change," and that includes the relationship with the U.S. The U.S. is being blamed directly by Japan's new financial services minister Shizuka Kamei for the global credit crisis because of its "unbridled capitalism."

Unlike his predecessors who admired America's rock icons, Hatoyama has a hit tune of his own now that he is president. He recorded it when first elected to parliament as a fund raising utensil. Not only does he think he is as good a singer as any American icon – he is not a drunk karaoke junkie. Any wonder he wants Japan to be on an equal political footing with the U.S.?

"The close and equal alliance between Japan and the United States is the foundation of efforts to secure regional peace that would benefit Japan, Asia and the entire world.

"Being equal means a relationship in which Japan can also actively propose roles and concrete actions that the Japan-U.S. alliance could perform for global peace and security." No question about what Hatoyama wants.

Hatoyama's election has worsened the U.S.-Japan relationship because he wants to relocate America's major military bases on Okinawa. The first I heard of the place was from a former rooming house roommate who was a Marine there. We both attended City College of New York, he majoring in oceanography and I in political science.

The flashpoint has been the U.S. Marine Corps Futenma Air Base on Okinawa, a facility long opposed by many local residents annoyed by aircraft noise, worried about accidents and angered by crimes committed by U.S. service personnel.

Hatoyama's government has said it will review a 2006 agreement to move the base from a crowded urban area to a coastal area of Okinawa by 2014, repeatedly suggesting the facility may be moved off the island.

President Hu Jintao gave Japan's new prime minister a reminder of the sensitive history between their countries and Taiwan-related issues in their first meeting in New York in September 2009 on the sidelines of the U.N. summit on climate change. Hatoyama used the meeting to raise his proposal for establishing an East Asia Community for economic cooperation and national security in the region, an idea he has championed since winning his landslide election, breaking an almost steady 50-year reign of America's ally, the Liberal Democratic Party.

China supports the Japanese plan in principal to establish an Asian answer to the European Union. The concept would tie China, Japan and South Korea into a union with the Association of Southeast Asia Nations, although members of the pact have yet to be sorted out. The long-term goal would be to have a common currency adopted across the new pan-Asian trade bloc. China, like Japan and South Korea, wants to turn the East China Sea from being a source of disputes into a "peaceful and friendly sea."

Since the late 1990s, Japan has kept in step with increasingly sophisticated U.S. military advances centered around networked and information-dominance strategies. The greater investments that Japan has had to make in keeping up with U.S. advances have transformed the traditional nature of the U.S.-Japan military alliance. The relationship has been steadily upgraded to make Japan America's lead attack lap dog for the creation of new tensions in the region over North Korea and Taiwan.

Japan was reportedly planning to identify Taiwan as a sovereign state in a new foreign residency permit scheme to be introduced in 2012. The new residency permit would list "Taiwan" as the nationality of Taiwanese living in Japan. Under the existing visa system, Taiwanese are classified under "China" for their nationality.

Just as America is coming to terms with Vietnam, and Germany has come to terms with its World War II follies, Japan will have to come to terms with its official hypocrisy and deception for its brutal wartime role in China and other countries it invaded, including America, before it can be a trustworthy partner. A country whose political establishment lives in denial must be denied international credibility.

The issue is highlighted at Japan's Yasukuni Shrine, which honors the country's war dead, including 14 war criminals. Japan's prime ministers make annual visits to the shrine, which has caused concern about separation of church and state. But because the shrine is also a symbol of Japanese militarism and imperialism to those countries Japan conquered in World War II, it has become extremely controversial. China cites the prime ministers, continued visits as the reason it barred top Chinese leaders from going to Japan, even though Japan is China's largest trading partner. Once Japanese prime ministers stopped making their annual pilgrimages to the shrine, President Hu Jintao visited Japan in 2008.

Hatoyama has pledged he will not visit the shrine while he is prime minister.

The hypocrisy is further magnified by a lawsuit filed by 32 elderly Japanese war orphans left in China after the war who returned to Japan at the dawn of the 21st century. They seek compensation from the government for its failure to promptly repatriate and resettle them. They received little or no Japanese-language education or job-search support after they returned.

"Japan is a nice country, but you have criminal leadership," former world chess champion Bobby Fischer said after being held for months by Japanese immigration authorities.

The highly acclaimed three-hour film *Japanese Devils* shows 14 former Imperial soldiers confessing their brutal roles during the war. One Japanese veteran confesses to 328 murders. A former army sergeant describes throwing babies into campfires for laughs. Another says he raped and killed a woman, then carved up her body to feed to his troops.

Japan's former Prime Minister Junichiro Koizumi suggested that Japan's self-defense forces constituted a "military" instead of simply a "force" and Article 9 of their constitution should be amended to allow Japan to be a military state that can take offensive measures – not just defensive. The U.S. imposed the military ban in the constitution after Japan's defeat in World War II. The fact that America now agrees to the amendment because of Japan's desire to support the U.S. missile defense shield is doubly worrisome and must be rejected and denied.

The U.S.-led "war against terrorism" in the Middle East saw the quiet re-emergence of Japan's naval forces from constitutionally mandated quarantine. Two Japanese destroyers and a supply ship sailed to the Indian Ocean to support America in Afghanistan, along with ships and peacekeeping troops in Iraq. This decision was supported by the U.S., but it has to be questioned. Just like Japan's decision to send two destroyers to the seas off Somalia to combat pirates "just because China did" must be questioned and denied.

Japan wanted the U.S. to nuke China in 1965 if war broke out between China and Japan under the U.S.-Japan security treaty, according to a recently declassified file. Is this the type of nuke-happy lap dog America needs in Asia?

Japan has the raw materials and technology to develop nuclear weapons in less than a year. That assumes it hasn't already done so. With plutonium for 25 bombs missing from the Japanese nuclear reprocessing plant in Tokaimura, one wonders if the conclusion of the 15-year probe into the shortage, which blamed it on shoddy bookkeeping, is believable. To attribute the missing material to faulty calculations in a country that prides itself on its precision engineering and quality control is highly suspect. To me it's a question of how many bombs does Japan already have?

The passage of a law allowing Japan to send self-defense forces to maintain peacekeeping in Iraq marks a dangerous new era of Japanese militarism and violates the constitution imposed by America after WWII. The constitution reads: "The Japanese people forever renounce war as a sovereign right of the nation and the threat or use of force as means of settling international disputes. Land, sea and air forces, as well as other war potential, will never be maintained. The right of belligerency of the state will not be recognized."

Building an aircraft carrier – a fearsome offensive weapon – "for defensive uses only" is oxymoronic and questionable when one considers the fact that Japan has one of the world's best-funded militaries that is backed by the U.S. military.

The Japanese right-wing faction makes George Bush's neo-cons look like innocent pacifist choir boys.

"Japanese Prime Minister Junichiro Koizumi, with Bush administration support, is pursuing a dangerous political course. By committing to military involvement in Iraq, he is trying to end one of the last vestiges of the

Second World War – the prohibition of Japanese military action on foreign soil," said William Beeman, who teaches anthropology at Brown University in Providence Rhode Island. This is something America cannot permit or encourage. For America to allow Japan to again become a regional military power because it believes it is an ally is delusional. Japan will never be America's true ally. Only a short-term, self-serving one.

Japan admits to an annual defense budget of $50 billion. It successfully launched its first commercial rocket at the dawn of the 21st century – the cost of which does not fall into any military budget. On March 28, 2003, it launched its first spy satellite, also as a non-military budget item. What is Japan's real military and related dual-purpose budget? Why is America not questioning and reporting this amount while it expresses outrage at China's military spending?

In 2004, Japan shifted its main defense focus away from Russia and toward China in a once-a-decade military review. Henceforth, the Japanese military is to regard North Korea and China, not Russia, as the main dangers to its home islands. China reacted with outrage. The Japanese defense outline stated that China is "pushing forward its nuclear and missile capabilities and modernization of its navy and air force. It is also trying to expand its scope of naval activities."

On Dec. 19, 2003, Japan announced it would spend at least $4.2 billion for a U.S.-built missile defense network to defend itself against North Korea. The network became operational in 2007 and will be fully deployed by 2011. Japan is on a 21st-century kamikaze mission. Japan also has lifted its long-standing ban on military exports – so it can cooperate more closely with the U.S. on a missile defense program.

Is it really necessary for America to support the amendment of the Japan constitution because of its support for the missile defense shield and potential support in an attack against North Korea? Wouldn't it be safer and more cost-effective to have a fleet of U.S. Aegis destroyers positioned in the Sea of Japan? The Aegis can track an incoming missile in a matter of 20 seconds or so, and determine where it will hit. North Korea's Nodong medium-range missile would take 10 minutes flying time to reach Japan from North Korea. A few Aegis destroyers are a lot safer, cost-effective and offer more protection than a dubious missile defense shield or an amended militaristic constitution.

And if the American-imposed Japanese constitution can be amended, why isn't the real McCoy on which it was modeled in America also amended to address the new realities of the 21st century? After all, if America is going to inevitably follow the economic course of Japan since 1990, with decades of stagnation and stock market depression, why not on the important constitutional front as well? I'm kidding, of course. The last thing America wants to do is emulate Japan on the political or economic front. It is a recipe for disaster.

Cross-Strait Peace

Taiwan, with its current policy of engagement with the mainland, has extended another olive branch to China. It has agreed to drop plans to develop missiles capable of hitting Shanghai and Hong Kong. Taipei has opted to slash troop numbers to 215,000 by 2014, and focus instead on self-defense rather than developing offensive weapons. It currently has the capability to build, with U.S. technology, missiles with a range of 600 to 800 kilometers.

In addition to developing its own missiles with American technology, most of Taiwan's missiles, including Patriot PAC-2 anti-missile systems and Avenger air defense missiles, come from the U.S. It has also obtained air-to-air missiles from France.

The U.S. again appears to be ignoring Taiwan's desire to cut back on military spending and insists on pushing multi-billion dollar arms deals, the latest being a $6.5 billion package in the fall of 2008. The U.S. is Taiwan's main supplier of military hardware. The continuing love-hate relationship between Taiwan and America experienced another hiccup when Washington demanded an extra $800 million for an upgraded missile defense system. The U.S. claims it needs the extra payment for the reopening of a production line as well as research and development costs of four sets of Patriot PAC-3 anti-missile systems.

It doesn't look as if things will change much with the Obama administration. National intelligence director Dennis Blair, Obama's top intelligence official, has suggested that Beijing's increased military spending "poses a greater threat to Taiwan" and will spur continued U.S. arms sales to Taiwan in order to maintain a military balance in the potentially dangerous Taiwan Strait. It was therefore no surprise that Taiwan took the political baton that Blair extended and asked the U.S. to sell it advanced F-35 fighter jets to bolster its new "defensive defense" national security policy that replaced its "active defense" and "pre-emptive strike" defense policies, the lynchpins of Taiwan's defense philosophy under former President Chen Shui-bian. Taipei also reportedly renewed its request to buy the advanced C/D version of the F-16 fighter that former President Bush had refused to sell.

China has in the past tolerated U.S. arm sales to Taiwan. Deng Xiaoping privately acknowledged to President Jimmy Carter that the U.S. could continue to sell arms to Taiwan after it switched diplomatic relations from Taipei to Beijing on Jan. 1, 1979. However, now that China and Taiwan are no longer hostile toward each other, China is taking offense to the continued arms sales by the U.S. It let the U.S. know its anger when it cancelled a senior military visit to Washington and shelved other military and diplomatic contacts to protest America's interference in an internal civil dispute. China went on to call for military cooperation with Taiwan to end the hostility between the two longtime adversaries once and for all, even though they are still technically at war. Reason is prevailing across the strait for a peaceful resolution of the ongoing civil war. Why can't America accept this reality? Hopefully it will now that the promising Sino-U.S. military talks resumed at the end of February 2009.

Cyberspace

Battles in the 21st century will no longer be fought only in the air and on the battlefield with conventional or nuclear weapons. They have already moved to cyberspace. The first shots America fired at Iraq were virtual volleys delivered in Arabic. The U.S. spammed military and civilian leaders with e-mails urging them to turn on Saddam Hussein.

President Bush signed off on National Security Presidential Directive 16, a secretive order to the government to develop a strategy to determine when and how America would launch cyber attacks against enemy computer networks. The full extent of the U.S. cyber arsenal is among the most tightly held national security secrets, even more guarded than nuclear capabilities – but not good enough.

Computer hackers have been able to break into U.S. government networks to research targets, deface websites or plant viruses. U.S. security consultants routinely enter secure and confidential military and government computers to expose America's vulnerability to electronic attacks and spying. The General Accounting Office concluded in July 2002, almost a year after 9/11, that "the government was not doing an adequate job coordinating efforts to protect its online systems." Security has not improved much since.

Most of the infrastructure of modern life is vulnerable to attack over the Internet. Cyber attackers can wreck the essential industrial, military and economic infrastructure of any country. To defend against such an eventuality, the Pentagon established the Air Force Cyber Command at Barksdale Air Force Base in Louisiana to respond to the millions of attack probes or scans from malicious computers on the Department of Defense's global information grid. The planned activation was suspended because of political maneuvering in Washington and confusion over its role – a typical Washington symptom whenever more taxpayer dollars are going to be spent on a new program.

America's antiquated intelligence architecture is frozen in time and lagging behind the fast-moving cyber bandits, said Jeffrey Hunker, a former member of the National Security Council. The National Security Agency, the largest and most secretive U.S. spy shop, vividly demonstrates the problem, Hunker and other experts say.

The U.S. has for too long failed to adequately protect the security of its computer networks, a fact finally being acknowledged by the government. President Obama said in May 2009, that this is a "transformational moment" for the country, where computer networks were probed and attacked millions of times a day. "We're not as prepared as we should be, as a government or as a country," he said, calling cyber threats one of the most serious economic and military dangers the nation faces. He echoed what I wrote in my book *Custom Maid War* in 2005. At the time, during the hundreds of radio and TV interviews I did on the subject of cyber terrorism, most of the hosts at the time ridiculed me for being a "fear monger" and did not believe that America was vulnerable on the cyber frontline.

"You know, Peter, I don't understand your patience and why you are not blowing your top with frustration if what you are saying is true," said Steve Chicorel one evening as we sat on his roof-top garden in Los Angeles in 2005 just after I had participated in a radio interview. Steve is techno-savvy and a lot of his Taiwanese wife's friends are in the high-tech computer software and hardware business. Cyber security is a topic that we all discussed on more than one occasion during my visits to LA. Listening to President Obama say that "It is the great irony of our information age – the very technologies that empower us to create and to build, also empower those who would seek to disrupt and destroy," echoed the essence of our rooftop discussions. A Pentagon military command to conduct both offensive and defensive computer warfare is long overdue.

NSA operates spy satellites and gathers information from radio, microwave, television, telephone and Internet signals. Experts say that even though it spends billions, its equipment is antiquated, it is overly bureaucratic and the lifetime tenure of employees with low pay discourages techno-savvy people from applying for positions. Isn't it time we swept out these low-paid, unimaginative bureaucrats and swept in policies that encourage the employment of technologically talented people at private-sector pay scales to insure America's safety? What good is the best equipment and technology if we don't have the best people running it?

Cyber War I

The emergency landing of the U.S. spy plane on Hainan Island in April 2001 triggered the first major public cyber war of the 21st century between the two Pacific superpowers. Chinese and U.S. cyber warriors hacked at each other with both offensive and defensive measures. The FBI's National Infrastructure Protection Center is still on the defensive. "To date, hackers have unlawfully defaced a number of U.S. websites, replacing existing content with pro-Chinese or anti-U.S. rhetoric," the agency said. Some U.S.-based hackers defaced websites in China in retaliation, said Rob Clyde, chief technologist of the Internet security company Symantec.

Websites run by the U.S. Department of Labor and the Department of Health and Human Services were defaced with tributes to the Chinese pilot, Wang Wei, killed in a collision with the U.S. spy plane. U.S. hackers retaliated with more than 300 attacks on Chinese websites. The Beijing City People's Radio home page was replaced with the home page of a pornographic site.

In March 2009, hackers broke into a senior Chinese State Council official's computer containing drafts of Premier Wen Jiabao's government work report for the year and were found copying it and other top-secret documents. The hacking was carried out from Taiwan.

Cyber terrorism is facilitated by the fact that it was not a high priority when Microsoft Windows was developed. Consequently, its very design makes it easy for this popular software to be hacked and difficult to secure.

The cyber war between China and the U.S. has been dubbed the "Red Guest" attack by Chinese hackers. The Chinese say the purpose of their actions is to encourage Americans to protest against their government and demand peace between nations. "We will attack to send a message to the people of the U.S. to tell them that we know we are all one, but they must stop their government from destroying the world," one of the Chinese hackers wrote.

The University of Toronto's Munk Centre for International studies said in March 2009 that mainland-based hackers had infiltrated at least 1,295 private and government computers in 103 countries, including those of the Dalai Lama. Many of these computers belonged to embassies, foreign ministries and other government offices.

Sophisticated cyber-spies are attacking the U.S. electric grid and key defense programs. In April 2009, *The Wall Street Journal* reported that hackers had breached the Pentagon's biggest weapons program, the $300 billion joint strike fighter and stole data.

More than two dozen Internet sites in the United States and South Korea, including that of the White House, U.S. Treasury Department, Defense Department, National Security Agency, Homeland Security, State Department, Homeland Security, Secret Service, Federal Trade Commission and Department of Transportation were attacked and all went down at some point and some were disabled starting July 4, 2009. Other targets included the New York Stock Exchange, Nasdaq and *The Washington Post*. The fact that U.S. government websites were still being affected three days after it began signaled an unusually lengthy and sophisticated attack.

South Korean media reported in May 2009 that North Korea had been running a cyber-warfare unit that had tried to hack into U.S. and South Korean military networks.

The U.S. got a real wake-up call to the vulnerability of cyber attacks in July 2009 when the White House, Pentagon, State Department and several other government websites were attacked and disabled for several hours. South Korea was subjected to similar attacks which were launched from Austria, Germany, Georgia, South Korea and the U.S., but are believed to have originated from North Korea on the heels of Pyongyang's missile launches that month. The distributed-denial-of-service attack, which plants viruses in thousands of computers, is believed to have been orchestrated by North Korea.

The vulnerability of the U.S. and its economic and military leaders is best exemplified by the fact that U.S. Federal Reserve Board Chairman Ben Bernanke became a victim of an identity fraud ring that stole millions. "Our family was but one of 500 separate instances traced to one crime ring," Bernanke acknowledged.

U.S. intelligence officials believe China is developing the capacity to damage and disrupt computer systems in America by hacking and spreading viruses. The main concern is that if China were to attack Taiwan, the Chinese military would then deploy widespread computer disruptions against U.S. and Taiwanese military systems to slow any effort by U.S. forces to intervene in Taiwan's defense. Wouldn't the U.S. do the same? And how do we know it isn't?

China and the U.S. are not the only cyber adversaries. The Crusaders of yesterday have turned in their steeds for laptops. Muslim Arab states and their Christian and Israeli adversaries are now battling it out just as intensely in cyberspace as they are in the desert sands.

The Pentagon is now building its own Military Command to focus on cyber security to coordinate the defense of Pentagon computer networks and improve U.S. offensive capabilities in cyber warfare to replace the security efforts currently divided between entities like the NSA and Defense Information Systems Agency. Cyber defense is the Department of Homeland Security's responsibility, so the command would be charged with assisting that department's defense efforts. The Air Force also runs a significant cyber security effort.

With so many bureaucratic cyber layers of competing interests, is it any wonder hackers can bypass the conflicting cyber defense forces? The Pentagon is also building its own Internet, the military's World Wide Web for the wars of the future. What the military call "Net-centric" warfare would change the military in the same way the Internet changed society. It is called the Global Information Grid. The goal is to give American commanders and troops "a God's eye view" of all foreign enemies, threats and battles. But Vint Cerf, one of the fathers of the Internet and a Pentagon consultant, wonders if the military's dream is realistic. "I want to make sure that what we realize is vision and not hallucination," he said.

"Cyberninjas" with security clearances are today's front-line commandos doing the most cutting-edge work, both in identifying weaknesses in Pentagon networks and in creating weapons for potential attacks. It is estimated that the Pentagon now has 3,000 to 5,000 information operation specialists in the military, as well as 50,000 to 70,000 soldiers involved in general computer operations. Adding specialists in electronic warfare, deception and other areas could bring the total number to as many as 89,000. Defense contractors with annual computer budgets of more than $10 billion – and rapidly rising – are now able to find the vulnerabilities in other countries' computer systems and then develop software tools to exploit them, either to steal sensitive information or disable their networks, the key tools being those that enable the U.S. to break into enemy computers. The most aggressive efforts involve anticipating how an enemy might attack and developing the resources to strike back.

Online gaming and battles offer the Defense Department some examples of how cyber wars of the 21st century will be fought. The peer-to-peer connections could also break down some of the time-wasting and bureaucratic hierarchies that obstruct military planning and operations.

Resentful Arrogant Perceptions

Long resentful that America and the West never treat them as equals, the Chinese are determined to control their military destiny in cyberspace as well as on the ground, sea and air. They want to match the U.S. on the world stage and dominate their hemisphere in the same way Washington dominates its own. China's approach to international relations may sometimes seem crude, but it underpins the deep anger with which China has greeted the string of American embarrassments: charges of campaign-financing corruption, the rebuff to Premier Zhu Rongji's concessions to win WTO endorsement, NATO's assault on a sovereign Yugoslavia and the bombing of the Chinese Embassy in Belgrade, which no Chinese citizen believes was accidental. The downing of the Chinese fighter jet after colliding with a U.S. surveillance plane added to the perception of American determination to subjugate China. Moving weaponry and equipment based in Germany and Italy in the last half of the 20th century to Asia at the dawn of the 21st century to "contain China" only magnified that perception.

The outrage, fear and concern expressed by America when China admitted in December 2008 that it was "seriously considering" building its first aircraft carrier to protect its national interests and as "a symbol of national strength," is hypocritical political spin. How can America be so disingenuous, when at the same time President George W. Bush commissions America's newest aircraft carrier, named after his father, which carries a lot more planes, is much bigger and is the 10th nuclear-powered Nimitz-class carrier to enter service with the U.S. Navy? Even though they are the world's largest warships, they will be replaced by 2015 by an even bigger and more advanced nuclear-powered class of carriers. Former Vice President Dick Cheney said in 2006 that these ships "will help ensure the sea power of the United States for the next half century."

To "defend its interests" in Asia and "contain" China, the U.S. has been steadily transferring more aircraft carriers and other warships from its Atlantic fleet to the Pacific. The result is that of America's 280 warships in active service, the Pacific fleet's share has risen from 45 percent to 54 percent and continues to increase. The fleet now includes six of the Navy's 12 carriers, almost all of the 18 Aegis cruisers and destroyers that have been modified for ballistic-missile defense operations, and 26 of 57 attack submarines.

To counter, China is not just getting into the aircraft business to compete. It is also developing ballistic missiles with non-nuclear warheads and guidance systems to hit moving surface ships in the Western Pacific before they can get within range of Chinese targets. If China can develop technology that can shoot down satellites in space, it won't be long before it perfects anti-ship ballistic missiles. These would have a range of up to 3,000 kilometers and be equipped with maneuverable re-entry vehicles designed to hit moving warships at hypersonic speed after being launched by rocket from land. This is a new technology and one the U.S. has never faced. If successful, the carriers that are the potent symbol of U.S. naval power would become "sitting ducks," in the opinion of Michael Richardson, a visiting senior research fellow at the Institute of Southeast Asian Studies.

China's announcement in November 2009 that it plans to put weapons in space is no surprise. A space race between China and the U.S. is inevitable unless both countries agree to cooperate. Washington and Beijing should explore the peaceful use of space and how both countires can work together on the development of space technology and weapons. A costly space arms race benefits neither.

Control of space means control of the world, said Senator Lyndon Johnson, before he became president. Is it any wonder China wants to develop its space weapons?

The Outer Space Treaty bans nuclear and other weapons of mass destruction from space, but does not ban conventional weapons or military-related systems.

China is believed to have developed a new anti-satellite laser weapon site in Xinjiang – an armament that potentially could "dazzle, blind, or destroy a satellite." The PLA is studying different technologies to jam U.S. spy satellites, including ground-based high-energy laser and electromagnetic waves. Both have been tested in military exercises.

A U.S. government agency revealed in 2006 that China had directed a ground-based laser at American spy satellites over its territory. Surely America would do the same.

"Future Military Capabilities and Strategy of the People's Republic of China," stated: "China already may possess the capability to damage, under specific conditions, optical sensors on satellites that are very vulnerable to damage by lasers."

The PLA did shoot down one of China's weather satellites with a ballistic missile in January 2007, making it member No. 3 in the exclusive club of the U.S. and Russia, who have mastered the technology. China has been actively trying over the years to catch up with the runaway leader – the U.S. China has also developed its own satellite navigation and positioning system – the Beidou, or Compass, network. It came into limited service in 2008. Once it is completed in 2020, it could rival the American GPS (Global Positioning System) in capability and range. To date, only the U.S. and Russia have independent GPS systems.

Beijing has never forgotten that the U.S. and former Soviet Union supported China to defeat Japan during World War II.

China decided in January 2009 to honor the scientific team from Dalian University of Technology that came up with the satellite zapper that can destroy a satellite nearly 1,000 kilometers above earth with the 2008 State Top Scientific and Technological Invention Award. It was a very public grand ceremony in the Great Hall of the People. China is definitely becoming more open and assertive. It is estimated that within a few years China will have more than 100 satellites orbiting the Earth.

China, with the world's largest military force, has been transforming and modernizing its military capabilities from a land-based, infantry-centered army into a fully mechanized, nimble active defense and rapid response fighting force capable of dealing with diverse security threats. According to China's defense policy white paper released in January 2009, the People's Liberation Army will pursue a three-stage development strategy for its military reform. The first step is to "set up a solid foundation by 2010, accomplish mechanization and make major progress by 2020, and reach full modernization by the middle of this century."

China's Defense Ministry announced in August 2009 that there will be cuts of up to 700,000 in its land forces while the navy and air force will be increased and the restructuring will be finished by 2012. It said the number of military commands will be trimmed from seven to five. Let's keep in mind that still leaves more than 100,000 drivers in the PLA, to chauffer people around and at least 50,000 entertainers and musicians, including at least 30 such non-combatant generals.

The recruitment of top entertainers had been an important tactic for the Communist Party to win the guerilla war against the Kuomintang during the civil war. The Red Army was poorly equipped and fed. "Revolutionary performances" helped boost the moral of soldiers. They are now being used in a musical offensive against Taiwan.

Chen Sisi, a senior colonel in the Song and Dance Troupe under the Second Artillery Corps, was the first PLA soldier to land in Taiwan in October 2009. Chen, a popular folk singer staged her historic performance at the National Dr. Sun Yat-sen Memorial Hall in Taipei. Chen reached a global audience when she performed at the closing ceremony of the Beijing Olympics.

Chen's musical offensive was followed by Major General Song Zuying, a special favorite of fprmer president Jiang Zemin. She also met the island's president, Ma Ying-jeou and former KMT chairman Wu Poh-hsiung. The camourflaged PLA landing caused a political firestorm with the opposition Democratic Progressive Party legislators demanding they be banned.

The Chinese air force and navy will take on the primary military roles while the massive Soviet-style army structure is reduced to smaller fighting units organized in brigades and battalions. A new Air Force Military Professional University was established in July 2008 to study new training methods suited to the weaponry and battle environments of the 21st century.

In August 2009, China conducted its largest-ever tactical mobilization, moving 50,000 troops over vast distances across the country over a two-month period using both military and civilian resources. Code named Stride-2009, the exercise was a rare opportunity to test the PLA's emergency response capability, after its slow response to the Uygur riots in Xinjiang a month earlier, which could be crucial in countering new security threats, particularly those from terrorists, extremists and separatists.

China is catching up fast on the military technology front with the U.S. It unveiled its most advanced fighter plane at the 2008 China Air Show. The J-10 is the centerpiece of China's military aerospace program – China's answer to the Pentagon's F-16, 150 of which America sold to Taiwan in 1992. Meanwhile, the U.S. is arming itself with more F-22s. An aerial arms race is clearly developing faster than many pundits anticipated. The Chinese show also featured various anti-ship missiles like the C-602 and C-705, which have a range of 200 kilometers and could be used to deter any U.S. naval interference in the Taiwan Strait.

The 21st century opened with the U.S. Air Force and the Space Warfare Center in Colorado staging its first military war games in space. The imaginary enemy in the conflict was China. The scenario was 2017 with the combatants fighting "Star Wars" style. Is this how America really wants to start the new millennium? Hopefully, former NASA astronaut Lee Morin's prediction of congenial relations between the Chinese and U.S. space programs will prove correct. But I am not optimistic.

Beijing sees the U.S. as a waning superpower, according to a Department of Defense report titled *Dangerous Chinese Perceptions: The Implications for DOD*. This report was submitted in the wake of an earlier one concluding that the U.S. would lose a naval confrontation with China in the region. Knowing this, why provoke one?

High-Flying Birds
China is close to fielding the world's first anti-ship ballistic missile, according to U.S. Office of Naval Intelligence. The missile has a range of almost 1,500 kilometers and would be fired from mobile land-based launchers and was "specifically designed to defeat U.S. carrier strike groups."

Five of the U.S. Navy's 12 carriers are based in the Pacific and operate freely in international waters near China. Their mission includes defending Taiwan should Beijing try to use force in its claim to the island. Beijing started to develop the missile after the March 1996 Taiwan crisis when the Clinton administration sent two aircraft carriers and escort ships into the Taiwan Strait and the surrounding area after the PLA fired missiles near the island before the presidential election.

China is making sure its territorial waters, including the Taiwan Strait, are a "no-go zone" for U.S. carriers.

The PLA Air Force has flown a long way since it was established with a handful of planes seized from the defeated Kuomintang force. The PLAAF celebrated its 60th anniversary on Nov. 11, 2009. For most of its history, it played a secondary role to the large land-based army. Its development did not really take off until the 1990s.

The catalyst that sparked the strategic change were the 1990-1991 Gulf War and the 1998-99 Kosovo war – the first conflict won exclusively by air power. Both wars demonstrated how powerful air forces were in relation to concentrated ground troops. The Chinese military leadership was shocked at how the Iraqi army, which was equipped with many Chinese-made weapons, was wiped out by the U.S. Air Force.

Until then, most PLA generals were following the outdated Soviet doctrine that relied on large mechanized ground forces to overwhelm enemies. Air power was used mainly as support. When the U.S. didn't follow the former Soviet Union's military tactics in Afghanistan, by sending a large land force to invade Iraq and Afghanistan, the Chinese military leadership realized they had to put more resources into high-tech weapons research and development that can be airborne.

China is acting no differently than any other rising economic power has throughout history – taking advantage of economic growth to invest in a modernized military.

History also teaches us that a world in which China is a superpower might not be as dangerous a place as many people think. I agree with historian John Keay, author of *China: History,* who says that if China does emerge as a superpower in the 21st century, it will not want to disrupt the new world order.

"I think history teaches us that a world in which China is a superpower might not be as uncomfortable as many people think. I don't think China feels the need to assert itself militarily and physically as many countries in the West have," says Keay.

Pacific Cruise Ship Delights
For thousands of years, China has been a land-focused nation that envis-

aged itself as the center of the Earth, the Middle Kingdom, and paid little attention to expanding its influence beyond its coastline. The wake-up calls came from a string of humiliating defeats by Western and Japanese navies during the Qing dynasty in the late 19th century, which prompted intellectuals in the early 20th century, such as Sun Yat-sen, the father of modern China, to contemplate the country's need to develop maritime strategies. Nevertheless, the concept of maritime power remained a low priority for most of the 20th century as the country went through a series of devastating man-made and natural disasters – including the Sino-Japanese war, civil war between the Kuomintang and the Communist Party, the Great Famine and the Cultural Revolution. Until it opened its doors to the world in 1979, China was largely an inward-looking, insulated country.

The open-door policy was a revolutionary change that hadn't taken place in 3,000 years and became the most important force driving the once land-loving Middle Kingdom to turn its eyes seaward. Additionally, the open-door policy created a manufacturing colossus forced to find ways to secure enough energy to keep its factories running. It is now a net importer of crude oil, which supports half its energy consumption, and 95 percent of that imported crude is shipped by sea. China also imported 52 million tons of mineral ore in March 2009 alone, with 99 percent coming by ship. Trade and economic incentives are the major reason behind the policy shift from land to sea.

Chinese leaders believe they must protect their own access to overseas resources and trade because they cannot count on the goodwill of any foreign power, especially the U.S., to maintain the steady flow of goods on the high seas. This was highlighted in October 2009 when China's bulk carrier De Xin Hai carrying 76,000 tons of coal was hijacked by Somali pirates in the Indian Ocean, 1,200 kilometers off the east coast of Somalia.

"Foreign trade is like a wife doing business abroad, and the navy is like the husband. The husband has to follow the wife wherever she goes, or he loses the money and his wife if she bumps into bandits," said Shanghai-based naval expert Ni Lexiong of the Shanghai Institute of Political Science and Law.

To take charge of its own seaborne security and protect its maritime trade, Beijing plans to build a new generation of large destroyers that will displace more than 10,000 tons as part of its effort to develop a modern blue-water navy. The new generation of destroyers is an important component of its long-term goal of building and operating aircraft carrier battleship groups. The new destroyers would feature fully developed stealth technology and most of the weapons systems and sensors would not be exposed externally, making the ships harder to detect on radar.

To be globally operational, big navies need friendly ports and bases. The U.S. has many such ports and bases around the world. China is now just starting to do so. It has secured ports from Bangladesh to Mauritius, in the South China Sea, the Indian Ocean and Arabian Gulf.

China's Navy

The PLA Navy was founded in Taizhou, Jiangsu, on April 23, 1949, bringing together vessels acquired from the Kuomintang and left behind by the Japanese after World War II.

As early as the 1980s, Deng Xiaoping directed Liu Huaqing, founder of the modern navy, to develop a long-term naval strategy that would be more in tune with China's outward-looking posture. May 2004 was the watershed in the evolution of Chinese maritime power when Beijing announced that the head of its navy would be assigned a permanent seat on the Central Military Commission, the highest national security decision-making body.

Another landmark was December 2008, when China publicly flexed its muscles by sending escort fleets to Somali waters, the first naval operation outside the Pacific, as well as a statement by the National defense Ministry that China needed an aircraft carrier.

China's state-of-the-art nuclear submarine, the Type 094, also known as Jin Class, and, space communications ship, a key player in the Shenzhen VII space program, kicked off the PLA Navy's three-day 60th anniversary party celebration in the northeastern coastal city of Qingdao in April 2009. The 222-meter Yuanwang-6 space communications ship is equipped with high-tech antennas that can transmit signals between the Earth and the moon. It can transmit and receive signals within a 400,000 kilometer radius of the Earth and can cruise for 100 days without making a port call.

Naval vessels from 14 countries, including the U.S., and naval representatives from 25 countries, joined in the celebration. Conspicuously absent was the Japanese navy. Japan was not invited for fear it might anger the Chinese public, still deeply scarred by the Japanese invasion in the 1930s and its attendant atrocities. Another important anniversary comes to mind

– the annihilation of the bulk of China's first modern naval force by the Imperial Japanese Navy in a battle 115 years earlier, a battle that shaped the courses of both nations.

The shocking defeat of the North Sea Fleet, considered the most powerful in Asia, came as a surprise to everyone at the time except the Japanese – who through careful reconnaissance discovered that the Chinese navy, while impressive in size, was so badly run that it was nowhere close to battle readiness. The Battle of the Yalu River in 1894 led to China's crushing defeat in the first Sino-Japanese war, marking the start of Japan's aggression toward its neighbor and a century of wars and social upheavals on the mainland. China had to wait half a century to assemble another credible naval force.

The reality is that China could not defeat Japan today either in a small regional conflict, yet alone a larger conflict that involved Japan's main ally – America. It will take decades for China to become a credible military threat to the U.S.

The idea of inviting an international array of naval personnel was to build foundations for further exchanges and the PLA Navy's integration with the international community. U.S. chief of naval operations, Admiral Gary Roughead, who attended the celebration, said he was there to clarify what China's intentions were regarding its naval buildup.

Chinese nuclear submarines cruise the Western Pacific and share the waters with the U.S. Pacific Fleet. By 2010 China will have about 85 submarines. Japan has 16 submarines with no plans to acquire more. Australia announced in May 2009, that it is planning to buy 12 advanced new submarines that will double its attack submarine fleet and buy warships capable of carrying ballistic missile shields in a $72 billion military upgrade. Australia has also signed a security pact with Japan, linking both countries into annual defense talks with the U.S., which China has criticized as an attempt at strategic confinement. China was assured that was not the case.

The Australian government released in May 2009 a 140-page Defense White Paper – *Defending Australia* in the Asia Pacific Century: Force 2030 – which "does not see the Chinese military as a threat." It says China by 2030 will become a major driver of economic activity both in the region and globally, and will have strategic influence beyond East Asia. China will also be the strongest Asian military power, by a considerable margin. A country of China's stature can be expected to develop a globally significant military capability befitting its size, the paper says.

China became Australia's largest trading partner in 2007. At the end of 2007, total Chinese investment in Australia was only A$670 million. In the 18 months leading up to June 2009, over A$30 billion worth of Chinese investment has been approved. A first-quarter Australia-China Business Trade report found that trade with China brings an average profit of A$3,000 to every Australian household annually.

"Why would Australia sell uranium to China, the key material used in atom bombs, if it really saw Beijing as a threat?" asked Australia's foreign minister in response to Australia's plan to sell China more uranium.

Southeast Asian countries are increasing their modern submarine fleets as well, with Indonesia planning to build 12 submarines by 2024 and Singapore, Thailand, Malaysia, South Korea, Bangladesh and Pakistan also on a sub-buying spree. Vietnam is reportedly planning to buy six Kilo-class submarines from Russia and India launched its first nuclear-powered submarine in July 2009.

The U.S. Pacific Fleet has 35.

"Their nuclear sub program has taken off like wildfire," said Eric McVadon, a retired U.S. Navy admiral who served as defense attaché in Beijing, said of China.

"…The Chinese are moving a whole lot faster on military modernization than anyone expected a short time ago," added Richard Holloran, a military affairs analyst based in Honolulu. The size of China's fleet could surpass that of the U.S. by 2020.

In response, the U.S. Navy is reversing an old Soviet-era formula, where the U.S. had 60 percent of its submarines in the Atlantic and 40 percent in the Pacific. The U.S. also set up an antisubmarine warfare center in San Diego. While doing so, the U.S. fast-attack submarine San Francisco ran into an undersea mountain on Jan. 8, 2005, killing one crew member and injuring 23. Hopefully, that will be America's only casualty in its aggressive efforts to contain China.

The reality is the deployment of Russian nuclear submarines to patrol the eastern seaboard of the U.S. in the summer of 2009 is a more serious and immediate concern. The episode, the first in 15 years, has echoes of the Cold War, when the U.S. and the Soviet Union regularly parked submarines off each other's coasts to steal military secrets, track the movements of their underwater fleets – and be poised for war. The new deployment of Russia's most advanced Akula II submarines follows the resumption in 2008 of Russian bomber runs off the coast of Alaska and Russian navy exercise with Venezuela. The U.S. cannot continue to ignore the growing threat from Russia in the Atlantic as it focuses its misguided attention on a non-threatening China in the Pacific.

Much of what is happening today in the Pacific is a repeat of what happened in 1908. Then President Theodore Roosevelt determined that America was to be a Pacific and international force, sent 14,000 sailors on 16 battleships and accompanying support craft on a world tour, which included a stopover in Xiamen. For a then-rising Japan, the message was plain: Don't mess with America. Today America is trying to send the same message to China – directly and through its military proxies in the region.

The crown jewel of the U.S. Navy is the aircraft carrier George Washington, which was sent on its maiden voyage to the Pacific in December 2008. Its primary mission was to "sanitize" the seas around it. That means using active and passive sonar, helicopters and a whole slew of secret gadgetry to inspect a large chunk of the surrounding waters for Chinese submarine activity. What a colossal waste of money.

Paul Bracken, a professor at the Yale School of Management and author of *Fire in the East: The Rise of Asian Military Power and the End of Western Dominance,* is right when he says: "This is the end of a Western monopoly on military technologies that began with gunboats and machine guns and extended to nuclear weapons, stealth bombers and cruise missiles."

"The United States may be ahead of the Chinese and others in military and other technologies, but the West's exclusive ownership of them is over with. China and others in Asia will soon have arsenals that will make any outside country think twice about moving forces there in a crisis," Bracken said.

Octoberfest
"The Chinese people have stood up," Mao Zedong declared on Oct. 1, 1949, from Beijing's Gate of Heavenly Peace overlooking Tiananmen Square. Mao put the world on notice after decades of civil war, political turmoil, foreign invasions and famines that China was going to stretch its economic

and military might as well as its limbs. At the time, China was one of the world's poorest countries. Life expectancy was 35 years then; it is 73 years now. The illiteracy rate then was among the world's highest, as education was considered an extravagance for an elite few.

Today, China claims to have the most people in higher education in the world. More than 90 percent of the 500 million-populace lived in rural areas back then, and the economy was almost entitely agricultural, without any meaningful industries.

Beijing was a city of ruins with shabby houses and dirt roads when Mao stood up to declare the People's Republic of China.

When President Hu Jintao, the fourth generation communist leader, stood at about the same spot Mao did to celebrate China's 60th anniversary, he saw a far different Beijing and presided over a vastly different military parade. At least 52 new-generation weapons were displayed in the National Day parade. These included the DH-10 long-range land-attack cruise missiles, which have a powerful 1,500 to 2,000 kilometer range that puts the U.S. military base in Okinawa at 700 kilometers within striking distance.

The DF-31A is China's first road-mobile nuclear ICBM with a range of more than 11,000 kilometers, which could reach Washington. It can carry at least three warheads. The DF-41 has a range of 11,000-13,000 kilometers and carries 10 warheads. China also paraded its ZTZ99 main battle tank, JL-2 Julang CSS-N-4 intercontinental missile, YJ-83 anti ship missile and numerous other medium range ballistic missiles.

The columns of troops and hardware, with the flyover displays by Jian 10-fighter jets, Zhi-10 armed helicopters and KJ series early-warning aircraft, are intended to send out messages of authority, strength and transparency – domestically and overseas. China wants its potential adversaries at home and abroad to know that it is no longer the supine China of ancient days, but a modern military powerhouse.

In its 2009 report on Beijing's military power, the Pentagon ranked Chinese defense technology below that of the United States, as it always has, but noted that the country's armed forces had improved their capacity to carry out operations away from its shores and deny other militaries access to its airspace and seas. Is it any wonder the U.S. wants more interaction with China's military to build trust over defense issues amid growing U.S. concerns about Beijing's rapid military buildup?

Display of Power

China's rising political, economic and military clout was put on its first full display in the fall of 2008 when it launched its first overseas mission since the 15th century. It sent three ships to join an international mission fighting pirates in waters off Somalia. More than 1,000 Chinese merchant ships passed through the Gulf of Aden in 2008, and seven were attacked by Somali pirates. The ships – China's most sophisticated destroyers DDG-169 Wuhan and DDG 171 Haikou, backed by the supply ship Weishanhu, now escort ships from China, Hong Kong, Macau and Taiwan. China provided Taiwan with a historic first naval escort in January 2009, quite a contrast to its primary political objective of capturing Taiwanese vessels. This has placed Taiwanese President Ma Ying-jeou's administration in an embarrassing position and subjected him to political fire from the pro-independence camp.

China still has a long way to go as a naval power, but it is only a matter of time before Chinese warships routinely deploy to the Middle East and Africa, the source of three-quarters of China's vital oil imports.

China's first aircraft carrier doesn't even begin to match the 12 carriers the U.S. has. The U.S. carriers do not operate by themselves, but with powerful and capable escort ships in carrier battle groups.

China needs a reliable infrastructure for projecting and sustaining naval and air power. The U.S. is the pre-eminent exponent of this strategy. It has a long head-start over China. Its 5th Fleet is based in Bahrain, in the Persian Gulf, drawing ships on rotation from both the U.S. Pacific and Atlantic fleets.

U.S. defense spending equals the defense budgets of the next 15 countries combined and will soon exceed all other countries combined. The reality is, that just as U.S. geopolitical analysis at the sunset of the 20th century and dawn of the 21st was flawed, so is its military dream. The weapons the "military industrial complex" builds, as I pointed out in *Custom Maid War,* are built without regard to enemies, costs, or trade-offs. In 2008 the General Accounting Office said cost overruns for the Pentagon's 95 biggest weapons programs – just the overruns! – added up to $300 billion, more than double that of China's $70 billion and Russia's $50 billion combined military budgets.

With an overall military budget of more than $655 billion in 2009 – almost

10 times that of China's, not counting the overruns – the U.S. is unmatchable. The 2010 budget calls for $750 billion in military spending, an amount that exceeds U.S. budget spending in all other areas except so-called "mandatory" spending on social security, health care and interest payments on the U.S. national debt. Russia imploded trying to keep up. The Europeans have given up. China is a different story. China already is developing a new stealth fighter jet to rival U.S. warplanes. Tentatively dubbed the J-X, it will rival the Lockheed Martin F/A-22 Raptor and F-35 Joint Strike Fighter.

The European Union has a population of 380 million people and a GDP of nearly $10 trillion, compared to a U.S. population of 300 million and a GDP of $13 trillion. Yet Europe barely spends $130 billion on defense – less than one-fifth of the U.S. amount, which rose sharply after 9/11. The post 9/11 increase alone is larger than the entire defense budget of Great Britain. Is it any wonder Europe wants to, and will, resume arm sales to China, the No. 2 military spender, that were suspended after the Tiananmen crackdown?

Why does the U.S. insist on pursuing military programs that are useless in today's wars in Iraq and Afghanistan – where much cheaper unmanned drones are much more effective – and other programs and budgets that were conceived during the Cold War and not applicable to today's adversaries? More importantly, why do American taxpayers allow defense budgets to continue to be so pervasively wasteful and not get outraged?

"American foreign policy has failed in recent years mainly because the United States relied on military force to address problems that demand development assistance and diplomacy," wrote Jeffrey Sachs, professor of economics and director of the Earth Institute at Colombia University.

China has become the world's second-biggest military spender behind the United States. China increased its spending by 10 percent to an estimated $84.9 billion in 2008, behind the U.S.'s $607 billion, according to the Stockholm International Peace Research Institute in its annual report on arms transfers released in June 2009. U.S. military spending is up more than 40 percent from 2001 to 2009, fueled in part by the wars in Iraq and Afghanistan. "China is continuing to acquire both domestic and foreign arms as it seeks to equip its armed forces for conditions of modern 'informationalised' warfare," it said. Such warfare involves the use of precision weapons and hi-tech information and communications technology.

What caught my attention in the report was the statement that "While they are certainly seeking to increase their regional and global influence ... there is very little evidence of any hostile intent in terms of the region."

Most of China's military budget is used to modernize its forces to retake Taiwan if it declares independence. The 2003 Annual Report on the Military Power of the People's Republic of China prepared by the U.S. concluded that the Chinese military doctrine emphasizes "surprise, deception, and shock effect in the opening phase of a campaign" to retake Taiwan. Who can really blame them? Wouldn't it be more constructive to pursue a realistic peaceful strategic dialogue that is mutually beneficial to both America and China?

The issue is not subject to a quick technical fix. It requires a new mindset and international system in which America's military superiority no longer goes unquestioned and its ability to enforce its vision of the economic and military future is carefully and thoroughly questioned.

Nuclear Transparency

A little known fact is that China has openly shared its nuclear capabilities with the U.S. The September 2008 issue of the journal *Physics Today* contains an account of the history of China's nuclear program. The article by Tom Reed, a U.S. nuclear weapons engineer and former secretary of the Air Force, details the two full tours his associate Danny Stillman was given of China's key thermonuclear weapons research, development and testing facilities across China in 1990. Stillman made seven more visits between 1991 and 1999. Why did the Chinese do it? "For one thing," Reed wrote in the article, "the Chinese probably sought deterrence. An American awareness of Chinese nuclear capabilities should lead to a more cautious American military posture around Taiwan and in the Pacific Ocean."

What is ironic is that the U.S. has prohibited Stillman from publishing his book *Inside China's Nuclear Weapons Program* on the grounds that it contains classified material. In other words, the U.S. is guarding military secrets for the Chinese, who have been perfectly willing to divulge them. It is one more example of U.S. bureaucratic political nonsense.

The bureaucratic nuclear stupidity reached its zenith in the summer of 2009 when the U.S. government accidentally posted on the Internet a list of government and civilian nuclear facilities and their activities. The 266-page document was published on May 6 as a transmission from President Barrack Obama to the U.S. Congress and posted on the Government Printing

Office Website. According to the document, the list was required by law and will be provided to the International Atomic Energy Agency. Some of the pages were marked "highly confidential safeguard sensitive."

Included in the report are details on a storage facility for highly enriched uranium at the Y-12 complex at the Oak Ridge National Laboratory in Tennessee and some sites at the Energy Department's Hanford nuclear site in Washington State.

While there is security at the facilities, the list could presumably be useful for terrorists or anyone else who would like to harm the United States.

China has also given to the International Atomic Energy Agency information and intelligence it has gathered on Iran's nuclear program because of its unease about how honest the Islamic Republic has been about its efforts to make a nuclear weapon. Suspected weapons-related work outlined in a February 2008 report to IAEA includes uranium conversion linked to high-explosives testing and designs of a missile re-entry vehicle; procurement of so called "dual use" equipment and experiments that could be used in both civilian and military programs; and Iran's possession of a 15-page document outlining how to form uranium into the shape of a warhead.

It should therefore come as no surprise that China is urging the U.S. and Russia to reduce their nuclear arsenals before it negotiates over its much smaller nuclear force with the International Commission on Nuclear Non-Proliferation and Disarmament. The Federation of American Scientists estimated in early 2009 that China had about 240 nuclear warheads compared to the 9,400 held by the U.S. and 13,000 by Russia.

What did come as a surprise was President Obama's threat in June 2009 to employ nuclear weapons against North Korea in retaliation for a nuclear attack on South Korea during South Korean President Lee Myung-bak's visit to the White House. The U.S. nuclear doctrine has been wrapped up in generalities and ambiguity intended to deter a potential adversary from a nuclear attack by keeping him guessing. That doctrine calls for never confirming or denying the presence of U.S. nuclear weapons anywhere. That all changed when Obama and Lee issued a joint statement saying that "the continuing commitment of extended deterrence, including the U.S. nuclear umbrella," provided an assurance that the U.S. would respond in kind if Pyongyang ever put into action its belligerent nuclear rhetoric against its southern neighbor.

Obama has called for a world without nuclear weapons, not as a distant goal, but as something imminently achievable. In 1992, after more than 1,000 explosions, the U.S. conducted its last underground nuclear test. The U.S., following Russia and France, announced a voluntary moratorium on tests and the other major nuclear powers – Britain and China – made the same pledge. Since then 180 countries have signed the Comprehensive Test Ban Treaty. Unfortunately, the treaty, which would go beyond the voluntary moratorium and legally bind states to not test, has never come into force. That is because the U.S. and eight other nuclear-capable states whose participation is required – China, North Korea, India, Pakistan, Indonesia, Iran, Israel and Egypt – have not ratified it. It is in everyone's interlocal universal national security interests to have the treaty ratified.

President Hu Jintao told world leaders at the U.N. in September 2009 that the nuclear powers should make "drastic and substantive" cuts to their arsenals and strive to make the planet nuclear free. "To realize a safer world for all, we must first and foremost remove the threat of nuclear war," Hu said. It was the first time he had addressed such a high-level summit on disarmament and nonproliferation.

It was the first speech by a Chinese president to the 1920-member General Assembly. He made no direct mention of Iran and North Korea, two countries with which Beijing has close ties, but which have been subjected to U.N. sanctions over their nuclear programs.

"We call on the international community to take credible steps to push forward the nuclear disarmament process, eradicate the risks of nuclear weapons proliferation and promote the peaceful use of nuclear energy and related international cooperation," Hu said.

Premier Wen Jiabao echoed Hu's statement a month later in Pyongyang during his state visit in October 2009 urging North Korea to rejoin the six-party talks addressing North Korea's denuclearization. "The international community universally agrees on denuclearization of the Korean Peninsula through dialogue and consultation," Wen told Kim Jong-il.

The nuclear Non-Proliferation Treaty signed in 1968 by the then five nuclear powers – U.S., Russia, China, France and Britain – was supposed to get the countries to gradually reduce and then eliminate their nuclear arsenals. That has not happened. In fact more countries now have nuclear weapons and others are seeking to develop them. It is up to America and Russia, which still possess 95 percent of the world's nuclear weapons, to lead the disarmament charge. China is happy to referee and will follow.

Future Cooperation and Transparency

America and China must find ways to ensure greater transparency, trust and cooperation on all fronts, but especially the military and nuclear ones. A world in which the U.S. and Chinese militaries work together to confront common threats such as terrorism, nuclear proliferation, natural disasters and limited natural resources is far more secure than one in which suspicion and distrust drive them into a greater arms race or, worse, armed conflict.

It was reassuring to read in June 2009 that both the U.S. and China hailed their recently concluded defense talks in Beijing as taking both countries "another step down the road towards more openness and transparency," said Michael Flournoy, U.S. undersecretary for defense. "The United States does not view China as an adversary. We think that as our relationship develops there will be a great deal on which we can act as partners."

America does not need to squander billions of dollars creating a new enemy at a time when it needs every dollar it can spare to save itself from its own worst enemy – the U.S. military industrial complex.

William Owens, who resides in Hong Kong and served as vice-chairman of the Joint Chiefs of Staff and as commander of the 6th fleet, said it best: "It is for the benefit of every man and woman in uniform and the citizens they protect – on both sides of the Pacific – that the U.S. and China lead our militaries to cooperate. We do not need to prepare for a new cold war – we need to prevent it."

The military power of America after World War II and its unilateral ability to dictate the structure of the U.N. to the world, or the U.N. itself, for that matter, are no longer applicable. It is time for the U.S. to re-examine how it can cooperate with China for the benefit of the people of all countries in the New World Order. America has much to gain by cooperating with China instead of bullying and challenging it. It is a bluff that China will call.

Chapter 5

American Buffet
– International Smorgasbord

Our form of government, inestimable as it is, exposes us, more than any other, to the insidious intrigues and pestilent influence of foreign nations. Nothing but our inflexible neutrality can preserve us.
– John Adams

G-20 Hypocrisy

The G-20 was created in the wake of the Asian and Russian financial crisis of 1998. It is a group of developed and developing nations that coalesced to prevent future global financial crises from developing – something they have obviously failed to do – again. The group accounts for almost 90 percent of global gross domestic product, or total value of goods and services. The member states are Argentina, Australia, Brazil, Britain, Canada, China, France, Germany, India, Indonesia, Italy, Japan, Mexico, Russia, Saudi Arabia, South Africa, South Korea, Turkey and the United States. The European Union is the 20th member.

Although the G-20 meetings in Washington at the end of 2008 and in London in April 2009 were the largest international financial summits held in years, the limited time scheduled for the meetings, a dinner and less than a full day of meetings, made the necessary comprehensive change of the world's financial architecture impossible – and a sincere warm-hearted embrace of financial powerhouse China even more remote.

The world's leaders came across as more interested in snapping souvenir pictures with each other than in dealing with the global economic crisis. They conveniently overlooked the lessons history has to offer on the close relationship between economic turmoil, protectionism and war. After the

Washington confab, they pronounced they were united against protectionism and yet 17 of the 20 enacted 47 different measures that "restrict trade at the expense of other countries," according to a World Bank report by economists Elisa Gamberoni and Richard Newfarmer released before the London gathering.

The third get-together of the G-20 in Pittsburgh in September 2009, the first hosted by President Obama, also failed to get the group on the right track to give it the traction needed to tackle the desperate issues of the 21st century for humanity to survive.

The sheer volume of global problems the two-day summit had to address – from the lopsided global growth model to climate change, tougher financial regulation, caps on bankers' pay and protectionism – meant any near-term concrete actionable results for defining a new economic direction for the world would be elusive – and they are.

With U.S. consumers holding back on spending after the collapse in house prices and rising unemployment, President Obama tried to push world leaders toward reshaping the world economy with a broad new economic framework that makes other countries the engines of global growth.

Global leaders in Pittsburgh had to tackle the $9 trillion tab they ran up rescuing the world economy from the deepest financial slump since the Great Depression. Unwinding and paying off the government debt that threatens to trigger the next crisis if not properly handled, dictates an age of austerity which inherently saps growth prospects, even during a recovery.

The International Monetary Fund says G-20 debt will reach 82 percent of gross domestic product in 2010, almost 20 percentage points more than 2007 and the equivalent of about $37 trillion. Former Federal Reserve Chairman Alan Greenspan has said U.S. debt, already about 84 percent of GDP, is "very dangerous" and threatens both treasuries and the U.S. dollar.

There was some good news out of Pittsburgh. Forcing banks to curb their leverage ratios and cap the salaries of their top executives did get some traction. It's about time. Why should traders' bonuses be based on unrealized gains that might never materialize instead of real booked profits? What is wrong with basing banker's bonuses on cash profits instead of paper gains? Why is it when people or businesses need to borrow money, bankers usually reject the loan applications – but are happy to loan money to the same people when they don't need a loan? Why don't the same rules apply to bankers? Why should public money be used to bail out bankrupt banks that use billions of the rescue proceeds to pay their executives bonuses? Executives at rescued banks should have their salaries and bonuses cut.

The bad news is that the world's leading economies have broken pledges made in Washington and London to refrain from protectionism. "On average a G-20 member has broken the no-protectionism pledge once every three days," said Simon Evenett, professor of trade and economic development at the University of St. Gallen in Switzerland who coordinates Global Trade Alert. Protectionism and economic nationalism are the twins that will destroy any new proposed global financial and economic architecture.

The imposition by the U.S. of a three-year punitive tariff on Chinese tires on the eve of the Pittsburgh summit, and shortly after the launch of the Doha Round talks, sent a negative message that protectionism and economic nationalism are acceptable, notwithstanding the G-20 pronouncements to the contrary.

Hard to Digest
China has a hard time accepting America's punitive protective measures. Beijing understands the need to impose them periodically to fulfill and achieve domestic political agendas, but asks why at China's expense?

The U.S. imposed its largest ever punitive protective measures against China in November 2009 after President Barack Obama completed his summit in Beijing – and agreed with President Hu Jintao to resist protectionism. The U.S. slapped anti-subsidy duties that range from 10-16 percent and anti-dumping duties of up to 99.14 percent on $2.7 billion worth of Chinese steel pipes imported to the U.S. annually.

Protectionist tendencies were the spark that ignited World War II after a meeting of global leaders at the London World Monetary and Economic Conference of 1933 failed to agree on a viable global trading and financial system. The fundamental circumstances in 2009 are worse than in the early 1930s. The debt burden is higher. The global economy is more tightly intertwined and economic viruses spread more swiftly. The damage that occurred from late 1929 to early 1931 has now been condensed into six months. Japan's exports fell 49 percent in January 2009 and global trade shrank 41 percent – annualized – from November 2008 to January 2009, according to Holland's CPB Institute.

The G-20's pledge of $1 trillion in loans and guarantees for distressed countries, agreements on linking executive pay and bonuses to performance, and "taking note" of secret tax havens named by the Organization for Economic Co-operation and Development are not the way to fix the global financial meltdown or prevent future meltdowns. They are populist responses to outrage and abuses highlighted by the financial crisis that merely increased the overdraft line of the world's dysfunctional financial system. The G-20 leaders failed to heed Karl Marx's admonition: History does repeat itself, first as a tragedy, then as a farce.

The long overdue global financial restructure, regulation and economic embrace of China must come sooner rather than later, otherwise America's geopolitical tragedy will become a farce.

Wrong Cooks in an Old Kitchen

The IMF and the World Bank are relics of World War II, created at the Bretton Woods conference in 1944 as the foundation cornerstones of the postwar world financial system. I advocated the abolition of both bodies, along with the United Nations, or at the very least, their restructuring, in my book *Custom Maid Knowledge,* to give China and other developing countries greater say. The bank's management structure reflects the world of the 1950s, with Belgium having more voting power than China.

A new global central bank relevant to the 21st century is long overdue. The world can no longer depend on the U.S. Federal Reserve to single-handedly micro-manage the global financial system with the IMF and World Bank playing second and third fiddle as its sidekicks. That is the only way to make sure that financial institutions doing business globally never again accumulate debt that is more than 30 times their capital and to insure that all central banks impose rational leverage ratios on their national banks.

It was hoped in some political circles that the Washington G-20 meeting in 2008 would turn into a "Bretton Woods II Summit," coming as it did amid the most damaging financial crisis since the Great Depression of the 1930s. But it was not to be because the Europeans wanted America to lead them in the charge to restructure a financial system that they continue to dominate.

The IMF, like its chief Dominique Strauss-Kahn, is too busy screwing its members to do them any constructive good. Strauss-Kahn's affair with Piroska Nagy – the wife of Argentina's central bank president – was revealed by *The Wall Street Journal*. This is the same guy who had said that rising food prices could have terrible consequences, including war, a few months earlier at the IMF spring 2008 meeting. So what does he do about it? Same thing the European Catholic Crusades did to the locals in South and Central America. Screw them. Crusades weren't limited to the Middle East. They were just spun as something more relevant to the "pagan" non-Jewish, Muslim and Orthodox Christians of the Middle East.

As if to make sure the world fully appreciated and recognized its incompetence, the IMF published embarrassingly erroneous exaggerated estimates of the external debt levels of crisis-hit Eastern European states in its Global Financial Stability Report released in April 2009. After the numbers for some countries were challenged by central bankers, analysts and journalists, the IMF was forced to revise and fix the data and publish the correct figures for the debt/reserve ratios of some Eastern European countries in May 2009.

The ratio for the Czech Republic was cut from 236 percent to 89 percent; Estonia's was reduced to 132 percent from 210 percent and Ukraine's was cut from 208 to 116 percent, with more revisions to follow for Lithuania and others. The fund added that it was reviewing "how the errors occurred" and would "amend the IMF's internal procedures according to the lessons learnt." Is it any wonder the IMF is despised in much of the developing world? "What might be at stake today is the very existence of the IMF," Strauss-Kahn warned its directors when he took over as managing director in 2007.

In 2009 the IMF repeatedly revised its 2010 growth forecasts while its chief contradicted other staffers. "Financial conditions have improved, confidence has recovered gradually and indicators of production and demand have firmed," IMF first deputy managing director John Lipsky told a conference in Turkey in June 2009. This statement not only contradicted another remark Lipsky made at the same conference when he said: "While the latest data points to a slowing of the global contraction, there is still great uncertainty regarding the timing and pace of economic recovery," but that of his boss Strauss-Kahn, who at the same time was saying in London that the world economy had yet to weather the worst of the recession.

The IMF doesn't seem to get many of its forecasts right. For example, in late July 2007, just as the credit crunch was beginning to bite, the fund's economists jacked up their forecasts for global growth, announcing that "the strong global expansion is continuing." They predicted the U.S. economy would expand 2.8 percent the following year; seven times as fast as it actually did.

Most infamously, in 1997, the fund decided that the best way to prevent a financial crisis in Indonesia would be to start closing down shaky banks; a decision that prompted immediate capital flight and precipitated a full-blown economic collapse.

The IMF has a lending capacity of only $250 billion, which is subject to the strict policies of the bank. A principal outcome of the April 2 meeting of G-20 leaders in London was an agreement to triple the IMF's resources to $750 billion – which it successfully collected – and to allow it to issue a further $250 billion on its own. China, on the other hand, has more than $2 trillion in foreign exchange reserves to lend to anyone it chooses.

The IMF reported in April 2009 that worldwide losses tied to rotten toxic loans and securitized assets – spun as "legacy loans" – may reach $4.1 trillion by the end of 2009. Banks would shoulder roughly 61 percent of the write-downs, with insurers, pension funds and other non-banks assuming the rest. Why should innocent non-bank taxpayers, laborers and consumers have to shoulder any of the shortfall?

Left to the stewardship of the West, the IMF has bankrupted the global economic order because of its impotence and incompetence. This was reluctantly acknowledged by the leaders at the London G-20 summit and European leaders will no longer have an automatic right to pick its managing director. And through a reform of its arcane shareholding or "quota" system, the domination of policy by the U.S. and other developed economies will give way to a more balanced system of governance. It remains to be seen whether these pronouncements become reality.

In fact, the exact opposite happened at the Pittsburgh G-20 summit. The IMF was given more power. The IMF was charged with figuring out the benchmarks for an exit strategy for the trillions of dollars of stimulus spending and to identify the warning signs of the new crisis. If they couldn't identify the looming current crisis in 2007 or 2008, what makes world leaders think they will in the future? How can the IMF monitor nations to ensure they are changing their economic policies to promote long-term growth?

The answer came from Strauss-Kahn himself. With a "substantial increase" in resources if it is to act as a guarantor of global economic stability. In other words, more taxpayer money to waste. Not just more money, but more meaningless talk. "Now we need to reflect and think about an extension of this idea of insurance," he said, to fix the so-called global imbalances where some countries accumulate huge reserves and others build up huge deficits.

"If you want to avoid countries, including China, building up such big reserves, contributing to global imbalances, we need to find another system," Strauss-Kahn said. In other words, he acknowledges that the current IMF system is broke and unsustainable but needs more money to come up with a solution.

World leaders reluctantly acknowledged that the developing world needs to have a greater say and promised action to better reflect China, India, Russia and Brazil's "real economic weights" and said a significant realignment of IMF quotas should be completed no later than January 2011.

The only way to avoid the widening fissures unfolding between the developed, developing and underdeveloped nations is to bring them all together and honestly recognize them for the economic powers they are today and will become in the future.

To its credit, China demanded greater "fairness" and that voting rights be fairly weighted and assigned to it and other developing countries in the U.S.-dominated organization before committing to loan any funds to the IMF. In recent years, China has pushed, with some success, to increase its voting power at the IMF and become a member of more multilateral economic organizations, citing its rapidly growing economic power and might.

More importantly, it has made it perfectly clear that it will no longer be dictated to or pushed around by America or Europe. French President Nicolas Sarkozy learned this lesson in a publicly humiliating way when he tried to push for the inclusion of Hong Kong and Macau on a blacklist of tax havens. In the face of French aggression, Chinese Premier Hu Jintao firmly put his foot down and booted the French proposal off the agenda. Beijing has made it clear that it wants positive results from global summits and that it wants to play an active role to achieve them.

The voting rights of Brazil, Russia, India and China in the IMF are 9.62 percent of the total, together accounting for about half of the voting rights that the U.S. holds, in addition to its sole veto power.

It is time for re-merging economic global powers like China, India, Russia and Brazil to be welcomed to the global financial policy-setting body with a far greater say and voting rights if the global economy is to be stabilized, properly and uniformly regulated, with effective enforcement bodies and penalties for the violators. China is, after all, soon going to surpass the U.S. as the world's largest economy.

Too Many White Cooks Spoil the Broth

The annual G-8 summit meeting started out in France in 1975 as a "fireside chat" with French delicacies and wines, known as the G-7 for the leaders of the U.S., Canada, France, Germany, UK, Italy and Japan, and became the G-8 when Russia joined in 1997. The "G" stands for group. The July 8-10, 2009 G8-plus-5 that took place in L'Aquila, Italy – the five being Brazil, China, India, Mexico and South Africa – plus Australia, Indonesia and South Korea who belong to the Major Economies Forum, Egypt and another 22 from Africa, Asia and the Middle East for a "Grand" total of 39 proved its outdated desperate efforts to remain relevant.

The cordial chat around a fire turned into a gabfest around a bonfire in Italy, a country that failed to meet commitments it made in 2005 to double aid to Africa by 2010. The earthquake-ravaged L'Aquila, along with the event's host, playboy Prime Minister Silvio Berlusconi, embroiled in a very public divorce, not just from his wife, but the G-8, and a lurid sex scandal, served as an appropriate metaphoric backdrop for the rubble of the G-whatever.

How can a three day chat with 39 egomaniacs possibly come to grips with a daunting agenda that includes the worst worldwide economic and financial crisis since the Great Depression, global warming, energy and food security, terrorism, nuclear proliferation, resuscitation of Doha trade negotiations, development, eliminating poverty – not to mention Afghanistan, Iraq and North North. In the face of all that, the Italian hosts failed to prepare an agenda and allowed the U.S. to hijack the agenda in China's absence.

Nick Deardon, director of the London-based Jubilee Debt Campaign, says that, by righs, the G-8 "should be dead and buried. It harks back to the days when a handful of countries could happily control the world economy without interference." I agree completely.

Deardon accurately described the L'Aquila summit as a mere "annual photo shoot." Commitments made at the previous few G-8 meetings didn't last much longer than the time it took the leader to make it to the airport on their way out of town. The legacy of L'Aquila doesn't look much brighter.

The time to toss out this overccoked and ill-conceived broth, stirred up by more than 10 times the number of chefs originally envisioned in 1975, is long overdue. And while we're at it, let's toss out the chefs, too. L'Aquila should be remembered as the group's wake. The Pittsburgh G-20 buried the G-8 gabfest. Now we have to wait and see how the chefs will be disposed of.

Dollar Value

From 1940 until the dawn of the 21st century, the U.S. dollar has been the primary universal currency. In 1940, much of the gold in the world was deposited in Fort Knox by governments terrified that Adolf Hitler would win the Second World War. When it became clear in 1944 that the Allies would prevail, U.S. leaders launched a number of conferences on postwar planning. One of them was the Bretton Woods Conference. Seven hundred and thirty delegates attended from 44 countries.

The two main protagonists were the Allied leaders America and Britain. America made the U.S. dollar the dominant currency that decided the value of other countries' currencies because the trove of gold in Fort Knox gave the U.S. immense power to bend recalcitrant countries to Uncle Sam's will.

A global currency must have three strengths to be accepted around the world. Most important is that it always delivers the economic value expressed on coin, paper and now electronic numbers. Second, a global super-currency must be prevalent enough to finance capital anywhere and anytime. And third, it must be a safe haven. A fourth unofficial rule is that all notes of all denominations must be the same color so they won't be confused with anybody else's. Just kidding.

The unraveling of the American super-dollar began during the Vietnam War. In March 1968, then-President Lyndon Johnson announced that he would not run for reelection. The bulk of his speech was not about the war, but about the gold crisis. And in 1971, President Richard Nixon announced he would cut the link between the U.S. dollar and gold. Nixon made the right decision and in the same year accepted an invitation to visit China and embrace it as a geopolitical partner to contain the Soviet Union.

The American currency's dominance in international trade was further eroded when the euro was introduced in 1999, so much so that in 2006, the total value of euro notes in circulation overtook that of dollar bills. Twenty seven percent of 2008 foreign official reserves were held in euros, up from 18 percent in 1998. Over the same period, the dollar's share fell to 63 percent from 71 percent.

The Afghanistan and Iraq wars have accelerated the decline of the dollar. Hurricane Katrina sealed its fate when the government announced it would rebuild New Orleans without taxing Americans. The only way that could be done was to become more dependent on foreign governments buying U.S. treasury bonds. While the dollar has been declining in value, the Chinese yuan, like China itself, has been quietly growing as a global currency that

America must embrace and learn to live with in the 21st century.

Dollar a Deflated Soufflé

The dollar collapse is a growing concern in Beijing. The dollar could collapse like a soufflé if U.S. policies do not change. The U.S. currency fell 10 percent since it hit a three-year high on a trade weighted basis in March 2009. In late May 2009 it reached its lowest point against a basket of currencies since December 2008. Emerging market and commodity-linked currencies rallied the most against the dollar over the same period. The Australian dollar was up 20 percent, the Brazilian real 15 percent and the South African rand was up 16 percent.

The demand for commodities, combined with improved risk appetite has pushed investors to seek yields in emerging markets and commodity currencies, away from the fiscal deficiencies of the U.S. economy. The dollar had rallied strongly after the collapse of Lehman Brothers in September 2008 as massive deleveraging sent investors scrambling for the safety of the U.S. currency. Just as the dollar benefited when investors scrambled out of risky positions, so it will suffer as they seek out yields in a stabilized global economy.

"The dollar will be the main casualty, since the U.S. growth will come with lower interest rates, higher inflation expectations and greater financing risk than most other economies," said JP Morgan's John Normand in May 2009.

Normand added that investors risked repeating a frequent mistake: underestimating growth at turning points. "Given the amount of money stockpiled in cash after the Lehman bankruptcy and still undeployed after this spring's equity market rally, any upside surprise would renew the dollar's downtrend." JP Morgan put this stockpile in May 2009 at $700 billion.

That is why Treasury Secretary Timothy Geithner's assurances that China's dollar investments were safe during his June 2009 visit to China – and that the U.S. will cut its huge fiscal deficits as he tried to persuade Beijing to continue buying U.S. Treasuries – were met with skepticism and laughter. China cannot afford to continue bankrolling the recession-hit U.S. economy indefinitely without grave political and economic consequences. His Chinese audiences made it clear they thought Beijing's vast stockpile of foreign reserves could be put to better use to raise living standards in China.

The rating agency S&P's downgrade of its outlook on the U.K.'s sovereign debt in May 2009 accelerated the downward spiral of the dollar because the U.S. went into the financial crisis with a worse debt to gross domestic product ratio than the U.K. – 63 percent against 44 percent – and most organizations, including the International Monetary Fund and the Organization for Economic Co-operation and Development, expect the U.S. ratio to hit 100 percent before the U.K. The change in the U.S. ratings outlook is just a matter of time. It is no longer a question of if, but when.

The question is when will market participants speculate that U.S. policy-makers are engineering a weaker dollar as part of the overall plan to fight deflation? Many have already started and are slowly moving away from the dollar as the world's reserve currency. The process started in March 2009 when the U.S. Federal Reserve announced it would purchase $300 billion worth of long-term bonds and $850 billion worth of institutional bonds in the following six months. The news soon gave rise to worries about the risks of mid to long-term inflation and U.S. dollar depreciation across the globe.

Nobel laureate Paul Krugman wrote in his *New York Times* column that "China had driven itself into a dollar trap," and that "it can neither get itself out nor change the policies that put it in that trap in the first place." I respectfully disagree. The U.S. is also caught in the same trap and has fewer options and space to maneuver than China, which can afford to take a dollar hit a lot easier than the U.S. The U.S. government cannot print its way out of the trap. All it does is get itself deeper into the trap as China and others slowly claw their way out.

While China publicly question's the dollar's role as the world's reserve currency, it actually increased its holdings of U.S. Treasuries to $800 billion in July 2009, compared with $767 billion at the end of the first quarter. China knows that selling off greenbacks too quickly would wipe out much of its own wealth. China is in effect "near-pegging" the yuan to the dollar because it recognizes the dollar conundrum is as much its problem to solve as the U.S.'s.

Beijing has a lead role with Washington to mange the looming dollar debacle. China recognizes it cannot continue accumulating dollars forever and does not want to repeat Europe's mistake of the 1970s.

During the 1950s and 1960s, Europeans amassed a huge stash of U.S. Treasury bills in an effort to maintain fixed exchange-rate pegs, much as China has done today. Unfortunately, the purchasing power of Europe's dollars shriveled during the 1970s when the costs of the Vietnam War and a surge in oil prices ultimately contributed to a calamitous rise in inflation.

America's thirst for foreign capital to finance its consumption binge and wars, like in the 1970s, played a critical role in the build-up of the current crisis.

It is not just the Chinese government that has excessive dollar holdings. It is all ethnic Chinese, including those in the mainland, Hong Kong, Taiwan and overseas, that may collectively account for half of the foreign holdings of dollar assets. One has to check the asset allocation of wealthy ethnic Chinese to fully appreciate and understand the dollar's unique status.

The Chinese love affair with the dollar began in the 1940s when it held its value while the Chinese currency depreciated massively. Chinese memory is long, especially when it comes to currency credibility. The Chinese yuan remains a closed currency and is not yet a credible vehicle for wealth storage. Also, wealthy ethnic Chinese tend to send their children to the U.S. for education. They treat the dollar as their primary currency.

Diluting Chinese savings to bail out America's failing banks and bankrupt households, though highly beneficial to the U.S. national interest in the short term, will destroy the dollar's global status. Ethnic Chinese demand for the dollar is already waning. China's overweight foreign exchange reserves reflect the lack of private demand for dollars, which was driven by the yuan's appreciation. Though this was speculative in nature, it shows the yuan's rising credibility and its potential to replace the dollar as the preferred vehicle of wealth storage for ethnic Chinese.

America's fiscal policy is forcing China towards developing an alternative financial system. Since the late 1980s, China's entry into the global economy relied on making cheap labor available to multi-nationals and pegging the yuan to the dollar. The dollar peg allowed China to leverage the U.S. financial system for its international needs, while domestic finance remained state-controlled to redistribute prosperity from the coast to interior provinces.

This dual approach worked remarkably well. "China could have its cake and eat it too. Of course, the global credit bubble was what allowed China's dual approach to be effective; its inefficiency was masked by bubble-generated global demand," observes Andy Xie, an independent economist and former chief economist for Asia Pacific at Morgan Stanley. China recognizes that it must become independent from the dollar.

China's decision to turn Shanghai into a financial center by 2020 reflects it's anxiety over relying on the dollar system. The year 2020 seems remote, and America will not pay attention to something so distant. However, if global stagflation takes hold, as many economists expect, it will force China to accelerate its reforms to float its currency and create a single, independent and market-based financial system. When that happens, the dollar will collapse.

The U.S. dollar has the most to lose as the global role of China's yuan increases.

Take-Out Dollars

With near-zero U.S. interest rates and easy funds readily available, investors have borrowed huge sums of money in dollars to purchase higher-yielding assets overseas in carry trades to achieve better returns. Estimates are that carry traders have taken more than $550 billion in the first half of 2009. The size of the dollar carry trade can be measured from the increase in net foreign assets of the U.S. financial sector. A large proportion of these trades appears to have taken place overseas through foreign banks that have borrowed dollars from their U.S. branch offices. At the height of the yen carry trade, transactions were said to have hit $1 trillion, accumulated from 2004-2007, and look what happened to Japan. The same is now in store for the U.S.

The Federal Reserve will probably keep interest rates low for some time to come. The carry trade gained momentum in the third quarter of 2009 as risk appetite rose and the cost of the benchmark interbank dollar funds fell below those of the yen. Is it any wonder that China, now that it has effectively pegged the yuan against the dollar at an undervalued parity, is keeping its currency low?

The dollar's continued depreciation risks major global economic damage that will further complicate recovery from the current worldwide recession.

Paper Bag Lunch

The U.S. Federal Reserve is the world's biggest currency manipulator – not China. Not only does the Fed keep put the short-term interest rate at zero through its vast purchase purchase program for mortgage-backed securities. It also keeps credit spreads and bond yields artificially low. Its manipulation stops money, bond and credit markets from pricing either the Fed's policy or the U.S. economic plight. All the firepower is packed into the currency market, giving speculators a sure bet on a weaker dollar and everything else rising.

The U.S. Treasury writes an annual report, judging if other countries are manipulating their exchange rates. "It should look in the mirror," writes independent economist Andy Xie. "Even though the Fed is not directly intervening in the currency market per se, its manipulation is equivalent to pushing down the dollar by non-market means."

The Fed is playing with fire. With such massive speculative outflows, the dollar could collapse, sparking hyperinflation, like in Russia in 1998. The main reason this is not happening is because China's currency is pegged to the dollar. Speculators believe there is no downside, only upside from holding yuan. Hence China's foreign-exchange reserves are bulging on the inflows.

The foundation for another emerging-market crisis has already been laid. The people responsible for the last crisis were not only not punished, but rewarded with positions in the new Obama administration in Washington and bonuses on Wall Street. So why should anyone in Washington or on Wall Street have any incentive to do the right thing?

It should therefore come as no surprise that Beijing is upset and critical of Washington's low U.S. interest rates. Chairman of the China Banking Regulatory Commission Liu Mingkang said the Federal Reserve's pledge to hold down borrowing costs and the weak dollar have emerged as a "new systemic risk."

"This situation has already encouraged a huge dollar carry trade and had massive impact on global asset prices," Liu said in a speech at a financial forum in Beijing in November 2009. Liu also said the global economic recovery gives little grounds for optimism, as it is driven largely by stimulus spending by governments rather than real corporate activity.

Should the Federal Reserve be stripped of its role as a bank regulator as some in Congress suggest? At the very least it needs to be significanty modified and have more oversight, but not by Congress.

A realignment of the dollar is long overdue. Its overvaluation began with the Mexico peso crisis in 1994, and was officially enshrined by the "strong dollar" policy adopted after the East Asian financial crisis of 1997. That policy produced short-term consumption gains for America, which explains why it was popular with Washington politicians, but it has inflicted major long-term damage on the U.S. economy and contributed to the current crisis.

The overvalued dollar caused the U.S. economy to haemorrage spending on imports, jobs and investments offshored to countries with undervalued currencies. In today's era of globalization, marked by flexible and mobile production networks, exchange rates affect more than exports and imports. They also affect the location of production and investment.

China has been a major beneficiary of America's strong-dollar policy, to which it pegged its own weak yuan policy. As a result, China's trade surplus with the U.S. rose from $83 billion in 2001 to $258 billion in 2007, just before the recession. As of November 2009, China's surplus has accounted for 75 percent of the total U.S. non-oil-goods trade deficit. The undervalued yuan has also made China a major recipient of foreign direct investment, even leading the world in 2002 – an amazing achievement for a developing country.

When combined with China's rapid growth in manufacturing capacity, the ongoing global inbalances promise to be around for a few more years.

America's lingering cold war mentality and arrogance, combined with the presumption of U.S. economic superiority, has meant that economic issues are still deemed subservient to geopolitical concerns. That is what best explains the neglect of U.S.-China economic relations, a neglect that is now dangerous to the U.S., given its weakened economic condition.

Any wonder funds are migrating to gold and other commodities? India's central bank bought 200 tons of gold from the International Monetary Fund in October 2009, raising speculation that more governments will follow suit as the dollar slides.

Yankees and Their Dollar Not Welcome

Picking up on my author's note at the end of *Custom Maid Knowledge,* the second of the Custom Maid trilogy, where I discussed – after the dollar had depreciated 40 percent since its peak in 2002 – why the yuan is in the process of replacing the U.S. dollar as the international currency, I want to share some personal enlightening experiences that confirmed my concern and prediction.

I was in Dubai in November 2007 and went shopping at the local spice bazaar for dates, figs, apricots, saffron and frankincense. When I took my money clip out of my pocket to pay, "Chinese money, not dollars" said the salesman as he saw me leafing through the 100-yuan notes to get to the dollars.

Commodities guru Jim Rogers declared a few weeks earlier that he was pulling out of all his U.S. dollar assets and buying the yuan. He said the yuan is the best currency to buy, predicting its value will quadruple in the next decade.

Groups of Chinese tourists were everywhere in the Emirates – in the Dubai Museum, on the dhows in Dubai Creek, souks and restaurants – no different than Europe, the Middle East, Africa, Asia and the Americas. Their currency dominated at the exchanges and cash registers. Tourists are the best ambassadors of their national currency.

Just as the yuan is replacing the dollar, the ugly, loudmouthed American tourists have been replaced by their boisterous Chinese counterparts. American tourists are becoming an endangered species because they are too busy being wage slaves to spare any dollars for overseas travel to get to know foreigners, their country, history, or enjoy the sights, sounds and smells of the world's bazaars.

Dubai's $59 billion debt pie debacle in November 2009 was another year-end reminder that the global recession is far from over. European and U.S. banks were the primary debt holders of Dubai's defaulted loans.

Just as Bear Stearns was a harbinger of a string of failures of overly leveraged investment banks, people should be concerned that Dubai could be the canary in the coal mine for heavily indebted countries.

Dollars for Euros

The only exception to this generalization about American tourists that I experienced in recent travels was euro-spending Irish Americans on the Dublin Literary Pub Crawl in May 2009. Their euros were gladly exchanged for whiskey and Guinness at the pubs where Sam Becket, James Joyce and Oscar Wilde tippled a few, listening to anecdotes of these and the many other Irish literary giants.

Walking from The Duke to O'Neals, two prominent local literary pubs near the Trinity College campus where Oscar Wilde attended, we were regaled with stories of Oscar's wild lecture tour to America and the Wild West where he easily drank under the table many a tough miner. Wilde is the most quoted writer of our times. His quip that "America is a country I would not live in even if I could afford to pay my own passage there" became the opening volley and fodder for a lively discussion of the historical abuses of businessmen and politicians in Ireland and America.

Hearing I was an American nonfiction political writer living in Hong Kong, the alcohol-fueled discussion heated up as I was challenged to opine on China's global threat and how it "must" be contained by America if Western civilization is to survive.

"Chinese is the second most spoken language in Ireland after English, followed by Polish, and Gaelic is a distant fourth," said Colm Quilligan, one of our two hosts on the pub crawl, as he acknowledged the growing influence of China in Ireland.

Thankfully, the basketball playoffs in America allowed me, the sole Lakers fan surrounded by a dozen Celtic supporters, to change the subject to the Houston Rocket's Yao Ming's impressive performance against Kobe Bryant in the opening game of their playoff series and the Celtics, poor performance against the Pistons and Magic – and unlikely survival against Orlando to get the chance to play against the Cavaliers – let alone replay the Lakers in the final as they did in 2008 and won. How I survived the evening remains a mystery to this day.

I never cease to be amazed by the mellowing effect of whiskey and ale, especially when I later found out that a Chinese business consortium had bought a minority interest in the Cleveland Cavaliers – even as the Cavaliers took Game 2 to tie the series 1-1 in one of the all-time comeback wins as LeBron James netted the game-winning 3-pointer in the final second to tie the series in the presence of the new owners sitting at courtside. The fact that the Cavaliers started trailing fast in the following games should not be a surprise. Why announce another Chinese super-sized gulp of an American icon during the playoffs? Having spent time with NBA Commissioner David Stern in New York discussing the China opportunities in the early 1990s, I was not surprised.

With an eye on spreading the game on a global scale, the NBA has been quietly pushing for international groups to become involved in the ownership of NBA teams on a minority level. With China's huge NBA fan base, inspired by All Star Yao Ming's play in Houston, it is just a matter of time before hungry Chinese investors start taking bigger bites of U.S. icons – not just sports teams – which they are aggressively exploring.

According to Columbia University professor Robert Mundell, the 1999 Nobel economics laureate and "Father of the euro," the dollar will regain strength and China will succumb to international and political pressure for the yuan to appreciate. I respectfully disagree.

Investment bankers and their pundits rarely made any sense to me about anything they did. Watching Manchester United on its way to the European championship the night before in a pub in Ballycastle, where I stayed before my visit to Bushmills and its world renowned whiskey distillery, I couldn't get over the fact that here was the world's best soccer team playing with the blazing bankrupt AIG logo on its shirt – knowing AIG had been posted in the Foreign Correspondents Club, Hong Kong, for not paying its over-due bills incurred while its officers celebrated their U.S. taxpayer-supported bonuses – and the company was desperately trying to change its heavily marketed name, brand and image while the team it sponsored, unlike the bankers it paid, actually delivered on their talent costs and overhead.

Going into the Champions League final against Barcelona with the losing AIG logo, they were doomed and destined to lose, as they did 2-0. A lesson I hope investment bankers will digest and learn from. Branding and market-ing alone do not justify the Wall Street mantra "Take the Loot and Scoot" when it comes to bonuses. It is performance.

Dollar Doldrums

The dollar hit a historic low during my 2007 Dubai visit as speculation mounted in international financial circles that the Gulf states were ready to either revalue their currencies or do away with their peg to the dollar and switch to a basket of currencies to quell the mounting exchange rate losses and domestic inflation. The same happened during my visit to Ire-land, where the economy was in the bottom of a Guinness barrel. The only difference being it could be exchanged for Euros.

To hedge against their potential loss if the dollar continues to decline or collapse, Arab oil money and China know they need to support the dollar because they have a lot to lose with its decline.

China keeps the currency composition of its $2 trillion foreign exchange reserves – compared to America's $44 billion and Japan's $923 billion – a state secret. It is estimated by some analysts that more than two-thirds are probably held in dollars. China is understandably nervous about its dollar reserves. The dollar isn't a safe haven anymore because most of the prob-lems facing the world economy are coming from America, Japan and the Arab oil-producers. The Greenback Blues are here to stay for as long as America needs more than $65 billion a month to fund its current-account deficit.

By the end of 2008, the yuan had gained more than 20 percent since Beijing's currency reforms in 2005. The Chinese currency will be fine tuned to take on its greater regional and global role.

Inflation

Inflation is the transfer of wealth from creditors to debtors – essentially from China to the U.S. The inflation monster that reeked havoc across the world in the 1970s and 2007 raised its ugly head again in June 2009 because of the massive U.S. public debt and the fact that the money supply, thanks to the Federal Reserve's printing presses, had spiraled out of control. The hike in oil prices from about $40 a barrel in March 2009 to more than $70 a barrel and a 20 percent increase in raw material prices during the same period were indications that inflation had started setting in. Another indication was gold futures, which crossed $1,000 an ounce as the dollar started its descent.

Given the loose monetary policy, it is not surprising to see U.S. government debt ballooning from about $500 billion to more than $2 trillion in just six months, from September 2008 to May 2009. The U.S. debt is set to mount further because of the Fed announcement in March 2009 that it would continue to try to buy its way out of America's financial problems, starting with $300 billion worth of Treasury bonds by September 2009. It will follow it up by buying $200 billion in bonds and $1.25 trillion in mortgage-backed securities issued by Fannie Mae and Freddie Mac by the end of 2009.

More inflationary pressure was applied by countries that adopted U.S. style tactics to emerge out of recession as well. According to IMF estimates released in June 2009, public debts of the 10 leading economies will rise from 78 percent of GDP in 2007 to 114 percent by 2014. That means these governments will owe about $50,000 for each of their citizens. More importantly, it indicates there is a high possibility of these governments depending on inflation to help clear their debts.

The good news is that many homeowners in the U.S. who managed to hold onto their homes because of the government mortgage refinance programs, will see the price of their homes rise again and will be the beneficiaries of inflation.

For about a generation, the U.S. surfed on a growing wave of debt. The ratio of debt to personal disposable income was 55 percent in 1960. Since then it has more than doubled, reaching 133 percent in 2007. Total credit market debt – throwing in corporate, financial and other borrowings – has risen apace, surging from 143 percent of gross domestic product in 1951 to 350 percent of GDP in 2008. The leverage wave crashed in the autumn of 2008. Facing the possibility of systemic collapse, the government stepped in and replaced private borrowing with public borrowing.

The Federal Reserve balance sheet went from $800 billion in September 2008, to $2 trillion by January 31, 2009, and the Fed guaranteed another $7 trillion to $8 trillion debt, so it was a total of $10 trillion at the end of 2008.

As of December 2009, when this book went to press, the U.S. government had $11.4 trillion in outstanding debt that was growing by over $6 billion per day. The average maturity of the federal debt is only four years, and hence, a quarter of it needs refinancing every year. With $2 trillion net financing for 2009, the federal government needs to raise about $10 billion per day. If the Treasury yield continues to surge, the expected interest burden for the federal government may spiral out of control. At some point, the market may stop lending to the U.S. government, if it expects it to go bankrupt.

The continuing rise of inflation in America could easily lead to a pull-out of global investors from U.S. bond markets. This will almost certainly trigger a crash in the dollar's real effective exchange rate, which in turn would add further inflationary pressure. Inflation on top of rising unemployment could be the straw that breaks the camel's back. Stimulating inflation is another dirty, quick-fix strategy, like so many of the bank rescue packages in operation. To restore balance, according to Reuven Glick and Kevin Lansing of the San Francisco Federal Reserve, Americans will have to increase their household savings rate from 4 percent to 10 percent by 2018.

The "economic stimulus" didn't do the stimulating that politicians expected it to because most of the money went to favorite political constituencies to promote parochial interests and fashionable causes rather than to the kind of projects that can revive an economy.

The reality is, the U.S. is going to need at least one more round of fiscal stimulus packages to get out of the financial trough it is in. Hopefully, this time around, the funds will be used as a real economic stimulus rather than a political vote stimulator. I agree with Laura D'Andrea Tyson, a member of the panel advising President Obama, who said at a seminar in Singapore in July 2009: "We should be planning on a contingency basis for a second round of stimulus."

The Great U.S. Recession

The 2008-2009 financial meltdown in the U.S. is shaping up as the Great Recession. With job losses rising, credit facilities diminishing and the billions of rescue dollars to save the pillars of capitalism failing, it is the longest U.S economic recession since World War II – and the worst may be yet to come.

"The recessions that follow in the wake of big financial crisis tend to last far longer than normal downturns, and to cause considerable more damage. If the United States follows the norm of recent crisis, as it has until now, output may take four years to return to its pre-crisis level. Unemployment will continue to rise for three more years, reaching 11-12 percent in 2011," according to Kenneth Rogoff, the Thomas D. Cabot professor of public policy and economics at Harvard University, and Carmen Reinhart, professor of economics at the school of Public Policy at the University of Maryland.

Contrary to popular belief, banking crises tend to be far more of an equal opportunity menace. Indeed, a failure to recognize the historical vulnerability of rich countries to financial crises lies behind the incredible conceit of Anglo-American policymakers in thinking their gold-plated systems were invulnerable.

Assuming the U.S. continues going down the tracks of past financial crises, perhaps the scariest prospect is the likely evolution of public debt, which tends to soar in the aftermath of a crisis. A base-line forecast, using the benchmark of recent past crisis, suggests that U.S. national debt will rise by $8.5 trillion from 2009 through 2011, according to Rogoff and Reinhart.

Debt rises for a variety of reasons, including bailout costs and fiscal stimulus. But the No. 1 factor is the collapse in tax revenues that inevitably accompanies a deep recession. Eight and a half trillion dollars may sound like a lot. It is more than 50 percent of U.S. national income. But if one looks at the Obama administration's budget deficit projections, with exceedingly optimistic projections on growth and bank-bailout costs, Rogoff and Reinhart think the U.S. is on track to reach that astronomical number. I actually think they are somewhat conservative in their projections because the U.S. is at the epicenter of the crisis.

This recession, which officially began in December 2007, is not only the longest and most severe, but the most devastating. More than half a million Americans, from financial analysts to factory workers, lost their jobs in November 2008 alone. Another 681,000 were added to the jobless rolls in December. Rarely has a labor downturn affected such a broad swath of income levels – and the worst is continuously coming in slow-kill mode in 2009. Some economists predict that the U.S. economy could lose as many jobs in the first six months of 2009 as it did in all of 2008. More than seven million jobs have been lost since the start of the recession in 2007, two-thirds of them since September of that year.

The current U.S. recession entered its 17th month on April 1, 2009, making it the longest economic slump since the 1930s, surpassing the 16-month downturns that ended in March 1975 and November 1982, which were the longest since 1945. The Great Depression lasted 43 months from August 1929 to March 1933 and the world experienced a two-thirds shrinkage in trade in that period. The combination of housing market, credit market and financial market collapses is a rare and unprecedented combination. Unemployment in July 2009 reached 9.4. percent.

Discussing the impact of the recession with Kevin and Mary Catherine McBride over coffee one morning, Kevin announced that he had just read something called the Top 12 Signs That America Is in a Deep Recession.

"It's so funny," he said. "I printed out the e-mail for you, Peter because I know you'll get a kick out of it." And I did. With apologies to David Letterman, here they are:

12. CEOs are playing miniature golf.

11. You receive a pre-declined credit card in the mail.

10. You go to buy a toaster oven and they give you a bank.

9. The stocks of Hotwheels and Matchbox toy car companies are trading higher than GM.

8. President Obama meets with small businesses – GE, Pfiser, Chrysler, Citigroup and GM – to discuss Stimulus Package.

7. McDonald's introduces the quarter ouncer.

6. People in Beverly Hills are firing their nannies and learning their children's names.

5. The best-paid job now is jury duty.

4. Mothers in Ethiopia are telling their kids, "Finish your plate. Do you know how many kids are starving in America?"

3. Motel Six won't leave the lights on.

2. The Mafia is laying off judges.

1. If the bank returns your check marked as "insufficient funds," you have to call them and ask if they meant yours or theirs.

"The real danger is that we don't let 2010 become 1937 over again," said Alan Blinder, a former vice chairman of the Federal Reserve. He points to a push to avoid inflation and deficit spending in 1936. "Those two things just killed the economy. We have to make sure we don't do that again."

Amity Shlaes, author of *The Forgotten Man: A New History of the Great Depression* and a senior fellow of economic history at the Council on Foreign Relations, says that massive spending had been tried in other countries, leading to "the appearance of growth, some real growth, and then a very big sorrowful morning after."

The U.S. recession that started in 2008 will probably stretch into 2011 and possibly longer, raising the need for more stimulus packages in America – at least as large as the first one consisting of $287 billion in temporary tax breaks and $500 billion in public spending and the public-private plan to rid banks of $1 trillion in toxic assets.

As this book went to print in December 2009, the U.S. Standard & Poor's 500 Stock Index had climbed about 50 percent from its low in March, while U.S. stock-market capitalization increased by almost $4 trillion during that period. As good as that looks, things look a lot better in China. The benchmark Shanghai Stock Index has been up more than 80 percent in 2009 because of a rise in property and equity markets. China is expected to return to double-digit growth by 2010, whereas America faces an unemployment epidemic.

More than 7 million jobs have been lost in the U.S. since December 2007, something not seen in the past 60 years. A third of the unemployed have now been out of work for more than two years. And the unemployment rate is not expected to top out until the U.S. economy gets strong enough to create at least 100,000 jobs a month.

In July 2009, U.S. home foreclosures set another record as more than 360,000 households drew foreclosure filings. Since January, the notices of default, auction or repossession have reached almost 2.3 million. The drastic rise has been attributed mostly to unemployment.

America has a trillion-dollar-plus budget deficit, extraordinary recession and a broken financial system, with less than 15 percent of the $787-billion stimulus package filtered into the U.S. economy.

While the U.S. economy sputters, China's hot pot simmers on. The Conference Board forecasts a 2.5 percent drop in GDP in 2009, but sees the Chinese economy growing by 7 percent for the year. Goldman Sachs puts China's number even higher at 9.4 percent for the year, well above Beijing's target of 8 percent.

China has compelled state-run banks to unleash a flood of credit, lending more in the first four months of 2009 than in all of 2008. In the meantime, China trimmed its holdings of U.S. treasury bills. Its April 2009 purchases were the smallest in 11 months since the purchases started building up in June 2008. Nevertheless, China is still the top purchaser of these U.S. debt instruments.

China is America's lead bank and largest foreign creditor, a fact that is generating anxiety in Washington. With more than $1 trillion of U.S. debt, in addition to more than $2 trillion cash, officials in Beijing are also anxious as their decision to invest in America and the dollar was more of a political decision than an economic one. But it was a conscious decision and represents the culmination of more than two decades of assiduous efforts on the part of the Chinese government and U.S, companies to bind the two economies together.

The future growth of U.S. companies will be driven by sales to Chinese consumers – as GM China has demonstrated – and at the same time provide support for China's industrial build-out. The Chinese government has actively tethered its economic and political fortunes to the U.S. With so much invested in the U.S., China can no more tolerate a severe U.S. implosion than Americans can. Any action taken by China to imperil the economic stability of the U.S. would be an act of mutually-assured destruction.

How do the two countries with the most to lose cooperate to make sure they and the rest of the world minimize the financial pain and make sure everyone benefits globally? They cooperate more with each other to stop protectionism and take a proactive-cooperative lead in global and regional organizations – and in bilateral dialogue – to learn from each other and build together as partners.

Capitalism with Communist Characteristics
Near the end of U.S. President George W. Bush's term in office he said: "I'm abandoning free-market principles to save the free-market system." It was the ultimate "Bush speak." Bailout capitalism in which profits are privatized and losses are socialized is nothing short of capitalism with communist characteristics. It works great for the bankers and the bailout artists who lined their pockets with millions until they bankrupted their banks,

insurance firms and automobile manufacturers and then got the government to put up taxpayer dollars and the Fed's printing presses to bail them out. The socialization of risk to pay for greed bankrupted Western financial institutions brought to mind Lenin's famous saying that a capitalist would sell you the rope to hang him with.

Who does the government of the people represent? The people or the corporate capitalists who get the people's money after they lose sight of good business judgment because they are blinded by their greed?

The answer is simple. The politically powerful capitalists who effectively spend millions of the people's bailout money on lobbyists to perpetuate corporate welfare and the people be damned. This form of capitalist-communism is unsustainable and cannot be allowed to continue.

"Given the possibility of bigger losses in the future, the government's evident unwillingness either to own banks or let them fail creates a heads-they-win, tails-we-lose situation. If all goes well, the bankers will win big. If the current strategy fails, taxpayers will be forced to pay for another bailout," Nobel laureate Paul Krugman wrote in one of his New York Times columns in May 2009. I share his concerns.

Few could have foreseen the paradox presented by U.S. capitalism with Chinese characteristics. Mao Zedong famously philosophized on the nature of contradictions, first in a 1937 essay, in which he stated: "The law of contradictions in things, that is, the law of the unity of opposites, is the fundamental law of nature and of society."

In China, like America, about one-third of the private entrepreneurs are members of "The Party," – Communist, Democratic or Republican – membership helps them get state finance, more protection and legitimacy.

This corrupt or predatory form of capitalism also has some obvious global implications. When foreign companies try to invest in China, or Chinese companies try to acquire holdings abroad, the decision-making process can be vitiated by arbitrary political interference, underhand dealings, kickbacks and influence-peddling.

Where has this left America? The U.S. government intervention in its own capitalist economy has made it the nation's biggest lender, insurer, auto-maker and guarantor against risk for investors.

Between financial rescue missions and the economic stimulus program, government spending accounts for a bigger share of the U.S. economy – 26 percent – than at any time since World War II. The government is financing 9 out of 10 new mortgages in the United States. People who buy cars from General Motors are buying from a company that is 60 percent owned by the government. Those who buy life insurance from AIG are buying from a company that is almost 80 percent government owned.

The big question is, how much more will the U.S. government own after the double-dip forecast for 2010? My guess is more than the Chinese government does of its capitalist enterprises because of its privatization drive.

Confucian Capitalism

America and China have more in common than either side wants to ac-knowledge. Neither trusts freewheeling capitalism and when it comes to the crunch, both governments take over industries for the political protection of the governing parties and the economic stability of their countries. Govern-ment intervention and ownership of private companies is very Confucian – a belief that public-private partnership of the wise ones will benefit the people. I don't for a moment believe in this model, as I believe government should be kept out of business and should be shrunk, not expanded by get-ting involved in the private sector. Getting government involved in business only benefits greedy self-serving capitalists at the expense of the people.

Before I address Confucian capitalism, I want to give an example that sup-ports my argument to keep government out of business at all costs. The Mustang Ranch in Nevada is a legal whorehouse and bar that was very profitable. It was busted on a variety of racketeering charges and the gov-ernment took over its daily operations. After trying to run the place for a couple of years, the ranch was put into receivership because the govern-ment operators lost money. Now, I don't want to speculate as to what hap-pened to the profits, but if the government can't run a simple cathouse and saloon, how the hell is it going to run the complicated financial services industry of America?

I witnessed and lived through a sneak preview of the U.S. government inter-vention and bailout of the pillars of U.S. capitalism during the Hong Kong stock market crash of August 1998. On a much smaller scale, to counter the short sellers and speculators that had battered Hong Kong stock prices, the Hong Kong government, with China's approval, decided to intervene in the market – and I want to emphasize stock market and not individual companies or the financial sector – with public money. It spent $15.1 billion to acquire 7.3 percent of the companies in the blue-chip Hang Seng Index. At the time, the Hong Kong government was severely criticized by free-market advocates for its intervention as a dangerous precedent. The fact is, it helped stabilize the market and then sold the stock at a substantial profit once the speculators left.

Billionaire investor George Soros, who led the attack on the Hong Kong currency, gave credit to the government for its defense of the Hong Kong dollar during the Asian crisis 11 years later in June 2009 in an interview with China Central Television.

"I actually think they [Hong Kong's finance officials] did a very great job defending the dollar, so they deserve credit," Soros said. "This is the way markets function…There was absolutely nothing wrong with it, and I don't feel any sense of guilt," he said. "This is the point people have difficulty understanding. I do speculation in the financial markets, but I do so accord-ing to the rules that prevail. If it is forbidden to speculate, I won't speculate. I am a legitimate participant in the financial markets," said Soros. He added if there were any problems, the regulators should take the blame. Problems stem from those who set the rules of the game, not from the players.

Seeing that the U.S. model of capitalism has bankrupted more than a few countries, Iceland, Ireland and Hungary being the only three willing to ad-mit to that fact by the end of 2008, there is no reason to believe developing countries will attempt to embrace Western capitalism anymore.

Brazilian President Luiz Inacio Lula da Silva summed it up nicely at the London G-20 in April 2009 when he said the global financial crisis had been created by "white-skinned people with blue eyes." Blue-eyed palefaces are responsible for saddling the world with a financial system that has crashed and will take generations to restructure and correct. The modern financial system grows out of a series of "Dutch finance" innovations in 17th-century Netherlands that traveled over the Channel where the English borrowed Dutch ideas to build a stock market, promote global trade and establish the Bank of England, going on to build a maritime empire of commerce and sea power that dominated the globe until World War II.

Dutch finance became "Anglo-Saxon capitalism." When the British system fell apart, the center of world finance crossed the water again to New York and Washington which replaced London and Amsterdam as centers of global politics and finance after Bretton Woods – all of which I discuss in great detail in *Custom Maid Knowledge*.

Walter Russell Mead, the author of *God and Gold: Britain, America and the Making of the Modern World,* summed it up best. "This financial and political system is the operating system on which the world runs: the Dutch introduced version 1.0 in about 1620; the British introduced 2.0 in about 1700; the Americans upgraded to version 3.0 in 1945, and as an operating system, it works pretty well – most of the time." China will have a major say in version 4.0.

The Chinese government owns more than two-thirds of all fixed assets like telecommunications lines, power plants, and real estate in the country. State- controlled companies represent some 70 percent of the major stock markets. And while the private sector still controls a little more than half the total economy, most China watchers believe the stimulus package will turn the tables. In other words, China would be more like America and America more like China.

The global financial meltdown could perhaps have been averted if we had listened to Confucius. Just take out the word "ruler" or "family head" from his guidelines listed in his *Analects* – a continuous collection of brief statements and short dialogues that Confucius' disciples collated from the master's teachings – and replace it with "CEO" and you have a wonderful formula for success in corporate governance.

The Hong Kong example of Confucian capitalism is a far cry from the U.S. quasi-nationalism with taxpayer dollars bailing out the country's bankrupt leading banks, insurance companies and automobile industry because of institutional incompetence. What is clear is that America's corporate demo-cratic capitalists, who repeatedly lecture China on how to run its Confucian capitalist economy, have capitulated to Confucian communist capitalism on a humongous hypocritical U.S. scale.

Markets

The market exchange – direct transactions between merchants and custom-ers – appeared gradually 3,000 or 4,000 years ago. The customer was free to buy whatever he wanted, whenever and from whomever he chose, often bargaining with the seller over price.

For several thousand years, the free market system was comprised of indi-viduals, craftsmen, traders and consumers. Capitalism, when it arose three centuries ago, was simply the same activity on a larger scale. Steam engines and electricity enabled a large number of people to work together, and cor-porations could attract a large number of small investors, who themselves became capitalists.

By the time of the French Revolution, the standard of living of the world had hardly doubled since the Roman Empire. Courtesy of capitalism, it is 150 times higher today.

Adam Smith's market never stood alone. Market economies are dependent on each other and human values more than they are on the dominance of capital. Amartya Sen, who received the 1998 Nobel Prize in economics and teaches economics and philosophy at Harvard University, wrote a new in-troduction to the 250-year anniversary edition of Adam Smith's *The Theory of Moral Sentiments* released in 2009. Smith is best known for his book *The Wealth of Nations,* but it is in *The Theory of Moral Sentiments* that he investigated the powerful role of nonprofit values. While stating that "pru-dence" was "of all virtues that which is most helpful to the "individual," Smith went on to argue that "humanity, justice, generosity, and public spirit are the qualities most useful to others." Confucian or communist capital-ism, or both?

Dr. Sen points out that Smith never used the term capitalism. What exactly is capitalism? The standard definition seems to take reliance on markets for economic transactions as a necessary qualification for an economy to be seen as capitalistic. In a similar way, dependence on the profit motive, and on individual entitlements based on private ownership, are seen as archetypal features of capitalism. However, if these are necessary requirements, are the economic systems we currently have in America and Europe genuinely capitalistic, asks Dr. Sen, when they depend on transactions that occur largely outside the markets, such as unemployment benefits, public pensions and other features of social security – and government bailouts? American capitalism and the worldwide financial system that supports it continues to survive because of the repeated government bailouts. Capitalism is definitely evolving in an open market that is becoming more protectionist and paternalistically Confucian. That is because left to their U.S. devices, these economic systems repeatedly fail to properly allocate risk.

Poor-Tasting Appetizer

The historic G-20 meeting in Washington in November 2008, on the cold Atlantic seafront, was the warm-up act to the Asia-Pacific Economic Cooperation forum that took place in Lima, Peru, a week later. The APEC meeting of leaders from 21 Pacific Rim countries that account for half the world's economy endorsed the Washington Declaration of the G-20 and pledged not to implement protectionist measures for 12 months – no matter how punishing the global downturn got. Yeah, well they lied again.

APEC 2008 was President Bush's global summit swan song before handing over the Washington reins to his successor on Jan. 20, 2009. President Obama presided over the April 2009 G-20 meeting and met his first global crisis summit head on. He grappled with the global financial issues personally with his new economic team, in contrast to what he did when he was the president-elect and sent a bi-partisan team of two out of respect to Bush and his presidency, as he did at the G-20 November 2008 summit.

When Obama got to the 2009 APEC summit in Singapore in November, he pushed the restart buttons on stoves cooking America's fusion menus. Thankfully, Obama actually understands what is being discussed and if he doesn't, he makes sure he eventually does. The same cannot be said about his predecessor.

Because of the collapse of the Doha negotiations, some APEC leaders are moving ahead with regional and bilateral agreements. China and host nation Peru did just that. China's Hu Jintao arrived in Lima two days before President Bush. Hu received an extravagant welcoming ceremony, including a procession with horses as he wrapped up a bilateral free-trade agreement with resource-rich Peru. China did the same with Thailand at APEC 2009.

It's payback time. After America repeatedly rejected China's attempts to buy Unocal or 3Com, it is only natural that China shy away from America's repeated requests that China participate in America's global rescue package. It prefers to invest at home to benefit its owncitizens. Over 114 million Chinese still live on less than $1 per day. Who can really be intellectually honest and blame China for also focusing on bilateral agreements in South and Central America, Africa, Asia and the Middle East?

China studied the 1997 Asian financial crisis even though it suffered the least from it. While America stood by and did nothing other than offer polite advice and destructive IMF prescriptions to the countries that suffered most, China made sure there was no replay. It coordinated and engineered an $80 billion East Asian states self-insurance plan against financial crisis, dissing the IMF.

Sweeping out Bush and his gang of self-serving oiligarchs was a millennium cathartic experience, much like a session at any good spa in China – and actually throughout Asia and most civilized communities in America and Europe. Having experienced the pleasures of Asia's spa cleansing on more than one occasion – and many with U.S. elected officials – is something everyone should experience. Sweating out and sweeping away the nonsense and political spin we are brought up with by parents, family, education system, religious beliefs and party dictates must be done in favor of clean, unbiased, objective ideas and political philosophies untainted by preconceived notions of ideal economic model, political or religious beliefs and convictions, regardless of sexual orientation, gender, ethnic grouping or color.

Political pollution, not only in America and China, is what has created not only a global climate and financial crisis – but an overburdened taxpayer leaving a legacy of over-tax-saddled grandchildren. Not a nice picture when so many in America are moving back in with parents and grandparents.

How are they realistically going to make those tax payments when their parents, and grandparents homes will have to be sold to pay probate taxes and their parents and grandparents' debts? Why isn't this calamity being addressed today? Meanwhile, Chinese families, who have been living with each other for centuries, can't wait to get away from not only the family home, but village, province, and in many cases country. Who's on the right roll in this picture?

A capitalistic America that believes in free enterprise, individualism, minimal government interference – and, God forbid, intervention – allows the government to bail out and become a shareholder in America's financial pillars of capitalism. AIG, Bank of America, Bear Stearns, Citibank, Fannie, Freddie, Wachovia, Washington Mutual. And guess who is picking up the tab? American taxpayers, as their homes are foreclosed, their fuel and food prices and neighborhood crime rise and the standard of their children and grandchildren's education plummets. Not a pretty picture of the starving eagle.

The lesson is that, when government pollutes capital markets by implicitly guaranteeing debt, market participants recognize that they will be protected if the enterprise runs into difficulty. There are exceptions. Lehman Brothers overplayed this hand. That is why foreign investors, including the People's Bank of China, hold more than $1.3 trillion in Fannie and Freddie bonds alone.

The subprime lending crisis that started the financial tsunami is at its base a crisis of markets tainted by government intervention, along with the failure of the Federal Reserve to tighten monetary policy. It is also a failure of regulation to effectively monitor lending practices in the subprime market.

China's financial sector is far more tainted by market socialism than is the U.S. market. But at least China calls a spade a spade and deals with the matter on its terms for its people, and the world be damned. China is heavily involved in credit allocation, and various entities hold large stakes in the big banks. Most listed stocks are state-owned enterprises, and political connections are essential in entering the capital markets. Consequently, corruption is a major problem.

Both America and China must keep in mind – and be periodically reminded – of their taxpaying public that keeps them in power. Governments in America and China are swayed by the well-connected lobbyists with *guanxi*. It is time America and China, and the respective global constituencies they carry, agree to move to a global financial system where owners and investors, not taxpayers, bear responsibility for their losses, as that creates rather than destroys wealth.

Fused Recipe

The Sino-U.S. road map toward achieving consensus on the lofty strategic goals within a mutually agreed timeframe is the great millennium challenge. When the world's sole superpower and the biggest developing giant talk to each other to resolve a wide range of bilateral issues with global implications – there is hope, especially when they agree that America needs to rein in its appetite for cheap foreign imports and stem its insane borrowing binge.

This joint vision to engage in ongoing intelligent dialogue to resolve complex economic, military and political issues is a major constructive adjustment for America.

Anything else is self-destructive and would create a magnitude 9 global economic earthquake and tsunami. The shock waves would rupture corporate America. A stronger yuan would make household-name brand companies like General Motors, Microsoft, Boeing or even Exxon-Mobil prime takeover candidates for the acquisitive Chinese with their trillions of excess dollars.

The diplomatic significance of the December 2006 high-level U.S. delegation to China was that it only went to China. Not Japan, South Korea, or any other major U.S. trading partner in Asia. There is no doubt that China is the foremost strategic global partner for America, especially after it surpassed Mexico in 2006 as the No. 2 U.S. trading partner.

The weak yen has left Japan mired in its "zombie" strategies of the past. China knows this, and until the yen rises sharply, the yuan won't either. The fact is America is living unsustainably beyond its means. Consumer spending accounts for 70 percent of the U.S. economy. A stronger Chinese currency won't change the unbalanced nature of U.S. growth. We must remember that the Plaza Accord of 1985, which sharply weakened the dollar versus the yen, did little to improve the U.S. balance of payments. Instead, it contributed to the asset bubble that led to Japan's lost decade of the '90s. Is it any wonder that China is in no rush? To try and push China into an unjustified economic crisis with the threat of protectionism is not only short-sighted – it won't work, is self-destructive for America, and is a waste of time and taxpayer dollars.

Sky-Scraping Smokestacks

New York skyscrapers, like Detroit's Big Three automakers, symbolized America's almighty meteoric rise as a world power. It's iconic Empire State and Chrysler buildings – and let us not forget the World Trade Center Twin-Towers – in New York city and Sears Tower, now the Willis Tower in Chicago, at one time the world's tallest buildings, symbolized power, modernity and economic wealth that other countries emulated as soon has they had the financial ability to do so. This is most noticeable today in Asia where the world's tallest buildings seem to reach up higher each decade.

Taiwan's 508 meter-high Taipei 101 is Asia's current tallest , with Shanghai doing its utmost to surpass it. Steve Chicorel who lives a few blocks away, marvels at the engineering feat it represents, but like me is concerned about people's safety in the top floors should a fire break out. "The one thing 9/11 taught us that people seem to have forgotten, is that it is impossible for people to get down to the ground floor safely or for firemen to reach them in time. I don't understand why buildings are allowed to be built to a height that people's lives are deliberately put in danger," Steve lamented as we compared our different life styles in Asia. Mine living in a quite village in a scenic cove, a dramatic contrast to his noisy city lifestyle.

The number of skyscrapers going up in every major city in China today surpasses anything in New York in terms of height and energy consumption. China is in the middle of the greatest building boom in human history. Six of the world's 10 tallest buildings completed in 2008 were in the mainland. While Dubai and other cities in the Middle East are building a handful of lofty structures, nothing can compare with the mainland for the sheer mass of super towers being planned or under construction. It is estimated China will erect up to 50,000 new skyscrapers by 2025. Buildings in China will account for a quarter of the mainland's energy consumption. Over 50 percent of the square footage under construction globally in 2009 was in China.

In the 1990s I lived in Shanghai and one of my clients was the Lujiazui financial district in Pudong that was determined to build China's tallest building – hopefully Asia's and then the worlds'. It achieved its first objective with the Shanghai World Financial Center which stands at 492 meters. At the time I was approached by Donald Trump, who was determined to build the world's tallest building, a Norman Foster design. His original plan was to build it in Tokyo Bay. When those plans fell through, I was contacted to see if he could build it in Shanghai. We had several meetings in New York and his representatives spent weeks in Shanghai trying to find a suitable location, of which there were many, and mutually acceptable financial terms, of which there were none.

The lessons I learned from the experience about the environmental degradation caused by their construction, ensuing traffic pollution and dangers these sky-high human smokestacks pose to humanity stunned me.

"The energy needed to heat, cool, light and operate the elevators alone in these buildings, all coal-powered, is phenomenal," I said to Steve Chicorel as we continued our discussion on my three-story village house rooftop. "People living in and around these buildings literally have their heads in polluted clouds of toxins and viruses circulated by the ventilation systems in and around the buildings. The same polluting ventilation systems and shafts then double-up as chimneys to help fire and smoke spread rapidly if a fire breaks out," I added. "There is no fire equipment or technology that I know of that can save people on the higher floors. They are effectively signing their death warrants by moving in – and that of the planet they live on."

Pax Americana is Passé
The U.S.-led, post-World War II Euro-American-centered world executive committee is done and over, thanks to America's failure to adhere to the principles of the Founding Fathers. Compromised national and global leadership, more than $10-trillion in debt and the gas lighter that sparked the global financial crisis in its hands, have all contributed to America's shining

city upon the hill losing its luster.

Concerns about U.S. mismanagement was pointedly expressed by China'sVice Premier Wang Qishan in December 2008 when he said: "The teachers have much explaining to do."

The world's sole superpower abused its global sheriff's role with unnecessary wars, failed financial instruments and basic misreading of people's needs – at home and abroad. America is no longer the Mecca of modernity, innovation and economic prowess. The era when America was the global locomotive that dictated the rules of international trade, finance and political affairs is over.

America is now perceived as a moral and political failure, as well as a financial and capitalist catastrophe by the developing world. China, on the other hand, because of its centrally controlled prudent fiscal, development and capitalist model that endowed it with more than $2 trillion in reserves, is fast becoming a viable and more acceptable alternative model. Cash-rich China is in a much stronger geopolitical position than cash-strapped America to move aggressively in the developing world and gain access to their commodities and natural resources.

The new world order that will succeed Pax Americana is one in which China will play a dominant and leading role, if for no other reason than it is the biggest holder of U.S. government bonds, accounting for more than 35 percent of the total held by foreign central banks. It is common knowledge in any bankruptcy proceeding that the lead creditor has a lot to say and the debtor has to listen, whether they like it or not. America must accept the fact that its failure to heed the admonitions of the Founding Fathers of the Republic has rendered it morally impotent.

Most people in Japan, South Korea and China favor a Northeast Asian free trade area including the three countries. Most Americans, on the other hand, are opposed to regional or bilateral agreements.

China must be viewed as a partner, not a competitor. If America insists on viewing China as a competitor, it will lose the competition. It already has. America has to accept China as a willing collaborative partner. America can no longer ignore the more than 230 years of U.S. business success in China and the political collaboration that goes hand in hand with that success. U.S. exports to China have grown much faster than to any other trading partner. In 2007 they grew by 18 percent and since 2000 they have grown by 300 percent. The U.S. is enjoying a resurgence in exports to China, which is driving productivity gains at a time when the U.S. economy critically needs it. The good Sino-U.S. relationship that exists today is a foreign policy success, built since January 1, 1979, when the two countries established diplomatic relations.

The 2008 Olympics in Beijing showcased China's ascendancy, not only as a sporting powerhouse with its record haul of gold medals, but in the global competition for economic supremacy. The Wall Street financial meltdown that cast its depressive shadow on the global economy has made capitalist America a "bailout nation" as communist China has become the center of U.S. capital and the new Confucian capitalism. China is fast becoming the world's economic leader.

America is losing its perch of global supremacy. In 2000, U.S. stock exchanges accounted for about half the value of global stock markets; at the beginning of 2008, they accounted for just 33 percent – and shrinking. The Chinese economy has been doubling in size every 10 years since 1978. In contrast, it takes the U.S. economy about two decades to double in size.

Not all is lost. America is still the head chef, but must now learn to share the kitchen with China if it wants to protect and preserve its considerable global stake holding for not only the country, but for all of its citizens, individual and corporate.

America's resilience, its fighting pioneer spirit, will-power and determination to win is engraved in the fabric of the country's inherent makeup and culture – the Constitution and Bill of Rights. America's founding ideals of openness, tolerance, diversity, equality and freedom will allow it to remain the head chef planning future geopolitical menus. No one should count it out because of its current hopeless decline, especially when no one, including China, is willing so far to step up to the plate to replace America. Questioning and challenging America is a far cry from taking over or replacing it. America can still come out of the current crisis on top of the ongoing geopolitical cook-off. The menu of geopolitical issues on the table is extensive and must be addressed honestly and harmoniously.

America's long-term spirit of determination to win, especially when it comes to dealing with China and its business and political culture, is represented by the National Football League. Despite dropping the China Bowl between the New England Patriots and Seattle Seahawks in 2007 and again in 2009, the NFL – which dwarfs other professional American sports leagues in revenues and viewership – is still chomping at the bit for the hearts and minds of Chinese sports fans. It is now planning a preseason game in either Beijing or Shanghai in the summer of 2011.

America, like the NFL, can take serious economic, political, military and terrorist body blows and bounce back, thanks to its founding cornerstones. A contemporary reminder is the reopening of the Statue of Liberty to the public on July 4, 2009, eight years after the 9/11 attacks. Another reminder: The last 10-meter steel beam to be removed from the rubble of the World Trade Center after those attacks has been returned to Ground Zero, festooned with commemorative graffiti and duct-taped with posters and photographs. The column will be part of a permanent exhibit in a planned National September Memorial and Museum.

Another reaffirming moment for America came when President Barack Obama was awarded the 2009 Nobel Peace Prize.

"Let me be clear," Obama said when he learned of his controversial selection. "I do not view it as recognition of my own accomplishments, but rather as an affirmation of American leadership on behalf of aspirations held by people in all nations.

"I will accept this award as a call to action, a call for all nations to confront the challenges of the 21st century."

The launch of America's Ares I-X rocket to the moon a few weeks later is just the latest millennium reminder.

Warren Buffett's decision to pay $26 billion to buy up the remaining three-quarters of Burlington Northern Santa Fe Corp, America's No. 1 railroad by revenue – a hefty 31.5 percent premium over BNSF's closing stock price, and 18 times the railway's estimated 2010 earnings – is a bet the nation's largest rail company will benefit from a recovering U.S. economy. It is another prime example of America's entrepreneurial spirit, resilience and determination.

"It's an all-in wager on the economic future of the United States," said Buffett, who has been building up his rail holdings for several years. "I love these bets." His All American bets include Coca Cola and American Express, two companies which Buffett's $150 billion Berkshire company is the largest shareholder.

He told the Burlington Northern employees that he would not sell the railroad's assets to pay debt and planned to continue investing in the company's infrastructure.

"I'd be crazy if we didn't," Buffett said. "We're not going to buy a business and starve it."

Buffett is betting that trains and the coal that power them will replace trucks and fossil fuel as America comes to grips with the reality of global warming. I agree. I have said on more than one occasion, in my previous books and blogs, that when possible, I prefer to travel by train because of the people and landscapes. Another major reason to travel by train is that it cuts carbon emissions. Shipping goods by train is also cheaper and cleaner than shipping them by truck

American power and determination is rooted in the ideals and principles laid down by the Founding Fathers, and that determination is still alive today. I was reminded of that spirit and determination at a book talk I gave in 2008 at the Westlake Yacht Club in Southern California, which helped sponsor an attempt by Zac Sunderland to become the youngest person ever to sail around the world alone. Sunderland completed his historic voyage in July 2009, the first to accomplish the feat under the age of 18.

"Amazing," I remarked at the time to the club's Michael Broggie, as Sunderland was sailing the Pacific on the first leg of the voyage. "What a great way to remind the world of the American spirit, determination and values."

Broggie was a member of the production team that produced *Poor Charlie's*

Almanack, The Wit and Wisdom of Charles T. Munger, Warren Buffett's partner. Buffett wrote the foreward. Broggie is also an author in his own right and has written several books about trains, including those at Disneyland.

Mike Perham, the British teen who is a few months younger than Zac, completed his solo sail around the world without assistance one month after Zac in August 2009, and reaffirmed the Anglo-American ideals of determination and resilience enshrined in the Magna Carta and Constitution.

What really brought the point home to me was the four-day Hong Kong port call in December 2009 of China's missile frigates Zhoushan and Xuzhou, back from their mission in the pirate-infested waters off Somalia. The monotomy of the four-month mission was a greater challenge to the PLA Navy than the pirates. The biggest complaint of the sailors was the length of time at sea with nothing to do.

"It's very easy to feel sick after drifting endlessly on the high seas for more than four months … We found that we had to deal with many more practical difficulties than we had imagined," said Zeng Liang, a lieutenant colonel aboard the Xuzhou.

The knowledge and ability to travel across high seas for extended periods of time is inbred in the Anglo Saxon genes. It has been practiced, perfected and the skills passed on to subsequent generations for centuries without interruption – Zac Sunderland and Mike Perham being the latest examples. The Chinese, on the other hand, had the ability to circumnavigate the globe before Anglo Saxons – and even before Christ was born. This was best exemplified by Admiral Zheng and his global circumnavigational voyages, which I discuss at length in *Custom Maid Knowledge,* before China decided to dry dock its overseas expeditions and burn its vast fleet of high sea vessels in the 16th century in a political power struggle. China's return as a global naval power came about only when it re-emerged as a world power in the 20th century.

The America's Cup race is the premier sailing competition. The 2010 race with America's trimaran yacht sponsored by BMW Oracle exemplifies not only America's creativity, spirit and determination to win, but what global sport competitions should be – environmentally sensitive and friendly. Formula 1 should take a page from America's Cup and learn how to put on races that address climate change now that its gas-guzzling teams and sponsors have dropped out.

China is re-emerging as a global seafaring power and it won't be too long before they it be an America's Cup contender.

The U.S., not withstanding the litany of foreign and domestic policy blunders that have bogged it down in two current wars and the near-total meltdown of the global economy, still commands credibility, respect and admiration around the world.

Indeed, China is one of those admirers, but Beijing is not blind to the blunders of America's career politicians. As China ascends, America can only help itself by forging a strong cooperative partnership for the future. The time for fear-mongering and China-bashing is finished. It's time for Washington to see China as part of the solution and not the problem. America must begin – sooner rather than later – to take the long-term view of its beneficial relationship with China.

Garbage Disposal

America, the world's No. 1 consumer society, has also become the world's No. 1 garbage disposal. That is why in America's creative manufacturing days in the '50s, garbage disposals were invented in America. Americans throw away a lot of their money as garbage, especially food. The Chinese gladly buy America's garbage for a song and then recycle it back to America at a profit.

From used clothes to computers, most of it manufactured in China in the first place, Americans, discarded garbage finds its way back to China, gets refurbished and recycled back to the U.S. There has to be a change of cultural mindset – recalibrating outdated ideas of lifestyles, credit and savings – to start getting close to closing the U.S.-China trade gap.

A good example of what America can do with its garbage when the entrepreneurial spirit of the Founding Fathers is applied to 21st century America, is clearly visible in the sleepy East Texas town of Huntsville, 110 kilometers north of Houston. Quirky homes for the poor made out of discarded materials. Roofs made of license plates, ceilings made of picture frames.

A lot more can be done. Consumers are on the frontline of the global warming war and can make the real difference by changing consumption and disposal habits – while politicians do what they do best – shoot the bull.

Over-Steamed Financial Bully

Former U.S. Treasury Secretary Henry Paulson, like most bankers, didn't always get it right – short term or long term. In May 2008 he predicted that the credit crisis, then in its ninth month, was probably more than half over and said the U.S. economy would keep growing.

"We are closer to the end of this problem than we are at the beginning," Paulson said in a television interview.

The former head of Goldman Sachs was echoing the CEOs of other Wall Street firms including JP Morgan Chase and Lehman Brothers in viewing the credit turmoil as nearer the end. Nothing could have been further from the truth. Is it any wonder America is in trouble and the Chinese take whatever economic predictions America makes with a grain of salt?

"America has to be nice to the countries that lend it money," warned Gao Xiqing, president of the China Investment Corp., which manages $200 billion of the country's foreign assets. Americans have to stop believing they can live on other people's money forever – with attitude.

America should know by now that it will not get far with China by giving it a public lecture in the media. The Chinese do not like "losing face." Polite diplomacy and magnanimity are a lot more productive.

It is time for America to get its own financial house in order instead of badgering China and other sovereign nations to disclose their secretive workings, holdings and become more transparent. It is America that must first tackle the issue of financial transparency, or rather the lack of, in the workings of unregulated financial U.S. institutions. Financial deregulation that started in the 1980s when I was a lawyer-banker in the U.S. has gotten completely out of control in the opening decade of the 21st century.

Paulson is an old China hand who has contributed greatly to the success of the Strategic Economic Dialogue. His successor in the Obama administration, Timothy F. Geithner, is not only a close ally of Paulson, but is no stranger to the dialogue or China either. He reportedly speaks Putonghua fluently. So let's get down and rap.

One-on-One-Ganbei

Ganbei, bottoms up, down the hatch. It is time the U.S. and China sit down and hoist a few and get down to real business. Not the way former Assistant Secretary of State for East Asian and Pacific Affairs Christopher Hill did with his North Korean counterpart at the Waldorf Astoria Hotel in New York in early 2007, when both staggered out of the hotel and the talks collapsed notwithstanding their drunken pronouncements of success, but civil toasts in constructive moderation. The thought that Hill is now the U.S. ambassador to Iraq does give me a hangover.

It is sobering to see that even though anti-Beijing politicians control both the House and Senate, Sino-U.S. relations appear to be heading into calmer seas. House Speaker Nancy Pelosi, who opposed normal trading relations, was against Beijing being awarded the 2008 Olympics. She has also criticized China's human rights record, and supports Taiwan. The fact that U.S. policy toward China has become more cordial as the 2009 Democratic-controlled Congress got down to business with a Democratic president is encouraging. The U.S. is on the right Sino-U.S. relations track. There will be bumps in the road, but as long as they continue on the constructive dialogue trajectory they embarked on in 2009 – there is hope that the relationship will blossom and bear fruit and the end of the arduous winding road and vine.

Drawing a line in the political sand and pulling the trigger on sanctions as has been the past practice of Washington may seem like smart economic policy, but it is not. America's harsher rhetoric toward China and its preoccupation with shortsighted domestic issues only benefited China, which has been boosting its own diplomatic profile globally – especially in Asia and the developing world – at America's expense.

America and China must initiate an end to the economic and political terrorism that permeates Sino-U.S. relations today. America's paranoia of economic encirclement by China, like China's fear of American military encirclement, must be abandoned by both if they are to lead a harmonious interlocal world in the 21st century and beyond. Dialogue between American and Chinese leaders is essential to avoid a military or economic confrontation. A constructive first step is for America to sign a "fourth communiqué" with China to confirm China's sovereignty over Taiwan. The U.S. has signed three communiqués with China pledging its support of a one-China policy and opposing Taiwanese independence. But it still pledges to come to Taiwan's defense if China were to attack. The fourth communiqué must dispose of that policy once and for all.

America has to acknowledge that China is emerging in the 21st century as a global superpower for the third time. The first was with the Jesuit missions of the 16th century; the second with Britain during the Opium Wars of the 19th century. In the 19th century, the imperialist West, led by Britain, famously carried out a three-way trade: Opium was sold to China for silver currency, which was used to buy tea in India, which was then shipped to Britain for consumption. When China tried to stop the sale and importation of opium, war erupted. The current third encounter, the "dollar-yuan war" will be longer lasting than the first two.

"China's Peaceful Rise" describes its non-ideological long-term foreign policy that contrasts dramatically from America's short-term "containment" policy. It can prevent the current inevitable conflict if Chinese values are acknowledged and accepted. The current mistrust and hostility that permeates the Sino-U.S. relationship must be replaced with a bedrock policy of bilateral and global partnership. As it stands, the political establishment in Washington is more of a threat to America than China.

America and China must take a realistic and pragmatic approach to forging their strategic alliance. There has to be a fusion of military thought and might – a meaningful engagement with the goal of achieving pan-Pacific integration. A union of peaceful and prosperous ideas with regional as well as global appeal will benefit all humanity.

Arnold J. Toynbee concluded in his definitive *A Study of History* that the ultimate cause of imperial collapse was "suicidal statecraft." The phrase applies to the policies pursued by America today domestically and toward China in particular. America's efforts to contain China and dissuade it from seeking to become a regional power have had the opposite effect. In December 2005, China launched the first East Asian Summit, which excluded America. China follows the advice of its ancient strategic guru Sun Tze, who taught that the best way to win is to let your rival defeat himself America should heed the words of its 2005 Nobel laureate, Thomas C. Schelling, a political economist who said it was in the best long-term interest of parties to foster cooperation rather than conflict. His 1960 book, *The Strategy of Conflict*, pointed out that a party could have long-term success by giving up some short-term advantages, even if that meant worsening its own options. By making concessions, the stronger party could build trust with the other party and that long-term relationship could be more beneficial to both.

Chapter 6

Chinese Banquet – Sweet and Sour Hotpots

There is a rank due to the United States among nations which will be withheld, if not absolutely lost, by the reputation of weakness.
– George Washington

China at Center Stage

China means "Middle Kingdom" or "Central Country" and Mao Zedong, modern China's founding father, is central to the state's patriotic and economic values. Mao quotes are recited by China's leaders, Mao-themed restaurants are the rage and Mao statutes are being feverishly erected across the mainland. One of my favorites is a 32-meter bust of a young Mao with a George Washingtonesque '60s longish mod hairdo in Changsha.

In a country that does not look or feel communist most of the time, the Communist Party is command central driving assertive nationalism and economic growth while encouraging nationalist intellectuals to express their anti-Western sentiments. One of the most prominent, Wang Xiaodong, says China should stop buying U.S. Treasuries and put the money into domestic infrastructure, defense and social security – a move that could quickly turn America's recession into a depression. He also rejects the Central Bank's support for creating a new currency run by the International Monetary Fund, as Wang believes it is to America's advantage. "Isn't the IMF also under the control of the United States?" he asks?

China has also become the global central bank. It is definitely living up to its name as its global financial role increases. It already is the No. 1 or No. 2 trading partner of virtually every country in Southeast Asia.

China's huge foreign reserves forced the spotlight at the G-20 Washington, London and Pittsburgh summits to be shined on Beijing to step up and take a bigger financial role in addressing the global economic crisis. Because China holds the biggest inventory of foreign exchange reserves in the world, and because it looks to be one of the few major economies to show significant growth in the near future, it was urged to boost the resources of the IMF. Pressure was brought to bear on China because Japan, which holds $1 trillion in foreign reserves – the second-largest cache – pledged $100 billion in loans to the IMF.

China is reluctant to give huge loans to the IMF because some of the European countries that would benefit from Beijing's contribution have been outspoken critics of China. Yu Yongding, president of the Institute of World Economics and Politics at the Chinese Academy of Social Sciences and formal central bank advisor, summed up China's perspective. "Their pitches are even higher than some Western countries sometimes when they protest against China," said Yu. "We have no reason to help them."

China is ranked 100 out of 192 U.N. members in terms of per-capita GDP despite the fact that it is the third-biggest economy in the world after the U.S. and Japan. Many of the troubled countries the IMF wants to rescue have a per-capita income that is much higher than that of the average Chinese. They have also enjoyed at least one decade of economic prosperity and their living standards are still far higher than China's. "If we do so, it will seem like the poor is rescuing the rich wouldn't it?" asked Yu.

"Even if China decides to inject a large sum of money, it is pointless to increase its weight in the international financial organization," said Yu. That is because the U.S. still holds veto rights in the decision-making process of the IMF. "The most substantial step, if any, should be the removal of the U.S.' right to veto," said Yu, "But it is a difficult task," he concluded.

China announced at the opening of the G-20 Washington summit that in addition to the $586-billion economic stimulus package it announced to bolster domestic demand and consumption, it had offered $500 million in aid to financially teetering Pakistan, calling it "an urgent agreement based on the countries' long-term friendly relations," and that it was prepared to do more globally once it had a say proportionate to its size and financial clout. China also demanded the abolition of protectionist legislation in America and Europe that limits its export ability.

China wants the global trust and respect it thinks it justifiably deserves. It is frustrated and angry that despite all its economic progress, the "developed world," led by America, is denying it the proper respectful place at the table, yet alone the head of the table alongside America where it belongs. America can no longer take for granted a world leadership role in capitalist banking, finance, insurance and automotive industries. America became arrogantly and belligerently drunk with its own power, destroying the global financial markets and world economy in the process. All China wants is its fair say in multilateral economic and political organizations because of its rapidly growing economy.

China's New Deal

China's announcement that it would pump $586-billion into infrastructure projects and other stimulus measures to bolster domestic demand and shore up its weakening economy five days ahead of the December 2008 G-20 session in Washington which gave global stock markets a limited boost, highlighted Beijing's global financial muscle and its determination to treat the financial crisis with a responsible and prudent attitude. It also put America on notice that China can contribute to global stability and that it wants to play a bigger role with America and Europe in running the world economy.

"The Chinese government will continue to take effective measures to strengthen macroeconomic control and stimulate consumer spending within the country, transform its economic structure and raise rural income in order to maintain stable economic growth and stabilize the world economy," said President Hu Jintao when the stimulus package was announced. Hu advised America and the world at large to learn from the global financial crisis and overhaul the existing financial architecture and encourage regional as well as global cooperation. He also called for increased coordinated efforts to regulate the world's financial sector by defining credit-rating standards, stepping up monitoring for global capital flow, and boosting the transparency of financial products and markets.

Beijing's stimulus package prompted regional Chinese governments to launch or speed up their own stimulus plans. Hubei announced it would spend over 500 billion yuan to build nine eco-cities around its capital Wuhan by 2020. Guangdong earmarked 2.3 trillion yuan for infrastructure projects and upgrading the manufacturing sector, while Shanghai announced it was expediting the construction of several infrastructure projects worth more than 500 billion yuan through 2010. Hainan, Hong Kong and other provinces announced less ambitious spending plans but which collectively added up to billions more.

The stimulus package amounts to one-sixth of China's annual economic output. Not a concern for China with its $2 trillion in foreign reserves and a reported fiscal surplus of $175 billion in the first half of 2008. China's foreign reserves are expected to grow by $218 billion in 2009, the smallest increase since 2005, after leaping by $419 billion in 2008 and by $462 billion in 2007. The huge policy stimulus is expected to keep the Chinese economy rising at a respectable rate in 2009 and 2010, but a robust recovery is unlikely given global weakness and soft non-government investment.

China's immediate main aim is to keep its economy from slowing down too much too fast in order to avoid social and political instability. Tens of thousands of Chinese factories have closed down as export orders evaporate. China faces a grim and worsening unemployment market as jobless workers strike, protest and riot. Stabilizing employment at home is China's top priority. China's phenomenal growth to date was based on exports and investment. China's economic output grew by 11.9 percent in 2007, 9 percent in 2008, although the economy expanded only 6.8 percent in the fourth quarter of 2008 compared to the same period in 2007, the lowest rate in seven years. It is projected to drop as low as 6.5 percent or lower in 2009 by some economists, but can achieve the 8 percent growth the government has targeted. Although such numbers would be music to any U.S. politician's ears, few countries, China included, can absorb a more than 3 percentage point fall in annual growth without problems.

To make matters worse, some of Beijing's economic stimulus money is being wasted on projects for which local governments may never be able to repay the mainland's central bank, chief Zhou Xiaochuan warned in July 2009. There is no proper way for local governments to raise money. That meant they resorted to providing hidden guarantees for development projects or used their investment arms to secure bank loans. No proper check-and-balance mechanism is in place. To better monitor the credit risk, Zhou favors changing mainland laws to allow local governments to issue bonds. "It is better to open the front door than to drive people to walk through the back door or jump through the window," he concluded.

China's trade picture at the end of 2008 plunged into negative territory for the first time in seven years. In November 2008, exports came in 2.2 percent below November 2007. China has felt the pain of the global credit crunch harder than expected. To make matters worse, China experienced a 36 percent fall to $5.3 billion in foreign direct investment over the same period as foreign investors showed they no longer find China attractive as the yuan appreciates.

Although China has benefited from its liberalization of trade and investment policies, it recognizes and is concerned that much of the benefit has gone to foreign invested or owned firms that account for more than 50 percent of exports. These firms do not cater to the domestic market. It is the state or quasi-state enterprises that cater to the domestic market.

The government hopes its stimulus package will fire-up consumer spending to make domestic consumption the engine of sustained growth. Household consumption made up more than half of China's GDP in the 1980s. Today it contributes less than a third. Chinese household savings have been as high as a quarter of disposable income. Corporate and government savings have also soared. China has been saving close to 60 percent of GDP.

China announced in May 2009 a draft plan to allow local and foreign firms to launch consumer-finance companies so that Chinese consumers can have an additional channel to finance the purchase of durable goods, travel and education. It will be interesting to see if these lending institutions will work. Going into debt to buy a television or go on vacation hasn't been the Chinese way. Easily available consumer loans may change that, but savings habits are deeply rooted and I doubt they will change any time soon.

China is embarking on a major policy shift with initiatives to shift growth from focusing on capital investment to a more sustainable model that gives domestic consumption a more important role. But the transition from an export-led model involves a long restructuring of the financial system and household behaviour, and a major turn away from political structures and industrial policies that powered growth in the past.

To jump-start consumer spending, farmers are now allowed to secure a collective bank loan using their farmland as collateral, a groundbreaking deal considering such loans had been illegal. Both the Rural Land Contracting Law passed by the National People's Congress in 2003 and the Property Law in 2007 forbid the use as collateral of operational rights to farmland. The government has given tacit approval to introduce an experiment allowing farmers to leverage their land for loans.

If 93.3 million hectares of farmland nationwide could be used as collateral for bank loans, rural families could enjoy up to a trillion yuan worth of loans – a massive boost to China's rural economy.

Another booster to lift the Chinese economy was a billion-dollar designer name brand sale held in Macau in February 2009 that lured thousands of cashed-up women from the Pearl River Delta. The fair's advertisement featured two women fighting over a handbag.

The market for luxury goods, art, furniture, top-dollar jewelry, gems and fine wine has made a tectonic shift from New York, London and Geneva to China. Sotheby's, the world's largest publicly traded art-auction house, and Christie's International, have moved their premier auctions to Hong Kong. Mainlanders buy the priciest antiques, wines, oil paintings by masters and contemporary art. This was highlighted when a Chinese buyer from Hong Kong bought Michael Jackson's iconic white glove that the King of Pop wore when he premiered his trademark "moonwalk" in 1983.

The two-year stimulus package, which includes tax cuts, loosening of credit and government spending through 2010, includes construction of low-income housing, transportation systems, rural infrastructure, technological innovation and disaster relief in the hope it will boost consumer spending. In other words, China spends its stimulus dollars on goods and services, unlike America that is investing stimulus dollars to clean up financial institutions, balance sheets. China's economic stimulus package also benefits U.S. multinationals doing business in China, which will have a positive effect in America. The most important part of the Chinese stimulus package is the educational and charitable component.

Education Stimulus Bar
China has called for the formulation of an education reform plan that will focus on improving rural education, vocational training and teachers' welfare, citing the global crisis as a call to arms to bolster education. The 2009 to 2020 evolving educational plan will take into account the nation's evolving population structure, rural-urban wealth gap and rural-urban migration, and meet the talent requirements for industrialization, urbanization and modernization.

The central government will create 50,000 teaching jobs in the country's backwater regions in a double-barrel effort to help fresh graduates get jobs and improve educational standards in rural areas. The 50,000 posts, for "special vacancy" teachers, are in addition to a three-year initiative from 2006 to send 60,000 young college graduates to teach at grass-roots schools to bolster the level of teaching. Shouldn't America be doing the same?

Students in rural areas of China, like America, have been increasingly failing to get access to quality education as the widening gap between urban and rural salaries and better working conditions lures many qualified rural teachers to more promising jobs in the cities.

Premier Wen Jiabao said educational planners must be prepared to shatter old mindsets and structures and be daring in exploring reforms in school management, pedagogy and assessment. "Education will take a prominent position as we seek to mitigate the impact of the global financial crisis on our economy," Wen said. "Education has become the cornerstone of national development" – music to my ears. I advocated that America do the same in my 2007 book *Custom Maid Knowledge*. Why isn't America, like China, investing in an education stimulus program that educates its citizens in the ways to acquire the knowledge and the tools necessary to compete in an interlocal economy instead of pumping $1 trillion of newly printed money to salvage failing, greedy financial institutions and short-sighted automobile manufacturers?

Chinese do not have the religious, sexual or moral hang-ups of Americans when it comes to earning a living and will do what it takes to make ends meet. Pole dancing is one such example. In America it means girlie bars and sex. In China it means entertainment, exercise and work. A good number of the unemployed in China are taking up pole dancing as a way to make a living – guys and gals.

A group of overweight people aged 18 to 28 and weighing between 100 and 225 kilograms in Zhengzhou, the capital of Henan province, have even formed a dance troupe called "Pang Pang," meaning fat in Chinese, to dance and sing commercially around the country.

China has set the bar for America and other countries to follow. China's New Deal FDR economic model to boost local and global economic stability is one that America and the rest of the world should also adopt. The fundamental solution to today's global financial crisis lies in the plugging of America's deficits with China's savings. America has to save more as China spends more and America has to educate more just to keep up.

China is in effect telling America and the West that their financial and economic models do not work as well as China's. For the first time, China has the credentials to articulate and showcase its financial and economic model on a world stage with the world listening to its sermon of "non-interference" assistance, a dramatic contrast to America's "interference" model.

Charitable Stimulus

China announced in early January 2009 that it would issue more than 9 billion yuan in special subsidies to the needy in the lead-up to the Chinese New Year as the ongoing global financial crisis further eroded living standards. There are 74 million Chinese living below the poverty level that were eligible. In China the poverty level is an annual income of less than 1,067 yuan – a little higher in cities. Impoverished urban dwellers received 150 yuan each, while rural residents received 100 yuan because of their lower living costs. Those who either joined the Communist Party before 1949 or made a special contribution to the country but are still living in poverty received 180 yuan each.

Many also received additional support from their provincial and city governments. China, like the U.S., has a central/federal government made up of provincial states and cities. One such city, Chengdu, Sichuan, issued a 100 yuan shopping coupon to each needy person to stimulate the retail sector and about 150,000 training coupons worth 500 yuan each to those wanting to upgrade their skills – including those potential pole dancers.

Great Military Firewall

The People's Liberation Army was called upon to play a more active role in helping China combat the deepening global economic crisis after President Hu Jintao made a rare call for the military to "contribute to the nation's economic development and social stability." It was the first time in many years that a top state leader had directly asked the military to help in economic matters. The PLA was extensively involved in economic affairs until the late 1990s, when former President Jiang Zemin demanded the army shed its business operations and focus on becoming a modern, professional fighting force.

Beijing now believes the likelihood of a war with a foreign power or Taiwan in the near future is remote and that China's main security threats now came from rising social tension, the economic slowdown, religious-ethnic uprisings in Tibet and Xinjiang – and natural disasters. As a result, the army is now becoming involved in more non-military missions such as infrastructure building, disaster-relief work and maintaining internal security amid spreading economic woes and sensitive political anniversaries.

The Communist Party's head of public order, Zhou Yongkang, demanded strengthening internal security to confront the new set of problems the party is confronted with because of the global financial meltdown.

"Faced with the present international and domestic situation, particularly the deep change in the economic environment, it is imperative to soberly recognize the new scenario and new challenges facing public order," Zhou was quoted as saying by state media on April 1, 2009.

Among China's greatest concerns at the end of 2008 was its 50 million bloggers and 298 million netizens, a 42 percent rise from 2007. The millions of unemployed netizens and bloggers and continued job losses in 2009 come at a time of sensitive anniversaries that could trigger political unrest. Despite the "Great Firewall of China," the Internet has allowed many people to voice dissent – and find others with similar grievances. Taxi strikes in southern China in 2008, like many other strikes and clashes across the country, were triggered by online and mobile phone communications.

Clashes also broke out in Shishou city, Hubei province, when more than 10,000 angry residents blocked police from entering a well-known local drug-dealing hotel in which local government officials and the local constabulary had an interest, to retrieve the body of Tu Yuangao, a 24-year old chef, whose body was found outside. More than 1,000 riot police were sent after a three-day standoff with as many as 50,000 protestors who had gathered outside the hotel – brought out by fellow supporters through the Internet and SMS messaging – and simmering anger over official corruption. The public refused to accept the official verdict of suicide because of a string of suspicious deaths over a 10-year period.

The deaths all appear to have resulted because of alleged threats to disclose the drug dealing and political corruption because of the decedents' refusal to co-operate or be quiet over their unpaid wages. The families of most of the victims of suspicious deaths were bought off and silenced.

Tu's father refused to be bribed and placed his son's body in the hotel lobby and demanded an investigation. Police insisted his son had committed suicide and demanded the body be handed over for cremation. An Internet posting by a local resident said police promised to pay 30,000 to 50,000 yuan if Tu's father agreed to cremate the body and remain silent. He refused.

Internet postings said the crowd threw bricks, beer bottles and stones when police officers approached. Protestors also set up barricades at major intersections. Some postings said Internet bars and hotels in the city experienced blackouts, which some netizens attributed to an attempt by authorities to stop information from getting out. Nevertheless, online video clips show helmeted riot police with batons dispersing protestors as they marched through the streets.

One Internet posting said residents were raising funds to buy a refrigerator to store Tu's body after a local mortuary turned down Tu's father's request to transfer the body. Residents said they believed police had insisted on a quick cremation to destroy evidence of a murder. Residents made it clear they had learned a lesson from a 2008 riot in Wengan county, Guizhou, when 30,000 residents took to the streets to protest against the mysterious death of a 16-year-old girl. "We are more willing to stand up for our rights since the Wengan riot. Officials can no longer ask us to keep quiet by paying a few hundred thousand yuan," said a local resident.

Police being held hostage by outraged citizens is becoming a familiar story. Three policemen were held hostage by villagers in Guangdong for eight hours until 100 officers were sent to their rescue. There were many grievances that triggered the crises. What triggered the stand-off was a government firm using explosives on a hill to extract limestone. Mr. Lai, a local resident, said they had taken the policemen hostage because they wanted to attract the attention of senior officials. "We said we would release the policemen after provincial leaders pay attention to us."

Netizens are getting police and government officials to back down or act as necessary. One of my favorite stories is one involving the arrest of two schoolgirls for allegedly being prostitutes. Their parents were fined. It turned out the girls were virgins and the police had to return the fines and compensate the family because of how they were pilloried on Internet forums.

A photo splashed across the Internet showing an alleged prostitute, naked and being pulled by the hair by a policeman, sparked criticism of excessive force and forum discussions about suspects' right to privacy.

More than a 1,000 police officers were deployed to a rural area on Hainan island in southern China to stop clashes between two feuding villages over a land dispute that left one dead, many wounded, destroyed government buildings and torched official vehicles. Nearly 1,000 villagers from the area around Zhaoqing in Guangdong clashed with hundreds of police outside a government building after the authorities stopped their protest against land requisitions.

There are many disputes over these land requisitions across China, which are expected to escalate as the infrastructure programs in Beijing's economic stimulus plan are rolled out across the country. The most disturbing development is PLA soldiers on guard duty being shot or stabbed and their weapons being stolen by unknown assailants.

There were 90,000 such events in 2006, according to a January 2009 article in China's *Outlook Weekly*, a policy magazine published by Xinhua, the official state agency, up from 60,000 in 2003. How many there are today is a state secret.

What really outrages Chinese citizens is the role of armed police. Considering their massive military exercises with different PLA units, why couldn't either or both with a joint command and control tackle the riots in Xinjian head on, or better yet, nip it in the bud?

First established in 1982, the People's Armed Police is a special half-police, half military force entrusted with the umbrella mission of "protecting internal security." However, its chain of command and administrative status have never been clear – hence political and bureaucratic paralysis at time of crisis.

The 680,000 strong PAP has fallen under the jurisdiction and control of the State Council and and the Communist Party's Central Military Commission.

The fact is that China's grip on its police security apparatus is being questioned and challenged daily. China's dreaded police force has lost control and the respect of the people because of its corrupt and unprofessional behavior. They are usually outnumbered by angry mobs and flee the scene of a disturbance, protest or riot, as was vividly demonstrated to the world in Urumqi on July 5, 2009, when Uygurs went on a killing rampage of rival Hans. Police officers remained absent for five hours after the riots started and the carnage continued.

"Where were the police while people were being killed?" asked Cheng Wei, 41 a landscaper whose neighbors, poor fruit vendors from Henan province, lost a son in the riots. "They were completely useless."

Government censors have long regarded the Internet as a major threat to their efforts to control the flow of sensitive information, a problem that grows daily as more and more mainlanders go online. Continuing to control and censor the media, especially the Internet, is a top priority of the government as political unrest among the unemployed masses spreads and the police are seen as toothless tigers.

Bannana Party Split

The Internet is also fueling the rumor mill about divisions within the Communist Party that threaten to rupture the party. China's one-party Communist system is gradually splintering into two-party factions – that look to become two parties – within the party. The Shanghai faction of elitists, including the princeling children of high-ranking officials, favor an increase in coastal development and place a far greater emphasis on economic growth and free trade, is headed by former President Jiang Zemin. It is lined up against the populist nationalistic faction headed up by President Hu Jintao, which favors improving China's social safety net, introducing greener policies, and balancing development between the wealthy east coast and the poor western hinterlands.

The two factions are divided by geography and by real economic and political issues. The Shanghai faction favors market and trade liberalization and pursuing China's export-driven economic model which tends to favor the cities and its big factories at the expense of the rural areas. The populist faction is more nationalistic and if it consolidates its power, it could auger a more prickly economic relationship with the U.S.

To avoid the appearance of a party split, the party declared at a 2009 Central Committee plenum that "intraparty democracy" is the party's "lifeblood."

The split between the elitists and populists has resulted in brutal criticisms being leveled against each other and party officials being arrested and jailed for corruption. In 2006, Shanghai's party secretary became the first Politburo member in years to be purged and imprisoned for corruption. His arrest helped Hu Jintao consolidate populist influence.

The Chongqing Party secretary, a princeling identified with the elitist bloc, declared war on the deeply entrenched Chinese crime syndicates in Chongqing in 2009. He arrested more than 2,000 people, including the city's former deputy police chief, three billionaires, 50 government officials, six district police heads, two senior judges, and more than 20 triad bosses. One of those bosses is a local parliamentarian.

Both factions recognize that their differences have to be contained and compromised for the Communist Party to remain in power. Both sides are mindful it was the open confrontation between conservatives and liberals in 1989 that led to the Tiananmen demonstations and bloodshed. Neither faction wants to risk an open rupture in the Internet age. They are keenly aware of how People Power can be galvanized by mobile Internet technology and social networking sites. The People Power movements in nearby Philippines, Thailand, Japan and South Korea that brought about political change at the top is not an option.

There is increasing reflection and criticism in China today that the price of China's progress and economic success has been inequity – especially towards the peasants and workers – and entrenched corruption.

Reform within the party system and an aggressive crackdown on corruption are preferable to revolution. That is the only way the Communist Party can remain in power.

Sensitive Allergies

The Year of the Ox – 2009 – marked several politically sensitive anniversaries. The 90th anniversary of the 1919 May Fourth Movement, triggered by resentment over the Treaty of Versailles at the end of World War I – which handed Germany's colonial concessions in Shandong to Japan rather than China – has special significance for the Communist Party. The student-led movement ushered in what has been described as China's patriotic renaissance.

The movement awakened hundreds of millions of Chinese people to the enthusiastic patriotic spirit and achieved unprecedented social mobilization with its incisive slogan "Defend our sovereignty and punish the traitors." Because it was such an unprecedented and profound social movement, it not only became a milestone in China's modern history, but also instilled long-term meanings that last to this day. "Patriotism," "science" and "democracy" were the national axioms set by the movement.

Lu Xun, a famous writer of the time, illustrated this attitude in his masterpiece *Na Lai Zhu Yi*, meaning grabbing whatever is useful. He acknowledged the advanced civilizations in the world and calmly dissected and criticized the traits of the Chinese nation. Like Lu Xun, the movement adopted a rational attitude from the West, and hence wrote "science," which was rare in Chinese society, and "democracy," which had never flourished in China onto the banner that urged the nation forward.

Top state officials met mostly as a formality to mark the anniversary. All nine Politburo members, including President Hu Jintao and Premier Wen Jiabao, attended a two-hour gathering at the Great Hall of the People, marked by lectures given by model youth workers, scientists and students.

Campuses across Beijing were quiet – even Beijing University, where student protesters set out on a historic parade on May 4, 1919. The protest eventually turned violent and marked a surge in nationalism. Authorities clamped down on student demonstrations during the Youth Festival – a title given to May 4 after the Communists came to power in 1949 – which aroused memories of the Chinese elite's painful and so far futileever quest for democracy. Party leaders usually visit a university in the capital on May 4. In a normal year that would be Beijing University. That did not happen in 2009.

May Fourth is a reformist movement, not merely a historic event, but a living legacy for the Chinese nation today and the future. Fundamental values like science and democracy, and progressive and critical thinking, will become more important as China prepares for the next era of reform.

Student protests have played a big role in democracy movements in China, the most recent being the 1989 uprising, on which the government cracked down. The 20th anniversary of the Tiananmen Square pro-democracy protests of 1989 is one of the main reason authorities played down the Youth festival in 2009. That did not stop protesters seeking redress from a litany of grievances by stringing up banners from a Beijing hotel and throwing handbills from its roof to get media attention. The banners complained of everything from corruption to the use of fake medication in hospitals.

April 2009 marked the 20th anniversary of reformist leader Hu Yaobang's death, which kicked off an ultra-sensitive period for the leaders in Beijing as it was forced to revisit the period that led up to the crackdown's anniversary on June 4. Hu was ousted as head of the Communist Party in 1987 for his weak response to student protests in December of the previous year. When he died on April 15, 1989, students used his death to call for democratic reforms. Hu was the symbol of the political reforms that had been stopped following his removal.

I helped bring surf rockers Jan & Dean to China for a two week concert tour in November and December 1986, and was witness to the student protests in Shanghai that year. The concert tour in Shangai ended on a heavy note. Overzealous security personnel started cracking heads after several student protest leaders joined a crowd spontaneously dancing to the music in the isles.

The mayor of Shanghai, Jiang Zemin, had attended the opening-night concert, at which we toasted "peace, harmony and understanding" between China and America.

But the mass student demonstrations in Shanghai were mostly peaceful, and helped get Jiang elected to the pinnacle of the Communist Party leadership in 1989 because of the party's inability to contain the student protests in Tiananmen Square and the resulting bloodshed.

I was in Beijing in late May and early June 1989 and witnessed the student protests in Tiananmen Square as I tried to navigate our car from a meeting with government film and television officials at one end of the square to my hotel at the other through the protesting throngs. Students in the mass of humanity would flash me V signs or punch their fists in the air.

The protests began with about 700 students gathering in Tiananmen Square on April 17. The next day, in front of Zhongnanhai, the headquarters of the Communist Party, up to 1,500 people called for Hu Yaobang's political rehabilitation. By the eve of Hu's funeral on April 21, class boycotts had been called at 20 universities and the next day 200,000 students gathered in Tiananmen Square demanding a dialogue with the nation's leaders. Tensions mounted on April 25 when the People's Daily published an editorial accusing the students of seeking to overthrow the Communist Party. The protests snowballed as students were joined by other sectors of society, including workers, marching through Beijing led by students parading portraits of Hu, because a fractured leadership could not agree on how to handle the demonstrations.

With the international media converging on the capital, the protest boiled over in May as students held a vast hunger strike in Tiananmen Square. Finally, in early June, PLA troops marched into Tiananmen killing an untold number of people to end the demonstrations.

Hu was popular because he tried to rehabilitate victims of the Cultural Revolution and admitted mistakes in the handling of Tibet, which he said needed real autonomy. The year 2009 also marked 50 years since the Dalai Lama went into exile and the 10th anniversary of 15,000 Falun Gong practitioners holding a protest in Beijing outside Zhongnanhai that resulted in the government banning them on the mainland. It also marks the 60th anniversary of the founding of the People's Republic of China. Is it any wonder Beijing police are mobilizing 800,000 residents for a two-month crimewatch campaign in a bid to boost public security ahead of the 60th anniversary of the founding of the People's Republic on Oct. 1. Basically, a rehash of what Beijing did for the Olympics in preparation for the anniversary of October 1. The campaign would focus on settlements of migrant workers, old residential areas, borders between urban and rural areas, public service areas and places known to be centers of crime, with Minister of Public Security Meng Jianzhu calling on police around the nation to prepare well for the security mission related to the 60th anniversary. "Attempts at violence and terrorism must be foiled before they are turned into real action," Meng said.

Beijing police arrested more than 6,500 crime suspects in the two months preceding the October 1st 60th anniversary National Day celebrations.

Tourists were banned from Tibet in the run-up to the anniversary celebrations. No travel permits were issued to foreign tourists several weeks before the anniversary. Beijing also ordered close scrutiny of tourists already there.

China was determined to stand up and show its strength without any distracting incidents – except for the women's military militia on National Day.

The glaring difference from the Olympics was that the Oct. 1 parade at Tiananmen Square was not open to the public. There was a lockdown in Central Beijing, with security forces on maximum alert ahead of the military parade. Tiananmen Square and the Forbidden City were cordoned off. All flights at Beijing Capital International Airport were grounded for 3 hours. Nearly a million security volunteers in yellow uniforms and red arm-bands – mostly retired women in their 50s and 60s – patrolled the entrances of almost every residential building across the city. Hotels along part of Chang'an Avenue near Tiananmen Square had their rooms booked by the government to house security personnel from Sept. 28 to Oct. 2. No other guests were allowed to occupy the hotel.

Ethnic Hot Dishes

The Dalai Lama and Tibetan political activists were contained on the 50th anniversary of the uprising that led to his Holiness leaving Tibet because of the Tibetan political protests that turned violent a year earlier in the run-up to the 2008 Olympics. Tibetans and Uygurs chose the Olympics as the event to highlight their plight and heat up Beijing's political kitchen.

Uygur militants gained international attention in August 2008 after an attack on a police station in the Silk Road city of Kashgar killed 17 police on the eve of the Beijing Olympics.

The massive parade and pageantry planned for the nation's 60th anniversary commemoration in Tiananmen Square is set to eclipse the opening ceremony of the 2008 Olympics. On such occasions, Beijing likes to make a point of celebrating its ethnic minorities, which it says have benefited greatly from the economic and social progress that has been brought to China by the ruling Communist Party.

Sun Yat-sen, the father of modern China, advanced the idea of a republic constituting five ethnic groups – the Han, the Manchus, Mongols, Hui or Muslims, and Tibetans. The Communist Party presented a more sophisticated picture of the Chinese people when it came to power. The Communists say China is made of 56 ethnic groups, including the Han majority. One of the four small stars on the Chinese flag represents China's ethnic minorities.

The riots on July 5, 2009 in Urumqi, the largest city in Central Asia, Kashgar and other cities across Xinjiang and protests at Chinese embassies in the Netherlands, Munich and Istanbul were triggered by the sexual molestation of Chinese Han women by Uyger workers in a Hong Kong-owned factory in Shaoguan, northern Guangdong. The molestations took place over a period of time going back to early May until June 25, when a worker being molested called for help from her boyfriend and others, triggering a massive fight between Ugyers and Hans that left two Uygurs dead and 118 people injured.

Electronic media spread the news about the incident quickly around the world. YouTube, video-and text-messaging linked these disparate peoples and places like never before, contributing to perhaps the world's first "ethnic pandemic," wrote Dru Gladney, author of *Dislocating China: Muslims, Minorities, and other Subaltern Subjects.*

The resulting explosive ethnic violence in Urumqi, which killed at least 197 and left more than 1,600 injured, the worst known bloodshed in China since Tiananmen, was another reminder of the widespread social vulnerabilities and concern confronting the Communist Party – shared with the world when China's Hu Jintao left the G-8 summit in Italy before it started – an unprecedented move by a Chinese leader. Never before has a Chinese leader cut short an overseas trip because of domestic concerns.

Many people in both of the Urumqi's main ethnic groups believe the true figures are much higher than the numbers the government has released. People think the scale of the killing was whitewashed because the government doesn't want to admit what a bloodbath it really was. The government's failure to update the figures after mass Han reprisals on July 7 fueled suspicions further.

The fact that the protests erupted in Urumqi, where Uygurs are only about 13 percent of the population and Han are 75 percent, is significant. Previously, most of the violent incidents took place in towns such as Kashgar, Khorla and Khotan, where Uygurs are much more numerous. China released a detailed report to back up its claim that the riots across Xinjiang, also known as Eastern Turkestan and protests at Chinese embassies in Washington and Europe, were coordinated and planned via the Internet by the Washington-based World Uygur Congress which is partially funded by the U.S. government's "independent" NGO, the National Endowment for Democracy.

Published NED reports show it gives the Uygur Congress $215,000 a year for "human rights research and advocacy projects." The NED was intimately involved in financial support to various organizations behind the Lhasa violence in March 2008. Allen Weinstein, who helped draft the legislation to set up NED, said in 1991: "A lot of what we do today was done covertly 25 years ago by the CIA."

The NED gets a yearly stipend from the U.S. Congress through four "core foundations": the National Democratic Institute for International Affairs, linked to the Democratic Party; the International Republican Institute tied to the Republican Party; the American Center for International Labor Solidarity, linked to the AFL-CIO labor federation and State Department; and the Center for International Private Enterpride, linked to the U.S. Chamber of Commerce.

On May 18, 2009, the NED, according to the Uygur Congress Website, hosted a seminal human rights conference on "East Turkestan: 60 Years Under Communist Chinese Rule." A salient question is what has the NED been doing that might have fanned the unrest in Xinjiang and why? How would the U.S. like it if China started funding restless Native Americans on the reservations across America who want to secede and become independent from the U.S.? After all, they are blood brothers. My educated guess is that America would get upset. Very upset. Political indigestion on a global scale.

China cannot afford a restless Xinjiang because the resource-rich region makes a significant contribution to the mainland's energy security. The province sits atop as much as 20 percent of domestic oil reserves and is expected to account for one-fifth of the mainland's coal output. Xinjiang's long borders with oil-producing Central Asian countries is what differentiates it from Tibet. That is one of the main reasons China established the Shanghai Cooperation Organization with Russia and its Central Asia neighbors – a regional association I discuss at length in *Custom Maid Knowledge for New World Disorder.* A geopolitical alliance Washington feels threatened by. Why? It can become an observer and maybe someday a participant in the global fight against terrorism.

Another salient question is was it mere coincidence that the Urumqi riots took place just days after the 2009 SCO annual meeting and the announcement of the Sino-Russia joint military exercise code-named "Peace Mission 2009" held every two years? The primary purpose of these exercises is to help both countries protect core security interests against terrorists, separatists and extremists. Russia, like China, has many ethnic groups and faces similar challenges along the 4,300-kilometer border the two countries share. The problem is they don't trust each other. A concept President Nixon recognized and seized upon to America's long-term advantage and the U.S.S.R.'s eventual demise.

It is time America and China establish a joint military command to fight terrorism and start joint military exercises, similar to what Russia and China are doing.

Islamic countries reacted mostly with silence to the ethnic clashes because they do not want to damage lucrative trade deals with Beijing or draw attention to their own attitudes towards political dissent. Al-Qaeda, on the other hand, vowed to avenge the deaths of Muslims in Urumqi by targeting China's extensive workforce and projects across northwestern Africa and urged Muslims in China to launch a holy war against their oppressor. It is the first time Osama bin Laden's terrorist network has directly threatened China or its interests – illustrating the international price China is paying for its policies in Xinjiang and its quest for resources in Africa and the Middle East.

The good news, if it can be called that, about the Al-Qaeda threat, is that it has brought the American and Chinese anti-terror teams closer together. Washington and Beijing can now expand their anti-terror and intelligence cooperation efforts in Africa, South East Asia and the Middle East. The U.S. and China now, more than ever, have a common interest in countering the threat of terrorism.

Beijing's aggressive and ambitious plans to construct refineries, pipelines and power grids across Xinjiang could backfire if these facilities become terrorist targets. In addition, much of the oil and gas extracted in Kazakhstan is transported inland via a 3,000-kilometer pipeline that passes through Xinjiang.

As if that wasn't a big enough hangover, the Tarim Basin in the center of the province is believed to hold trillions of cubic meters of natural gas. A 4,000-kilometer pipeline has been constructed to take the fuel through Xinjiang to Shanghai. Without this energy reserve, China recognizes that Xinjiang can be written off. Fortunately, because of the province's vast energy resources, both Beijing and Washington recognize that Xinjiang's vast reservoir of natural resources can attract long-term investment from both countries that will justify further cooperation.

Xinjiang is ground zero of China's "Go West" campaign. The province's gross domestic product jumped from 220 billion yuan in 2004, to 415 yuan in 2008. It's GDP has seen six consecutive years of double-digit growth since 2003. The number of railroads, major oil pipelines, electricity grids and factories has mushroomed since 2000, making it economically one of the best performing minority-populated regions in China. Uygurs claim they have received far fewer of the economic benefits than the millions of Han Chinese encouraged to move to Xianjiang to help exploit agriculture and mineral resources, including large oil and natural gas deposits in what Beijing views as a strategically vital gateway to Central Asia.

I regret not taking up Nelson Wong's often extended invitations in 2007 and 2008 to join him on his many business trips from Shanghai to Urumqi, where he and his business associates from across China would meet before catching a connecting flight to Kazhakstan.

"Peter, you must come with us," Nelson would implore me. "The opportunities are unbelievable. The government is spending so much money in Xinjiang, as is the government of Kazhakstan. The vacuum left in Kazhakstan after the Russians left is unbelievable and China has been offered so many business opportunities that both places are like Wild West boom towns. Construction everywhere. Money being given away for any project that sounds feasible, even if it is not." Nelson would repeat variations of the same theme whenever we got together in Shanghai or Hong Kong.

"I don't know. After watching Borat, I'm not sure I buy your rosy picture," I told Nelson one evening after I had just seen the movie.
"No, Kazakhstan is nothing like that," he responded. "It is a modern progressive city where if you know the right government officials, you can get anything, and I mean anything done."

Maybe I should have taken up Nelson's invitation. Someday I probably will.

I caught up with Nelson in Shanghai in September 2009. We decided to have dinner in Tahar, a new Xinjiang restaurant that had opened in the Xu Jia Hui district near his home. Restaurants across China serving Middle Eastern food are one of Xinjiang's biggest exports and contribution to the Chinese dining experience.

"You know Peter, there are thousands of restaurants like this all over China that are owned, operated and staffed by Uygurs who can move freely to other provinces to start businesses. It is not just the Han Chinese moving to Xinjiang," Nelson said. "The Uygurs are allowed to move freely across China to pursue business opportunities just like anyone else. But the Western media don't discuss this. The Uygurs complaint that they are oppressed and not given the same opportunities as the Han Chinese is absolutely not true," he continued as we ordered another round of *Arak*.

Such has been the scale of the influx that Han Chinese, who accounted for just 6 percent of Xinjiang's population in 1949, now make up more than 40 percent of the total population. Uygur resentment has grown increasingly nationalistic and separatist, emboldened by the defeat of the Soviet Union in Afghanistan and the independence granted to three neighboring former Islamic Soviet republics.

Uygurs seeking independence used the Guangdong factory incident as the spark for the unrest in Xinjiang, an energy and resource-rich province which accounts for one-sixth of the country's territory, where the majority Uygurs feel exploited because the Han Chinese dominate economic and political life – a good reason for Chinese President Hu Jintao to leave the G-8 summit in Italy before it started – to tend to the melting tip of the explosive ethnic iceberg in Beijing's kitchen.

Smoked Meat

China is the world's largest producer and consumer of tobacco – and the leader in fake cigarettes. China churns out an unprecedented 400 billion counterfeit cigarettes a year that are sold worldwide. According to U.S. Customs, 99 percent of the counterfeit cigarettes seized in America originate in China. It is a country that sees about a million tobacco-related deaths a year, a quarter of all such deaths worldwide.

China is a signatory to the World Health Organization's Framework Convention on Tobacco Control, which aims to reduce global demand for tobacco products by encouraging developing nations to adopt anti-smoking measures that are now commonplace in developed countries. China signed the convention in 2003, ratified it in 2005 and became a full member in 2006.

The mainland is home to about 350 million smokers, with about 3 million people taking up the habit annually. Nearly 60 percent of males aged 15 or above are smokers. More than one million Chinese die each year – one every two seconds – from smoking-related diseases. And 540 million people suffer from passive smoking. China's culture of cigarette smoking runs very deep and is very pervasive. Most of the founders of the People's Republic, including Mao Zedong and Deng Xiaoping, were chain smokers. Just how engrained smoking is in Chinese culture was exemplified by the Mao and Deng wax figures at an exhibition in Hong Kong in September 2009, at a 60th anniversary National Day exhibition – they were both holding cigarettes.

Getting Chinese to stop smoking is a tall order even for Yao Ming, who has teamed up with the wife of China's vice president to lead an anti-tobacco crusade.

One of the biggest difficulties the country faces in banning smoking is the fact that more than half of male doctors are smokers – the highest ratio in the world. The government plans to ban smoking in all hospitals in 2011, when the convention's timetable kicks in. But according to the convention, China is required to ban smoking in all indoor public venues, office buildings and public transport from 2011.

The central government did not ban smoking in public entertainment venues, including movie theatres, stadiums and bookshops until 1991, nor in airport terminals until 1997.

The nation grows a third of the world's tobacco crop and manufactures a third of its cigarettes, according to WHO. The State Tobacco Monopoly Administration has more than 500,000 employees in more than 1,000 companies across 33 provinces. China's massive tobacco industry employs more than 20 million farmers and more than 10 million retailers. Pre-tax revenues from the tobacco industry amounted to 388 billion yuan in 2008 and accounted for about 8 percent of the country's fiscal revenues. Is it any wonder Chinese are smoked meat?

My biggest advertisers and sponsors of concert tours, radio and television shows when I was in the radio media distribution business in China in the 1980s and '90s were tobacco companies. Their commercial impact on entertainment and sporting events is huge, because their budgets seemed to be limitless. Reading that the Shanghai World Expo 2010 has handed back 200 million yuan in sponsorship funds from the Shanghai Tobacco Group's contribution to the China national pavilion to promote a "healthy World Expo" brought a big smile to my face and a chuckle as I yelled out, "Right On! Finally!" – there is hope for a lot less smoke in China.

I agree with professor Zou Fangbin, an economics professor at the Guangdong University of Business Studies who has proposed scrapping the state monopoly and allowing private companies to compete in this lucrative deadly sector. How can the government regulate an industry it owns and controls? It can't. The commercial and regulatory arms of the industry must be separate. China is the only one of the 164 signatories to the WHO convention to have such a monopoly.

Poisoned Meat

Thousands of China's children and pregnant women have been poisoned by rogue chemical plants and illegal factories that dump their toxic waste into local streams and rivers. Corrupt officials have turned a blind eye to these pollution tragedies in the past, but starting in 2009, are being arrested and charged on an unprecedented scale, along with the owners of these death factories.

Fifteen thousand people in 10 villages in Jiyuan, Henan province, who live close to the mainland's biggest lead smelting area had to be moved elsewhere – so that the plants that may have poisoned 1,000 children can keep working.

Lead smelters around the world have been shut down because of pollution fears, allowing the industry to blossom in China. The price of lead spiked to its highest point in September 2009, when some smelters in Jiyuan had shut down for two months after tests revealed excessive levels of noxious lead in the blood of children.

Untreated chemical waste dumped by the Xianghe Chemical plant in Liuyang city, Hunan, killed at least five people over a six-year period and left hundreds sick before it was closed in 2009. When the factory opened, people were told it would be processing animal feed. Instead, it made batteries and liquid crystal displays and the chemical fumes and waste from cadmium and indium used in their manufacture was spewed into the air and discharged at night into local water systems, poisoning villagers in its wake.

The metal poisoning scandal in Liuyang, has become a case study for tens of thousands of people across the mainland who are suffering under corrupt local administrations and from the effects of pollution. The cadmium poisoning has been widely reported after a large protest by more than a 1,000 residents besieged the local police station and government office demanding the release of their elders who had been detained because of their demands for compensation.

Poisoned villagers across the country are traveling to Hunan to learn the town's lessons. They return home and stage protests demanding the closure of illegal pollutant factories, free medical checkups and compensation from the government for their ruined lives and land. Increasingly, the victims of pollution have started to band together and learn from each other's experiences. Ironically, local officials are doing the same. Many civil servants have been traveling to other administrations to learn how to handle pollution-triggered protests. Pollution is now among the prime causes of social unrest and protests on the mainland.

Out to Lunch

China's one-child policy has resulted in male births since 1980 outnumbering female births by 38 million, sparking fears among demographers that a rising number of single males could threaten social stability. These boys are spending their free time desperately trying to find a wife. Many of them will wind up single with no families to support them later in life and they will have to depend on the social security system after retirement.

The preference for boys in a male-dominated culture has resulted in abortions and infanticide. To make matters worse, China has one of the world's largest populations of infertile men and women. One in eight married couples is unable to have children. There are an estimated 40 million couples in China who are infertile and seen as a serious threat to the nation's population structure and social stability.

China's Triple-Fisted Handful

The reality is that China cannot afford to follow in the financial footsteps of America and the Western world it leads. With its gross domestic product slowing dramatically each quarter since March 2008 and continuing into 2009, China has opted for more flexible macroeconomic measures to maintain stable multi-sector growth in a non-inflationary manner. Furthermore, there is no domestic support for such action. China has been adversely affected by the Wall Street meltdown and needs to spend its reserves domestically to support its economy and create new jobs to replace the millions of factory jobs lost because of the global recession and shrinking export orders.

China must find 24 million jobs in 2009 to ensure social order. Jobless university graduates, unemployed migrant workers and disgruntled retired military personnel, of which there will be more than 3 million with their families in 2009, protesting government policies is a lethal political social cocktail. That is especially true in the major cities where most of the unemployed homeless migrant workers make up the multi-million "floating population." With more than 60 percent of China's population moving to cities by 2030 – that's 900 million urban dwellers – economic stability and prosperity are essential for the Communist Party to retain public order and power.

The Chinese leaders know their power is slipping away when they are confronted by retired military officers protesting their failure to receive pensions and farmers who refuse to grow crops. In 2008, about 100 retired army nuclear engineers, representing over 60,000 suffering from radiation exposure while working on China's atomic weapons program, staged public protests over pensions that they had not received. Grain and pig farmers – who have made or broke Chinese dynasties, including the Communist Party – also created a food crisis that threatened to bring down the communist dynasty by refusing to farm their land for food. Famines have been one of the primary causes that toppled Chinese dynasties. Global prices for key grains – rice, wheat, corn and soya beans – have risen steadily since 2005 because of pressure from farmers who would rather plant crops for biofuels than food. China has 7 percent of the world's arable land to feed 22 percent of the world's population.

Pork and Grains
The cost of Thai rice, the world benchmark, more than doubled in 2008. The price of pork also more than doubled. Many Chinese prefer to be paid with bags of rice rather than cash, a common practice historically. Arable land has given way to growing urbanization which has left millions of unemployed migrant workers with no farm to return to. China now imports more than 75 percent of its soya beans for domestic consumption. The most populous nation in the world has the most severe imbalance between population and land. Even as the population grows, grain production and the supply of pork are dropping.

To battle the shortage, China has approved reform to enable 730 million peasant farmers to trade their land-use rights – sell or rent out their rights to use their land – more freely and provide greater legal protection for existing landholders. The Central Committee of the Communist Party set a target to double the per capital disposable income of rural residents by 2020, and pledged to increase government spending on social welfare in the countryside. China is determined to modernize its agricultural sector and integrate the rural and urban economies.

Pork is a staple in China. Sixty five percent of the meat Chinese eat is pork. The Chinese are hooked on pork the way Americans are on oil. Pork has been a mainstay of the Chinese diet for millennia. Beijing maintains vast warehouses where it stockpiles frozen carcasses, which operate much like

America's strategic oil reserve. The government releases stocks onto the market during natural disasters, crisis points in the hog cycle, and whenever it needs a political boost. China's hunger for meat will have global financial ramifications, just like America's hunger for oil has.

Many Chinese farmers continue to skirt the ban on chemical additives in food for pigs, increasing the risk of disease and illness in humans. In February 2009, more than 80 people in Guangdong province experienced stomach aches and diarrhea after consuming pig organs contaminated with an illegal feed additive called Clenbuterol. It is added to pig feed to keep the animals lean. Leaner pork brings a higher price.

China's leaders are well aware of this and would rather deploy their foreign exchange reserves to buy any food or commodity the country is short of on the global market – especially as commodity prices bottom out after the Food and Agriculture Organization of the United Nations said in 2008 that food prices will stay high for another 10 years or so. China will then have to spend more on food subsidies to keep prices down and its citizens properly fed. In 2008, China had stockpiled between 150 million and 200 million tons of grain to keep prices down. China has also raised its grain output target by 10 percent to more than 550 million tons by 2020. China is well on its way to achieve its call as it had its fifth consecutive record harvest in 2008, with grain output rising 5.4 percent year on year to 528.5 million tons. China can afford to feed its people. Can America?

Not without China's support. U.S. soybean prices rose by almost a third since the start of March 2009 amid strong demand from China and production problems in Argentina and Brazil. Prices rose because U.S. stocks at the end of the 2009 season shrank to 77 million bushels, well below the U.S. Department of Agriculture's inventory forecast of 130 million bushels. Just another bureaucratic miscalculation that explains why Americans are going hungry.

Clipping the Wings of High-Flying Hogs
While making more arable land available to farmers and increasing grain production, China is also clipping the wings of its high-flying earners in financial institutions to prevent a widening income gap that can trigger social unrest. A concept the Obama administration toyed with and then dropped and appointed a salary czar to address. The Ministry of Finance issued a circular in April 2009 asking state-owned banks, insurers and securities firms to cut pre-tax income by at least 10 percent for top executives from 2007

salaries if the companies were more profitable in 2008 and by 20 percent if company profits declined. The ministry also announced a salary cap for financial services executives.

The government's concern for the widening salary gap between rural and urban dwellers was triggered by a report that the 2008 average disposable income for urban residents was 15,781 yuan while that of rural residents was 4,761 yuan. Top executives in the financial sector, like their counterparts in America on the other hand, earned millions.

"The salary reduction is aimed to maintain social equality, protect rights and interests of the nation and shareholders and improve corporate governance," the ministry said. Why isn't America doing the same? Governments do need to rebalance the relationship between the state and the markets to create a fairer, more equal distribution of rewards. China did the right thing.

Pay Cut
All American bankers have to do is apologize for their mistakes, get their bonuses and go back to business as usual.

"We participated in things that were clearly wrong and have reason to regret," said Lloyd Blankfein, CEO of Goldman Sachs, issuing an apology for its role in the financial crisis amid public anger over its record bonuses in 2009.

Wall Street's utter disconnect from the rest of the world was laid bare for all to see when Blankfein was quoted as saying he's doing "God's work" at a Chinese business conference in New York. He went on to say that "everybody should be happy" that he and his peers are on track to take home billions in bonuses in 2009.

In November 2008, Treasury Secretary Hank Paulson, another former Goldman Sachs CEO, announced a dramatic shift in the U.S.'s strategy to deal with the rolling financial crisis. Rather than use the $700 billion in TARP funds to buy troubled assets from banks, as originally promised, he would inject capital straight into banks and other financial institutions in exchange for preferred stock – the so called nuclear option.

That self-serving banker decision is at the root of where the U.S. finds itself today, with record bonuses, zombie banks, and bipartisan suspicion that nothing has changed. It hasn't. Is it any wonder China, America's banker, is upset?

Side Dishes – Hong Kong, Macau and Taiwan

China is not only concerned, focused and preoccupied with the needs on the mainland during the global financial and economic meltdown, but also the needs of Hong Kong, Macau and Taiwan as well. Besides helping itself with its stimulus plan, China has to dish out billions to assist the economies and citizens of Hong Kong, Macau and Taiwan. All three provinces saw their GDP shrink more than predicted with their future outlook looking bleaker than anticipated. Hong Kong's goods exports fell the most since 1954, plunging 22.7 percent in 2009. Taiwan had the biggest slide since it started keeping records in 1962, and Macau's high rollers were nowhere to be seen as its casinos did everything in their power to stave off bankruptcy.

China liberalized yuan trade rules to bolster Hong Kong's economy during the global meltdown. Beijing adopted a 14-point plan that allowed companies to conduct cross-border trade between the mainland and Hong Kong using yuan.

The plan allows individuals and companies to set up currency swap facilities and encourages mainland financial institutions to (1) develop international services via Hong Kong; (2) support more mainland firms listing in Hong Kong; (3) encourage the early start of the Hong Kong-Macau-Zhuhai bridge; (4) press ahead with the Hong Kong-Shenzhen airport and Hong Kong-Guangzhou express rail links; (5) foster development of a "world-class metropolis" in the Pearl River Delta; (6) support Hong Kong companies building the next Shenzhen metro line; (7) support Hong Kong development of the border zone; (8) facilitate coordination between delta container ports; (9) raise export tax rebates; (10) take other steps to help Hong Kong firms on the mainland, allow out-of-towners living in Shenzhen to get visas for Hong Kong there rather than in their home provinces; (11) consider opening the mainland market to more local service firms; and secure stable food, water and fuel supplies from China to Hong Kong.

For years, Beijing successfully blocked Taiwan's participation in everything from international organizations to informal beach volleyball games – and gave it zero financial support on any front. Beijing's ferocious venom for a Taiwan that at any moment might declare formal independence scared everyone off. Today the politicians and citizens of the mainland and Taiwan are working feverishly to unite a common people economically and politically.

One of the most significant political milestones to achieve that goal was the meeting on the shores of Little Kinmen, a Taiwan-controlled inlet just off the coast of mainland China in March 2009, when the mayor of Xiamen, the Chinese port across the strait, met the county magistrate of Kinmen on a beach dotted with spears embedded in the shallow ocean floor, to remove them to make way for the crossing's first swimming competition in the summer of 2009. That event, coupled with the successful third round of high-level bilateral talks aimed at improving trade relations across the Taiwan strait, propelled Taiwan's benchmark index to its biggest one-day gain in almost 18 years. Orders from the mainland have also been responsible for a 35 percent rise in the value of Taiwan's export orders since the beginning of 2009.

China pledged 130 billion yuan in loans to Taiwanese businesses operating on the mainland as part of an economic cooperation package to help the island weather the global financial crisis. Taiwanese firms will also be allowed to work on mainland projects under its stimulus plan. China also agreed to buy $2 billion worth of flat-screen displays made on the island. Beijing also pledged to do its utmost to provide whatever aid Taiwan needed during the global economic crisis.

China at Crossroads

China is at a political and economic crossroad that few in America or the West fully appreciate. For the first time since China embarked on its economic reforms in 1978 and lifted hundreds of millions of people out of poverty, it's political leadership is faced with its greatest test of political survival. President Hu Jintao has gone so far as to say that turning the challenges posed by the global credit and economic crisis into opportunities will be a test of the Communist Party's capacity to continue to govern. China recognizes it needs to stand on its own two feet and not rely on exports.

The task is daunting. Household consumption in 2007 made up just 35.3 percent of China's gross domestic product, a record low for a major country in peacetime. In the 1980s, it was over 50 percent. By comparison, household consumption in the U.S. in 2007 made up 72 percent of GDP.

China must make radical spending changes from infrastructure to social investments, which requires giving people more disposable income. More

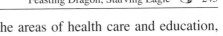

household subsidies, especially in the areas of health care and education, are needed. The problem, believe it or not, is that China does not have the bureaucratic infrastructure in place to minimize waste and corruption.

The other reality is that returning money to the people through lower taxes or spending on social programs is not a high priority in China because its leaders do not have to run for re-election. In China, officials are held accountable to their superiors, not voters. Hence most officials are afraid to make a mistake and take the same bureaucratic road as their counterparts in America. They just want to make it to retirement without taking any risks that could cost them their job.

Thus, Chinese citizens who are unable to vote out their leaders or collect compensation from the courts express their rising anger in protests, riots, strikes and political demonstrations that are unnerving the Communist Party leadership. One must keep in mind that public demonstrations are not permitted in China. So when people do take to the streets at great personal risk, they do so because they want their leaders to notice and do something about it, or lose their "mandate from heaven."

Millions of laid-off workers and Chinese investors in the local stock market who lost trillions of yuan – Shanghai was the worst-performing market in 2008 – across China are protesting, smashing windows, offices, overturning police cars and scuffling with police. Even police have gotten into the act. Auxiliary officers in Hunan Province surrounded a Communist Party office in December 2008 to demand higher wages. Chinese investors in China's collapsed market are also demanding an American-style bailout.

With millions of college graduates unable to find work joining the ranks of millions of unemployed migrant workers who have lost their factory jobs and don't have land to go back to farm, the current economic crisis presents China's political leadership with its biggest challenge since the bloody 1989 student protests at Tiananmen Square. This floating population of the unemployed and desperate homeless is the government's biggest nightmare. Add to their ranks the middle-class Chinese who are relative novices to investing in the stock or real estate markets and are quick to blame the government when what they thought could only go up goes down instead – and the nightmare, with restive minorities and roving migrants thrown into the mix, can easily become a living hell.

It is estimated that more than 20 million peasant workers have lost their urban and factory jobs. The actual number is unknown. The Ministry of Human Resources and Social Security also doesn't know how many of the 200 million rural workers who have been laid-off have found new jobs. The government admitted this when it introduced measures in July 2009 to promote employment among the country's large army of rural-based migrant workers. These unemployed migrants and new college graduates are the most vulnerable in the ever-shrinking job market in China. By June 30, 2009, 23.8 million peasants had been covered by a pension program, 41.53 million covered by medical care programs and 15.8 million registered for unemployment insurance. The government has downplayed the importance of unemployed peasant workers as this group has turned out to be less worrisome than urban residents, especially college graduates.

In Shanghai, hundreds of disgruntled property owners protested – and came to blows with local security forces – at an apartment complex in August 2009, when construction workers began to remove the remains of the 13-story building that toppled in June, killing one worker.

In Anyang, Henan, thousands of workers at a state-owned steel plant staged a protest against the takeover of their plant by a private firm because they were angered at the "manipulated" privatization. The firm was sold for 64 million yuan less than the initial bid at auction without the workers' consent. The workers had been pressing for suspension of the takeover, higher wages and a resolution of issues concerning unpaid wages during the restructuring.

Party authorities have to not only address the rising number of protests by locals across the country and ethnic minorities in Tibet and Xinjiang – but Africans in Guangzhou. The city is home to the mainland's largest enclave. It is estimated there are more than 100,000 Africans around the Xiaobei district, known to irreverent locals as "Chocolate City." In July 2009, more than 200 Africans dragged what they thought was the body of a Nigerian clothes trader to the local police station and started a siege. For four hours they vented their fury at officers and onlookers and forced traffic on a busy road to grind to a halt. The protest is believed to be the first by a group of foreigners anywhere on the mainland objecting to the government's visa policies.

The protestors thought the Nigerian trader had died when he fell from a second-story window of a market when he attempted to flee a visa check. He had blood pouring from his head and although unconscious had survived the fall and was later treated at an a local hospital. With Africans protesting in China, you know Black Power has gone global and created a political nightmare for the authorities in Beijing who pride themselves on being the leader of the developing world, especially Africa.

Although China's unemployment rate is not expected to top 4.5 percent, compared with America's near 10 percent in early 2009, without double digit economic growth, China is headed for a serious economic and political "hard landing" that can result in social turmoil on an unprecedented scale.

This is especially worrisome, because after the 1989 Tiananmen protests, an implicit understanding was reached between the people and the Communist Party. People are happy to give up their demands for democracy and free speech in exchange for jobs, wealth and prosperity. In China, historically, there has always been a connection between economic growth, social stability and dynastic rule. The Communist Party is the current dynasty.

In December 2008, more than 300 prominent members of China's intelligentsia signed a petition demanding political change. "In the world, authoritarian systems are approaching the dusk of their endings," the document says. Many of the signatories have been arrested and now languish in jail. So much for democracy and free speech.

The Bubble

The China stimulus package has forced banks to force-feed the economy with liquidity. The purpose of the so-called "quantitative easing" was to generate domestic demand amid slumping exports. But much of the liquidity has flowed into property and stock markets instead – and has partly become government fiscal revenue.

Stocks and properties in China may be 100 percent overvalued. Only two decades of relatively high inflation can justify their prices. However, persistently high inflation leads to currency devaluation, which triggers capital flight and, eventually, an asset market collapse.

The stories coming out of China of millionaires losing their deposits in financial institutions, corrupt, fast and loose lending by rural credit cooperatives and bankrupt consumer lending institutions hollowed out by employees and borrowers make me shudder at the thought of the lending bubble being inflated by Beijing. Kickbacks to officials who review and approve loans regardless of the borrower,s credit worthiness is a replay of what happened in America.

Beijing's decision in 2008 to embark on a monetary easing policy in tandem with its stimulus package encouraged financial institutions to grant loans to fund infrastructure projects – Confucian capitalism at its worst because most of the money was spent on personal businesses, stocks and real estate. Worries are mounting that the lending spree will lead to a mountain of bad assets in the banks as well as the misuse of funds. Mainland financial institutions extended a record 7.37 trillion yuan of loans in the first six months of 2009, nearly three times the amount a year earlier.

In 1989, after the government decided banks could no longer be treated as personal ATMs and had to be run as commercial enterprises, it had to transfer 1.4 trillion yuan of bad loans from the banks into asset management companies. The AMCs issued bonds to the banks. Given the low quality of the bad loans, the AMC's hopes of ever repaying the principal on the bonds is close to zero. As the decade-long "breathing space" ended in 2009, many expected the Ministry of Finance to pay for the AMCs.

The government decided not to pay off the bondholders and advised banks to roll over the bonds for another 10 years. The effect of the roll-over is that the government can delay recognition of the non-performing loans issued in the mid-1990s until the country's 70th birthday. A giant Ponzi scheme similar to the one the U.S. has created in which the income of the current generation goes to pay off the bad debt of past generations.

Official statistics show that rural credit cooperatives had piled up about 590 billion yuan in non-performing loans by the end of 2008. Bad loans at rural commercial banks stood at 19.28 billion yuan at the end of the first half of 2009.

Having started a few thrift and loans, savings and loans, federal and state banks in California in the 1980 go-go years, both as a lawyer and a principal, I can relate to how financial institutions get hollowed out by owners, shareholders, employees and borrowers.

John Greenwood, an adviser to the former Hong Kong monetary authorities and who still advises the HKMA, also known as the "father of the peg" in Hong Kong, was back in July 2009 and warned at a Foreign Correspondents Club luncheon that China's massive stimulus package could cause serious trouble for the mainland economy within two years.

"If China continues with the current rate of money and credit growth, there is an inflationary danger," warned Greenwood. When something seems to good to be true, it usually is. World trade – the engine of global growth – has collapsed. Employment is still contracting throughout the world. There are no realistic scenarios for the global economy to regain high and sustainable growth, which means the Chinese stock market and property bubble inflated by the government's massive stimulus plan will burst.

How Beijing weans the economy off the state stimulus life-support system can only be worked out with the U.S., its largest export market and dollar manipulator. The two countries must work out a mutually sustainable rebalancing of both economies.

Yuan Power Flexing

China's Christmas Day 2008 present to America and the world was an announcement that, effective immediately, companies in Hong Kong and Macau would be allowed to use yuan to settle trade in goods with partners in Guangdong and the Yangtze River Delta under a pilot program. The currency will also be used to settle the tangible trade of companies in Guangxi and Yunnan with counterparts in the 10 Southeast Asian countries which comprise the ASEAN bloc.

The People's Bank of China followed up with a Chinese Lunar New Year gift in January 2009 – an agreement with the Hong Kong Monetary Authority on a 200 billion yuan currency swap to bolster financial stability in the region.

Beijing and Hong Kong sealed the long-awaited agreement announced in December on June 29, 2009, on the eve of the 12th anniversary of the July 1 handover of Hong Kong to China. Cross-border yuan trade settlement could result in about $2 trillion of the country's annual trade being conducted in the mainland currency within three years, says HSBC. The bank said that would equate to up to half of the mainland's total trade and make the yuan into one of the worlds' top three currencies. To get there, the yuan faces a long and lonely road, especially if it plans to dethrone the dollar.

The yuan is well on its way down that road. Yuan-denominated funds will soon be the favored fundraising and investment option in the Chinese venture capital and private equity markets. Twenty four yuan funds were set up in the first half of 2009 and raised $1.13 billion worth of capital. The yuan funds once again surpassed offshore funds in terms of the number of new funds, and accounted for more than 70 percent of the new funds raised in the first half of 2009.

The outstanding performance of the Chinese economy and underlying ability to spur economic activity amid the worsening global financial crisis reinforced the confidence of neighboring countries in the yuan and their commitment to hammering out currency swap arrangements with China. China started 2009 by signing in January with South Korea a 38 trillion won ($30 billion) currency swap agreement to ensure financial stability.

The larger-than-expected scale of the pilot program underscores Beijing's intention to minimize risks brought on by the unstable dollar – the currency in which most trades are settled – and to strengthen the position of the yuan in the international currency system, at the expense of the U.S. dollar. China is concerned that the U.S. will try and print its way out of its crisis by issuing more currency. China is also paving the way for a greater role in the international monetary system with yuan settlements in Northeast Asia, Russia and other regions. It has become an aggressive emerging international currency.

If China loses faith in the dollar, it will collapse. It is only a matter of time because of the unique situation of the U.S. dollar. The U.S. borrows its own money which is also the world's dominant reserve currency. Consequently, the U.S. can disregard its creditors concerns' for the time being without worrying about a dollar collapse.

When U.S. central bankers decided in March 2009 to buy as much as $300 billion of long-term Treasuries and more than double mortgage-debt purchases to $1.45 trillion, aiming to lower home loan and other interest rates – in effect using the Federal Reserve's power to print money – they signed the dollar's death warrant.

When China's State Council issued its directive to develop Shanghai into a global financial center by 2020, something that would only be possible if the yuan were fully convertible, it announced the date by which the yuan will become a fully convertible currency. In other words, China has put America and the world on notice that it plans to make the yuan fully convertible by 2020.

China has few illusions that its currency will replace the dollar as a reserve currency any time soon. Economist Michael Pettis wrote in 2009: "One of the necessary conditions for currency reserve status is that the home country must be able and willing to run trade deficits, since this is the only way the rest of the world can permanently accumulate reserves." The U.S. has been willing to run huge deficits, most notably with China, enabling the rest of the world to use the dollar as a reserve currency.

Making the yuan fully convertible by 2020 can be done. "Having it accepted as an international reserve currency is something entirely different. China has pointed out the advantage the U.S. enjoys by having the dollar as an international reserve currency. But it must also realize that there is a huge price tag attached," *South China Morning Post* columnist Frank Ching said as we discussed the subject at fellow Foreign Correspondents Club Hugh Van Es' wake at the club at the end of May 2009. "Is China prepared to pay it?" he asked as we raised our glasses in one of the many toasts to Hugh's memory.

"Good question," is all I could say. For the yuan to play a bigger global role, China will have to make a lot of changes by 2020 – the most significant ones being unrestricted capital accounts and the rule of law.

China is well aware that it must allow unrestricted capital accounts and adhere to the rule of law if it is to become independent from the dollar. America's policy is forcibly pushing the Chinese toward developing an alternative currency, financial system and adhere to a corruption-free rule of law.

New Global Super-Currency

It was therefore no surprise when China proposed an overhaul of the global monetary system in March 2009, a week before the London G-20 summit, outlining how the U.S. dollar could eventually be replaced as the world's main reserve currency by the IMF's special drawing rights. The SDR is an international reserve currency created by the IMF in 1969 that had the potential to act as a super-sovereign reserve currency. The unit is valued against a basket of the world's major currencies. People's Bank of China Governor Zhou Xiaochuan spelled out in great detail Beijing's dissatisfaction with the primacy of the U.S. dollar, which has led to increasingly frequent global financial collapse since the failure in 1971 of the Bretton Woods system of fixed but adjustable exchange rates.

A super-sovereign reserve currency would not only eliminate the risks inherent in fiat currencies such as the dollar, which are backed only by the credit of the issuing country – not by gold or silver – but would also make it possible to manage global liquidity, Zhou argued.

"When a country's currency is no longer used as the yardstick for global trade and as the benchmark for other currencies, the exchange rate policy of the country would be far more effective in adjusting economic imbalances. This will significantly reduce the risks of future crisis and enhance crisis management capabilities," Zhou said. He made it perfectly clear that as far as China is concerned, the U.S. must bear the brunt of its mismanaged of the global economy.

American Nobel prize-winning economist Joseph Stiglitz, a long-time proponent of ending the dollar's role as the world's dominant reserve currency, welcomed China's proposal.

"We may be at the beginning of a loss of confidence [in the U.S. dollar reserve system]," he said. "There is a need for a global reserve system." A system based on a single currency whose strength depends on confidence in its own economy is not a good basis for a global system, Stiglitz said. "Questionable" is how he challenged the dollar's role as a good store of value.

Relinking of the currencies of major global economies with SDRs, including China's yuan, is a better system than the current world financial chaos in which countries compete to depreciate their currencies against the dollar – much as China has been doing with the yuan.

The U.S. debt bomb consisting of government securities, Social Security and Medicare does pose a growing risk to China. If China and other countries, central banks become less willing to hold U.S. debt, the Federal Reserve may become the buyer of first resort. If that happens, China will become the biggest loser as the U.S. will then probably use inflation to reduce the real burden of its debt. That is why, for the first time, Chinese leaders are publicly voicing their concerns about the future of the dollar as a reserve currency.

The London G-20 decision to create $250 billion in new SDRs marks a major step toward establishing the SDR as a new global reserve currency to replace the dollar.

"The global currency buffet table should add the yuan and others to the dollar, European currencies and yen to make it more appetizing to developing countries led by China" Suyin Stein piped in during a dinner at a Thai restaurant in Sebastopol, California.

"You mean trading nations should have the variety of currency dishes as people do in cuisines around the world?" I asked her as a dish of pineapple rice arrived.

"Exactly!" Suyin replied.

It is essential that a banquet table of expanded currencies that includes the yuan be set up in the new world interlocal wired trading order.

Halal
China is the next big Islamic finance market, as demand grows for ethical funds. A large Muslim population and growing wealth provide a ready retail Islamic banking market in China. China has a Muslim population of about 37 million.

Islamic law requires investments to be based on a specific asset and bans excessive speculation, interest-based lending and gambling, alcohol and pornography-related activities.

The $1 trillion Islamic finance industry is targeting rapidly growing investment opportunities in China where, unlike America and many European countries, it is welcomed with open arms.

Yellow BRIC Road
When the leaders of Brazil, Russia, India and China – known by their acronym BRIC – held their first stand-alone meeting in the Russian city of Yekaterinburg on June 16, 2009, it was a wakeup call – and a shake down of the G-8, dollar and global financial system. On the second day of the summit, the U.S. dollar fell sharply, indicating the BRIC nations had found the magic power of making the dollar ride a roller coaster with only a few words.

The BRIC leaders proposed investing their reserves in each other's currencies, settling bilateral trade in domestic currencies and striking currency swap agreements. It was even suggested to include the five central Asian states of Kazakhstan, Uzbekistan, Turkmenistan, Tajikistan and Kyrgyzstan within the framework of using the yuan as a settlement currency, which some point to as an attempt to create a miniature European Union type of arrangement in Central Asia.

The idea of replacing the dollar as a global currency does have some significant traction. "The BRIC countries can lead the world towards global monetary stability by supporting the researching and planning for the next global currency to replace the U.S. dollar," said Morrison Bonpasse, president of the Single Global Currency Association, a U.S. think tank. Bonpasse believes that "when such a single global currency supports a number of countries with 40-50 percent of the world's GDP, the 'tipping point' will have been reached, and other countries will join quickly."

The handwriting of the new global currency menu is on the BRIC wall. BRIC nations already account for 50 percent of world growth, based on purchasing parity power. While collectively their gross domestic product amounts to only 14.6 percent of the $60.7 trillion global economy, within 20 years it is estimated that it will reach 50 percent. Their collective populations account for 42 percent of the world's total and 26 percent of the world's landmass. Goldman Sachs now predicts that in 20 years, the four countries could together dwarf the Group of Seven leading industrial nations, and that China's economy will overtake that of the U.S. in size.

The summit concluded by calling for a "fairer world order" and a more democratic and just "multipolar" world order.

The IMF's 2009 plan to raise $500 billion by issuing bonds for the first time attracted emerging countries looking to diversify their dollar holdings. Both Russia and Brazil committed $10 billion each, while China aimed at $50 billion. Russia publicly announced it would sell U.S. Treasury bonds to buy IMF bonds. The IMF bonds will be offered in the fund's SDRs, whose value is based on a basket of currencies, rebalanced daily, in which the dollar represents only a 41 percent share.

Considering that the BRIC economies seem to have emerged out of the global financial meltdown earlier than the U.S. and other developed countries, they do merit wider global attention. The stock markets in the four countries rebounded by 40 to 70 percent between February and early June 2009 – and had an annual growth rate of 10.7 percent between 2006 and 2008 – emerging as major contributors to the global economy.

The rapid recovery of BRIC is helping global capital to flow back into emerging markets, and stimulating the rebound of resources and assets prices. Invigorated by the recovery of RIC, the once, sluggish capital markets of the U.S., the European Union and Japan started to rally.

At the conclusion of the BRIC summit, Arkady Dvorkovich, Russia's chief economic aide to President Dmitry Medvedev, called on the IMF to expand the basket of SDRs to include the yuan, commodity currencies such as the ruble, Australian and Canadian dollars and gold.

It is the dollar's relative weakness in SDRs that has raised market concerns that some countries are seeking to distance themselves from the greenback. The announcements by China, Russia and Brazil are troubling rumbles for the dollar.

"It is a clear sign that these countries are not comfortable with their large dollar holdings and should be read by the U.S. as an additional signal of market unease about their large budget deficit," said Desmond Lachman, a resident fellow at the American Enterprise Institute.

"The fact is that the process of decoupling from the U.S. dollar has already begun in many countries' bilateral and multilateral trade arrangements. Of course, the evolution of the U.S. dollar's status will be a long , drawn-out process," an editorial in the June 16, 2009, overseas edition of the *People's Daily*, the official newspaper of China's Communist Party, proclaimed during the BRIC summit.

When to Hold and When to Fold

The fact is that China is already helping the global financial situation by holding onto U.S. Treasury debt. Not only holding on, but also continuing to quietly buy, even as late as September 2008, knowing full well that doing so could bring great additional losses. The fact is that China has lost billions of dollars on its global financial forays. The State Administration of Foreign Exchange has invested 15 percent of its $2 trillion foreign reserves in global stock and bond markets, according to a *Financial Times* report in March 2009. The loss is expected to be more than $80 billion. This is solidarity. Nevertheless, it is understandable why China is feeling nervous about its U.S. dollar holdings and investments and why Premier Wen Jiabao voiced his concerns at the closing meeting of the National People's Congress in March 2009 and urged the U.S. government to protect its investment. It should therefore have come as no surprise to China when Nobel Laureate Paul Krugman said: "They give us poisoned products, we give them worthless paper."

"There is reason why even in the midst of this economic crisis you have seen actual increases in investment flows here in the U.S.," was President Obama's response. "I think it is a recognition that the stability not only of our economic system but also our political system is extraordinary," he continued in his response to Beijing's concerns.

That worked. Beijing decided to go on a $15 billion shopping spree in America to buy real hard American hi-tech machinery and environment-related equipment, in addition to the depreciating paper Treasuries of questionable long-term value, after Presidents Obama and Hu Jintao met on the sidelines of the London G-20.

The global financial meltdown has presented China with a golden platter of buying opportunities in America. China knows it has to safely off load its dollars – and what better place than America? With the demise of investment banking in the U.S., China sees more golden acquisition opportunities – starting in Detroit.

Total holdings of U.S. equities by all Chinese entities more than tripled to $100 billion by the end of June 2008 from mid-2007 and from just $4 billion in June 2006, according to the U.S. Treasury 2008 annual report. It is therefore no surprise that Chinese companies are stepping up their international merger and acquisitions activities to take advantage of falling asset values amid the global financial crisis, despite their poor track record on such deals in the past.

China's foreign reserves have already been invested – more than half in U.S. Treasury issues and other American bonds and much of the rest in euro-denominated assets – and it isn't easy or practical to transfer hundreds of billions, or tens of billions of dollars without causing serious disruption to the currency market, which wouldn't be in China's self-interest either. If it sells the U.S. Treasuries it holds, global interest rates would rise and the dollar would collapse. On the other hand, the fewer Treasuries China buys as a result of the 2008 financial tsunami, the sooner America will see the end of its money-printing spree.

Financial crises don't last forever. But this one could last a lot longer unless Washington policymakers start basing their actions on more realistic assessments of where things stand and what is likely still to come from the line chefs in key government departments.

Shanghaied

The benchmark Shanghai composite index had gained more than 50 percent by November 2009 when this book went to bed, making it one of the world's top performing indexes. More than 30 companies that had received regulatory approval have been waiting for as long as a year to go public since the government quietly suspended IPOs in September 2008. It is estimated that once these companies do go public another 105 billion yuan in new shares will be raised.

In March 2008, the State Council, China's cabinet, approved Shanghai's plans to develop into one of the world's top financial centers by 2020. This was done at a time when established financial centers such as New York and London were hit hard by the financial crisis, the worst since the Great Depression.

In November 2009, after almost 10 years of negotiations, Shanghai finally gave the green light to build a Disney theme park there. Before the Communists came to power in 1949, Shanghai was known as the Paris of the East or the Whore of the Orient, depending on who was describing the city state. It was the financial center of China and inarguably the most exciting city in Asia. The last colonial industrialists and white Russians mixed and socialized with triads and anti-Japanese revolutionaries in bars and jazz clubs.

Having lived and worked in Shanghai since the mid '80s as a lawyer and media executive, I personally witnessed and experienced the rapid transformation the city has made in re-establishing its traditional way of doing business in all-night girlie bars and karaoke lounges.

It was during one such all-night session with media executives from Shanghai TV in 1987, that the now world-class Shanghai TV Festival was born. I was appointed to be the financial advisor to the festival organizers for the debut festival in 1988.

Given time, there is no doubt in my mind that Shanghai will again be acknowledged as the dominant world commercial and financial center.

London was one of the earliest international financial hubs and Britain left a lasting influence on the banking system and capital market, since most relevant rules, regulations and legal frameworks were formed in the country. With the U.S. economy becoming more powerful, the dollar eventually replaced the British pound as the global reserve currency, and New York replaced London as the premier financial and trade center in the world. Despite the shift, the British framework underlying the financial system did not change.

The underlying elements enabling New York to evolve into the leading global financial center were the English language, the dollar, capital accounts and the Anglo-Saxon legal system.

"Shanghai is not a threat to either Hong Kong or London. This is just like New York, it does not replace London," said Alderman Luder, the mayor of London, during a visit to Shanghai in June 2009. "The development of Shanghai will not cut down opportunities for the other two cities, but rather it is sharing pieces of a bigger cake," he added.

Journalist Martin Jacques predicted in early 2009 in Britain's *The Guardian* that Shanghai would soon replace New York as the leading world financial center. I believe China is poised to be among the first choices for global investors in the coming years, but it will be decades before it comes anywhere close to replacing New York as the leading financial center.

Shanghai does not plan to emulate Wall Street and London as development models because Beijing believes it's the bankers in these global financial hubs that caused the worldwide financial crisis. The crisis raises serious questions about the global acceptance of the "free market" model of finance. China's Shanghai model will be interesting to watch as China's preference for gradual change and prudent regulation – "crossing the river by feeling the stones" – goes into effect in 2020. Will Shanghai revert to its historical legacy as an open international city with Chinese characteristics after it Shanghais the best of the West's financial models?

Head Financial Chef
China knows it can and will lead the world out of the financial crisis that America led the world into, especially when it is constantly reassured it will,by financial gurus like Jim Rogers, George Soros – and even the U.N.

"I certainly expect China to come out of it sooner than the U.S.," said Rogers, chairman of Singapore-based Rogers Holdings. "They seem to be spending the money on the right things. China is doing a far better job than the others," he added as he announced plans to sell his remaining U.S. dollar holdings because the world's largest economy isn't a "safe haven" for investors anymore. In his opinion, it is China's farmers who will have the

Lamborghinis in the future and not the brokers on Wall Street.

The reason why is simple. U.S. policy makers focused on stimulus rather than reform. U.S. asset prices will implode when the dollar printing press bubble bursts – and China will pick up the pieces for pennies.

Paleface Knight?

China cannot and will not be America and Europe's white knight. The suggestion made by some columnists that China lend as much as $500 billion of its $2 trillion foreign currency reserves to the U.S. Treasury to help bail out failed banks in America and Europe is absurd. Such a gesture would not help China's stature rise as has also been suggested, especially now that China is also a casualty of the global financial meltdown. China needs these reserves to support its economic agenda and to ensure it has the capital to feed its people and pay external obligations. China is still a developing country with hundreds of millions of people – more than the entire population of America – living on less than a dollar a day. China needs to save itself before it can save any one else, and definitely not a China-bashing country.

All China can do is to continue buying U.S. Treasuries and support the U.S. deficit because of the sheer size of the Treasury market, especially if it wants to continue a monetary policy aimed at promoting exports to the U.S. – and continue to run a trade surplus.

There is no incentive for China to stop buying U.S. Treasuries; it needs a safe investment for its dollar reserves, and its growth depends on a healthy U.S. economy. That policy will hopefully get America and China to jointly develop global policies that are mutually beneficial and positive for the rest of the world.

Chapter 7

Chinese-American — Chop Suey
It is best to win without fighting.
– Sun Tzu

Tête-â-Tête

Just as China swept out the homeless in Beijing ahead of the 2008 Olympics and America did for Barack Obama's inauguration in Washington, both countries must sweep out the antiquated U.S.-Sino policies and sweep in a strong, vigorous, ever-expanding and long-lasting bilateral relationship.

The China and U.S. agreement at the conclusion of the 5th Strategic Economic Dialogue talks in December 2008 to give traders of both countries $20 billion in financing credit to boost bilateral commerce was the first right step in the direction of upgrading the SED into a biannual meeting between the two countries that now includes top diplomats as well as the bankers. The export-import banks of America and China will offer $12 billion and $8 billion respectively to credit-worthy importers in developing countries.

The U.S. also said it would support China's joining the Financial Stability Forum, a club of central banks and finance ministries from the world's richest nations.

Notwithstanding my earlier criticism of former Treasury Secretary Henry Paulson, he does deserve full credit as the architect of the SED, one of the few successful foreign policy legacies of the recently departed Bush administration. The SED has been upgraded to a cabinet-level forum between the two who held their first meeting in Washington in July 2009.

The most important task for both countries is "to work more closely to address the international financial crisis, resolutely oppose protectionism in trade and investment, promote reform in the international financial system and tighten oversight of the international reserve currency so as to ensure the stability and growth of the Chinese and the American economies and the world economy," Premier Wen Jiabao told Timothy Geithner during his visit to Beijing in June 2009.

Premier Wen Jiabao, in a speech to U.S.-China business leaders in New York in September 2008, said the two countries "are not competitors, but partners."

"Two countries that appreciate each other and learn from each other should be able to live together in amity and achieve common progress," Wen added.

After President Obama's election victory, the Chinese congratulatory message emphasized that Beijing is ready to strengthen its relationship with the U.S. and further promote friendly and constructive cooperation. President Obama agreed with President Hu that the development of Sino-U.S. relations is not only in the interest of the two countries, but the interests of the world. Let's hope Obama sticks to that agreement and brings about the necessary "change" in U.S.-China relations and doesn't get sidetracked by Congress, or his Secretary of State Hillary Clinton, a former senator and aggressive China-basher during her primary campaign and Senate confirmation hearings as Secretary of State.

She made it clear that Washington will continue to rely on Japan as the "cornerstone" of U.S. foreign policy in Asia – confirmed by President Obama in February 2009 when he welcomed Japanese Prime Minister Taro Aso to the White House. Aso was the first foreign leader invited to visit Obama in the Oval Office as his party and country was doing everything they could to get rid of him – and did in July 2009. Come on, America, let's get it right for a change instead of being repeatedly stuck with the loose change.

Clinton took another side swipe at China with a subtle lecture when she warned China that Sino-U.S. relations will depend largely on Beijing's behavior at home and abroad. "We want a positive and cooperative relationship with China, one where we deepen and strengthen our ties on a number of issues. But this is not a one-way effort – much of what we do will depend on the choices China makes about its future at home and abroad."

Making Japan her first foreign stop as Secretary of State and China the fourth and last on her first overseas trip, the Chinese character for four also meaning death, was the kiss of death for U.S. foreign policy in Asia. Still, her positive comments about strengthening Sino-U.S. economic, political, environmental and military cooperation and engagement were encouraging. Acknowledging the old Chinese saying, "When you are in a common boat, you need to cross the river peacefully together," Clinton told the Asia Society in New York before her trip to Asia.

"This aphorism is from The Art of War," Premier Wen Jiabao told Clinton during her visit. "And there is another line after it, and that is 'To march forward hand in hand just like the right hand holding the left hand.'"

The quotes confirmed the two countries' dependence on each other and that neither one can afford to turn its back on the other or reverse course. I hope that is the case, and that U.S. political agendas of future presidential campaigns and administrations don't sink the American ship of state that George Washington saved crossing the Delaware.

Clinton's veiled warnings during her confirmation hearings were followed by a direct threat from Treasury Secretary Tim Geithner during his confirmation hearings. He accused China of "manipulating" its currency – much the way he manipulated his tax payments. Forcing China to revalue the yuan will be "economic suicide."

I agree with fellow Hong Konger Stephen Roach, Morgan Stanley's Asia chairman, who said: "I've never seen an economy in recession voluntarily raise their currency. It's horrible advice."

Thankfully, both Clinton and Geithner's remarks were political spin expressed to ensure their swift nomination. Both their words and actions during their trips to Beijing in early 2009 confirmed the political and economic path America wants to pursue and go down together with China as they develop and pursue a new era of ties.

"World events have given us a full and formidable agendas," Clinton said during her February visit to Beijing. "As we tackle it, the U.S. is committed to pursuing a positive, cooperative relationship with China, one that we believe is important to future peace, progress and prosperity for both countries and for the world."

America must wake up to reality. The finance, banking, insurance and real estate sectors together rose to represent more than a fifth of U.S. gross domestic product, while once mighty American manufacturing contributed less than 13 percent. Millions in China had work and Americans' purchasing power was artificially boosted as they bought cheap Chinese-made goods and ran up more debt.

America may be waking up. The U.S. trade deficit shrank 28.7 percent in November 2008, the biggest contraction in 12 years, as weak consumer demand and plummeting oil prices caused a record drop in imports, according to the Commerce Department. This book went to print before fresher numbers became available, but I would be surprised if the numbers haven't dropped even more since.

A treaty formalizing biannual meetings between the leaders of the two countries is long overdue. Any treaty with China requires a two-thirds vote by the U.S. Senate, a potential hurdle with Democrats retaining their overwhelming majority in both houses. Thirty years after diplomatic relations were established between the two countries, there is still an overwhelming lack of trust in China by the American Congress.

Hopefully, Congress will listen to an American public that favors co-operation and engagement with China. A poll conducted by the Chicago Council on Global Affairs in the summer of 2008 showed that 64 percent of Americans favor "friendly cooperation and engagement" as the appropriate response to China's rise. America and China are interlocally connected and dependent on each other. The sooner America embraces this reality, the quicker the Sino-U.S. relationship will blossom into a pragmatic and constructive one that is mutually beneficial and rewarding.

America cannot afford to risk a trade war with China while it is in the economic danger zone just because Congress yields to powerful lobbyists from the producers and manufacturers association, labor unions and business. U.S. business and labor groups are pushing lawmakers to take a harder line with China. Steelmakers, paper producers, textile companies are all getting ready to file trade complaints. Just about everyone who counts for career politicians' re-election campaigns – donors. Not when America is trying to spend its way out of a recession with Chinese financing. America needs more than $2 billion a day just to stay afloat. It's not smart to bite the hand that feeds America.

On the eve of Barack Obama's inauguration, the retired deputy chief of the People's Liberation Army general staff, General Xiong Guangkai, called on the president-elect to relax restrictions on Sino-U.S. military exchanges, saying such a move would be crucial to resolving crises and eliminating misunderstandings between the two countries. He did so as a star-studded list of old China hands from American politics – including former President Jimmy Carter and ex-Secretary of State Henry Kissinger – were in Beijing to celebrate the 30th anniversary of the re-establishment of diplomatic ties between the two countries.

"There is no more important diplomatic relationship in the world than the one that has grown between the People's Republic of China and the United States of America," Carter said.

Toasting the occasion with glasses of champagne is the way forward as both sides ply each other with their political and economic alcohol.

What should now be America and China's goal?

"In a dynamically changing world our relationship cannot be static; it will either expand or narrow. The world will benefit, and so will our countries, if it expands. In the post-Cold War era, the deepening and widening of the American-Chinese partnership is not designed against others – and it does not diminish the importance of the U.S.' or China's close ties with other major powers – but it reflects an increasing awareness of our shared responsibility for global well being," said Zbigniew Brezezinski, National Security Adviser to President Jimmy Carter from 1977 to 1981, in a speech at a seminar in commemoration of the 30th anniversary of the establishment of diplomatic relations between the U.S. and China.

America and China should spend 2009 celebrating the three decades of the world's most crucial diplomatic relationship. Figuring out ways to develop it further, rather than tearing down the existing infrastructure, should be the focus of the Obama administration. It should take to heart, as it appears to have done, China's call for a multipolarization and multilateralism to address and resolve global issues rather than America being a hegemonist trying to unilaterally impose its will in a unipolar world.

China's leadership, like America's, faces its biggest challenge since the Communists won the civil war in 1949 and America won the Cold War in 1989. The fringe advocates of extremism and distrust in China and America must be pushed aside in favor of the constructive players regardless of their party affiliation.

Backdrop

A brief history of the Sino-U.S. relationship is in order so that it can be appreciated from an objective and constructive point of view. President Richard Nixon broke the ice of the Cold War mindset of America when he made his groundbreaking visit to China in 1972. The U.S. then switched diplomatic recognition from Taipei to Beijing in 1979, recognizing "One China" and closing the door on economic and political isolation. In three decades, China has gone from being a Cold War Communist backwater into one of the world's top economies.

However, since the fall of the Berlin Wall, the collapse of the Soviet Union and communism in Russia and Eastern Europe, the U.S. and China now find themselves trying to overcome new challenges and finger-pointing and build a relationship that will help move the whole world forward in peace and prosperity.

China is almost fully recovered from Chairman Mao's failed social policies. When will America recover from its failed foreign policies and stop making more? Granted the top priority for the Obama administration is the domestic economic crisis, which is a tremendous political handful. China, with its vast foreign reserves, can be part of the solution because of its desire to protect its massiveinvestments in U.S. Treasuries and other securities.

The Sommeliers

The Sino-U.S. Strategic Dialogue is sort of like a wine-tasting where Chinese and American executive chefs get together for honest conversation and free-flowing exchanges, seeking the economic and political flavors they perceive as best for both countries and the world. The U.S. Secretaries of State and Treasury and their Chinese counterparts are bent on making their executive chefs, recipes more palatable.

The meeting of American and Chinese sommeliers in Beijing in December 2006, however, was a reminder of how China continues to be misperceived by America. The U.S. delegation – seven cabinet secretaries, and the head of the Federal Reserve – were there to lobby and bully China. While the Americans came to lecture China on currency revaluation and market theories, the Chinese fired back with a call for Washington to clean up its own act by reforming its economy and breaking its addiction to the Chinese goods and loans that underwrite the massive U.S. trade and budget deficits.

The Chinese prefer gradualism. After all, they represent the biggest economic experiment in history. Transforming a highly centralized, state-controlled economy into a market economy, and transforming an export-driven economy into a consumer-driven economy that affects a quarter of the world's population is, to say the least, a challenge. China is not a threat to America. It is America's most important ally if the eagle is to survive, thrive and continue to guide in the 21st century.

U.S. politicians received a Chinese Power Point history lesson on the country's 5,000-year history of poverty, colonial subjugation and civil wars. But Americans to this day don't know or understand China.

China must maintain an annual investment growth rate of around 20 percent if it is to avoid a crash landing and implosion – with devastating global consequences, especially in America. China's per capita GDP in 2008 was just under $3,000, while the per capita GDP in America is nearly $47,000. The fact is that the Chinese government is beholden to China's vast export sector, which accounts for more than one-third of the country's economy. Letting the yuan float upward could massively weaken the export-driven economy and create political instability. For example, the textile industry alone supports 90 million workers but makes miniscule profits. The consequence of millions of textile workers being unemployed or the government extending more subsidies to the textile industries while it is trying to reform its market economy would have a devastating political impact.

America gave China the green light to join the Inter-American Development Bank. In return, China signed an $8-billion contract to buy four nuclear power plants from U.S.-based Westinghouse. The deal creates 5,500 U.S. jobs and is a concrete first step in reducing America's trade deficit with China. Westinghouse also agreed to transfer to China technology that could be used in the construction of more nuclear reactors in China. It's a pity Westinghouse is no longer owned by America. It is owned by Japan's Toshiba Corp. However, the two-day session failed to produce any short-term solutions to the schizoid Sino-U.S. relationship, other than an agreement to meet again, which they have been doing every six months.

The Main Dish
The fifth U.S. China high-level get-together in Beijing on Dec. 4 and 5, 2008, under their Strategic Economic Dialogue Agreement, was the main event to watch as America shifted gears with a new president and Democratic Congress.

The SED was conceived as a civilized and mellow way of dealing with prickly and sensitive issues without anyone at any time ending the process acrimoniously. The dialogue, held twice a year in China and the U.S. in turn, has so far achieved 150 agreements ranging from the macro economy to environment protection.

With all the noise and media coverage of the need for China to revalue the yuan because currency reform is "as important now as it has ever been," the fact is that the yuan has appreciated more than 20 percent in the four years since it was de-pegged from the dollar, a detail that has been conveniently overlooked. Granted, but not surprising, the yuan recorded its highest one-day fall against the dollar during the December 2008 dialogue. Just a re-minder of who controls currency fluctuations. Many economic and political experts speculate that China let its currency weaken to help its exporters during the crisis. The yuan will continue to appreciate with time.

Another significant fact that is overlooked is that for every gain the yuan makes against the dollar, the lesser the value of China's holdings in dollars becomes. Being the largest holder of America's debt, that can be a signifi-cant financial hit. Why should China follow in America's footsteps? Just because America says so? America was again reminded that its unceasing pressure to revalue the yuan is tantamount to interference in China's eco-nomic affairs.

Congress should recognize that it is in China's own economic interest to let the yuan appreciate, to avoid inflation. When the Chinese currency's value in U.S. dollars increases, it means the People's Bank of China does not have to create as much domestic currency to buy U.S. dollars.

It is not a surprise that Chinese officials urged the U.S. to stabilize its own economy and protect China's U.S. dollar-based investments as the two sides opened their cabinet-level economic talks in Beijing in December 2008, the first since the global financial meltdown.

China pointed out that it had made important contributions to the glob-al economy by keeping its own growth steady, adopting pro-active fiscal and monetary policies and raising domestic demand. China also assured America that it would sustain its growth and financial stability. "Excessive consumption in the U.S. and over-reliance on debt are the key reasons be-hind the global financial crisis," said China Central Bank Governor Zhou Xiaochuan, lecturing America about its economic frailties.

China expressed concern over the constantly shifting U.S. regulatory environment, which makes it difficult for China to invest in U.S. companies. U.S. Treasury Secretary Henry Paulson, the architect of the dialogue agreement, took most of the criticism on the chin like honest bankers do.

China's GDP growth dropped to 9 percent in the third quarter of 2008, the lowest in five years, and 6.5 percent in the fourth quarter, the lowest in seven years. The forecast for 2009 doesn't look any brighter, according to the World Bank. It has slashed its forecast to 7.5 percent, the lowest in almost two decades. Although China also faces a rapidly slowing economy and rising unemployment, the tone of the critical comments reflected the shift in power. China made it clear that it is more productive for the country to put its foreign reserves to work at home rather than to continue underwriting America's debt.

The U.S. has no basis to lecture China, or any other country really, about prudent financial policies. It really should devote its effort to get its own financial house in order. The U.S. system, once the epitome of modern economic thinking and an example to emulate, suddenly imploded and is not really respected or trusted anymore.

Former U.S. Federal Reserve Chairman Alan Greenspan told the House of Representatives Committee on Oversight and Government Reform in October 2008, that he was "shocked" at the breakdown in U.S. credit markets, and concluded that he had been partly wrong to resist regulation of some securities.

"This crisis has turned out to be much broader than anything I could have imagined," Greenspan said. "I have found a flaw. I don't know how significant or permanent it is. But I have been very distressed by that fact." Any wonder China is distressed and distrustful?

China also has welcomed U.S. companies with strengths in energy and the environment because it has a huge appetite for the technologies. China and America signed seven deals on ecological partnerships. These included electricity generation, transportation, clean water, clean air, and protecting wetlands and other natural areas. In 2006, China used 15 percent of the world's energy to produce 5.5 percent of global gross domestic product. China recognizes it has paid too high an environmental price for its growth.

The U.S.-China dialogue mechanism has been a valuable and productive way of getting the two countries to tackle thorny issues honestly and develop ongoing stable economic relations. But it must be adapted to the realities of the new decade, *Global Trends 2025: A Transformed World,* published by the National Intelligence Council concluded. America's intelligence community also concluded that America is losing world dominance to China and India.

America can no longer sustain itself as the world's only superpower, even when bankrolled by China and other countries. The world today is multipolar. Trying to isolate China is a futile mistake, no matter whether the attempt is with Japan, India or both. The efforts to do so by American administrations have repeatedly failed. All this does is weaken America and generate more hostile foes. That does not mean America won't remain powerful. It just won't be the sole super power. America must give up the bully pulpit because it has been a self-destructive one and has outlived its usefulness. It's a much healthier, cheaper and refreshing way to recognize, acknowledge, educate and come to terms in order to prepare future generations to this new global reality.

Super-Sized Main Dish

America and China have expanded the scope of the bi-annual SED meetings and renamed them as the Strategic and Economic Dialogue, adding the "and." The inaugural meeting took place in Washington on July 27-28, 2009. The meetings are no longer limited to financial and economic matters discussed between the U.S. Treasury Secretary and his Chinese counterpart, but now include the U.S. Secretary of State and her Chinese counterpart to also address global geopolitical issues.

The Chinese S&ED co-chairs who joined their U.S. counterparts Clinton and Geithner at the inaugural meeting were State Councilor Dai Bingguo and Vice Premier Wang Qishan. Various heads of U.S. and Chinese departments, bureaus and commissions are invited to participate, depending on the issues being addressed.

The S&ED should be elevated even further to include at least one annual presidential level meeting. Why not make them even stronger? America and China must step up their dialogue and cooperation in areas of trade, energy, environmental protection, food safety and military cooperation and sign a mutually beneficial bilateral treaty governing their relationship in these areas.

A comprehensive bilateral treaty that brings the two countries closer together would be just as miraculous as Obama's election victory was. The China challenge is, first and foremost, really about money and military might. Energy and the other geopolitical issues are secondary. The other benefits of a bilateral treaty are that it would allow U.S. firms to invest in China's industrial sector and allow U.S. firms in China to settle disputes by international arbitration rather than subject them to the arbitrary rule of law that currently exists in Chinese courts. In turn, China would have an incentive to improve its legal system and better protect private property rights and intellectual property.

"The global economic downturn we are experiencing here in the U.S. is also being felt in China, reminding and emphasizing that both countries need each other now more than ever if we are both to remain the top super giants" Mary Catherine McBride said during a dinner in Newbury Park, California, in February 2009 as Obama was settling into the White House and a feeling of euphoria enveloped the country.

"You're right," I said. "Let's hope Obama recognizes this imperative of mutual dependence. He hopefully got some insight from his half-brother who lives in Shenzhen, across the border between the mainland and Hong Kong, who went to Obama's inauguration," I continued as we took our drinks and moved to the living room. Well, so far so good. The Obama administration clearly recognizes the importance of the Sino-U.S. mutually destructive-dependency diet that needs to be changed for the two countries to lead the world through the 21st century.

Now that America and China recognize each other as potential global partners and are signaling their newfound "cooperative and comprehensive partnership," it is time to resume more direct military-to-military exchanges and create a joint military command. The U.S. and China did initiate a dialogue on nuclear strategy in April 2008, between the two defense ministries involving the U.S. Strategic Command and the People's Liberation Army's 2nd Artillery Command. This is a dialogue the U.S. had sought for many years. After one meeting, it was suspended as part of the broader Chinese suspension of military-to-military exchanges in retaliation for the outgoing Bush administration's decision to sell $6 billion worth of arms to Taiwan in October 2008.

The Obama inaugural euphoria felt across America was transformed to the inaugural S&ED as the president addressed the opening ceremony of the talks.

"The relationship between the United States and China will shape the 21st century, which makes it as important as any bilateral relationship in the world," Obama said. Serious words to digest, but the perfect antacid to unnecessary repeated burning economic, financial, ethnic, terrorist and military indigestion attacks.

China's Hu Jintao sent a message to the meeting in which he said China sought a "positive, constructive and comprehensive relationship." He went on to add: "As two countries with significant influence in the world, China and the United States shoulder important responsibilities on a host of major issues concerning peace and development of mankind."

The only thing of significance to come out of that meeting was an important memorandum of understanding between the two nations regarding global warming, energy and environment that they are both pushing from their own radical extremes. That is one issue they really have to duke out honestly and harmoniously as the future relationship depends on it. If they can't solve this one, then humanity is doomed.

Watching the Chinese media portray U.S. Commerce Secretary Gary Locke and Energy Secretary Steven Chu as "bananas" – a derogatory term meaning yellow on the outside and white on the inside – two weeks before the historic meeting during their visit to Beijing, I chuckled to myself. As an "egg," white on the outside and yellow on the inside who has felt like a banana on more than one occasion, I can relate to grining and bearing it. The key is to keep talking harmoniously and constructively without unnecessarily provoking each other by continued deal breaker-delayer actions on the military fronts. That is the only way each party can get to know and trust each other. Hopefully, they are in those food lines. That is the only way they will become true equal, adoring partners, loved by their global family.

With a U.S. federal budget deficit that could reach $1 trillion in Barack Obama's first year in office, a national debt of more than $11 trillion that requires more than $2 billion a day in interest just to stay afloat, with China owning over half-a-trillion dollars in U.S. government bonds – more than any other country – how many other options does America have to finance its national debt and the more than $700 billion financial industry bailout? America can't just spend its way out of the financial crisis alone. It desperately needs a long-term partner that can help it prudently develop a plan that gradually ends America's deficit financing as it tries to preserve the dollar's global dominance and value as best it can without bankrupting China. "To sleep in the same bed but dream different dreams," an ancient Chinese saying, sums up the new economic dialogue. North Korea is in both their dreams, as well as their nightmares.

Looking down on the endless carpet of white cotton-candy clouds on my last flight from America to China at the end of December 2008, with bright clear blue skies above them as cold rain and snow blanketed the West Coast below, I couldn't help reflecting on how bright and clear Sino-U.S. relations could be. The chilly confrontational perception created by career politicians, fanned by China-bashing and fear-mongering, obscures how calm, clear, bright and constructive a Sino-U.S. partnership could and should be.

I couldn't believe my delighted, bewildered and foggy eyes after a night of revelry the first Sunday morning in May 2009, when I opened the morning paper and read the headline "Obama seeks balanced ties but won't preach at Beijing, aide says." Finally, I thought to myself, America is getting it right and is heading down the right geopolitical track. Obama wants a more balanced trade relationship and closer military ties with China and will not lecture it on human rights, said Jeffrey Bader, senior director for Asian affairs at the National Security Council. Speaking to the Committee of 100, a prominent Chinese-American group, Bader said Obama would also look to China to exercise a leading role in world affairs.

"President Obama sees China as a major global player, as a leader. He does not see China as an inevitable threat or foe," Bader said. "President Obama does not believe in lecturing people" and would reach out to the Chinese people. "He believes in leading by example, not by finger-pointing. He has no instinct to impose first-world models of development or artificial timelines on developing countries as to how they should achieve democracy or protection of human rights," he added.

America must acknowledge that what China has done. Keeping 1.3 billion people fed as China prospers is no small feat. America also has to acknowledge that trying over the years, as it has, to get China to accept more international responsibility and Western norms of political and economic behavior is just another means of trying to keep China down. China's rising star and global role will not be controlled or dictated by America. China will define its role and terms of international engagement as it deems best for China. Beijing refuses to dance to Washington's tune or dine at an international buffet when the price is set by America. A Chinese banquet is more than enough. China prefers America's a la carte menu to pick and choose from.

Having done business in China for more than 20 years, starting back in the early 1980s, when the only good food one could get in there was Chinese, I can attest to the difficulty and frustration of negotiating with the Chinese – regardless of whether they are in the stronger or weaker position. As long as the food and drink is Chinese – China wins. If the food is Western or American, they win faster and the cost is higher as they want to get going so they can have their Chinese food fix.

Giving China greater recognition would send a strong signal that the U.S. is not opposed to China's peaceful rise, prosperity and ability to invest in or buy U.S. companies the way it attempted to do in 2005, when China National Offshore Oil Corp. tried to acquire Unocal, the U.S. oil and gas company, for $18 billion, much more than Chevron eventually paid for it. America would also affirm its confidence in a policy of engagement and its distrust for protectionism. Chinese reformers would also benefit and gain a stronger hand, benefiting America, China and the world.

The Banquet of Great Expectations

President Obama's November 2009 state visit to China gave him a first-hand opportunity to see the human face of China as he tried to convince Beijing that Washington is its partner, not its rival. It was the most important political "chewing the fat" banquet on earth as Obama's low-key approach promised to achieve a lot more than America's traditional swaggered lectures. Bringing a carrot without the stick to stir up any contentious issues was sweet.

"The United States does not seek to contain China, nor does a deeper relationship with China mean a weakening of our bilateral alliances," Obama said. "On the contrary, the rise of a strong, prosperous China can be a source of strength for the community of nations."

What impressed the Chinese public the most about Obama was a report that he had insisted on paying for his own hamburger at a Washington restaurant and the fact that he carried his own umbrella when he got off Air Force One in Shanghai.

The unrealistic expectations, and unfair criticism, of Obama's China November summit by the Western media and American talking heads of all political hues, for its lack of concrete accomplishments, reflects America's lack of understanding of the inherent distrust both countries have towards each other.

How can China trust America overnight when the U.S. National Intelligence Strategy 2009 identifies China as a "global challenger" on par with the so-called axis of evil to U.S. interests? This on the heels of U.S. Secretary of Defense Robert Gates saying China's ever-advancing arms would create a "new threat" to the U.S. military and weaken its military power in the Pacific region? America's determination to sell more advanced weapons to Taiwan, coupled with its increased surveillance activities of China's military expansion, as it increases the volume of its accusations that China is expanding its espionage activities in the U.S. – and protectionism – are not endearing gestures of trust.

The question on Chinese minds is whether America was being capricious because of its economic difficulties, which force it to be nice, or is this a genuine change of U.S. attitude towards China?

Nevertheless, the leaders greeted each other at the door of the Great Hall of the People after President Obama's motorcade slithered its way past thousands of onlookers crowding around Tiananmen Square, in front of the giant portrait of Mao, to catch a glimpse of the American president.

The leaders shook hands and walked up the red carpet, Chinese military leaders facing them. At the conference table where the first bilateral meeting was held, President Obama sat flanked by senior cabinet members, including Secretary of State Hillary Clinton and Larry Summers, director of the National Economic Council. Their meal was a state banquet.

It was a constructive first step in a budding romance over a state banquet, which bodes well for the future engagement of the two world super powers.

What a difference to the pedestrian heckled reception President Hu received on the White House lawn, followed by a mere social lunch. Who really had whom for lunch?

Go, the strategy game invented in China more than 2,500 years ago, is known for its simple rules and parity. Two players alternately place black and white stones on a grid, with the simple objective of winning a larger portion of the board. But as any Go player will testify, it may be the most complex of games involving constant reading ahead, plotting and strategizing.

So the set of Go that President Obama bore as a gift for President Hu Jintao accurately reflects and symbolizes the character of Sino-U.S. relations over the coming years. Two of the world's greatest powers have finally sat down as equals at the same banquet table, in a relaxed manner knowing they will be involved in constant maneuvering to capture or save stones, always mindful of the overall board as each country adopts a different strategy to address global problems as vital partners and competitors.

Presidents Hu and Obama, in their joint statement to the media, did serve up some reheated dishes: bilateral cooperation, building and deepening strategic trust, economic cooperation and global recovery, regional and global challenges, climate change, energy and environment.

There were several new dishes served as well, including a host of clean energy initiatives and an accord to combat climate change, cooperation in law enforcement, intelligence and counterterrorism, science and technology sharing, including possible outer space exploration, significantly increasing youth and student exchanges (increasing American students to China fivefold), expanded civil aviation flights, joint research in public health, cooperation in high-speed rail and a new agricultural accord. A pleasantly surprising dish was the "strategic reassurance" framework that would allow a regular consultation to seek agreement, or at least an agreement to disagree, on main starategic issues between the two nations before they are debated internationally.

The two sides recognize and respect each other's core interests and major concerns. They addressed the sensitive area of building strategic trust, saying they "share a responsibility" to cooperate on regional and global security challenges. China specifically said it welcomes the U.S.'s contribution to peace, stability and prosperity in the Asia-Pacific region, clearly seeking to reassure America's neo-cons who fear that China is seeking to push the U.S. out of the region.

President Obama reciprocated when he expressed U.S. respect for China's "sovereignty and territorial integrity" concerning Taiwan and Tibet.

Being a foodie, Obama knows how to chill and change the U.S.-China relationship one bite at a time.

Suspicions continue to linger on both sides. Especially after Obama returned home and hosted his first official state visit for Indian Prime Minister Singh during Thanksgiving week. The challenge for both countries is to overcome their suspicions, build credibility and turn their words into action. They must play the game of Go until they achieve harmonious trust with each other to lead a bipolar world as trusting partners.

President Obama's maiden voyage to China has elevated the Sino-U.S. relationship to a new high frontier. The 21st century reality is that China and the U.S. must build a "positive, cooperative, and comprehensive" relationship, as neither country can fulfill many of their goals without the other.

Thanksgiving

Thanksgiving is a uniquely American holiday, thanks to the Pilgrims who survived their first harsh winter in Massachusetts and celebrated the first Thanksgiving in 1621. They set aside time to give thanks for their bountiful harvest and to live in peace with their Native-American neighbors in the Land of the Free. A land where they could live and worship freely.

In his Thanksgiving Proclamation of 1789, George Washington urged Americans to give thanks "for the peaceable and rational manner in which we have been able to establish constitutions of government for our safety and happiness." He also asked them to beseech the "Lord and Ruler of Nations" to "render our National Government of wise, just and constitutional laws, discreetly and faithfully executed and obeyed ...."

Turkey has been a mainstay of Thanksgiving dinners from the very beginning. But the modern bird, like Americans, is much different than its ancestors. Earlier turkeys were naturally smaller and more wiry, and they had less breast meat than today's birds, which have been bred to satisfy American preferences for white meat. Today's male turkeys, like many leading American politicians, are so top-heavy that many can't fly or even walk without toppling over, and most are incapable of mating. Were it not for artificial insemination, the species would be extinct.

Thanksgiving is similar to the Chinese tradition of celebrating the Mid-Autumn, or harvest, Festival. Families get together and give thanks and celebrate their "bountiful harvest" and prosperity.

Mooncakes, the Mid-Autumn Festival delicacy, like turkeys, have gone through a major transformation that reflects today's Chinese tastes – and politicians. They are no longer the traditional baked cholesterol-packed salty egg treat, but modern-style health-conscious snowy mooncakes that require no baking, so they are not oily.

Thanksgiving, like the Mid-Autumn Festival, is a time to reflect on Sino-U.S. relations and give thanks for what each country has enabled the other to achieve – and how much more they can achieve together for each other and the world as true global partners.

Leaner, Greener Detroit – Shanghai

I remember when I came to America in 1964, General Motors, Ford, Chrysler and Detroit were synonymous with America's might, dynamism and power. The "super-charged" engines of America's globalization plan. That's why I first went to Detroit when I came to the U.S. – to work in the hood and under it – working the American Dream. I worked at Grant Machine Shop in Detroit and its related company, Precision Automatic in nearby Pontiac, making parts for GM, Ford and Chrysler. Making parts for America's top global automobile brands, especially pistons for the hot new Ford Mustang, was a buzz. Having been there and worked with so many great Americans, as the Motown sound and Vietnam War were accelerating, was exhilarating.

I bought my first car in 1966 in Los Angeles – a GM-built 1962 Chevy Impala convertible. With the American Dream waving in my hair, I drove down Hollywood and Sunset boulevards and up the Pacific Coast Highway. Today, driving smaller fuel-efficient Korean and Japanese cars for the sake of conservation, as I do at home in Hong Kong, can bring on a sad nostalgia.

But the sadness as Motor City crashed and burns because of short-sighted, profit-centered business decisions is mixed with excitement as other car makers, including China's, doing something about emissions and the environment.

The GM bankruptcy is a metaphor for the meltdown of America and why its corporate icons have become mere crumbs on the bankruptcy court table for China to pick over and choose which ones to gobble up. As a former auto parts worker and lawyer who represented Detroit's car makers, I have serious doubts whether the Big Three can change its corporate culture to compete with the likes of Chinese, Japanese and Korean manufacturers. There is no sound reason for the U.S. to bail out Chrysler and GM, only political, since the UAW and other big unions are in the Democratic Party's camp.

It's only a matter of time before GM and Chrysler – and maybe Ford this time – are back in the government soup line, begging for one more hand-out.

Hummer and Sickle

For someone who started his working career in America in machine shops in Detroit and Pontiac in the 1960s, and legal career in the secured lending arena representing corporate America in the 1970s, who for several years worked his way through the bankruptcy court system representing secured lenders, creditors, trustees and receivers, including Detroit's giants and America's leading financial institutions, watching GM seek refuge in bankruptcy court is not only a sad epitaph for an era, but a double dose of nostalgic memory. First as an auto parts worker who made parts for what became America's automobile dinosaurs, and then as a lawyer representing the corporate-financial institutions whose misdeeds and missteps led America to be technically bankrupt.

Living in China and reading that GM's gas-guzzling Hummer brand is being sold to a Chinese company for a cool $500 million, even though the purchaser has said it plans to keep production in America, so that 3,000 workers and 100 dealers can retain their super-sized burger diets, was a symbolic reminder of how China's Confucian capitalism is devouring America. After all, the Hummer is different from other American car brands because it invokes a sense of American pride. A Hummer conjures up American soldiers dashing around in Humvees in Iraq and Afghanistan. Hummer is symbolic of Americanism – the iconic gas-guzzling celebrity- driven road-hogging oversized SUV status symbol. Driven by the likes of actor-turned governor of California Arnold Schwarzenegger, who is reported to have once owned as many as seven, Playboy magazine founder Hugh Heffner, basketball star Shaquille O'Neal, soccer star David Beckham, former boxing champion Mike Tyson, socialite Paris Hilton and 700 to 800 wealthy owners in China, even though GM has no authorized dealership in China. It is understandable why Tengzhong Heavy Industrial Machinery, which has the finances to swing the purchase, sees the market potential. A definitive agreement is just a matter of time.

The Hummer-deal needs to be approved by both Washington and Beijing. The U.S. Department of the Treasury must give its nod to the deal, as must the Committee on Foreign Investment in the U.S., and Beijing's policy for a "green and environment-friendly vehicle industry" poses a hurdle for the buyer Tengzhong. The company plans to meet new fuel-efficient green standards in both China and the United States.

Hummer's expertise in producing heavy-duty SUV's is a significant asset to Tengzhong, as is the Hummer brand to wealthy Chinese looking for a new status symbol – no different than the brand's proud American owners. These two reasons, and the fact that Tengzhou has a successful track record in its short four-year history, are reasons enough for the sale to be approved on both sides of the Pacific.

Top Dogs, Hot Rods

With America's automobile industry fighting for survival with its "Cash for Clunkers" program as it depends on government lifelines, China's auto-mobile industry is thriving. The big financial winners of the U.S. program were Asian automakers and the small cars they manufacture. Toyota was the biggest winner. It accounted for 19 percent of all sales and had two of the three top-selling cars.

Detroit's Big Three automakers accounted for less than 40 percent of the vehicles sold. That was a substantially lower figure than the 45 percent combined market share that the Detroit companies had posted in the first seven months of 2009.

It wasn't long ago that China produced only 5,000 cars a year. Today it is the world's largest car market. No one expected China to be in first place in the global auto market race until 2020. The pundits and experts were wrong again. China sold more cars in the first quarter of 2009 than the U.S. This was due to Chinese stimulus policies which halved the retail taxes on small cars and gave 5 billion yuan in vehicle subsidies in rural areas to drive car sales. American auto makers in China also benefited from that stimulus package. GM doubled its 2009 forecast for China's market growth as the tax cuts and subsidies revived demand.

Mainland vehicle sales surged at a record pace in June 2009. Total sales, including passenger cars, multi-purpose vehicles, sports-utility vehicles, trucks and buses, exceeded 1.14 million units in June, as the government implemented stimulus measures to push sales to a record 36.5 percent increase from last year. It was the fourth consecutive month sales had surpassed 1.1 million units. Sales of passenger units reached 874,000, up 48.5 percent from 2008. Mainland vehicle sales beat U.S. figures for the first time in January 2009, making it the world's biggest car market.

China's stimulus package with more than $733 million in tax breaks for rural buyers of small cars drove sales through the Middle Kingdom's roof. Let's not forget China also allocated $220 million to boost new green automotive technologies, especially in alternative-energy vehicles that are the wave of the future. To help offset the high cost of buying clean-energy vehicles, subsidies of nearly $8,800 are being offered to local government agencies and taxi fleets in 13 cities for each hybrid vehicle purchased.

Beijing's 2009 car sales target was 10 million units, an increase of 10 percent from 2008, and a figure that will cement its position as No. 1 with an estimated 1 million more unit sales than America. It is estimated mainland sales will reach 13 million units in 2009. China is the world's leading car consumer.

China's dominant role will allow it, rather than Detroit and Washington, to dictate world fuel consumption and emission standards, including fuel-efficient Hummers.

Buffet on Wheels

Chinese auto manufacturers are on an international food-tasting spree trying to decide what to buy. Beijing Automotive Industry Holding Corp., a top-five Chinese carmaker, was interested in bidding for GM's Opel brand but might go after Ford's Volvo dish instead. Germany confirmed that the Chinese firm made an offer for Opel. Beijing Auto is also looking at every potential item that troubled hungry United States carmakers have on offering.

Ford, the only major U.S. carmaker not to file bankruptcy, or take government money, is shedding international luxury brands to focus on rebuilding its namesake cars and trucks to avoid having to ask for a federal handout. The company is seeking about $2 billion for Volvo, less than a third of what it paid for the maker of rock-solid sedans and station wagons a decade earlier. I know first hand having owned one in Los Angeles driving my two children, Alexandra and Jonas, and their carpools. The carmaker put Volvo up for sale in December 2008 as the brand's U.S. sales slipped 31 percent. Ford, the second-largest U.S. carmaker, sold Britain-based Jaguar and Land

Rover to India's Tata Motors for $2.4 billion in June 2008.

The five top-selling brands in China are Volkswagen, Hyundai, Toyota, Honda and Nissan, in that order. No American car made the list.

The two Chinese joint ventures of General Motors, now emerged from bankruptcy, reported record monthly sales for May 2009. Shanghai GM said vehicle sales jumped more than 50 percent from a year earlier to 56,011 cars, buoyed by the top-selling Buick brand. GM's minivan joint venture sold 100,258 cars, the first time that a Chinese automaker sold more than 100,000 cars in one month. GM's total vehicle sales in China surged 75 percent from a year earlier to more than 156,000 in a month. This was in stark contrast to its performance at home, where sales plunged 50 percent in the first quarter of 2009.

GM, which sold its first car in China in 1920, sold 1.09 million vehicles in China in 2008, and said it expected to double annual sales in the country to more than 2 million cars over the next five years.

While car factories in America and Europe are hitting the brakes, China's automakers are accelerating. Geely, the maker of the popular Panda car, is increasing production in 2009, while Volkswagen rolls out its Lavida, a car that shares components with VW's Golf, but was conceived, born and is sold only in China. Europe's largest carmaker now sells more VW-brand vehicles in China than it does at home in Germany.

China's biggest car makers Chery Automobile Co., announced in June 2009 that it had raised 2.9 billion yuan from private Chinese investors. "The capital will be used in our clean energy program," said a spokesman for the company. Chery sold more than 140,000 vehicles in the first four months of 2009. The company aims to sell 419,000 vehicles in 2009, compared to 356,000 in 2008.

Chery is expanding its global manufacturing and dealership network with the construction of six more assembly plants outside China, boosting its global production network to 15 countries and regions. The six new destinations are Taiwan,, Thailand, Syria, South Africa and Venezuela. It has dealerships in 60 countries. In 2009 it opened 55 dealerships across Brazil and plans on building an assembly plant in Brazil, the world's ninth-largest automobile market, in the next few years.

Goldman Sachs announced in November 2009 that it had invested $250 million to buy Geely's convertible bonds and warrants, which will give it a 15 percent stake in Geely.

Porsche introduced its Panamera sedan at the impressive Shanghai auto show in April 2009, where international and domestic carmakers vied for the attention of Chinese consumers, a departure from the Porsche traditional coming out parties in Europe and the U.S.

The 2009 Shanghai Auto Expo was the greenest A-list car show in history. Although none of them represent cutting-edge technologies, China's homegrown electric and hybrid vehicles were visible everywhere. Chery, exhibited four alternative-energy cars. China is fast becoming the global trendsetter. Its emphasis on fuel efficiency plays well in all countries, including America.

China's cell phone battery maker BYD Co. introduced the F3DM in December 2008, a car that can run in full-electric or gas-electric hybrid mode and retails for around $20,000 in China. It will be available in the U.S. in 2011. Warren E. Buffet is an investor in the company and made a $1 billion paper profit after the mainland's securities regulator approved the deal in July 2009.

Buffet's Mid American Energy Holdings agreed to buy 225 million shares, or 9.98 percent of BYD at HK$8. While waiting for the regulatory approval, the share price increased fivefold to HK$42.95, boosting Berkshire's initial HK$1.8 billion investment to HK$9.67 billion. The carmaker's acronym stands for Build Your Dreams, which it has. Wang Chuanfu, the company's founder, sometimes jokes that it really means "Bring You Dollars." It is China's largest maker of rechargeable batteries and Wang wants to build BYD into the world's biggest car company by 2025.

BYD displayed its models at the Detroit Auto Show in 2008 and 2009. The F3DM car is being sold to local government departments and state-backed firms and will be launched to the public after Beijing announces its subsidy plan for environment-friendly vehicles at the end of 2009 or early 2010.

While its car business hits its stride, China is also a global leader in solar power. It has also developed solar-powered cars and is the world's top supplier of photovoltaic cells, but uses very few domestically. If China were to cover 10 percent of the Gobi Desert with photovoltaic cells, it would have unlimited energy forever. America could do the same in Nevada. No different from what happened in California when America needed railroads, levees and farms.

Solar power will rival coal-fired electricity in China within a decade. The country is already a major user of solar energy to heat water for homes, using rooftop solar panels. More than 30 million Chinese households have these relatively low-technology devices, accounting for 80 percent of the world market. China is also the world's largest producer of solar cells, which convert light directly into electricity.

China's desire to invest in the U.S. energy sector should be welcomed, not rejected as it was in 2005 when China tried to acquire Unocal. The same holds true for Chinese carmakers interested in buying Chrysler or General Motors. In the meantime, China is aggressively courting the 6,500 Chinese engineers working for Detroit's struggling carmakers.

Why does Ford's new Fiesta have an instrument panel that resembles a mobile phone? Because that is what is familiar to its target audience of 20-30-something Chinese. It is also why Chinese versions of the Fiesta come in sedan size, with four doors, rather than as hatchbacks, which are anathema in China. Ford started selling its new Fiesta – with an engine displacement of 1.5 litres – in China a little more than a month after the new tax cut. It sold more than 4,000 cars in six weeks.

Coked Out
The hypocrisy of America's double standards and destructive approach to China is exemplified by the complaint filed by the United States and European Union claiming China is preventing some products from being exported. China is damned if it does and damned if it doesn't. It is criticized on the one hand for being the factory of the world, exporting billions of dollars worth of cheap manufactured products – and now for hoarding and not exporting coke.

Coke is an essential material used in making steel tubes. China produced 336 million tons of coke in 2008. By putting export restraints on the raw material, of exports were limited to 12 million tons, which upset U.S. and European buyers who could not buy cheap coke. Ironically, China put the limits on the exports for environmental protection reasons. Coke is derived from coal in a process that results in heavy air pollution.

"Beijing's logic goes that by imposing restraints on exports, it can subdue the urge of domestic firms to increase capacity and thus reduce pollution," said Xu Zhongbo, the chairman of steel industry consultancy Beijing Meitak.

Other steel making products involved in the latest complaint – bauxite, fluorspar, magnesium, manganese, silicon metal, silicon carbide, zinc and yellow phosphorus, like coke – were often overly mined on the mainland and major contributors to China becoming the global leader in emitting destructive greenhouse gases. By cutting their exports and resulting pollution – and continued warehoused profitability – the case was the first complaint the U.S. filed against China with the WTO since President Obama took office. Corporate America has again emerged from the shadows of its failed and destructive corporate practices to lead the China-bashing campaign as it tries to falsely recapture its financial dominance in the local market.

Original Recipes

China is also a world leader in the number of applications for new patents filed and is set to pull ahead of Japan – the current leader – by 2012. It will become the "most prolific basic patenting authority in the world," concentrating more on innovation in areas such as chemical engineering, according to a 2008 report by *Thomson Reuters Scientific*. For the first time, China has also overtaken the U.S. in the number of engineering papers published in 2007, with the gap expected to widen. China published 78,200 papers in academic journals, mostly in English, as indexed by Engineering Information, a leading engineer database.

The achievement is remarkable and only the tip of the iceberg because almost every U.S. scholar writes in English, but only a small percentage of Chinese authors do so. Adding political fuel to the achievement fire, British historian Gavin Menzies claims Leonardo da Vinci's drawings of machines were derived from Chinese originals brought by a Chinese fleet to Venice, Italy, in 1434. The Chinese brought encyclopedias of technology unknown to the Europeans at the time. From Venice, a Chinese ambassador went to Florence and presented the material to Pope Eugenius IV. Menzies postulates that the Chinese technology is what really ignited the Renaissance in Europe and that Leonardo and Galileo built on what was brought to them from China.

China, like the Chinese-Americans who came to America to contribute their skills and labor to help build it and make it what it is today, has a lot more talent and resources to contribute to America's domestic and global ambitions. Billions of people and dollars, both of which America desperately needs. An example of such cooperation is China's Loyalty Enterprises Group which recycles electronic waste. It has teamed up with E-World Recyclers of California and together they have developed a cost-effective cutting edge approach to separating and recycling glass and electronic waste.

China has pushed its emissions of greenhouse gases above those of the U.S., which had long been the world's biggest emitter, according to many experts. Under the Kyoto Protocol, China and other Third World economies have no required goals to contain emissions. The U.S. refused to ratify the Kyoto pact, saying that the lack of caps on China and other big developing emitters make it ineffective. China and America should start working together to come up with a mutually acceptable framework that both countries can live with for the treaty that will replace Kyoto when it expires in 2012.

The Politics of Art

Museums, opera companies and charitable arts foundations in America, like Wall Street and the U.S. economy, have nearly destroyed themselves because of their failure to keep their eyes on the bottom line. The Museum of Contemporary Art in Los Angeles, one of the most dynamic museums in the country – the opening of which I attended in 1979 – is a prime example. MOCA, and all artistic groups in America, should emulate the partnership between the World Monuments Fund, a private nonprofit New York-based preservation group, and China's Forbidden City Palace Museum to restore the Juanqinzhai studio – "Studio of Exhaustion From Diligent Service" – a two-acre retreat in the northeastern corner of the Forbidden City that was built in the 1770s by Qing dynasty Emperor Qianlong for personal use after his retirement. In fact, it is the cooperative model America and China should adopt on the political front as well.

The emperor personally oversaw every inch of design and creation and issued an edict that nothing could be altered by future generations. Few had set foot in the studio since 1924, when Puyi, China's last emperor, vacated the palace and locked the door behind him. The studio was used as a warehouse.

The $3-million restoration, which took nearly a decade to complete, marks an extraordinary partnership of Chinese artisans and American expertise to refurbish one of the historically important interiors to survive from China's imperial period. It was the first time the Palace Museum had cooperated with a foreign organization. Palace officials visited the Peabody Museum in Washington, D.C., to view firsthand U.S. techniques of restoration. Both sides are satisfied with the results and looking forward to more collaborative projects.

The refurbishing partnership can and should be emulated on the economic and political front in the 21st century. Just as China's outstretched hand in the arts has been clutched by America, China's repeatedly extended political hand to the U.S. must also be grasped. Global economic and political leadership by America and China can bring about peace and harmony and an end to global conflicts sparked by religion, ideology, ethnic conflict and nationalism that are pushing the world to the precipice of Armageddon.

Chapter 8

Dessert – Cooling Off a lá Mode
Kiss Mother Nature Goodbye
– Hank Williams Jr.

Super Bowl

        The navies of China and the U.S. have many common goals they could sail toward as allies, instead of against each other as they are today. Fighting pirates off the coast of Somalia and in the Malacca Straits, global terrorism, winning in Afghanistan, containing North Korea's nuclear proliferation and criminal activities, the environment and climate change are six areas in which America and China can tee up and team up their navies to seek progress that will not only benefit the citizens of both countries – but all of humanity.

The U.S. and China should head up an anti-piracy naval task force supported by countries whose oil supplies and cargo are at risk in the Gulf of Aden and through the Malacca Straits. Pirate attacks worldwide more than doubled in the first half of 2009, according to a report released in July 2009 by the International Maritime Bureau's piracy center in Kuala Lumpur. The number of attacks rose to 240 between January and June, up from 114 incidents in the same period in 2008. Ships were boarded in 78 cases and 31 vessels were hijacked, with 561 crew taken hostage, 19 injured and six killed. The spike in attacks was due mainly to increased Somali pirate activity off the Gulf of Aden and the east coast of Somalia. Piracy is a renewed scourge from the 19th century that has to be dealt with today as it was then, with the U.S. again leading the charge, this time with China alongside leading other countries interested in joining the anti-piracy coalition.

There is no doubt in my mind that Presidents Hu and Obama discussed Sino-U.S. military ties. My hope is they actively explored how to join military commands and forces to jointly lead the fight against piracy.

China's military leadership has made no secret of its desire to play a leadership role to defeat the pirates that made it lose face with the hijacking of the *De Xin Hai* and its 25 Chinese crewmen. It was the first Chinese vessel to be hijacked since the arrival off Somalia of China's naval task force in January 2009. It no longer wants to just hang around a naval kitchen of admirals with no head chef. It is prepared to become the head chef or souz-chef and has made a formal request for the job.

Beijing hosted a two-day conference of its international naval counterparts from Japan, India, Russia, the European Union and NATO, in November 2009, in a bid to take on a greater leadership role in its effort to boost anti-piracy policies off the Horn of Africa. China proposed that individual navies become responsible for a specific sector of responsibility. Currently, navies coordinate escorts across specified protected sea lanes. The navies involved are split into three flotillas under NATO, the EU and the so-called Combined Task Force 151, led by Turkey. China's ships, as well as ships from Russia, Japan, Malaysia and India, operate independently but stay in close touch.

Hopefully, when General Xu Caihou, China's second-highest-ranking military officer, and the most high profile Chinese military commander to travel to the U.S. in years, visited the U.S. in October 2009, he discussed with U.S. Secretary of Defense Robert Gates how the U.S. and China can not only cooperate in combating piracy, but how they will lead the charge.

The daylight helicopter raid in Somalia by U.S. commandos in September 2009 that killed Saleh Al Saleh Nabhan, the most-wanted Islamic militant in Africa, is an example of what America can do when its political and military will are synchronized – a far cry from the dark Black Hawk Down days in Somalia.

America has to stop going to war alone and picking up the tab for the war budget as it is doing in Iraq and Afghanistan. The coalition contribution to the military boots on the ground and the military budget is miniscule. The time is long overdue for America to embrace China as its 21st century comrade-in-arms and lead the world back to basics – starting in Somalia.

The Somali pirates have updated an ancient criminal trade into a model modern business. These fly-infested-poverty-ridden fishermen with satellite dishes and state-of-the-art communication systems, ignore international law, and with their pitiful and leaky skiffs make a mockery of the world's great industrial and military powers as they reel in tankers, dry bulk and container ships the size of several football fields, containing millions of dollars worth of cargo and citizens. The ransoms they get paid to release their ill-gotten property is estimated to have been more than $80 million in 2008, which has certainly already been topped in 2009. Their long-established tribal money-moving networks avoid electronic transactions. Doesn't sound right to me.

Living in Hong Kong, I get to regularly cruise the local Fragrant Harbor and South China Sea waterways on anything from an 8-foot zapcat to a 120-foot yacht. Doing so with a ship owner, through Hong Kong's empty container terminals in early November 2009, piracy and the recent hijacking of Beijing and Qingdao Ocean Shipping's *De Xin Hai,* that was carrying 76,000 tons of coal from South Africa to India, naturally became a heated topic of discussion. Fully loaded and riding low in the water, it was a sitting duck. The bulk carrier was attacked as it passed 550 nautical miles northeast of the Seychelles – far from the area covered by the international armada and a sign that the pirates are extending their reach by using "mother ships" as staging posts for attacks. The carrier had yet to cross to the 60th meridian – the point at which ships are advised to take anti-piracy measures, such as posting extra lookouts and preparing fire hoses. The consensus was that America and China must lead and deal with piracy more effectively.

The pirates have to be given credit for taking good care of their captive-hostages. The pirates periodically hire caterers to provide Western or Asian food – a luxury in a country with one of the most malnourished populations in Africa.

What is the point of America and China building state-of-the-art navies, air forces, armies and intelligence gathering infrastructures to protect their citizens and international commerce on the high seas if they can't be used? Taxpayers paid for them so they and their businesses can be protected and pirates defeated – especially in a failed state like Somalia – and legitimate authority restored.

Why are no navies willing to risk a confrontation on Somalia's lawless coast despite another toothless U.N. Security Council resolution allowing the use of force in Somali waters? The pirate attacks are acts of war that justify an invasion of the pirates' strongholds and Somalia. America and China must establish and lead the Somalia Restoration Task Force to rehabilitate the failed state of Somalia.

This is a topic I address at length in my book *Custom Maid Knowledge*. The 21st century war on terrorism at sea is very similar to the 19th century war against piracy that resulted in colonization. It was America that initiated the first campaign against pirates in the 19th century. It did so again after 9/11 but went to the wrong land-based battlefields in Afghanistan and Iraq. It should be on the high seas fighting the terrorist-backed pirates.

In the 18th century, most civilized states accepted the Roman Law definition of pirates as "enemies of the human race." By the end of that century, the rulers of Algiers, Tunis and Tripoli had become notorious for harboring pirates, and engaging in piracy and the slave trade in whites, chiefly captured seamen. European countries found it easier to ransom these unfortunates rather than go to war. Admiral Horatio Nelson, commanding the British Mediterranean fleet, was forbidden to carry out any reprisals.

"My blood boils," he wrote, "that I cannot chastise these pirates." Sound familiar to anyone up on the news on piracy today?

By contrast, America was determined to do so. Pirates were the main reason Congress established a navy in 1794. In 1805, U.S. Marines marched across the desert from Egypt to Tripoli, forcing the Pasha there to sue for peace and surrender all American captives – an exploit recalled by the lyrics of the U.S. Marine Corps Hymn, "From the halls of Montezuma to the shores of Tripoli." Why not add "and Mogadishu." Make the hymn – and the U.S. Marine Corps – relevant to the 21st century.

The war against piracy in Asia, like the Mediterranean, was directly linked to colonization – British, French, Dutch, Portuguese and Spanish – a fact finally recognized by the U.S. when it annexed the Philippines after the Spanish-American War. It established a large naval base at Subic Bay, where one of the main duties was pirate hunting. The lesson learned was that suppression of well-organized criminal communities, networks and states was impossible without government coalitions and cooperation to ensure political control – a replay of which is now long overdue in North Korea and Zimbabwe. Then as now, civilized powers preferred to act in concert. It is therefore no surprise that China, like America, is today expanding its naval capability to protect its oil tankers and cargo ships sailing through the Gulf of Aden and Malacca Straits where terrorist attacks and piracy are rife. Together, these two powerful navies, and other nations willing to join in, can stomp out this menace on the high seas.

Karzi's Korma

China shares a 76-kilometer border with Afghanistan and is doing a lot of business there without commiting any boots on the ground.

Watching President Obama in China getting blown away by what he was experiencing, but not really prepared about what his half-brother and political advisors had told him as the U.S. public, political and military estalishments debated what America should do in Afghanistan was an eye-strainer. The U.S. president trying to decide what troop commitments America should make to support a corrupt, vote stealing, heroin dealing regime doing business with China.

Without China, Afghanistan will become America's worst military quagmire – making Vietnam and Somalia look like a traditional family picnic in the park.

China and America have agreed to cooperate on ensuring that neither Afghanistan nor Pakistan is used as a terrorist base. Because of China's long border with Afghanistan, it fears Islamic extremism is bleeding into its Western frontier which has been racked by unrest.

Beijing is also discussing intelligence cooperation with the U.S. of the sort that took place in the '80s, when America, China and Pakistan worked together to boot the Soviets out of Afghanistan.

The original U.S. goal when it launched "Operation Enduring Freedom" in Afghanistan in 2001 was to capture Osama bin-Laden and his al-Qaeda cronies and bring them to justice in the wake of the 9/11 terrorist attacks. But meantime, Osama and al-Qaeda have moved to the Pakistan side of an unpatrolled border and into Somalia, China and other Muslim battlegrounds while America continues to misdirect its military resources in Iraq.

While America is squandering billions on the war in Iraq, after its fleeting shortsighted victory of routing the Taliban in Afghanistan in 2002, the Taliban has returned with a vengeance, and now has a presence in 80 percent of the country. Of the 42-nation International Security Assistance Force, 56 percent want their troops brought home – and that includes America. After eight years, more than 1,500 ISAF soldiers have died.

Meanwhile, China Metallurgical Group paid $3 billion in 2008 to prospect for copper deposits worth some $88 billion in Afghanistan's Logar province. So who is really winning and why isn't America engaging China?

War for Peace

Watching President Obama accept his controversial Nobel Peace Prize a few days after he committed 30,000 more U.S. troops to Afghanistan, and listening to his acceptance speech promising to use the prestigious award to "reach for the world that ought to be," I couldn't help think "Right on, America and China leading the world as true partners to where the world ought to be."

"To say that force is sometimes necessary is not a call to cynicism, it is a recognition of history," Obama said in his speech. And why not with the most obvious practical ally China? It has close political, military, intelligence and economic ties with both the Afghanistan and Pakistan governments and military establishments.

America can could benefit greatly from China's relationships in the region, developed over centuries along the Silk Road because of the three countries, common borders, ethnic groups and Islam.

The Nobel Laureate Obama has to watch his military mis-steps. On his watch, the number of U.S. troops in Afghanistan has grown from 34,000 to about 70,000 en route to 100,000 when he accepted the Peace Prize.

China worked with America and Pakistan to rid Afghanistan of its Soviet occuoiers in the 1980s. China's panhandle-shaped corridor border is close to territory held by insurgents and proved strategic as Beijing quietly assisted Washington in arming the Afghan mujahideen during their fight against the Soviet Union's occupation. It can do the same today to rid Afghanistan of the Taliban and al-Qaeda. It can be America's economic development partner that can help build a vibrant domestic and export economy, similar to what it did on the mainland – and also eliminate heroin as Afghanistan's number one export.

It is highly unlikely that China will send any fighting forces to Afghanistan. Why would it want to join the ranks of Alexander the Great, Rome, Britain or the Soviet Union and soon to be America, unless China and India are added as lead coalition partners? Forget about the Europeans. They never got it right in the first place. China did. That is no reason for China not to send medical teams and all the other military personnel it now provides to U.N. peacekeeping forces around the world. That in itself is a major financial contribution that China would probably be happy to make, especially if the investment is in dollars.

It is going to take at least 20 years for Afghanistan to become economically and militarily self-sufficient without U.S. support. Look how long U.S. military forces and bases have been in Germany, Italy and Japan – to this very day since the end of World War II!

With al-Qaeda leaders urging Uygurs to launch a holy war against oppressive China, is there any doubt in any political realist in America, regardless of party affiliation, that this is America's best Afghanistan option? America has to fast start discounting its military menus in favor of the far more lucrative big-tip economic options.

Seeing all the *ObaMao* T-shirts and other souvenier memorabilia which blanketed Shanghai in the winter rains, and Beijing during the winter snows in anticipation of President Obama's first visit to China – and the man himself – are a clear signal that together America and China can and must jointly lead the Chiefs of Staff to get America and its coalition allies, China, Pakistan and Afghanistan, to save not only their face – but their asses. And I'm not talking about the Democratic Party symbol. I'm talking about the anatomy of America's future and the economy that depends on them.

Kim's Kimchi

The U.S.-China naval coalition must also work together to contain North Korea's weapons proliferation programs – conventional and nuclear. The U.S. Navy should have the backup and support of the Chinese Navy to track all vessels, especially North Korean ships leaving any of the country's ports suspected of carrying weapons to rogue regimes or aspiring regimes of terrorist groups in violation of the U.N. resolution punishing Pyongyang for its nuclear test and missile launches in May and June of 2009. Kim Jong-il has not only promised to test-fire more short-term or mid-range missiles but to hit South Korea with a "fire shower of nuclear retaliation." It is time to hose Kim and his family out of power – and out of country – a piece of kimchi, if America and China join forces and forget about the U.N. and its widely mocked and unenforceable sanctions.

Forget about the stalled six-party talks or the five working groups aimed at ending North Korea's nuclear program. Forget about more useless sanctions. Forget about bipartisan recriminations. Forget about the blame game – especially picking on China and Russia. Forget about a nuclear East Asia.

The universal opposition and condemnation of North Korea's nuclear tests – the first in October 2006 and the second in May 2009 – demands an urgent alternative solution to the rehashed and recycled proposals that have been tossed around since the 1953 Korean armistice took effect.

China and Russia, which like America opposed the North Korean tests, have been humiliated and desperately want a solution they can jointly embrace with America. Kim Jong-Il's nuclear bluff must be called. The Dear Leader crows that he is ready for war. Bring it on and let's end the Korean War once and for all.

The Korean armistice signed on July 27, 1953, between North Korea and the U.N. forces in Korea led by the U.S. remains in force. No formal peace treaty was ever concluded. People have forgotten that more than 84,000 soldiers from 16 countries serving under the U.N. flag died during the conflict. More than a million Korean civilians also died, as well as an estimated 900,000 Chinese troops fighting with the North Koreans. A peace treaty is long overdue.

Why should China and Russia go along? Because the U.S. will agree that Taiwan is a province of China and that America will not defend Taiwan should it declare independence. The U.S. settles two thorny issues simultaneously. China and America have a lot to offer Russia to come along.

America, China, Japan, Russia and South Korea must initiate five-party talks without pre-conditions or sanctions, which only hurt and subject the majority of North Koreans to more misery and suffering because of their self-centered sycophant authoritarian military leadership.

The five-party talks should explore how best to find an honorable face-saving exit for Kim and Co. This is a negotiating tactic America has perfected with several Haitian dictators over the years, allowing them to live comfortably in exile.

North Korea borders economic powers China, Russia and South Korea. Japan is nearby, across the Sea of Japan. These four economic superpowers could set up cooperative cross-border economic zones on their mutual borders, the kind Kim has visited and admired in China and is hopelessly and helplessly trying to emulate.

These special economic zones would transform Pyongyang's central planned Stalinist communist economy into neutral economic buffer zones in the potentially explosive area and stop the accelerating destabilization rippling through the region and beyond. It is the only feasible way to bring stability to East Asia.

It is in the world's long-term strategic interest to neutralize North Korea's nuclear capability, create a North-South confederation and eventually a unified Korea that enjoys prosperous cooperative economic zones with its neighbors.

Economic prosperity also would prevent a massive North Korea refugee exodus and ensuing crisis that China and Russia are concerned about, especially if American and European corporate citizens embrace the economic zones the same way they did in China. This would allow North Korea to finally sign a peace agreement that would clear the way for gradual reunification with the South. The cost of reunification, unlike the case in postwar Germany, would be shared by the five in the interest of all humanity.

The five-party effort could transform the secretive and isolated Hermit Kingdom and its crippled economy into an open, vital, sunlit renaissance model for basket cases like Zimbabwe and other failed states.

Pancake Screws

The economic reality is that North Korea's economy and people are as flat as a dehydrated pancake – imagine a meal at the International House of Pancakes where no pancake is bigger than a quarter, economically, militarily and geopolitically. The reason the pancake is even there at all in the first place at its miniscule size, is because its neighbor China is caught between a nuclear-armed rock and a nuclear-inhibiting U.S. shaping East Asia security hard place.

The fact is that as China has gotten more embroiled in global politics, economics and security, its historic bilateral ties with North Korea have become more tenuous. That doesn't mean it can make North Korea march to China's nuclear tune. While Beijing feeds the starving millions of Koreans out of compassion and self interest, it also votes with the U.S. to impose sanctions against North Korea for its nuclear tests.

China's anger is well documented in authoritative journals and newspapers. Chinese political analysts are contemptuous and rudely critical of Kim and his regime. Such public criticism was unimaginable in the past. Looks to me like China has put Kim on notice of Beijing's intentions, which he has chosen to ignore for now for personal political nepotistic reasons.

China and the U.S. do not want to see the continuation of a nuclear North Korea.

This was confirmed by the leaders of China, Japan and South Korea at their summit in Beijing in October 2009, when they agreed to put pressure on Pyongyang to return to the six-party nuclear disarmament talks and discuss total denuclearization.

The U.S. is helping tighten the screws by talking to the pancake bakers at banks throughout Asia. Denying North Korea access to the global banking network to launder money from its various illegal activities, ranging from nuclear proliferation to counterfeiting, is a much more effective tool than military action, especially with China's support.

The five-party talks are a solution Kim Jong-il himself may be trying to cook up in direct talks with the U.S. on the heels of former President Bill Clinton's trip to Pyongyang in early August 2009 to gain the freedom of two American journalists held by the North Koreans. That was followed by a visit by two high-level North Korean diplomats to Governor Bill Richardson in New Mexico, after which Richardson said the reclusive regime "is now prepared to have a dialogue with us."

Could visions of the overthrow, trial and summary execution of Romanian dictator Nicolae Ceausescu in 1989 be dancing in the Dear Leader's head?

"What a jerk – make that patsy – Clinton was to go to North Korea," said Earl Klein, an American friend of mine visiting from Thailand as we shared drinks at the main bar of the Foreign Correspondent's Club in Hong Kong just after Pyongyang freed the two journalists. " ... I don't care if Obama sent him or his wife did. He should not have gone. The Obama administration and liberal media are spinning this release as something great. It's a travesty!" he declared loudly.

That got my dander up. "Liberal media? You must be joking, Earl! What planet do you live on?" I said, annoyed.

Just then, David O'Rear, another American and a Democratic Party activist, joined us and tried to calm Earl down by reinforcing my argument that dialogue is important to restrain and contain North Korea's nuclear program.

"But why Clinton?" Earl demanded.

"Probably because Kim's got the North Koreans believing through his controlled dynastic media that Bill Clinton is still president of the United States," I quipped, trying to ease the tension.

"You're right," Earl said. "The North Koreans would never believe a black man is president of America."

The three of us burst into laughter and raised a toast to America. For America to try and butter up North Korea to end its nuclear program, America will only re-experience the nuclear talks popping in failure like bad buttered popcorn. Even China is distancing itself from the Dear Leader. This is best evidenced in the city of Dandong, a major city in Northeast China's Liaoning province. There traders and smugglers alike are feeling the economic pinch of the cutback in trade and commerce between the two countries since the May 2009 nuclear tests that created serious strains in their relationship.

"How did China react to North Korea's nuclear tests and missile firings?" I asked Nelson Wong during one of our nightly phone conversations after the tests.

"Very angry," he responded without hesitation. "China did not know the tests were going to take place. In fact Kim Jong-il told the Chinese leadership he had no intention of conducting any tests. He lied!" Nelson exclaimed. "The Chinese leaders are furious. You are right that the North Koreans can't be trusted."

Nelson was referring to my book *Custom Maid Knowledge* in which I wrote: "Kim is smart and recognizes that the Bush administration will sign off on any deal today to claim a victorious success, and no more. After all, why should Dear Leader trust the Bush administration any more than the Clinton administration it succeeded – and promptly disavowed and dishonored the 1994 agreement? The Dear Leader is stuck in the '60s Cold War mentality and is waiting for America's political meltdown, because he believes that he can then get everything he is demanding of America. China will not allow him to continue on his delusional path and will continue to reign in its recalcitrant, overdependent neighbor...."

Hence, my recommendation on how to make Kim Jong-il the Gorbachov of a united Korea while he is Yeltzinized.

What is the alternative? More crippling sanctions, nuclear one-upmanship and political threats that can only lead to conflict, and potentially Armageddon. Since when did oppressive totalitarian dynastic thugs have the right to dictate regional and global geopolitical policies to America? I thought that ended with the death of Stalin.

Pacific Plastic Patches

While the U.S. and China naval commanders work together to come up with a game plan to tackle the piracy, North Korea and build a coalition they can lead, both country's politicians have to focus on how their navies and armed forces can join forces to tackle the longer term underwater threat to humanity – plastic.

The Great Pacific Garbage Patch is a marine plastic soup that may be twice the size of France. It is contaminating the Pacific Ocean and its ecosystem. It is an environmental catastrophe that has received limited political or media attention because of the billions of dollars the plastic industry – and its petroleum-based oil-producing supporters – has spent in the form of political campaign contributions and media advertising.

The garbage patch was discovered in 1997 by California sailor, surfer and volunteer environmentalist Charles Moore, who was heading home with his crew from a sailing race in Hawaii on his catamaran. For the hell of it, he decided to turn on the engine and take the short-cut across the edge of the North Pacific subtropical gyre, a region seafarers have long avoided. It is a perennial high pressure zone, an immense, slowly spiraling vortex of warm equatorial air that pulls in winds and turns them gently until they expire. Several major sea currents also converge in the gyre and bring with them most of the flotsam from the Pacific coast of Southeast Asia and North America. In the 1950s, nearly all that flotsam was biodegradable. Today it is 90 percent plastic, millions of tons of it.

Floating beneath the surface of the water, to a depth of 10 meters, was a multitude of small plastic flecks and particles, swirling like snow-flakes or fish food. The world's navies and merchant fleets make a significant contribution, throwing some 639,000 plastic containers and bags overboard every day. Eighty percent of marine plastic was initially discarded on land, according to a variety of studies. The wind blows plastic rubbish out of littered streets and dumps, trucks and trains on their way to landfills. It gets into rivers, streams and storm drains and then is funneled out to sea. Beaches are also a major source.

Plastic does not biodegrade. In other words, no microbe has yet evolved that can feed on it. But it does photodegrade. Prolonged exposure to sunlight causes polymer chains to break down into smaller and smaller pieces, a process accelerated by friction, such as being blown across a beach or rolled by waves. This accounts for most of the flecks and fragments in the enormous Pacific Garbage Patch and on most beaches and seashores. On most beaches today, even Hawaii's prisitine beaches, there are now more plastic particles than sand particles until one digs at least a foot down.

I experienced this first hand on the pristine beaches of Palau when a chemical engineer, working for a Taiwanese businessman trying to set up a plastic factory there, who was drunk and heartbroken and couldn't bear the thought of how polluted Palau would become – and at the risk of getting fired – educated me in the basics of plastics and their long term devastation of the environment. A U.N. report says there are 46,000 bits of plastic floating in every square mile of the world's oceans.

Worldwide, plastic kills one million seabirds every year and 100,000 marine mammals and turtles, according to the United Nations Environment Program. Many chicks die every year from eating pieces of plastic their parents mistake for food and bring back to the nest.

"Hi, Long time no see," I said to Karin Malmstrom, a Hong Kong based communications director with a U.S. agricultural association, as I stopped by her table on my way out of the Foreign Corrspondent's Club Main Bar one day in November 2009, after a business lunch. "Where have you been?"

"I was in the Plastic Vortex aboard the Scripps Institution science vessel New Horizon for 21 days," Karin responded after we exchanged greetings. "Really?" I said taken aback by her answer. "That Plastic Garbage Patch about twice the size of France. How did you manage that?" I asked as I joined her for a glass of wine.

"Oh, so you know about it," Karin responded, surprised that I knew what she was talking about.

"Project Kaisei, here in Hong Kong," Karin continued. "It was the most amazing trip I have ever taken," Karin enthused as she shared her recent memorable experiences on the plastic patrol with world reknown scientists and fellow volunteers.

"Some amazing creatures out there," Karin continued.

"Bejeweled light-reflecting lantern fish, scaly dragonfish, vampire squid, rattail and a deep-sea scyphomedusa vermilion jellyfish of the Family Periphyllidae. The lantern fish is of particular interest to the scientists as they, and other small fish, are a primary food source for numerous sea mammals around the planet – including seals in the Antarctic found with plastic in their stomachs."

"You should check it out," Karin said encouragingly as we said our good byes.

"I will."

Nearly all the plastic items people use begin as little manufactured pellets of raw plastic resin, which are known in the industry as nurdles. More than a billion kilograms of nurdles are shipped every year to processing plants around the world to make the plastic products, containers and packaging that we are all so familiar with.

French cultural theorist Paul Virilo observed that every new technology opens the possibility for a new form of accident. By inventing the locomotive, you also invent derailments and with the plane you create plane crashes. The invention of plastic by Belgian chemist Leo Baekeland in Yonkers, New York in 1909 has created an environmental oceanic nightmare in the Atlantic and Pacific that only the navies of the U.S. and China can effectively take on and win – a constructive use of stealth submarine plastic technology. The point was really brought home in June 2009, when red-faced Brazilian officials had to retract their claims to have recovered debris from Air France Flight 447 that went missing over the Atlantic because the items they thought were the remains of the plane were in fact sea trash. Even a big oil slick originally thought to have come from the plane probably came from a ship passing off Brazil's coast.

Honky Trash
Hongkongers and their dollars are referred to as Honkies by expatriates in

Hong Kong – and there are a lot of locals and expats who are Honky trashers – but that is not what I am referring to. It is the plastic waste and garbage that finds its way into Hong Kong waters and its shores that I find myself trying to avoid whenever I take a walk with my dog along one of the many beaches near the bay where I live on the Sai Kung peninsula.

More than 12,900 tons of trash was cleared from the waters around Hong Kong in 2008, a 5 percent increase over 2007, according to the Marine Department. This compares with 6,750 tons in 1998. The figures from the Marine Department do not include the 15,500 tons collected at beaches by the Leisure and Cultural Services Department, and Agriculture, Fisheries and Conservation Department and the Food and Environmental Hygiene Department.

"What a mess. Where does all this garbage come from?" asked Steve Chicorel on one of his visits to Hong Kong in 2008.

"Most of it, around three-quarters is locally produced, the rest from ships, the Philippines, Indonesia. A few months after the 2004 tsunami hit Thailand and Indonesia, we found debris from those two countries with markings in the local language on this beach," I told Steve as we walked around a pile of smelly tangled fishing lines wrapped around pieces of plastic and seaweed.

"Honkies suffer from a 'pick up after me' syndrome," I continued as we came across a pristine sandy beach around a cove that was shielded by a natural rock barrier. "People here just don't care about their garbage and just leave it wherever they are. I see fishermen and day trippers come out here and leave their empty beer cans, plastic bottles and lunch wrappings wherever their asses were parked, rather than taking it to the garbage bins sitting a few hundred yards away in the parking lot we passed earlier," I said angrily.

"It's not only here, I see it in some of the outlying parts of Taiwan as well," Steve replied. "But I must say, overall, Taiwan is a pretty clean place compared to other parts of Asia."

Hongkongers are demanding a cleaner environment and air, but they don't want to pay the price fearing the cost if shifted to the public in the form of increased cost of goods will put many out of business and crimp lifestyles. They are demanding the government do its duty and pick up the tab. The government is seeking public input for 19 measures it proposes to introduce to enable the city to set stricter air-quality objectives to bring it closer to the standards adopted by the World Health Organization.

While waiting for public input, the government decided to subsidize a nine-month trial of "green" fuel – ultra low sulfur diesel instead of the marine light diesel, reducing sulfur dioxide emissions by more than 90 percent as the actual sulfur content is only 1 percent that of marine light diesel – on local ferries. Ferries are a major source of maritime air pollution emissions, accounting for 40 to 70 percent of the air pollutants emitted from all local vessels. The government converted its marine fleet to the ultra-low sulfur diesel in 2007 with no major problems.

Honkies volunteer for many environmental causes. The Hong Kong edition of the International Coastal Cleanup Challenge organized by the Ocean Conservancy, clean up rubbish-strewn beaches. In 2009, more than 6,500 people comprising 121 teams cleared nearly 30,000 kilograms of waste from Hong Kong's beaches.

Lei Yue Mun is Hong Kong Harbor's last intact coastal village. This once rural waterside community resembles a ramshackle squalid squatter settlement more than it does the picturesque "traditional" coastal village the promotional tourist literature promotes. And as Jason Wordie, a local historian and columnist said: "Saltwater in the seafood storage tanks is mostly pumped up from the harbor below. Most of Lei Yue Mun village still has no modern sanitation facilities. Raw sewage drains straight out into the harbor, within sight, smell – and presumably water-tank-intake-pipe distance – of Asia's World City's most internationally hyped seafood restaurant strip. Nice! Fancy some e-coli with your steamed garoupa, sir? And perhaps a little cholera on the side?"

This scene is replayed daily at thousands, if not millions, of eateries around the world.

Hong Kong is one of the most environmentally clean cities in Asia. The tons of garbage it generates and leaves strewn about its country parks and beaches pales compared to the garbage generated elsewhere around the region and the mainland. Nevertheless, the government can and must take an even more commanding environmental and clean-air lead if it wants its coffers to start bulging again.

Hong Kong is trying. It launched the city's first Car-Free Day in September 2009. Its Chief Executive Donald Tsang, walked to work and other government officials, like most Hongkongers, took public transport.

A 49-square-kilometer tract of some of Hong Kong's most rugged land and seascapes has been designated China's 183rd national geopark in a move that officials hope will boost tourism and lead to World Heritage status as early as 2010.

Climate Terror

Time is of the essence, not only to defeat high seas piracy, plastic and human waste proliferation, but to deal with climate change. The matter is so urgent that I am taking the liberty of reprinting three pages from my 2007 book Custom Maid Knowledge in this subheading to emphacize the increasing urgency of the crisis.

The last decade of the first millennium was the warmest in 1,000 years. Greenhouse gases are warming up our oceans, changing their chemistry and becoming a greater threat to the world than terrorism. The oceans are humanity's canary in the coal mine. Greenhouse gases such as carbon dioxide emitted from power plants and automobiles are trapping heat in the atmosphere. The result is a warming planet, with melting glaciers and arctic ice sheets sending an unprecedented flow of fresh water into fragile saltwater habitats and raising sea levels worldwide.

Global warming is expected to create at least 1 billion refugees by 2050 as water shortages and crop failures force people to leave their homes, sparking local wars over access to resources.

Scientists predicted that average temperatures will rise by between 1.8 to 3 degrees Celsius this century because of greenhouse gas emissions, mainly from burning fossil fuels, causing floods in some areas, droughts in others, and putting millions of lives at risk. The researchers at the Massachusetts Institute of Technology, who were previously predicting a temperature rise of a little more than 4 degrees Celsius by the end of this century, are now predicting a rise of more than 9 degrees. The reality is that humanity, our civilization, is at risk.

The problem is so severe that some scientists are saying that drastic geoengineering may be our only hope in the race against global warming. Some of the ideas being explored include wrapping Greenland's glaciers in blankets to protect them from the sun's rays; dropping tens of thousands of seedlings from aircraft to reforest large tracts of land; spraying micron-sized particles of sea water into the air to make clouds whiter so as to reflect more light; deploying wave-powered pumps in the North Pacific to revive the phytoplankton that convert carbon dioxide into living matter; diffracting the power of the sun by placing trillions of lenses in space, in effect to create a 250,000-square-kilometer sunshade; and sending thousands of satellites into space to gather the energy of the sun and beam solar energy to Earth as microwave energy, which can be collected by antennae on the ground and converted to electricity. This would achieve a double whammy of cutting carbon emissions and supplying never-ending power.

Secretary of State Hilary Clinton during her visit to China in March 2009 opened a new chapter in environmental cooperation between the world's two largest greenhouse gas emitters. Clinton admitted that both America and Europe "didn't know any better" about protecting the environment during their industrialization and development. She urged China not to repeat their mistakes and called for a U.S.-China partnership to fight global warming.

Todd Stern, the U.S. special envoy on climate change, who accompanied Clinton on her trip, said there are "a great number of areas" for cooperation, such as clean coal technology, carbon capture and storage, hybrid and electric vehicles, energy efficiency and renewable energies. Stern applauded China's efforts in combating climate change as "very impressive" and made a point that the steps China has been taking needed to be better understood in the U.S.

The U.S. is the largest consumer of energy in the world. With energy use growing at 15 percent per year, China is catching up rapidly. Together the U.S. and China account for nearly 50 percent of global energy demand, and spew out a similar percentage of greenhouse gases. Dennis Bracy, chief executive officer of the U.S.-China Clean Energy Forum, said that "Both China and the U.S. want to be energy-independent. That means the two countries have much potential to cooperate on alternatives such as wind and solar energy." Bracy was in Beijing in July 2009 as part of the advance team ahead of the trip to China by U.S. Commerce Secretary Gary Locke and Energy Secretary Steven Chu to discuss cooperation on clean energy.

The U.S. is also looking at the establishment of special economic development zones. "Shenzhen, Tianjin and other cities are given special statuses and encouraged to do innovative programs," Bracy said, suggesting the two countries should create some sort of energy special zones with special tax laws to implement new energy technologies. A joint center or mechanism based on clean energy that promotes joint research and investment and improve the efficiency of both countries is being discussed. The U.S. and China announced the building of a joint clean energy center during the two U.S. secretaries visit to China in July 2009. With initial financing of $15 million and headquarters in both countries, the center will focus on developing clean buildings and vehicles. This would be the first government-level center between China and the U.S. to promote the use of clean energy.

Climate change topped the agenda of the inaugural China-U.S. Strategic and Economic Dialogue in Washington in late July 2009 and earlier that month during the visit of Chu and Locke to their ancestral homeland. The string of visits by U.S. political heavyweights to China in 2009, including President Obama, is the strongest sign possible of the warming ties between America and China. Climate change has taken center stage in the bilateral relationship.

Climate change transcends national interests. Cooperation between the world's largest developed country and the world's largest developing country is vital if efforts to forge a new global treaty are to succeed. The world is about to experience a climatic shift as profound as the last Ice Age – but in the opposite direction.

Cooking Greens

If each Chinese was to use the same amount of energy as each person in the U.S. does – the equivalent of 7.82 tons of oil – then China alone would consume nearly as much energy as the entire world does today. That is a scary and dangerous scenario. To avoid it, China is forging ahead in developing renewable energy and is urging America to do the same. China is a signatory to the Kyoto Protocol and, like America, is spending billions on developing alternatives to oil. China is a world leader in harnessing green renewable energy, particularly hydro, wind, solar and biomass power.

Climate change is a serious challenge to humanity and sustainable development. China recognizes this reality. In 2007, it established the National Leading Group on Climate Change, headed by Premier Wen Jiabao. That same year, China issued its National Climate Change Program, the first ever by a developing nation. The program has set an objective to lower energy consumption per unit of gross domestic product by 20 percent or so of 2005 levels by 2010 and, in its mid-and-long-term plan, for the development of renewable energy. It also aims to increase the proportion of renewable energy in the primary energy mix to 10 percent by 2010, and to 15 percent by 2020. To this end it has adopted a series of effective policies and measures, achieving remarkable progress.

First it has succeded in lowering its energy consumption per unit of GDP by 1.79 percent, 4.04 percent and 4.59 percent respectively for 2006, 2007 and 2008, which strongly suggests the prospect of meeting the 20 percent objective in 2010.

Second, between 2006 and 2008, China shut down small thermal-generation units with a total installed capacity of 34.21 gigawatts, phased out 60.50 million tons of obsolete steel-making capacity, 43.47 million tons of iron-smelting capacity and 140 million tons of cement-production capacity. Naturally, these steps reduced pollution significantly.

Third, between 2000 and 2008, China increased its wind power generating capacity from 340 megawatts to 10 GW and hydropower from 79.35 GW to 163 GW. It has also made great efforts to reduce agricultural and rural greenhouse gas emissions. By the end of 2007, more than 26.5 million rural households were using household biogas digesters, thereby avoiding carbon dioxide emissions by 44 million tons.

Fourth, China has increased the size of its carbon sinks by promoting reforestation. China's forest coverage rate increased from 12 percent in the early 1980s to more than 18 percent today. China's economic stimulus package has allocated 210 billion yuan for energy-conservation, pollution-reduction and eco-system-protection projects; 370 billion yuan for economic structural adjustment and technology renovation; and 400 billion yuan for new energy-efficient housing that will use environmentally friendly materials. A further 370 billion yuan will be used to improve rural living standards in an environmentally sound manner and sustainable way. This is already being done in the rebuilding of the villages of Sichuan that were devastated by the May 2008 earthquake.

Sichuan province is being rebuilt with green technologies. The State Council Leading Group Office on Poverty Alleviation and Ministry of Environmental Protection are working together on water and soil conservation initiatives that benefit agriculture rehabilitation. The Ministry of Housing and Urban Rural Development and the Architectural Design and Research

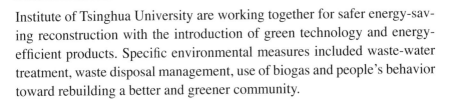

Institute of Tsinghua University are working together for safer energy-saving reconstruction with the introduction of green technology and energy-efficient products. Specific environmental measures included waste-water treatment, waste disposal management, use of biogas and people's behavior toward rebuilding a better and greener community.

America, like China, is spending billions of dollars of economic stimulus money to renovate public housing by creating so-called "green jobs" by making the dwellings more energy efficient – only $4 billion, not nearly enough when compared to China's 3 trillion yuan.

"China is making huge efforts to combat climate change despite the fact that it remains a low-income developing country with a per-capita GDP of about $3,000. Indeed, by United Nations standards, China still has 150 million people living in poverty. China has no other choice but to pursue sustainable development to meet the basic needs of its people and to eradicate poverty.

"The world can be assured that China will make every effort to address climate change," are the words of Xie Zhenhua, President Hu Jintao's special representative on climate change and vice-chairman of the National Development and Reform Commission.

"The global financial crisis has no doubt exacerbated the challenge of climate change. But since climate change is a more far-reaching and serious challenge, the world must not waiver in its determination and commitment to address it. Indeed, the financial crisis could well provide an opportunity for both climate protection and economic development. With a deep sense of responsibility for its own people and the entire human race, China will continue to implement proactive policies and measures to address climate change," Xie vowed.

China's installed wind power capacity has roughly doubled each year since 2005 after Beijing ordered power distributors to buy all of the nation's wind power output, and offered tax incentives to developers.

Construction has started on the country's first 10 gigawatt wind-power base in Jiuquan, Gansu. Dubbed "the Three Gorges Dam on the land," the planned wind power plants in Jiuquan in northwest China will by 2020 have an installed capacity comparable to the world's biggest hydropower project on the Yantze River. As one of seven onshore wind power bases that

Beijing is planning, the Gansu project will usher in a new era for the wind power sector.

China has said it will bring its total wind capacity to 100GW by 2020 from 2009's 12GW, as part of a broad energy target to generate 3 percent of its total electricity from non-water renewable resources.

China could soon become the world's largest wind energy market and producer. By the end of 2008 wind power capacity in China reached 12 gW, accounting for 10 percent of the world total and the fourth-highest output globally – with the potential to become No. 1 and power the entire nation by 2020.

China's potential wind power resources alone are sufficient to meet its entire electricity demand, according to the country's top wind power research institute. Xiao Zinju, director of the National Climate Center, said in June 2009 that China's onshore wind power potential has been evaluated at between 700 gW and 1,200 gW, exactly within the range of the country's 790 gW power generating capacity for 2008. The NCC released the numbers after 10 of its experts carried out an intensive investigation of wind power resources across all the provinces of China.

"This result assures us that the country's entire electricity demand can be met by wind power alone," said Xiao. The study also revealed that China has 250 gW of potential offshore wind power capacity.

China looks set in 2009 to overtake Spain as the world's third-largest wind power market by installed capacity and Germany in 2010 as the second largest behind the U.S. But the world's fastest-growing wind power market, where capacity has doubled in each of the four years since 2005, is facing infrastructure problems that could hinder its long-term development. According to the China Wind Energy Association, more than 20 percent of the nation's installed wind power capacity was not generating any electricity in 2008 because the plants were not connected to grids. The reason is the regions where wind resources are the most abundant tend to have the weakest grid infrastructure development

The National Development and Reform Commission allocated 280 million yuan to the NCC to conduct the investigation and work out a development plan for wind power resources by 2011.

The government has called for further development of renewable energy, including wind, as one of the country's strategic measures to cope with the economic crisis.

"China could soon become the largest wind energy market in the world. So we are intensifying our commitment to green technology to further expand our leading global position," said Richard Hausmann, CEO of Siemens North East Asia and president and CEO of Siemens China. China expects wind power capacity to hit 100gW by 2020, up eightfold from 2008.

China and the United States will remain the top two wind power markets. Texas oilman T. Boone Pickens announced to the world in 2008 that he, like America, should abandon oil and aggressively build a wind-driven green energy infrastructure across the windy corridors of America. What did surprise me is Pickens' retreat from wind energy development in 2009 because of the lack of political and financial support. Pickens is not alone in his backtracking.

China believes it needs to expand its economy to lift millions of more people out of poverty. New legislation aims at seeing carbon dioxide emissions peak around 2030, following a report by several government bodies and academics that said the mainland should "as soon as possible research and draft relative and absolute cuts in carbon dioxide emissions." The nearly 900-page "2005 China Energy and CO2 Emissions Report" said gross domestic product might exceed that of the United States by 2030, and its greenhouse gases would make up 20 to 25 percent of the world's total emissions. If China implemented cuts on absolute growth of emissions, carbon dioxide emissions would start to slow by 2020 and peak by 2030.

China gets 8 percent of its energy and 17 percent of its electricity from renewable sources – shares that will rise to 15 percent and 21 percent respectively by 2020 if the government's targets are met. America can help China achieve that goal and do the same for itself. All it takes is the political willpower to work together.

Dying Fossil Fuel
The world is running out of oil a lot faster than expected, according to the International Energy Agency in Paris. The day we will see the end of the oil era can be described as an oil-bomb implosion – more powerful than anything humanity has seen, and less than a few decades away. That is why it is imperative to pursue alternative energy options, something China rec-

ognizes and is addressing. It is a country shifting from a society built on oil looking at development beyond the "age of oil." That is why it is so heavily invested in renewable energy.

Big Oil, meantime, is turning away from renewables as the oil companies retreat to their core business of oil and gas. The sad reality is that Big Oil is not going to be at the forefront of clean, new tehnologies. Their fossilized corporate culture is much to comfortable, swimming in record profits, to seriously explore alternative renewable energy. Their obstinance would be funny if it were not so sad.

What is even more disgusting is Saudi Arabia's insistence that if wealthy oil consuming countries reduce their oil consumption to combat global warming, they should pay compensation to oil producers. I'm not kidding. What sheer arrogance to even make such an apalling suggestion when the very survival of humanity is at stake!

The kingdom has pushed this position since 1992 at climate treaty negotiations without much success, but their stubborn hard line unyielding stance has delayed or disrupted discussions. It is not only determined to pursue its hard line in Copenhagen, but *ad infinitem*, because the Saudis call their position a "make or break" proposition. Just another one of many delaying tactics used by the Saudis, other petroleum exporters and Big-Oil determined to stall climate talks.

But for me, any amusement turns to anger when I ponder the taxpayer-subsidized pipelines, refineries, tankers and politicians that feed Big Oil. The oil company executives continue to wallow in stubborn arrogance and apathy, free of responsibility as the world tries to find a way out of the mess it finds itself in.

It doesn't make sense to allow oil companies to make record profits from the public's dependence on oil and then allow them to use those profits to find more oil with polluting technologies to continue the public's oil-addiction as they are now doing with tar sand, coal to liquid and carbon capture and storage. That is why I renewed my 1979 horseback ride – protesting oil profits and urging alternatives be developed – in 2006 and 2008.

Power Lunchers

Unfortunately, it does take stunts to get the public's attention through the media, especially in today's age of reality T.V. My favorite climate warrior stunts that pointedly addressed the threat of climate change, from the ocean floor to outer space, are those of Maldivian President Mohamed Nasheed and Cirque du Soleil founder Guy Laliberte.

Nasheed, dived to the sea bottom with 11 ministers, the vice-president and the cabinet secretary, to stage the world's first underwater cabinet meeting on October 18, 2009.

"We should come out of Copenhagen with a deal that will ensure that everyone will survive," said the president as he bobed in the shimmering Indian Ocean after the meeting. He had good reason to get media attention. His resort paradise could be submerged by rising sea levels by the end of the century. In 2008, he stunned the world when he announced he wanted to buy a new homeland to relocate the population of the Maldives in the event that damage from rising sea levels became to great for the 1,192 coral islands that make up the archipelago of the Maldives.

The announcement had a major impact in India, Sri Lanka and Australia – all potential destinations cited by Nasheed for what could be the world's first environmental refugees.

Cirque du Soleil founder Guy Laliberte, went into outer space on the Russian Soyuz capsule as Canada's first space tourist wearing a clown nose. While in space, Laliberte hosted a global Web broadcast to promote his One Drop Foundation's crusade to preserve the world's water resources.

Former U.S. vice president Al Gore, U2 and Shakira were among the entertainers and activists who took part in the broadcast on earth, with participants appearing in 14 cities on five continents.

Power lunches are not limited to people with a political platform and money. Countries, U.S. states and consumers can do as much – actually, probably a lot more.

Norway is a good example of a country. It controls the largest sovereign wealth fund outside the Middle East, worth $435 billion, which invests the country's oil and gas revenues, with a pot that is growing fast. It made a smart timely decision to gobble up stocks at the start of 2009's global rally. The result is it now Europe's fatest equity investor, owning 1 percent of all the world's shares.

The fund does not hesitate to use its soft power to promote its clear environmental goals. In August 2009, it issued a list of measures on climate change that it expects from businesses in which it holds a stake, including an obligation to set targets for reducing greenhouse-gas emissions. In the future it plans to screen 500 leading companies and send each an annual scorecard marking its performance. What better way to control Big Oil than big oil. A lesson the Saudis and other countries better learn fast and join the climate change power lunch banquet table.

Hawaii is a U.S. state on the frontlines to break the shackles of fossil fuels. The state relies on imported oil to generate 77 percent of its electricity. It has energy experiments across its six main islands. With the most diverse array of alternative energy potential of any state in the U.S. Hawaii has set out to become a living laboratory for the rest of the country, hoping it can cut its dependence on fossil fuels.

Every island has at least one energy accent: waves in Maui, wind in Lanai and Molaki, solar panels in Oahu and eventually, if all goes well biomass energy from crops grown on Kauai. On the Big Island of Hawaii, seawater is also being converted to electricity. Other U.S. states should join Hawaii for a climate change surfing beach party and then collectively join other countries at Norway's power lunch banquet table. Honor it, not only for its foresight in the war on climate change, but award of the Nobel Peace Prize to President Barack Obama.

David Greenberg, a sustainable environment architect, authority and author about tree houses, who lives in Hana and commutes to China to consult on various sustainable master plans, resorts and other environmentally friendly developments, stops off periodically in Hong Kong on his commutes and we can catch up on our three decade debate about sustainable development. I've known David since the '80s in Los Angeles, where we both lived at the time and our sons of the same age played with each other. David, a native Angelino, and Gail, my wife at the time, another native Angelina, would reminisce about the memorable white sandy beaches of Santa Monica and Venice beaches and the clear blue skies of Los Angeles.

We, the consumers, are the most important force in the fight against climate change. We're the biggest and most powerful army on the frontlines. We have to become better informed about the carbon footprints of products and other important environmental information when shopping. We can make a huge difference – more than any politican, country or state – more than anyone. Our children and grandchildren's future depends on our responsible sustainable behaviour – durable and recyclable products and energy.

Sustainable Lifestyles

The American concept of sustainable lifestyles is not very different from what the Chinese have been practicing for generations. The concept of Lohas (lifestyles of health and sustainability) is gathering worldwide momentum. The term Lohas was coined by American sociologist Paul Ray in his 1998 book *Culture Creatives*. Lohas, or *Le Huo*, which literally means live happily, refers to a lifestyle that advances personal well-being and development, while taking into account the impact on the environment.

Chinese have a long tradition of living simple and sustainable lifestyles in harmony with nature. Examples of this include the use of Chinese medicine and the lunar calendar. Many Chinese keep potted plants and flowers on their balconies and some, especially the elderly, grow their own vegetables.

"The American concept of Lohas is a marketing strategy based on consumption," says Steven French, managing partner of Natural Marketing Institute. "But in China, it is more about a life philosophy guiding people to lead a simple yet happy life."

While Americans may eat organic food and purchase eco-friendly products, they are not necessarily Lohas because they use cars frequently and live in houses that guzzle energy. This is something I am reminded of daily whenever I take the train to and from work and it stops at the Tseung Kwan O station. A recorded announcement reminds people going to Lohas Park, a new highrise residential development in Hong Kong, that they have to get off and change trains.

Silver Blades

Trucks carrying silvery blades nearly 150 feet, or 45 meters, long have been snaking through mellow New England in the summers, backing up traffic as they slowly leave the main roadways. Huge, tubular chunks of tower also pass through. Tall pieces of machinery looking something like jet engines travel at night because they require special routing to avoid overpasses. As demand for clean energy grows, towns across America are finding their traffic patterns disrupted by convoys carrying pieces of tower that will reach more than 250 feet in height, as well as motors, blades and other parts. Escorted by police patrol cars and gawked at by clueless citizens, the equipment must travel long distances from ports or factories to their remote, windy destinations. The reality is that this fossilized thinking must be disposed of for a remade socially responsible attitude and approach that is relevant to all interlocal citizens.

Even though Big Oil doesn't get it, it's a good thing other politically-connected U.S. corporate iconic cowboy-pioneers sort of do, or at least go with the flow. General Electric is one such example in the "scandalous" corporate and personal culture of its corporate capitalist guru Jack Welch. It has decided to develop its water purification business, from a drop in the corporate bucket of earnings to a major growth driver within years, just as its wind unit did.

"What GE tries to do is to align the company with some of the mega trends, the mega challenges of the world. Energy is one, healthcare is the other, and the third one is water," said Heiner Markhoff, president and chief executive of GE Water & Process Technologies.

Let's not forget that GE corporate executives for the most part are made out of the same cookie cutter that their counterparts in Big Oil are. This is best exemplified by what GE Executive Jeff Immelt said in 2001 when wind turbine executives pitched him to get GE into the business. He dismissed the technology as a "hula hoop." Immelt later changed his mind when Enron's bankruptcy provided a cheaper way into the business, and wind turbines in 2008 generated almost $6.5 billion in revenue.

Overcooked Insects

The Lancet medical journal declared in a May 2009 commentary that "Climate change is the biggest global health threat of the 21st-century." As someone who has eaten more than my fair share of insects in China, where they are treated and considered delicacies, I was fascinated to read how they actually are the carriers that spread human diseases because of climate change. Tree-munching beetles, malaria-carrying mosquitoes and deer ticks that spread Lyme disease are three living signs that climate change is likely to exact a heavy toll on human health. As it becomes hotter, the air can hold more moisture, helping certain disease-carriers, such as ticks.

Pine bark beetles, which devour trees in western North America, will be able to produce more generations each year, instead of subsiding during winter months. They leave standing dead timber, ideal fuel for wildfires from Arizona to Alaska, said Paul Epstein of the Center for Health and the

Global Environment at Harvard University. Having personally fought a forest wildfire when I lived in the former guest house near California's Will Rogers Park in the 1980s – and being the father of a former U.S. Forest Service firefighter who fought fires across the Western United States in the 1990s – I shudder at the thought.

History offers many lessons that we ignore and, unfortunately, as a repeat in updated modern variations. One of my favorites, as a photographer and agricultural high school graduate – and of course English-born writer – is what happened in England during the industrial revolution. Compare modern photographs of colleges in the English university city of Oxford with those taken as recently as 50 years ago, and one can't help but notice the remarkable difference. Today the picturesque sandstone buildings are a near pristine golden yellow in colour. However, before the passage of the Clean Air Act in the United Kingdom in 1956, they were more or less uniformly black.

Years of choking fumes from open fireplaces and filthy emissions from cars in a country that was the cradle of the industrial revolution using coal as the primary source of energy, inflicted consequent damage, not only to buildings, but to the environment and human health.

One of those consequences for a particular life form can be found in the history of the peppery moth, as taught in biology classes to children learning about Darwin's theory of natural selection. Before the industrial revolution began in earnest, in the 18th century, most of these moths in Britain were a light color. However, some possessed mutated genes that made them much darker. These latter were fewer in number, it has been suggested, because it was easy for birds to spot and eat them. Then the environment changed and soot blackened the trees so that the lighter moths were more easily spotted and eaten while the darker moths blended better. The latter soon outnumbered the former.

That story illustrates the dilemma humanity faces with climate change, especially China. No country has managed to boost its economic growth substantially without a consequential effect on the environment. America, like Britain before it and China today, have paid the same price and caused the same damage to the environment. Fortunately, today the world is aware of the price the planet and human health has paid and is trying to mitigate such damage.

As global temperatures rise, expect more heat waves. The U.N. Intergovernmental Panel on Climate Change projects 25 percent more heat waves in Chicago by the year 2100. Los Angeles will likely have a four-to-eightfold increase in the number of heat-wave days by century's end. These "direct temperature effects" will hit the most vulnerable people hardest, according to the U.S. Environmental Protection Agency, especially those with heart problems and asthma, the elderly, the very young and the homeless.

Cooking With Explosive Gas

Both the United States and China are actively seeking solutions to curb emissions of carbon dioxide generated by burning fossil fuels. Some are more fanciful than others and frankly non-starters. The carbon capture and storage initiative being explored by the Obama administration tops that list in my book. The idea is to siphon off the carbon dioxide from the smokestacks of power plants and pump it into deep underground storage tanks before it enters the environment and warms the atmosphere. The government is spending $2.4 billion from the U.S. stimulus package on carbon capture and storage projects.

"A mere down payment…the administration may be digging a very expensive dry hole. I mean it literally," wrote Washington columnist Eugene Robinson in a June 2009 column. I agree but I would add that it is not only expensive, but explosive.

Scientists and engineers will have to prove that the possibility of a sudden catastrophic carbon dioxide release from a storage site is impossible. "Catastrophic" because carbon dioxide is heavier than air, and a ground-hugging cloud would suffocate anyone it enveloped. That is what happened in Cameroon in 1986, when naturally occurring carbon dioxide trapped at the bottom of Lake Nyos erupted and killed 1,746 people in nearby villages.

China, unlike the U.S., is looking at building more nuclear power plants to meet future energy needs as it struggles with what to do to minimize carbon dioxide emissions generated by power plants that are dependent on fossil fuels. Now that it has become the top greenhouse gas polluter, China is trying to grapple with U.S. and international pressure to curb its rising CO emissions. The dilemma Beijing faces is that its leadership does not want to be distracted from building its economy by accepting a ceiling on greenhouse gas output, which even optimistic mainland experts expect to keep rising until around 2030.

Now that there is new evidence that the planet itself has begun to contribute to global warming through fallout from human activity, time is of the essence. Huge amounts of gases such as methane – an even more powerful greenhouse gas than carbon dioxide – trapped for millennia in the Arctic permafrost may be starting to leak into the atmosphere, speeding up the warming process. The March 2009 IPCC report calls on policymakers to take urgent steps to keep average global temperatures from increasing more than two degrees Centigrade, compared to pre-industrial levels. The time for action is upon us.

"Rapid, sustained, and effective mitigation is required to avoid 'dangerous climate change' regardless of how it is defined," the report says. Achieving this goal, the report concludes, would require industrialized nations to slash greenhouse gas emissions by 25-40 percent from 1990 levels. Deep emission cuts are essential.

By 2030, annual emissions of carbon dioxide could reach 8 to 10 billion tons a year, unless tough action is taken, said He Jiankun, a professor at Tsinghua University who advises the government on emissions. "Ultimately, there will have to be compromise in Copenhagen, because these negotiations can't be allowed to collapse," He said. "If they do fall apart, that will be devastating, and nobody will be spared the repercussions."

Why don't the Chinese and U.S. governments spend their money and energy on solar, wind and other renewable energy sources instead of trying to deal with pollutants from nuclear and fossil fuels?

Cooking With Biogas and Planting Trees
Farmers in China are turning to biogas for their home cooking and lighting needs because of government initiatives and incentives that encourage farmers and rural dwellers to switch from coal. According to national statistics, 26 million households in China were using methane from biogas sources for cooking and heating by the end of 2007. That number rose to 31 million by 2008. China has invested more than 10.5 billion yuan from 2004 to 2009 for construction of biogas projects in rural areas, including 98,600 villages.

Animal and crop wastes are processed in biogas digester pools into clean methane that can be used for cooking, heating and lighting and replace carbon emitting coal. After five years of research, the Ministry of Finance and the Asian Development Bank initiated its Efficient Utilization of Agricultural Waste Project in 2003. The ADB offered $33 million in loans targeting rural Shanxi, Hubei, Henan and Jiangxi provinces. The provinces put up matching funds that trained thousands of farmers, biogas facility experts, construction workers and managers in the construction and operation of communal and home biogas facilities.

China encouraged the development of biogas as part of the Renewable Energy Law, which became effective last year, and also as part of the country's Mid-and-Long-Term Development Program for Renewable Energy.

In America, the government has decided to plant 18 million acres of new trees – roughly the size of West Virginia – by 2020, replacing both pastures and farm fields under a bill passed by the House of Representatives in June 2009. The bill gives financial incentives to farmers and ranchers to plant trees, which suck in large amounts of carbon dioxide. The trees not only lower carbon dioxide levels, but they would improve the water quality because they need lower levels of fertilizer and pesticides.

The United States, like China, should take a closer look at bamboo which has been used for thousands of years as a building material. It is gaining attention in China for its potential to arrest the destruction of forests due to its almost miraculous replenishment rate.

China has more than 400 species and more than four million hectares of bamboo forests. The biggest problem bamboo has to overcome, is its cultural perception as a poor man's timber which is deep rooted in Chinese culture.

Bamboo accounts for only one percent of the world's forests. Boosting its coverage would make a significant contribution to reducing the release of carbon dioxide caused by deforestation.

Tri-Color-Carbon Diet

If China, Japan and South Korea can work together to tackle pollution during the global financial meltdown – China and America definitely can and must. The three countries meeting for the 11th trilateral ministerial dialogue on environmental protection in Beijing in June 2009, agreed that tackling pollution during the economic meltdown was vital.

The trilateral ministerial dialogue on environmental protection began in 1999 and has already made "substantial achievements" in environment education, sandstorm prevention and fostering a circular economy. China has vetoed all heavy-polluting and high energy-consuming projects in its multi-trillion yuan economic stimulus package. Japan has agreed to cut its GHGs by 15 percent from 2005 levels by 2020, excluding the carbon credits purchased from clean development mechanism projects. Similarly, South Korea is promoting green growth as a priority and is determined to become a global model for low-carbon development.

Cooking Together

It was heart-warming to hear former China-basher, House Speaker Nancy Pelosi, express in Beijing in June 2009 her high hopes for co-operation between the United States and China, the two biggest emitters of greenhouse gases, ahead of President Obama's visit to China in November and of the 192-nation U.N. Framework Convention on Climate Change in Copenhagen in December 2009.

"We believe China and the United States can and must confront the challenge of climate change together," she said. "We have a responsibility to ourselves, to our country, to our people and to the world to work together on this."

Pelosi's change of tone exemplified how the two chefs can cook together instead of throwing boiling water at each other. Hopefully, the U.S. and China can lead their respective global constituencies to cook up a cooling climate recipe to replace the Kyoto Protocol when it expires in 2012.

In Pelosi's meeting with China's President Hu Jintao, he told her the differences between the two countries could be handled through dialogue and consultation, and that mutual efforts should be based "on equality and mutual respect."

"I think this climate crisis is game-changing for the U.S.-China relationship. It is an opportunity we cannot miss," Pelosi said at the U.S.-China Clean Energy Forum. "I am very optimistic about the cooperation...as a great deal of work between us has been done," she added.

I met Nancy back in January 1977, at a White House reception during President Jimmy Carter's inauguration. At the time, I was a member of the Democratic National Committee's Executive Finance Council, under then Party Chairman Bob Strauss and Finance Committee Chairman Lee Kling.

My initial impression at the time, like now, was that Pelosi is a serious political foodie – make that junkie – on a self-indulgent binge to get America on the right political diet as she saw it. We didn't agree on much then, except our daughters' name – Alexandra.

Her optimism in Beijing was shared by Congressman Ed Markey, who co-sponsored the draft U.S. Waxman-Markey climate bill and chairs the Select Committee on Energy Independence and Global Warming. He was "encouraged because of movement that was being made in a significant way in China on energy intensity, energy efficiency and fuel economy standards." Hopefully the U.S. and China will sign that treaty that will propel the two countries to explore new green recipes to create and cook clean green energy together.

"We are in the process of working on a deal the U.S. president will sign when he visits China in November," said Stan Barer, co-chair of the forum.

U.S. Senate Foreign Relations Committee Chairman John Kerry, who was in Beijing at the same time as Pelosi and Markey to attend the forum, after high level meetings in Beijing on energy cooperation, said: "I have been involved in this issue for 20 years... This has been the most constructive and productive discussion I've ever had with Chinese officials."

Todd Stern, U.S. climate change chief negotiator, echoed Kerry's words at the conclusion of the U.N. climate conference in Bonn: "I think what China has already done – the 20 percent energy efficiency target for the current five-year plan, renewable energy and nuclear power targets – is all very impressive."

The U.S. bill aims to cut greenhouse gas emissions by 17 percent from 2005 levels by 2020, falling short of a European Union pledge to reduce carbon dioxide emissions by an average of 20 percent from their 1990 levels by 2020 and boost renewable energy sources by 20 percent. In a position paper for the Copenhagen Conference, China is urging developed countries to reduce greenhouse gas emissions by 40 percent by 2020 from 1990 levels.

Green Tariff

The applause that welcomed the passage by Congress in June 2009 of the cap-and-trade law to limit America's emissions of carbon dioxide and other greenhouse gases, diminished by July when it was discovered a last-minute amendment inserted before the bill's passage imposes a green tax starting in 2020. A special import tax is imposed on goods from countries that have not enacted and enforced similar cap-and-trade controls on their global warming emissions. China condemned the U.S. for resorting to "trade protectionism in the disguise of environmental protection."

The U.S. concept of imposing a border tax on imports as a weapon to force countries like China to limit their own emissions triggered a warning from Su Wei, China's chief climate negotiator, that this will lead to retaliatory measures. "Green protectionism" is not a solution. China itself may be polluted, but its exports tend to come from modern, efficient plants, and the country already has higher efficiency standards for vehicles and appliances than the U.S., leading a Chinese official to remark at a Brookings Institution conference in Washington in 2008 that it may be China that should slap carbon tariffs on U.S. products, not the other way around. In fact Beijing is considering levying a "Green Tax," first on domestic and then foreign enterprises, a topic scholars have been debating in China since 2000. Protectionism in any guise is not a solution to a greener cleaner global environment.

China's opening invitation to America and other rich countries to commit 1 percent of their economic worth to help poor nations fight global warming is a start. China is aggressive in pursuing renewable energy sources and will press for a new international mechanism to spread green technology worldwide. It plans to showcase its commitment at the 2010 Asian Games in Guangzhou by improving upon Beijing's blueprint for clear skies during the 2008 Olympics. The city plans to close or relocate 123 heavy polluting manufacturers by the end of 2009. The government is keen to use the Asian Games as an opportunity to invest in environmental protection.

Guangzhou's 71-story Pearl River Tower due to be completed in October 2009 is one such investment being billed as the most energy-efficient skyscraper ever built. With wind turbines, solar panels, sun shields, smart lighting, water-cooled ceilings and insulation, the 310-meter tower is designed to use half the energy of most buildings its size and set a new global benchmark for self-sufficiency among the planet's high-rises. The tower could be enhanced to create surplus electricity to sell to the local power firm.

Surprisingly, buildings account for about one-third of global energy use. Tenants need to take the same environmental care with buildings that they do with cars.

The tower combines many of the world's leading energy-saving technologies on a scale never seen before. The most spectacular feature will be the four wind turbines built into the belly of the structure. The building has been shaped to drive air through the cavities at maximum velocity so the turbines can generate 1 million kilowatt-hours of electricity a year. The building will also produce electricity via the photovoltaic cells of the solar shades cooling its east and west facades.

According to Skidmore, Owings & Merrill, the U.S. architectural firm that designed the building, the energy efficient devices add about $13 million to the construction costs. But this could be recovered within five years by reduced electricity bills, lower maintenance costs and extra rent from the space not used for air-conditioning ducts. The tower's energy consumption will be 58 percent lower than that of a standard building of the same size. The irony is, the building's main tenant will be a tobacco company in cigarette-happy China.

The announcement in 2008 of plans to spend 40 billion yuan on water cleaning projects ahead of the Asian Games has sparked questions about transparency. Shouldn't America and China be cooking smarter together regardless of the water temperature needed to cook and cool both countries kitchens on all fronts?

Ice-Cold Danish

The blizzards that brought the East Coast of the United States and Europe to a standstill in the wake of world leaders failing to reach a meaningful agreement in Copenhagen in December 2009 were just the latest political and meteriological message from Mother Nature that inaction is not an option. The failure to reach a climate change agreement in Copenhagen in December 2009 makes it imperative for the U.S. and China to save the world from the looming climate crisis that knows no borders. Science dictates action now. Political rhetoric of future mid-century intent is not good enough nor acceptable to prevent a global warming apocalypse.

America's will to cut carbon emissions by only 17 percent by 2020 from 2005 levels, when compared to the European Union's 20 percent, Japan's 25 percent and China's 40 to 45 percent, is shortsighted and shameful.

Just cutting greenhouse gas emissions is not good enough either. China and the U.S. have to lead the world and get it to place a greater focus on the reduction of deforestation and on research for new clean technologies.

Reducing deforestation is the cheapest way to mitigate climate change in the short term. If we stop cutting and burning tropical forests in Brazil and Indonesia we can eliminate 17 percent of all global emissions. But to do so requires putting in place a whole new system of economic development that makes it more profitable for the poorer, forest rich countries to preserve and manage their trees than chop them down to make furniture and toys. Without a new system for economic development in the timber-rich tropics, the rainforests are doomed.

Brazil's President Luiz Inacio da Silva wants "gringos" to pay Amazon nations to prevent deforestation as a price for their environmental sins of the past.

Laser Inertial Fusion Energy, or LIFE, is a new clean cutting edge technology worth pursuing. It is a controlled nuclear fusion – fusing nuclei rather than splitting a nucleus, as happens in existing nuclear-fission power plants – can produce an endless supply of safe, clean energy. In a fission reaction, the nucleus of a uranium atom is split into two small atoms, releasing energy in the form of heat. The heat is used to make steam, which drives a turbine and generates electricity. In fusion energy, the second half of this process, that is heat makes steam makes electricity, remains the same. But instead of splitting the nucleus of an atom, you're trying to force a deuterium nucleus to merge, or fuse, with a tritium nucleus. When that happens, helium is produced that throws off energy.

Scientists at Lawrence Livermore National Laboratory in California have been given $3.5 billion of taxpayer money to develop this new fusion technology in a commercially viable way. It involves a small pellet that contains a few milligrams of deuterium and tritium, isotopes of hydrogen that can be extracted from water that is blasted with a powerful laser that creates a reaction like the one that takes place at the center of the sun. Harness that reaction, and you've created a star on earth, and with the heat from that star you can generate electricity without creating any pollution. It is real solar power that can replace nuclear, coal and oil power plants.

LIFE would produce energy with no carbon emissions, from a fuel that is cheap and abundant. Ten gallons of water could produce as much energy as a supertanker of oil.

Scientists believe utility companies could be building prototype "LIFE engines" by 2020, and have commercial plants up and running by 2030.

China is also pursuing nuclear fusion energy. Why dont China and the U.S. develop fusion technology together? Fusion energy is a potential solution to a looming crisis.

China, the front runner in the fight to address climate change, is prepared to lead the climate change charge alone or with the other BRIC countries. It certainly has the money to do so. If it does, it will literally leave the U.S. in its dust.

'Hopenhagen' Suicide Pact

'Hopenhagen' failed to live up to the pre-conference hype to safeguard the generations of tomorrow. The U.N. Framework Convention on Climate Change, the fruit of the 1992 Rio summit that convened in Copenhagen in December 2009, hosted 192 nations, joined by Iraq and Somalia – one of the largest gatherings of world leaders in history – with the misplaced hope that a treaty that would protect future generations would be signed. Instead, what was signed was a weak farcical face-saving global suicide pact in order to avoid a complete embarrassing global political collapse. More empty promises by empty political suits.

A non-binding agreement that does not spell out any global emissions targets for 2020 or 2050, or set a deadline for transforming the objectives outlined in the accord into a legally binding treaty. All the signatories agreed to was to "take note" of the agreement. "Take note?" They must be kidding. If not, if that is the best they can come up with, it is nothing short of a complete collapse of global political will and leadership that humanity can ill afford.

The lack of sincerity, political grand-standing by irresponsible delegates walking out of chaotic meetings and accusatory inflammatory rhetoric confirmed yet again the U.N.'s incompetence and irrelevance in the new world order. The lack of basic common sense of what must be done today in the scorching glaring face of the apocalyptic fate the world faces because of climate change is beyond comprehension.

China likened rich countries' refusal to help poor ones pay for the transition to cleaner economies, with "short-term financial aid" leading to the gradual establishment of "long-term support mechanism," to people eating at a fancy restaurant who are joined for dessert by a poor friend and then demand he pay a share of the cost of the entire meal.

"We are not asking for donations," said China's Deputy Foreign Minister He Yafei in response to U.S. climate envoy Todd Stern's comment that China should not expect any U.S. climate aid money and that the U.S. was not in any debt to the world for its historical emissions. "They have a legal responsibility, the U.S. included. Whoever created this problem, they are responsible," said Minister He. The deep public rift between the U.S. and China in Copenhagen is disconcerting. Nevertheless, the fact is that poor countries need help from the countries that grew rich off polluting industries to buy the technology required to develop their economies without adding to greenhouse gase emissions, and to cope with the drought, floods and other disruptions associated with global warming.

Women and children in those poor countries that have contributed the least to global warming are the ones suffering the most today, and will suffer even more tomorrow without a meaningful climate change treaty.

China, leading the developing world, objected to the verification procedures proposed by the U.S. and the developed world as an infringement of sovereignty hard to sell to local municipalities that have a difficult time accepting verification guidelines from Beijing, yet alone Washington or Copenhagen. Washington, of all capitals, should understand this basic political obstacle that all members of the U.S. Congress also face at the state and municipal level.

China was tough and assertive in Copenhagen, something Europeans and Americans are not used to. Well, they better start getting used to the idea, and more importantly, better start listening.

"We're not going to do Kyoto and we're not going to do Kyoto with another name," said Todd Stern in Copenhagen. That is not a very cool public stance for America to take if it wants to continue sitting at the head of the climate change banquet table.

The 1997 Kyoto Protocol, the world's only legally binding emissions-curbing treaty, which America did not sign, required rich nations' emissions to be cut by around 5 percent from 1990 levels by 2008, but not surprisingly was never achieved.

More political hot air was emitted by U.N. Secretary General Ban Ki-moon who after his dismal performance in Copenhagen, dared promise that a legally binding treaty on climate change will be reached in 2010. Not if the U.N. is running the show again.

The U.N. must be taken out of the climate change equation if a treaty that replaces Kyoto is to be signed in 2012. A new environmental organization with political clout and effectiveness headed up by the U.S. and China, together with a manageable group of representatives from the various environmental constituencies represented, is long overdue. No more global leaders conferences that create more carbon emissions than they reduce.

History has proven that strong international institutions are a precondition for building any successful global cooperation.

2012

The planet must be saved. Hopenhagen is a wakeup call to humanity. Citizens of Earth must unite to fight as environmentally conscious consumers and political activists. Otherwise Armaggedon will be upon us as depicted in the Hollywood blockbuster *2012*. The movie was a number one hit in both China and the U.S. It accurately depicted what will happen if *We the People* don't get our act together on climate change. Leaders of the world will have to embark on a mission to build an ark in the mountains of China to house people and animals that can repopulate the planet. Chinese military personnel saluting American refugees entering China, and a U.S. military officer saying that only the Chinese could build an ark of such a scale so quickly, will prove to be more than just a movie. It will be the biggest reality show on Earth.

That is the concern of the "Hollywood elite" that U.S. Senator James Inhofe ridiculed in Copenhagen when he showed up to let the delegates at the summit know that "We're not going to be passing a climate-change bill" in the Senate. The ranking Republican member of the Senate committee addressing global warming flew to the Danish capital hoping to undercut President Obama's pledge to take a leadership role on climate change.

Senator John Kerry, chairman of the Senate Foreign Relations Committee, visited the 192-nation summit a few days earlier to assure people that the U.S. would approve its first national plan to reduce carbon emissions. Inhofe said Kerry had misled the summit and feared Obama would do so as well when he showed up. Inhofe also brought Washington's China-bashing campaign to Copenhagen.

"Why would we in the United States give something to China to help them to meet certain goals when they own $800 billion of our debt? It doesn't make sense," Inhofe said. As a Senator responsible for the U.S. debt and the financial crisis America faces, Inhofe's inappropriate remarks are another good reason for Americans to consider abolishing the U.S. Senate as well as the U.N. in the 21st-century. It is an irrelevant historical self-serving political relic indebted to Big Oil that is out of touch with the people it is meant to serve and is no longer a necessary utility to empower small states.

Further negotiations are expected to take place in 2010 in Mexico City, with a legally binding treaty to succeed Kyoto at the end of 2012. A treaty will be signed a lot quicker at a global climate settlement conference after a global class-action suit has been filed by developing nations against the developed ones.

Since all the talk fests conclude with a bunch of empty suits full of hot air, maybe it is time to get the real suits – lawsuits – by developing countries to resolve the outstanding climate change issues. The environment is a property right that belongs to all citizens on Earth. Everone of us owns a piece of the environment. China and the developing world own the biggest piece. China should therefore initiate and lead the global class-action lawsuit against the developed world in any one of the international courts governing cross-border property right issues – and even the U.S. state and federal courts. There is no more time for political procrastination.

Interlocal Action

Cities around the world are taking immediate action against climate change. Copenhagen aims to become the first carbon-neutral city by 2025. It plans to reduce carbon emissions by 20 percent by 2015, with a total of 50 initiatives to push it down to zero a decade after that. These include a new geothermal power plant, use of more wind and biomass power, increased district heating and experiments with district cooling, as well as rolling out hydrogen and electric vehicles. Pedestrians and cyclists already have the right of way on roads designed to make life as smooth and speedy as possible for them.

New York Mayor Michael Bloomberg said it wasn't practical to wait for national governments to act because cities have to get on with the job of solving problems. New York pledged in 2008 to reduce its carbon emissions by 30 percent in 10 years. Bloomberg said New York had copied Copenhagen, and now had 260 kilometers of cycle paths. New Yorkers want more.

The Big Apple is also retrofitting old buildings to improve their energy efficiency. Bloomberg stressed that thousands of jobs were being created through the mandating of building upgrades. All public buildings will be retrofitted, and it is estimated that the work will have paid for itself, through improved efficiency, in seven years. All buildings are now required to carry out energy audits and publish the energy-efficient data online. This gives owners and tenants information and transparency, which in turn should result in even more-energy-efficient buildings.

Cities are the key to reducing emissions as quickly as possible and should be our main focus for political action to bring about the changes necessary to stem climate change.

Climbing the Climate Hurdles
The U.S. and China got over their first joint climate hurdle by signing their first bilateral memorandum of understanding on global warming in early 2009 in preparation for the Copenhagen climate change conference. Hopefully, their agreement will become the template for the other nations that attended in the hope of reaching an agreement in 2010 to succeed the Kyoto pact, to which the U.S. is not a signatory. The U.S. and China are responsible for 40 percent of the world's greenhouse gas emissions and can lead their respective developed and developing world constituencies to the dotted signature lines.

A 20 percent across-the-board cut in emissions is an excellent starting point. The target was first set by Governor Arnold Schwarzenegger in California, an average of 6.2 liters per 100 kilometers for all cars and light trucks by 2016, and has now been adopted by President Obama for the entire country. That will eventually cut U.S. vehicle emissions by 40 percent. It also means U.S. oil imports fall up to half by 2019.

By the time the U.S. reaches its 6.62 liters per 100 kilometers target in 2016, most other countries will have moved on to an average of 5.2 liters per 100 kilometers or better. China's current requirement is 5.5 liters per 100 kilometers. The U.S. is playing catch-up. But at least it is back in a game it can easily win and lead with China, which has clearly demonstrated its willingness to partner to make sure the rest of the world follows.

With the sun missing its spots, the solar cycle is speaking volumes about the impact of climate change. Ever since Samuel Heinrich Schwabe, a German astronomer, first noted in 1843 that sunspots grow and wane over a roughly 11-year cycle, scientists have carefully watched the sun's activity. In the latest lull, the sun reached its calmest, whitest, least pockmarked state in the autumn of 2008.

For operators of satellites and power grids, that is good news. The same magnetic fields that generate sunspot blotches also accelerate a devastating rain of particles that can overload and wreck electronic equipment in orbit or on Earth. A panel of 12 scientists assembled by the National Oceanic and Atmospheric Administration now predict only 90 sunspots during the peak month of May 2013. That would make it the weakest solar maximum since 1928, when there were 78 sunspots. During an average solar maximum, the sun is covered with 120 sunspots.

Some global warming skeptics speculate that the sun may be on the verge of falling into an extended slumber similar to the period of several sunspot-scarce decades during the 17th and 18th centuries that concided with an extended chilly period. Another Ice Age? If anything it will be the Ice Age in reverse. More like the "Roaster Age," "Hell's Age," "Fossil Age," or destructive "Human Age."

The sun, Danish scientists say, influences how many cosmic rays impinge on the Earth's atmosphere and thus the number of clouds. When the sun's activity is frenetic, the solar wind of changed particles it spews out increases. That expands the cocoon of magnetic fields around the solar system, deflecting some of the cosmic rays. Cosmic ray levels, reflected in concentrations of various isotopes, correlate well with climate extending back thousands of years.

Loss of Appetite
America has to lose its appetite and dependence on oil. Some states in the U.S. create more carbon emissions than several developing countries put together. The U.S. Senate cannot be allowed to again hold up legislation mandating the reduction of carbon emissions, as it did with the Kyoto accord. At the time, the Senate would not approve the ratification of the Kyoto Protocol unless it contained binding targets and timetables for developing countries as well as developed nations. The excuse given at the time was that signing Kyoto "would result in serious harm to the economy of the U.S." It was the only developed country not to climb aboard.

America's hot-air empty-suit career politicians, especially those from America's most polluting states, have to acknowledge the urgency for them to act now. There is hope.

The U.S. House of Representatives unveiled four bills in 2009 to foster closer relations with China on climate change, trade, energy and to boost teaching of the Chinese language in the U.S. The 55-member congressional U.S.-China Working Group is finally tackling climate change as seriously as China.

America and China must get their scientists to not only address all the ramifications of global warming at the dawn of this new century, but how the two countries can put aside their respective radical notions of how to achieve progress. It's time that science and the corporate world (sorry Big Oil), regardless of whether they follow the capitalist or Confucian model, begin thinking and acting in ways that can pay huge dividends for the people of the world, not to mention themselves and their shareholders. Otherwise, they will lose it all. Venezuela's Hugo Chavez is a 21st-century wake-up call.

An extensive study on a breed of wild sheep in Scotland shows that global warming has caused the animals to shrink in size by up to 5 percent, a finding that has frightening implications. Evolutionary theory says wild sheep should "gradually get bigger, as the stronger, larger animals survive into adulthood and reproduce." But the study shows the "local environment has had a stronger effect on the sheep than the evolutionary pressure to grow larger." If global warming can do this to sheep, I'm mortified to think what it might be doing to grains, vegetables, fruits, and of course, *We Human Citizens*. Humanity and the future of the world's climate rests on the ability of the governments of the U.S. and China to work together as partners, shepards, leading their local and interlocal flocks.

Rising global temperatures must be jointly arrested by the U.S. and China. Only they have the resources, scientific know how, and combined global number of local and interlocal citizens clamoring for more government intervention and economic stimulus support to ensure their personal and economic survival. China can't handle this alone, notwithstanding what many countries are asking it to do. It knows its only trusted partner can be America. But the U.S. must meet China half-way.

China knows it has to halt its current industrial path if the planet is to survive. While China is the world's largest source of carbon dioxide emissions, its per capita emissions are still way below American levels; and the great bulk of global warming that already happened was not caused by China – but by America and the developed industrial world it leads. China knows it can't keep polluting at America's pace because the Earth can't take the strain.

Former Utah Governor Jon Huntsman, a potential Republican presidential contender in 2012, has been named U.S. Ambassador to China by President Barack Obama. Fluent in Putonghua and Fukienese from his days as a Mormon missionary in Taiwan, Huntsman was a popular two-term governor who served in both Bush administrations and was national co-chairman of Senator John McCain's 2008 presidential campaign – a Washington insider who also knows China. In a 2006 speech at Shanghai Normal University, he spoke of the need for China and the U.S. to work together on environmental issues.

"The United States and China must be good examples and stewards of the Earth. We must match economic progress with environmental stewardship. The effects of industrialization are felt worldwide," Huntsman said. Now's his and America's chance to do just that in these exceptionally exciting and challenging times.

Chapter 9

Pitcher of Fresh Water
– What the World Needs
Come Together
– Beatles

Tidal Wave

The Intergovernmental Panel on Climate Change, an international group of scientists, says that by 2080 as many as 3.2 billion people – one-third of the planet's population – will be short of water, up to 600 million will be short of food and as many as 7 million will face coastal flooding.

Security experts fear that the ensuing tidal wave of forced migration will not only fuel existing conflicts but create new ones in some of the poorest and most deprived areas of the world. "A world of many more Darfurs is the increasingly likely nightmare scenario," the report warns.

Since 1965, a volume of water equivalent to the Great Lakes has melted in polar regions and flowed into the world's oceans, making them less salty. China is at risk from global warming as the Tibetan glaciers that feed and regulate many of China's rivers begin to melt and the country's agriculture becomes vulnerable to even small changes in temperature. The Panel on Climate Change has projected that sea levels will rise up about 0.91 meters by 2100.

The U.N. estimates that by 2025, two-thirds of the world's people will be living with water stress, with North Africa, the Middle East and West Asia hit the worst. Regions that get abundant rainfall may get it in the form of fierce rainstorms that cause flash floods rather than a useful drizzle that soaks into the ground.

People who live within 97 kilometers of a shoreline, or about one-third of the world's population, could be affected if sea levels rise as expected over the coming decades, possibly more than 1 meter by 2100. Flooded homes and crops could make environmental refugees of a billion people. Living on a bay that floods my street whenever there is a direct typhoon hit that brings with it high tides and ferocious winds, I have personally experienced the growing peril on a small scale and am naturally very concerned.

"The culprit responsible for warming has been identified. As far as I am concerned, the debate's over. What we need to be debating is what we're going to do about it," said Tim Barnett, an oceanographer at the Scripps Oceanographic Institution in San Diego. The Pentagon agrees.

A study commissioned and suppressed in 2005 by the Pentagon warns that major European cities will sink beneath rising seas and Britain will be plunged into a "Siberian" climate by 2020. Nuclear conflict, mega-droughts, famine and widespread rioting will erupt across the world. This threat to global stability vastly eclipses that of terrorism, say the few experts privy to the report. "Disruption and conflict will be endemic features of life," concludes the Pentagon analysis. "Once again, warfare would define human life."

The major threat of mayhem comes from large populations simply upping the stakes and moving into other people's territories. I don't know which way global warming will run, but won't it be interesting if the zones that suffer most are Europe and North America and the ones that remain or indeed become more habitable are in Africa and the southerly Asian lands. Colonialist imperialists on the move again – firing as they go.

Global warming should be elevated beyond a scientific debate to a U.S. national security concern, say the study's authors, Peter Schwartz, a CIA consultant and former head of planning at Royal Dutch/Shell group, and Doug Randall of the California-based Global Business Network. According to Randall and Schwartz, the planet is already carrying a higher population than it can sustain. By 2020, catastrophic shortages of water and energy will become harder to overcome, plunging the planet into war. They warn that 8,200 years ago, changing climate conditions brought widespread crop failure, famine, disease and mass migration of populations that could soon be repeated.

Randall told *The Observer*, which first reported the leaked Pentagon report in 2005, that the potential ramifications of rapid climate change could create global chaos. "It is a national security threat that is unique because there is no enemy to point your guns at and we have no control over the threat."

"You've got a president who says global warming is a hoax, and across the Potomac River you've got a Pentagon preparing for climate wars. It's pretty scary when (George W.) Bush starts to ignore his own government on this issue," said Rob Gueterbock of Greenpeace.

Jeremy Symons, a former whistleblower at the Environmental Protection Agency, said that suppression of the report was a further example of the Bush White House trying to bury the threat of climate change. Symons, who left the EPA in protest of political interference, said the Bush administration's close links to high-powered energy and oil companies was vital in understanding why climate change has been received skeptically in the Oval Office. "This administration is ignoring the evidence in order to placate a handful of large energy and oil companies," he said.

The Pentagon study is confirmed by numerous other reports, including one entitled "Meeting the Climate Challenge," prepared by a task force of senior politicians, business leaders and academics from around the world to coincide with former British Prime Minister Tony Blair's promise to advance climate change policy as the chair of both the G-8 group of rich nations and the European Union in 2005.

With this ecological time bomb ticking away, how much longer can *We the Apathetic People* afford to ignore the global warming threat? Not much.

Hot Global Soufflé
Four years of talks on the U.N. climate treaty to widen the existing Kyoto Protocol ended in the cook-off to the final climate banquet in Copenhagen in December 2009, in a 12-day meeting among 182 countries in June 2009, in Bonn, Germany, with the United States and Europe insisting that the private sector, not governments, finance the climate fight – passing the buck as usual. At the other end of the spectrum, developing countries called on developed countries to make more cuts of greenhouse gases. Poor countries say developed nations got rich on industrialization and want to be paid to avoid going down the same high-carbon road.

"We have only one atmosphere, and it is just like we are living in one house. If someone has occupied the main room for too long, as the argument goes, that person should be asked to pay the main part of the rent," You Nuo, a

China Daily columnist wrote after the U.N. talks. Thus the climate change fight is turned into a tussle between the haves and the have-nots as they jealously guard their own self-interests.

The draft text report had swollen like a soufflé from 50 pages to 200 with no breakthroughs. Some of the preliminary language for a new global climate treaty repeated earlier warnings: "The impact of climate change is already causing migration and displacement," the report began, adding that by mid-century, "the prospects for the scope and scale could vastly exceed anything that has happened before."

A 36-page report that summarized more than 1,400 studies presented at a climate conference in March 2009 in Copenhagen, where the U.N. meeting will be held in December to hammer out the successor to Kyoto, concluded that greenhouse gas emissions and other climate indicators are at or near the upper boundaries forecast by the U.N. Intergovernmental Panel Change, whose 2007 report has been the scientific benchmark for the troubled U.N. talks. Knowing that, the outcome at Bonn is not only pathetic, but disastrous.

The U.N., in my opinion, as I elaborated in great detail in a chapter devoted to the irrelevant global dinosaur in *Custom Maid Knowledge*, is a wasteful kitchen throwing away hard-earned global taxpayers dollars to over-tip incompetent overpaid bureaucratic cooks – make that crooks.

What confirmed the dire need to replace the U.N. was another humorous e-mail I received from Frank Kocher in California about the results of fictitious U.N. survey, this one about food shortage. The alleged world-wide telephone survey took place in the summer of 2009. The only question asked was: "Would you please give your honest opinion about solutions to the food shortage in the rest of the world?" The survey was a huge failure because in Eastern Europe they didn't know what "honest" meant. In Western Europe they didn't know what "shortage" meant. In Africa they didn't know what "food" meant. In China they didn't know what "opinion" meant. In the Middle East they didn't know what "solution" meant. In South America they didn't know what "please" meant. And in the U.S. they didn't know what "the rest of the world" meant.

For someone who has been as critical as I have of the U.N. and its leaders, I must confess it is difficult for me to compliment U.N. Secretary General Ban Ki-moon for anything. However, he does deserve to be universally applauded for his bold statement after the July 2009 G-8 meeting in Italy when he accused the leaders of missing a "unique opportunity" and "not [doing] enough" to tackle climate change. Making that statement after President Barack Obama announced that the group had reached a "historic consensus" on cutting pollution was not only necessary, but mandatory.

A study released at the end of July 2009 by researchers from the U.S. Naval Research Laboratory and Nasa's Goddard Institute for Space Studies suggests the Earth has been enjoying a cool spring and that in the next five years, temperatures will rise to 150 percent of the rate predicted by the U.N. Intergovernmental Panel on Climate Change.

By mid-century, according to Britain's Hadley Centre for Climate Prediction and Research, China and India alone, without any contribution from the U.S., can push carbon dioxide levels to 650 parts per million, the point where the Arctic's permafrost completely thaws, unleashing vast amounts of carbon dioxide and deadly methane, and with it, unstoppable warming. Some experts say that, in 35 to 50 years, the glaciers will be gone, leaving swaths of India and China at the mercy of droughts and floods. Already the melting of the glaciers on the roof of the world threatens to devastate the great Himalayan and Tibetan river system, the Ganges-Brahmaputra, Indu.

The industrialized nations plan to cut greenhouse gas emissions by between 15 and 21 percent below 1990 levels by 2020 is unacceptable to China because the targets fall far short of the steeper cuts China is prepared to make. China is demanding a cut of 40 percent while a panel of U.N. scientists has proposed cuts of between 25 percent and 40 percent.

An agreement to limit the rise in the Earth's average temperature to two degrees above its 18th-century level before the Industrial Revolution and cut emissions by 80 percent by 2050 isn't enough. China is right when it demands serious reductions be agreed to by 2020. Long-term goals without interim goals are meaningless.

The excuse given by the Obama administration for not coming up with an interim goal boggles the mind. John Holdren, Obama's chief scientific advisor, when asked why the U.S. would not commit to the same target for greenhouse-gas emissions by 2020 as the European Union, replied: "If we had not wasted the last eight years we would probably achieve that target. But we did waste the last eight years [so] it doesn't make a lot of sense for us to officially embrace a target that is not realistically within reach."

So, because America didn't do what it should have done for eight years under the Bush administration, we can't do what we should for the next 12 years either? Does anyone still doubt that Congress and the White House are owned and controlled by Big Oil that is leading this world straight to hell – with George W. and Dick Cheney leading a parade they can no longer spin?

While writing this part of the book and contemplating the alternative hot or cold options of a living hell, I received an e-mail from Bob Sherwood, a business associate living in New York. It brought a smile to my face because it explained the alternative hells in the most graphic righteous way. In big red capital letters "HELL EXPLAINED," is how it started. "The following is an actual question given on a University of Washington chemistry midterm exam. The answer by one student was so 'profound' that the professor shared it with colleagues, via the Internet, which is, of course, why we have the pleasure of enjoying it as well.

"Bonus question: Is Hell exothermic (giving off heat) or endothermic (absorbing heat)? Most of the students wrote proofs of their beliefs using Boyle's Law (gas cools when it expands and heats when it is compressed) or some variant. One student, however, wrote the following: First, we need to know how the mass of Hell is changing in time, so we need to know the rate at which souls are moving into Hell and the rate at which they are leaving. I think that we can safely assume that once a soul goes to hell, it will not leave. Therefore, no souls are leaving. As for how many souls are entering Hell, let's look at the different religions that exist in the world today.

"Most of these religions state that if you are not a member of their religion you will go to Hell. Since there is more than one of these religions and since people do not belong to more than one religion, we can project that all souls go to Hell. With birth and death rates as they are, we can expect the number of souls in Hell to increase exponentially. Now, we look at the rate of change of the volume in Hell because Boyle's Law states that in order for the temperature and pressure in Hell to stay the same, the volume of Hell has to expand proportionately as souls are added.

"This gives two possibilities: 1. If Hell is expanding at a slower rate than the rate at which souls enter Hell, then the temperature and pressure in Hell will increase until all Hell breaks loose; and 2. If Hell is expanding at a rate faster than the increase of souls in Hell, then the temperature and pressure will drop until Hell freezes over. So which is it? If we accept the postulate given to me by Debra during my freshman year that 'it will be a cold day in Hell before I sleep with you,' and take into account the fact that I slept with her last night, then number two must be true, and thus I am sure that Hell is exothermic and has already frozen over! The corollary of this theory is that since Hell has frozen over, it follows that it is not accepting any more souls and is therefore extinct....leaving only Heaven, thereby proving the existence of a divine being, which explains why last night Debra kept shouting 'Oh, my God!' This student received an A+."

Cold Cuts

Climate scientists are shocked at the rapid speed at which the polar ice is melting. The phrase "shock" entered their vocabulary when the International Polar Year, a global consortium studying the Arctic, froze a small vessel into the sea ice off eastern Siberia in September 2006. Norwegian explorer Fridtjof Nansen had done the same thing a century earlier, and his Fram, carried by the drifting ice, emerged off eastern Greenland 34 months later. IPY scientists thought their *Tara* would take 24 to 36 months. But it reached Greenland in just 14 months, stark evidence that the sea ice found a more open ice-free, and thus faster path westward courtesy of Artic melting.

The cryosphere – the regions of our Earth covered by snow and ice – has long been considered the "canary in the coal mine" for global warming. We have known since the first report of the Intergovernmental Panel on Climate Change published in 1990 that the Arctic was warming more rapidly, twice as fast as the rest of the globe. We have seen the glaciers topping Mount Kilamanjaro all but disappear, 85 percent gone in the past century. We watched the Larsen B ice shelf of Antarctica collapse in 2002. What we have in the environmental coal mine is a loudly ringing alarm bell in every corner of the cryosphere – the alarm bell of melting ice that will drown millions living in coalmine Earth.

The melting glaciers in the Arctic could lead to an ice-free Arctic Ocean, which is stirring military activity to carve up a strategic polar region where a thaw will open new shipping routes and allow oil and gas exploration. In 2008, Russia sent a nuclear submarine across the Arctic, under the ice, to the Pacific. The new class of Russian submarine is called the Borei – "Arctic Wind." Canada runs a military exercise, Nanook, every year to reinforce sovereignty over its northern territories.

Much is at stake. The U.S. Geological Survey estimated in 2008 that the Arctic holds 90 billion barrels of undiscovered oil – enough to supply current world demand for three years. Arctic shipping routes could be shortcuts between the Pacific and Atlantic oceans in summer even though uncertainties over factors such as icebergs, insurance costs or the need for hardened hulls are likely to put off many companies.

The standoff over who owns the seabed under the North Pole or how far Canada controls the Northwest Passage and how to cut and share the heretofore frozen and inaccessible Arctic between the U.S., Russia, Canada, Norway, Iceland and Denmark may have to be refereed by China.

Water

Water makes up 60 percent of our body, 70 percent of our brain and 80 percent of our blood. We humans are essentially made of water. While we can go about a month without food, our body cannot survive a week without water. The same water that existed on Earth billions of years ago still exists today. It covers most of the planet, but just 30 percent is fresh water and most of that is ice, albeit melting. Less than 1 percent of all fresh water is readily accessible for human use. In other words, less than 0.0007 percent of all the water on Earth is available for human consumption.

What is more depressing is that most people are not aware that a quarter of all the clean water that enters their home is used to flush toilets. One toilet flush uses three gallons of water. A single load of laundry uses 40 gallons, a 10-minute shower 50 gallons, brushing teeth with the water running four gallons, and brushing teeth with the tap off a quarter of a gallon.

A water crisis is looming. In the 20th century the world's population tripled. The use of water grew six times. By the middle of the 21st century there will be an additional 3 billion people. A number that would have been more than triple that had China not implemented a "one child" policy. Most will be born in countries already experiencing water shortages.

What does that mean for water use? Los Angeles County can support about 1 million people with its own water. Remember the movie "Chinatown?" L.A. ain't seen the half-of-it yet, because by 2020 its population is expected to reach 22 million. El Paso and San Antonio in Texas could run out of water sometime in 2019-2029. Central Florida could run out of water by 2014.

Millions of people in the world live on less than three gallons of water a day. The average American uses about 160 gallons a day. Some sobering statistics to keep in mind:

- 25 million refugees were displaced by contaminated rivers in 2008. That is more than were forced to flee from war zones in the same year;
- One in three people worldwide lack access to safe drinking water;
- According to the U.N., a child dies from a water-related disease every 15 seconds;
- We are going to run out of water before we run out of oil;
- Due to overpumping, the groundwater in several countries is almost gone;
- Depleted aquifers lead to cutbacks in grain harvests which lead to more food shortages and higher prices;
- China is already developing large grain deficits as a result, as are India, Pakistan and Egypt;
- Our water problem is fast becoming a hunger problem.

I ponder these mind-boggling numbers and statistics every time I water my plants or go for a swim in the nearby bay, which is quite often in the hot and humid summer months. One solution I've come up with that can save millions of gallons of water is a "Shower Free Day" once a month globally. Not only will it save water, but it is healthy because of the natural human oils that will be preserved on our skin.

Growing up in Cyprus in the 1950s, I still remember as a child how I had to walk to the communal village tap at the bottom of a low hill daily in the late summer and early fall with my mother to fetch our quota of two buckets of water. In the winter, the rainwater from the roof was piped into two big tanks in the attic of our house that got us through the early summer. Water was also a constant concern in Israel, where I went to attend agricultural high school in the early '60s.

Arriving in America in 1964 and not having to worry about water was almost more enjoyable than mingling with the abundant free-wheeling-and-dealing-love-children of the '60s.

Today, living in Hong Kong, it feels like I've come full circle. Now that I live in China, draughts and water shortages are again a haunting concern. Cities are charging residents more for water to decrease usage, while farmland is being abandoned because of the persistent draught, not only in nearby Guangdong where about 325,000 residents have no water, but throughout mainland China – and especially in its top 20 cities. Price increases known as water tariffs for water usage are now a common political issue in many municipalities, many of which have imposed higher tariffs throughout the mainland to encourage conservation – in the face of strong public resistance.

One thing that always amazes me about Hong Kong is the fact of how its Confucian-capitalist-political-free-wheeling-dealing Special Economic Zone status in China, continuously helps bail out the Motherland – it is now doing the same to help alleviate the water shortages of its neighboring provinces. Hong Kong is not taking the water quota it is entitled to under its contract from China so that those nearby cities like Shenzen – and farmers throughout the provinces in desperate need of water to survive can have it – especially when Hong Kong recorded an annual 10 percent rainfall shortage in 2009. Hong Kong may well become a pioneer in building water desalination plants in China. Studies conducted by the Hong Kong government show they are technically feasible in Hong Kong. However, being the Confucian-capitalist-wheel-a-dealer-negotiator it is, it is holding out for a better price.

It is believed that the drought in Guangdong could be associated with the El Niño phenomenom, which has become more common due to global warming and has reduced the risk of typhoons approaching the South China region. The result is that in nearby Macau, the water shortage is so severe that the local government is providing poor residents with bottled water at a nominal cost. The development of America's Las Vegas casinos has consumed and gambled the local water supply away together with the corrupt regional official's ill-gotten gains.

A scene that caught my attention in the Oscar-winning movie *Slumdog Millionaire* was where the brother of the main character is working in a factory illegally "sealing" used plastic alpine spring water bottles with tap water. It is a scene I have personally witnessed on many occasions in the Philippines, Cambodia, Indonesia and China. Water is a precious vanishing commodity that is fast becoming the world's No. 1 crisis.

Food
Without water there is no food for any menu. The world's primary use of water is to grow food. While only 17 percent of the world's arable land is irrigated, it produces more than one-third of total food supply. Asia is the heartland of global irrigation. It contains 70 percent of the world's 277 million hectares of irrigated land. While accounting for only 34 percent of

Asian arable land, the irrigated zone produces 60 percent of the continent's rice, wheat and other staple grains.

Irrigated farming is very water intensive, especially for growing rice in paddy fields. Asia uses 73 percent of the 2,664 cubic kilometers of water the world withdraws annually for agriculture. Surface water is being sucked dry in some major river basins in China and India.

As people become better off and join the urban middle class, they tend to eat less cereal. Instead they consume more fruit, vegetables, milk and meat. For example, meat consumption in China has more than doubled in the past 20 years and is expected to double again by 2030. Livestock production requires much more water than crops. For example, beef cattle take an average of three years before they are slaughtered to produce 200 kilograms of meat. In that time, each animal requires 31 cubic meters of water. It also consumes nearly 1,300 kilograms of grain as well as 7,200 kilograms of hay and other roughage. This requires even more water, bringing the total to more than 15,000 litres per 1 kilogram of beef.

The traditional political slogan "Where's the beef?" has to be replaced with the contemporary urgent request of "Where's the water?"

WC-20

The G-20 should change its name to WC-20. The initials do not stand for "Water Closet" and I do not mean to insult the group by implying that they will be a toilet, which is what most people think about when they see the initials WC. But that is where the world will wind up if world leaders don't come to grips with climate change and the looming water crisis it has created. WC stands for "Water Crisis."

Water scarcity is the underlying cause of many of today's conflicts. A water pitcher that is fairly designed by the WC-20 and its contents equitably shared, can bring about the elusive peace nations have been trying to impose on each other for millennia with destructive wars.

The conflicts from Chad to Darfur, Sudan, to the Ogaden Desert in Ethiopia, to Somalia and its pirates, and across to Yemen, Iraq, Israel, Jordan, Syria, Lebanon, Palestine, Pakistan and Afghanistan, lie in the great arc of arid lands where water scarcity is leading to failed crops, dying livestock, extreme poverty and desperation that continue to provide fertile recruiting grounds for religious extremists.

Governments lose their legitimacy when they cannot guarantee their populations' most basic needs: safe drinking water, sufficient food, and fodder and water for their animals on which communities depend for their meager livelihoods.

Career politicians, diplomats and generals in conflict-ridden countries typically treat these crises as they would any other political or military challenge. They mobilize armies, organize political factions, combat warlords, or try to grapple with religious extremism. But these responses overlook the underlying challenges of helping communities meet their urgent needs for water, food and livelihoods. As a result, the United States and Europe often spend hundreds of billions of dollars to send troops, drones or bombers abroad to quell uprisings or target "failed states," but do not send one-hundredth of the amount to address the underlying crisis of water scarcity and resulting underdevelopment. China on the other hand does. That is why the countries in desperate need of development and water prefer to trade their natural resources with China.

The WC cannot be flushed away. The stench of continued painful pointless deaths will only get worse unless a global pitcher of drinkable water and buckets – preferably reservoirs of recycled or desalinated water – are made easily and cheaply available to those in desperate need. Addressing the WC is the solution to peace.

The story is the same in all the world's arid and war-torn regions. The U.S. is heavily committed militarily at U.S. taxpayer's expense, while China exploits regional resources in exchange for infrastructure projects that deliver water. The precise nature of the water crises vary from region to region, with different pressure points in different regions depending on the size of their bulging populations. For example, Pakistan, an already arid country, will feel the stress of a rapidly rising population, which has grown from 42 million in 1950 to 184 million in 2010, and may reach an astounding 335 million in 2050, according to the U.N.'s "medium" scenario. Even worse, farmers are now relying on groundwater that is being depleted by over-pumping. To make matters worse, the Himalayan glaciers that feed China, India, Bangladesh and Pakistan's rivers may melt by 2050, courtesy of global warming.

Water is becoming a key security issue in Sino-Indian relations and a potential source of bitter discord. China and India already are water-stressed economies. The spread of irrigated farming and water-intensive industries, together with the demands of a rising middle class, have led to a severe struggle for more water. Bhopal, India's "City of Lakes," where water was always plentiful, has become a parched wasteland of high and dry lakes where the water shortage has turned deadly as residents fight to the last drop. Both countries have entered an era of perennial water scarcity, which before long is likely to equal in terms of intensity the water shortages found in the Middle East.

Tibet and Xinjiang, China's two westernmost regions, are not only in the forefront of China's ethnic conflict, but climate change as well. While Tibet is getting mired in a deepening drought and declining water resources in future years, the water table in Xinjiang is on the rise and the dry climate is gradually becoming more humid. While Tibet is drying up, Xinjiang's water reserves are growing at a rate equivalent to a rise in rainfall of 10mm per year.

Glaciers in Tibet have been melting for decades. From 1971 to 2002 they shrank by 5.3 percent, and between 2003 and 2008 they shrank a further 10 percent. Between 2002 and 2007 Tibet suffered a drop in total water resources – ice, snow, surface and underground water – equivalent to a 30mm reduction in rainfall. Tibet experienced a drought in 2009, with some monitoring stations not recording rainfall for more than 200 days, and temperatures rising up to 2.3 degrees Celcius higher. The Tibetan plateau is the source of China's major waterways, the Yangtze, Yellow and Lancang (Mekong) rivers.

Tibet is also the source of most major Indian rivers. The Tibetan plateau's vast glaciers, huge underground springs and high altitude make Tibet the world's largest freshwater repository after the polar icecaps. Indeed, all of Asia's major rivers, except the Ganges, originate in the Tibetan plateau. Even the Ganges' two main tributaries flow in from Tibet.

China is now pursuing major water transfer projects on the Tibetan plateau that threaten to reduce international river flows into India and other riparian states. The seeds of a potential water conflict have been sown. Water is now a political tool, not only on the Tibetan plateau, but globally.

China is contemplating the northward rerouting of the Brahmaputra river, know as the Yarlung Tsangpo to Tibetans and Yaluzangbu to the Chinese. It is the world's highest river and one of the fastest-flowing. Its diversion to the parched Yellow River is an idea China does not discuss publicly, because the project implies environmental devastation of India's northeastern plains and eastern Bangladesh, and would be akin to a declaration of water war on India and Bangladesh.

China's ambition to channel Tibetan waters northward has been whetted by two factors: the completion of the Three Gorges Dam, which China trumpets as the greatest engineering feat since the construction of the Great Wall; and the power of President Hu Jintao, whose background fuses two key elements – water and Tibet. Hu is a hydrologist by training and owes his swift rise in the Communist Party hierarchy to his effective rule as governor of Tibet.

It's the same story in the Middle East. After a five-year drought, the region is headed toward a water calamity that could overwhelm all peace efforts. The Jordan River now has large sections reduced to a trickle. The Sea of Galilee is at its lowest point ever. The surface area of the Dead Sea has shrunk by a third. Iraq's ancient marshes are now marked by large swaths of stalks and caked mud. In northern Syria, more than 160 villages in two years from 2007 to 2009 have run dry of water and been deserted by residents. In Gaza, 150,000 Palestinians have no access to tap water. In Israel, the pumps at the Sea of Galilee, its largest reservoir, are exposed above the water level, rendering pumping impossible.

The same holds true for many pumping stations across America's lakes and rivers. Not only are they running low, but what water and fish remains is polluted with high levels of mercury. The U.S. Geological Survey's test of fish pulled from 291 streams from 1998 to 2005 found every one of them contaminated with some level of mercury. The study found 27 percent of the fish had mercury levels above the level Environmental Protection Agency considers safe for human consumption. Previous research has found levels of concern in ocean and lake fish. Mercury is a neurotoxin especially dangerous to development in infants and fetuses.

I swam in the Sea of Galilee, the Dead Sea and the River Jordan on several occasions since the early '60s and enjoyed their refreshing history-soaked waters. Watching the waters at the cradle of Western Civilization and the Tibetan plateau that feeds the cradle of Eastern Civilization gradually disappear before our very eyes as we blindly and idly stand by as the world drowns itself in more wars and sorrow is not only unbelievable – but a self-inflicted human calamity. The potential regional and global devastation a water shortage in these seas and rivers can cause is nothing short of Armageddon.

Jeffrey Sachs, professor of economics and director of the Earth Institute at Columbia University, summed up the existing problem and the solution: "Most governments are poorly equipped to deal with serious water challenges. Water ministries are typically staffed with engineers and generalist civil servants. Yet lasting solutions to water challenges require a broad range of expert knowledge about climate, ecology, farming, population, engineering, economics, community politics and local cultures. Government officials also need the skill and flexibility to work with local communities, private businesses, international organizations and potential donors. A crucial next step is to bring together scientific, political and business leaders from societies that share problems of water scarcity to explore creative approaches to overcoming them."

That's where the WC-20 comes in. The world water problem is the most important cause and reason for world leaders and citizens to come together.

America and China must take charge and lead a global interlocal mobilization campaign to find cheaper and affordable ways of converting seawater into drinking water that will not only save communities and avoid conflicts in the arid arc, but save coastal communities from the rising waters from the melting glaciers. Humanity, as we know it, depends on that pitcher of drinkable water that will sustain its development and survival by quenching global thirst.

He who takes nature for his guide is not easily beaten out of his argument.

– Thomas Paine

Coffee, Tea Digestif? – Author's Note
In The Morning
– Norah Jones

Cross-Cultural Studies

China's booming economy, growing middle class, one-child policy and U.S. universities' aggressive recruiting policies have resulted in a record number of mainlanders attending America's 4,000 colleges and universities. Foreign students at U.S. institutions of higher learning in 2008 reached an all-time high of 624,000, according to the Institute of International Education. China sends the second-largest contingent to the U.S. after India.

In China, smarts, not sports, is what's cool.

Chinese students will do anything, literally, to get the grades and go to a foreign university. Stand-in candidates known as "Shooters" arc the cadre of fraudsters for hire who will sit in for the English-language exam mainland students must take to attend overseas universities. There are hundreds of shooters working for syndicates or as freelancers that openly advertise their services. Armed with foolproof counterfeit ID cards and sheer hutzpa, they pass themselves off as their handsomely paying customers to take the International English Language Testing System examination – a one-day English test taken by thousands of students across the mainland every month and usually a prerequisite to getting immigration clearance and heading for a university in the United States, Britain or Australia. More than 100,000 Chinese students take the exam every year.

International students and their families contributed more than $15 billion to the U.S. economy in 2008. Foreign students typically pay higher tuition and have therefore become an important revenue source for universities as the supply of U.S. college students has crested because of the high cost of education. That is another subject I critically address at length in *Custom Maid Knowledge*. Cross-cultural education is beneficial to both the host country and the countries that send their students overseas. In the words of B.B. King, "I don't think anybody steals anything; all of us borrow."

Returnees

Many foreign students stay on in America after their studies because of the opportunities, lifestyle and political climate. I am one such example. I went to America in 1964 to study veterinary medicine and wound up studying political science and law because I decided I didn't want to go back to a farm in Israel as a veterinarian. Many mainland Chinese students stick around after they complete their U.S. studies. The difference, however, is they do eventually return after spending several years or decades developing their career skills in America. They take home with them the best of what America has to offer.

Close to 800,000 Chinese students have gone abroad since 1978 when the government first started sponsoring them for overseas studies. Drawn by job opportunities overseas, less than a third returned, though the rate at which they are coming back is accelerating. In 2005, about 35,000 students returned, three times the number in 2000, according to official statistics that are significantly conservative. Many of the returnees, armed with cutting-edge technical and managerial skills, have helped kick-start new high technology businesses. At the same time, foreign venture capitalists are flooding China with unprecedented amounts of money. Combined with the mind- boggling opportunities from an economy expanding 10 percent annually, the result has been the creation of private wealth on an unprecedented scale.

The reality is that China would have remained a rural society were it not for these expatriates returning home. The homeward rush in the early 1950s, the return of some of the world's leading physicists, chemists, rocket experts and engineers, helped China to establish its modern industry, build its first nuclear bomb, send a satellite into space and, in September 2008, astronauts. The door was shut in the 1960s during the Cultural Revolution, but since the reopening policy of 1978, more than 1.2 million of China's most talented students have gone overseas to study and work. Only a quarter had returned by 2007, according to the Ministry of Education. That is rapidly changing with the 2008 global economic meltdown, not only for Chinese returnees, but foreign students studying there and expats willing to work in China rather than go back home.

Mainland cities are offering financial incentives and subsidies to returnees in the fields of IT, biotechnology and finance. Job fairs entice prospects, especially entrepreneurs, in major cities like Guangzhou and Shanghai. Chinese companies and foreign companies operating in the country are offering expats with expertise in research and development, high-tech, engineering, or pharmaceutical industry, good-paying jobs in China despite the global recession. The same offers are being made to foreign students in China studying Chinese.

Many Chinese-Americans are now returning to their roots in China because of discrimination in America. Chinese-Americans in the U.S. earn less than non-Hispanic whites of the same educational level. A study, jointly carried out by the University of Maryland and the Organization of Chinese Americans in 2008, concluded there are twice as many college degree holders among Chinese-Americans aged 25 and above than among the general population, but they earn less than whites of all levels of education. They earn anywhere from $5,000 to $15,000 less than their white counterparts.

To make the U.S. racist reality worse, prestigious Princeton University has been accused of placing admission caps on Asian student applicants. The civil rights case was brought by Jian Li, a Chinese-American who had perfect SAT scores and was in the top 1 percent of his high school class. He enrolled in Yale and Harvard, but wanted to go to Princeton because he grew up near the Ivy League campus in New Jersey. He sued believing he was rejected because of an existing cap on the number of Asians the university will accept. Is it any wonder they are going back to China where they are appreciated? One more reason America is losing out to China.

Language Studies

I grew up in Switzerland, Cyprus and Israel, where I learned to speak Russian at home from my Russian-born parents; Berne Deutch – German Swiss Miss style – from the kids in Berne; English at School, and Greek, Turkish and Hebrew in the schools and streets of Cyprus and Israel. Unfortunately, I've forgotten most of these beautiful classical languages for lack of practice and usage.

Living as I do now in Hong Kong and spending as much time as I do in China, I am frustrated and annoyed at myself for not doing a better job of learning any one of the many local dialects, Mandarin, Shanghainese and Cantonese being the most useful.

It is important, maybe even vital, to be bilingual or even trilingual in the New World Order. Learning a second and third language is more important for American children than any other subject – especially if America wants to continue to be a global leader in the 21st century. All high school and university graduates should be required to speak, read and write either Spanish or Chinese fluently, preferably both. Admittedly, once students have had a brief look at what is involved in each, there may be an overwhelming choice for one option, amigo. Only then will Americans be true global citizens able to survive in the 21st century.

Chinese officials are prepared to learn English to better serve their country – and do. Norman Pritchard is an English teacher living in China who has produced multimedia teaching materials at China Central Radio and TV University and Beijing Foreign Studies University for more than 10 years and has the privilege of teaching Chinese officials English. One characteristic that he says was shared by all of the Chinese officials he taught, was their enormous and intense motivation, studying 15 hours a day.

"Westerners have a generally cynical view of politicians, and here in China sometimes the phrase 'officials' is more often described with adjectives like 'greedy' and 'corrupt' than 'sincere' and 'diligent.' I did not expect to be touched at the emotional level by a group of trainees at the National School of Administration," said Pritchard, who spent an intense three months teaching government officials. "I think I learned more about China and the Chinese in the last three months than I had in the previous 10 years as a teacher in China," he added.

"I think my fellow foreign experts and I were privileged to gain an insight into the quality of some of the people who govern China in a way that only a few foreigners share, and the West in general is completely ignorant of. These were valuable men and women. They were cultivated and honorable, diligent and sincere. They represent truly the ideal of the good public official. I came to a closer understanding that this belief in education for its ministers is a central tenet of the Chinese government," Pritchard said.

"China demands excellence in their officials, and they are prepared to invest heavily in it. There is no analogue to this practice in Western democracy that I know of. I think China is the stronger for it, and the West the weaker for its absence," Pritchard concluded.

The Pentagon is now including Chinese studies in its long-overdue 21st-century linguistic arsenal – the National Security Language Initiative – which also includes Arabic, Farsi, Korean and Swahili. Students who take the Chinese course are paid a $1,000 stipend and competition for admission is fierce. More than 1,000 students apply for 69 places.

The languages involved skew heavily toward current or potential global trouble spots. The initiative aims to direct U.S. foreign language education away from European languages towards languages that are perceived to be more useful in the 21st century. At the U.S. Military Academy, where future Army officers are educated, the number of students taking introductory Chinese has steadily risen, from 65 in 2000 to 94 in 2007. The Pentagon identified about 5,000 service members who speak Chinese in 2007, up from just 1,400 in 2000.

The White House and Congress have finally agreed to spend more than $100 million on the National Security Language Initiative. The Pentagon also plans to spend $750 million over five years to increase foreign language proficiency in the armed forces.

The intensive Mandarin immersion program that kindergarten children in Lorain, Ohio, are subjected to for three years with teachers from China is to be applauded, as is the dual immersion program at the Glenwood Elementary School in Chapel Hill, North Carolina. In Lorain, children ages 4 and 5 are placed in classrooms where Mandarin is the only language spoken, while teaching the same curriculum as other classrooms. Chapel Hill has its pupils – half native Chinese, half native English speakers – do their lessons in both languages. In the U.S., Chinese language is giving Chinese food a run for its money.

The number of students in America who are learning Chinese is still relatively small, about 24,000, most of them in elementary and high schools. That compares with 3 million or so who study Spanish, the most popular language in America's schools. Second is French, with about 1 million students. A number of big urban school districts have launched Chinese language programs, including Chicago, Philadelphia, Houston and Boston. The most ambitious program is in Chicago. It was started in 1999, and there are more than 5,000 students, virtually all of them native English speakers, studying Chinese in 17 elementary and 10 high schools. Now that Arne Duncan, the former head of the Chicago school system, has become secretary of education, that will hopefully happen nationally.

Hopefully President Obama and Michelle, will get their daughters to learn Mandarin. With the support and extr tutorial services of their uncle Mark Okoth Nolesandjo, who lives in Shenzhen, China, they will become the model international Americans carrying through the ages the dreams and principles of America's Founding Fathers.

The biggest obstacle to expanding Chinese instruction in U.S. schools is finding qualified teachers. The problem is complicated by the federal No Child Left Behind program, which requires all teachers to be certified. Most states don't have a language certification program and need to get one started.

The number of students in two-and four-year college courses studying Chinese rose by 20 percent between 1998 and 2002, to slightly more than 33,000. "Now that the pipeline is active at the high school level, we expect many more students to be enrolling in advanced courses," said Rosemary Feal, executive director of the Modern Language Association. More American families also are employing Chinese nannies so their children can grow up speaking Chinese.

The Senate Foreign Relations Committee is considering a proposal to allocate $1.3 billion to boost Chinese language and culture classes in secondary schools. What's to consider? China is assisting by establishing Chinese cultural centers under a program called Confucius Institute, to teach Americans, and foreigners worldwide. By year-end 2008, there were 21 such institutes in America – the latest at the University of Oklahoma – and 305 worldwide in 78 countries. China started to push Mandarin as a second language worldwide in 1987, but the scheme did not really take off until 2004. Confucius Institute takes the form of a joint venture, with venues and basic hardware provided by local partners.

The institute teams up with local partners, acquiring space in their buildings or getting the host government to pay for their housing. Instead of sending teachers who will instruct foreigners directly, the institute sends teacher-trainers who work to upgrade the skills of local Chinese teachers.

The Chinese strategy is smart. Beijing has figured that promoting education and language as tools for understanding is the most effective way to spread its influence far and wide. It learned the hard way that gunboats frighten people into temporary submission, but a shared language can make them life-long friends. Shouldn't America also embrace this strategy and be doing the same instead of building military bases?

The Chinese government has sent language teachers to nearly 300 schools in 70 countries. Chinese language or culture-related classes are taught in more than 2,500 colleges and universities in more than 100 countries. China's Ministry of Education hopes to teach 100 million foreigners to speak Mandarin by 2010. Some estimates say that number has already been achieved.

Confucius was an educator, but also represented peace and harmony, values that China insistently proclaims, hoping to disarm fears about its rapid rise. Confucius also taught principles of filial piety and social obligation, concepts that are mostly alien to Americans.

Confucius revolutionized education in China 2,500 years ago by making it accessible to commoners. There are more than 30 million commoners learning Chinese worldwide at his namesake institutions, according to the Ministry of Education.

As growth industries go, learning Mandarin is right up there. In 1988, only 8,000 foreigners studied the language in China. By the dawn of the new millennium, the number was up to 50,000. By the time of the 2008 Beijing Olympics, the government put the number at more than 120,000 – and by the end of 2008, more than 220,000. The foreign students hail from 189 countries and are studying in 592 mainland universities. The largest contingents are from South Korea, the U.S. and Japan. China is developing and nurturing its "soft power" through students. An estimated 50 million people around the world study the language as well.

I had the privilege of hosting one such student for a few days in Hong Kong in January 2009. Caitlin McBride is a graduate of Newbury High in Ventura, California, and a student at Redlands University in Redlands, California. She went to Beijing University in the fall of 2008 for her junior year as part of her Global Business Major program to learn Chinese by immersing herself in the language. She spent the first semester living in a dorm on campus and the second semester living with a Chinese family. I have known Caitlin since she was but a gleam in her parents' eyes. I was delighted we were able to share some time comparing her experiences as a student in America and China and the difference she has observed between U.S. and Chinese college students.

"Attitude. Students in America are lazy, fat and spoiled," Caitlin said when

I asked what she thought was the major difference between the two. "In China, the students work so hard studying. Many of them can't fall asleep at night worrying about what would happen if they didn't study enough and failed," she continued. "They study all the time. They take nothing for granted."

Studying Chinese written characters is compulsory for those who want to learn more than just the language. By learning the characters, one gains insight into the culture, economics, law and philosophy, something Caitlin and many American students are doing.

Learning a second language should be mandatory in all U.S. high schools. If the rest of the world is mandated to learn English, shouldn't U.S. high schools require Mandarin, Spanish or Arabic as a second language required for graduation? The hard part is that classroom teaching of languages to ambivalent children does not have a high success rate and never did. Better off having them practice in Chinatown or the barrio.

Original Human Recipe

The 2009 discovery of 38-million-year-old fossils in Myanmar could prove that the common ancestors of humans, monkeys and apes evolved from primates in Asia rather than Africa – several million years earlier than any anthropoid found in Africa and the second-oldest found in Asia. The fossils belonged to an extinct family of Asian anthropoid primates known as Amphipithecidae. Eosimias is the world's oldest known species of primates, which lived between 40 million and 45 million years ago and roamed in rain forests on the eastern coast of China. That may help explain why the Chinese repeatedly develop, advance and re-emerge as a progressive and prosperous civilization that offers other cultures and peoples their inventions, ideas and philosophies. It is doing so again in the 21st century.

Human Capital

China has invested heavily in human capital that promises to sustain growth and create greater prosperity. Parents in China spend $90 billion a year on their children's education. This is over and above what the government spends. Government and families constantly increase their investment in primary and secondary education. Elite English private schools are setting up campuses in China to capitalize on this hunger for education. Given the excellent core curriculum available across China to its 230 million students, the country is well positioned to continue to upgrade its human capital over the next few decades. Shouldn't America be doing the same?

Why are U.S. universities investing and losing billions of dollars of their endowment funds in the stock market instead of investing them in needy bright Americans who need scholarships? Harvard said its $36.9 billion endowment fund had lost 30 percent of its value since the Wall Street meltdown of 2008. Many other universities lost a lot more. Some like Ohio's Antioch College went out of business. In early 2009 Harvard was forced to tap the bond market for $1.5 billion, Stanford and Princeton borrowed $1 billion each and Yale $800 million just to support their liquidity. After all, universities are nonprofits and they are not supposed to "hoard" their endowments, accumulate large surpluses, or profits.

Let's hope American universities have themselves learned a lesson and that, instead of gambling their endowments in speculative investments, they begin investing in scholarships for more bright inner-city youngsters and underprivileged kids in all 50 states.

I don't know what percentage of U.S. university endowment money is spent on scholarships for needy kids, but I'm sure it's nowhere near the 45 or 50 percent level that I believe it should be. If it were, many fewer young people would wind up as criminals on the street, and more bright human capital would be invested to make America once again into a viable competitive force in the world.

As I was exploring the objectives of this book, I sat down around the dinner table in Sebastopol, California, with the Steins – Suyin, her husband Jim, son Alaric and daughter Melody. There we collectively came up with the "Contents on the Table" heading that introduces the chapters of the book.

Suyin confessed that she doubted the book's concept at first, but had come to appreciate the thread that holds it together – the fact that the United States and China have the power and the opportunity to lead a troubled world to a better place, here at the dawn of the 21st century. The lighting of the upper floors of the Empire State Building in red and yellow spotlights for the first time ever on October 1, 2009, in commemoration of the 60th anniversary of the founding of the People's Republic of China, is a constructive first step in the right direction.

"I believe … in a global community," Suyin said, "Where we think and strategize as one, in order to make the planet work."

I can't say it any better. And indeed, if *We the People* want to survive the

21st century, America and China must likewise sit down at the dinner table, learn to live together as a caring family and develop a warm and loving and progressive relationship.

The alternative is Armageddon.

The Utensils – Chapter Notes
Learn to Live
– Darius Rucker

After Meal Cravings – Bibliography

A knowledge of books is the basis upon which other knowledge is to be built.
– George Washington

Extensive bibliography is available for your reading pleasure at
http://www.custommaidbook.com

Index

So convenient a thing it is to be a reasonable crea-
ture, since it enables one to find or make a reason
for everything one has a mind to do.
– Benjamin Franklin